AUSTRALIAN POLITICS IN THE TWENTY-FIRST CENTURY

OLD INSTITUTIONS, NEW CHALLENGES

Australian Politics in the Twenty-first Century brings to life the key institutions, theories and concepts by considering the question: How are Australia's political institutions holding up in the face of the new challenges, dynamics and turbulence that have emerged and intensified in the new millennium? This approach equips students with the requisite foundational knowledge, and encourages them to critically examine the complex interplay between a centuries-old system and a diverse, modern Australian society.

This text presents the many moving parts of Australia's political system from an institutional perspective: the legislative and judicial bodies, as well as lobby groups, the media, minor parties and the citizenry – institutions not often considered but whose influence is rapidly increasing. Student learning is supported through learning objectives, key terms, discussion questions, further readings and breakout boxes that highlight key theories, events and individuals. The extensive resources available in the VitalSource enhanced eBook reaffirm comprehension and extend learning.

Written in an accessible and engaging style, *Australian Politics in the Twenty-first Century* is an essential resource that will give students the tools to navigate the contemporary Australian political landscape.

Glenn Kefford is Lecturer in the Department of Modern History, Politics and International Relations at Macquarie University.

Hannah Murphy-Gregory is Lecturer in the School of Politics and International Relations at the University of Tasmania.

Ian Ward is Honorary Associate Professor in the School of Political Science and International Studies at the University of Queensland.

Stewart Jackson is Lecturer in the Department of Government and International Relations at the University of Sydney.

Lloyd Cox is Lecturer in the Department of Modern History, Politics and International Relations at Macquarie University.

Andrea Carson is Associate Professor in the Department of Communication and Media at La Trobe University.

AUSTRALIAN POLITICS IN THE TWENTY-FIRST CENTURY

OLD INSTITUTIONS, NEW CHALLENGES

Glenn Kefford
Hannah Murphy-Gregory
Ian Ward
Stewart Jackson
Lloyd Cox
Andrea Carson

CAMBRIDGE
UNIVERSITY PRESS

CAMBRIDGE
UNIVERSITY PRESS

University Printing House, Cambridge CB2 8BS, United Kingdom

One Liberty Plaza, 20th Floor, New York, NY 10006, USA

477 Williamstown Road, Port Melbourne, VIC 3207, Australia

314–321, 3rd Floor, Plot 3, Splendor Forum, Jasola District Centre, New Delhi – 110025, India

79 Anson Road, #06–04/06, Singapore 079906

Cambridge University Press is part of the University of Cambridge.

It furthers the University's mission by disseminating knowledge in the pursuit of education, learning and research at the highest international levels of excellence.

www.cambridge.org
Information on this title: www.cambridge.org/9781108577564

First published 2018 (version 2, June 2020)

Cover designed by Anne-Marie Reeves
Typeset by Integra Software Services Pvt. Ltd
Printed in China by C & C Offset Printing Co. Ltd, April 2020

A catalogue record for this publication is available from the British Library

A catalogue record for this book is available from the National Library of Australia

ISBN 978-1-108-57756-4 Paperback

FOREWORD

People often quote Otto von Bismarck saying 'Politics is the art of the possible, the attainable – the art of the next best'. It's an easy pose to be cynical about politics and its many and obvious failings. It's much easier and safer to remain pure, above the fray and aloof.

I hope the reason you have picked up this book is that you realise what a cop out that is.

If politics today is not good enough, what is your responsibility, as a citizen of the country you love, to make it better? And how would you go about doing that?

Rather than the art of the possible, I would say politics is the science of convincing your fellow citizens that, what previously had seemed impossible is not only achievable but also necessary. It's also working out how to make those big changes happen. From the 8-hour day, to action on climate change; from widows' pensions to the National Disability Insurance Scheme; from needs-based funding for schools to rebuilding our aid program; or a Makarrata Commission for our First Nations people.

What have we learnt from history about how to use the institutions of our democracy to deliver on these ideals? How do we win government, then use our time wisely to change our country and the world for the better? How do we manage legitimate and competing interests in a fair manner? How do we ensure politics is about the power of ideas, not just power for its own sake? And how do we ensure that we leave our democratic institutions strengthened when our time in government is done?

I hope you have chosen to study politics because you realise, like Teddy Roosevelt said:

> The credit belongs to the man who is actually in the arena, whose face is marred by dust and sweat and blood … who spends himself in a worthy cause; who at best knows in the end the triumph of high achievement, and who at the worst, if he fails, at least fails while daring greatly.

Because, as men and women of Australia, every one of us should know how our precious democracy works; should work to strengthen and protect it; and should play our part as a citizen to make our country better. And a manual for that is kind of handy.

by the Hon. Tanya Plibersek MP, Deputy Leader of the Opposition,
Shadow Minister for Education and Training, Shadow Minister for Women

CONTENTS

USING YOUR VITALSOURCE EBOOK

Once you have registered your VitalSource access code (see the inside front cover for instructions), you will have access to the enhanced eBook via your VitalSource Bookshelf. The navigation instructions below provide a general overview of the main features used within the enhanced eBook.

ICONS

This icon is used throughout the textbook to indicate the presence of an interactive component in the eBook. A descriptor below indicates the type of content available.

NAVIGATION AND SEARCH

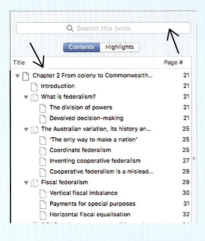

Move between pages and sections in multiple ways, including via the linked table of contents and the search tool.

HIGHLIGHT

Highlight text in your choice of colours with one click. Add notes to highlighted passages.

skills that serve the interest of patients are reviewed. Interacting with professional colleagues is presented in the context of team communication and collaborative working relationships. Guidelines in communicating through written document ... and legal ...

All ... practice must be effective at producing shared meaning between people. For this reason, the chapter begins with an overview of the process of interpersonal communication and what makes it effective. The emphasis is on the formation of professional relationships with patients and colleagues, as communication is the means by which relationships develop.

Key term for chapter

KEY TERMS

Hover over bold terms to display pop-up definitions of key concepts.

archers being concerned about the l...

Demographic: the characteristics and dynamic balance of a population. The term is used widely in sociology and sociocultural contexts.

on the student demographic, age o...

AUTHOR PANEL

Start each chapter with the author panel podcast. These audio clips provide an extended discussion of the topics within the chapter. Click the icon to listen.

Author panel

- What is a federal system?
- What advantages do federal systems have over unitary systems?
- Is it important to see Australia's federal system in historical context?
- How has Australia's federal system evolved since Federation in 1901?
- What role does The Council of Australian Governments (COAG) play today?

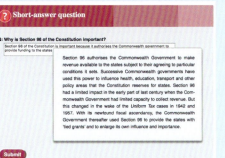

SHORT-ANSWER QUESTIONS

Read the question and type your answer in the box. Submit your answers to view the guided solutions and assess your results. Note that the solution pop-ups can be moved about the page.

REFLECTION QUESTIONS

Throughout the chapter, respond to the reflection questions and use the prompts to assess your responses. Note that the solution pop-ups can be moved about the page.

RESEARCH QUESTIONS

Engage in further reading to respond to the research questions and use the prompts to assess your answers. Note that the solution pop-ups can be moved about the page.

VIDEOS

View relevant video content to extend your knowledge on the topics presented in the book. Click the icon, which links to the video.

DISCUSSION QUESTIONS

Respond to the discussion questions at the end of each chapter and use the guided solutions to assess your responses. Note that the solution pop-ups can be moved about the page.

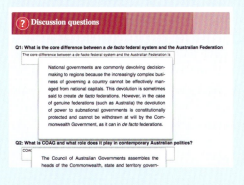

ABOUT THE AUTHORS

Dr Glenn Kefford is a Lecturer in the Department of Modern History, Politics and International Relations at Macquarie University. His research focuses on Australian and comparative politics with an emphasis on political parties, elections and campaigning. He has published widely on these topics and is a regular contributor to the media.

Dr Hannah Murphy-Gregory is a Lecturer in the Politics and International Relations Program of the School of Social Sciences at the University of Tasmania. She specialises in the roles and impact of NGO campaigns on contentious social, economic and environmental issues. Her published works analyse the roles and impact of NGOs in policy-making at the local, national and global levels in diverse issue areas including marine governance, public health, international trade, labour standards and foreign investment rules. Dr Murphy-Gregory's research is published in a range of international outlets including *Environmental Politics*, *Review of International Political Economy* and *Global Policy*.

Ian Ward is an Honorary Associate Professor at the University of Queensland where he previously taught politics for many years. He has contributed to various introductory Australian politics texts, including several editions of *Politics One*. He has written extensively about political parties and politics and the media.

Stewart Jackson is a Lecturer in the Department of Government and International Relations at the University of Sydney, Australia. He researches green and environmental parties in the Asia–Pacific region. He also has research interests in the structure and composition of social movement mobilisations in Australia. His previous book, *The Australian Greens: From Activism to Australia's Third Party*, was published in 2016, and he is currently working on a new monograph on the life and times of Australian antinuclear activist and former Greens Senator, Jo Vallentine.

Dr Lloyd Cox is a Lecturer in Politics and International Relations at Macquarie University, having previously taught at La Trobe University and the US Studies Centre at the University of Sydney. His varied research and publications include articles on Australian politics, US politics, nationalism and globalisation, and revenge in international politics. More recently, his research has turned to exploring the relationship between politics and collective emotions. He teaches units on Australian and US politics and is particularly interested in the pedagogy around more effectively communicating political ideas to undergraduate students.

Dr Andrea Carson is an Associate Professor lecturing in media and communication at La Trobe University. Her work examines changes in the news media – with a focus on investigative journalism – and the role of digital media technologies. She is a Chief Investigator of an Australian Research Council Discovery Award (2018–2020) examining influences, such as the media, on public policy decision-making. She has done extensive research on journalism, Australian politics and public policy. Other research interests include party representation, voter behaviour and election campaigning. Andrea has taught courses on political communication, politics and the media, and campaigns and elections. She has worked as a print journalist (*The Age*); radio (ABC) and TV producer (ABC *7:30*), and as a radio broadcaster (3RRR).

ACKNOWLEDGEMENTS

The authors and Cambridge University Press would like to thank the following for permission to reproduce material in this book.

Figure 1.1: Courtesy Museum Victoria: https://collections.museumvictoria.com.au/items/2005107; **2.1**: © Getty Images/DigitalVision Vectors; **3.1**: Courtesy Parliamentary Education Office; **3.2**: © Commonwealth of Australia (Australian Electoral Commission) 2018. IF derivative: This product [*Australian Politics in the Twenty-first Century*] incorporates data that is © Commonwealth of Australia (Australian Electoral Commission) 2018. The Federal Electoral Boundaries Map 2016 ('Map') has been used in *Australian Politics in the Twenty-first Century* with the permission of the Australian Electoral Commission. The Australian Electoral Commission has not evaluated the Map as altered and incorporated within *Australian Politics in the Twenty-first Century*, and gives no warranty regarding its accuracy, completeness, currency or suitability for any particular purpose; **6.1**: © Getty Images/Stefan Postles/Stringer; **7.1**: Wikimedia Commons, State Library of New South Wales; **7.2**: Watson, James, Approximately, Engraver, and Joshua Reynolds. Edmund Burke, head-and-shoulders portrait, facing left, in medallion / Sr. Joshua Reynolds pinxt. ; James Watson fecit. [London: Printed for J. Watson …, June] Photograph. Retrieved from the Library of Congress, <www.loc.gov/item/2001696982/>; **13.1**: © Getty Images/Peter Parks/Contributor.

Every effort has been made to trace and acknowledge copyright. The publisher apologises for any accidental infringement and welcomes information that would redress this situation.

CHAPTER 1

INTRODUCTION TO 21ST-CENTURY AUSTRALIAN POLITICS

LEARNING OBJECTIVES

After reading this chapter, you should be able to:

1. Describe some of the approaches used to understand politics

2. Explain some key features of Australian federal politics

3. Understand how and why we study Australian politics

4. Identify some of the recent domestic and international challenges to Australian federal politics

INTRODUCTION

political institutions: Bodies that influence the distribution of power, and can be formal, informal, bureaucratic or cultural such as parliament, federalism, political parties, churches and the state.

political actors: Individuals who seek to influence the distribution of power either directly, for example, by standing for parliament, or indirectly, for example, by lobbying or campaigning, including politicians, bureaucrats and judges.

liberal democracy: Representative democracy, rather than direct democracy, that includes free and fair elections with individual rights enshrined in a constitution and an active civil society.

geo-political: The political environment taking into account geographic considerations; geo-politics and the regional environment are critical to foreign policy.

AUTHOR PANEL

With the Australian Federation now well into its second century, important questions have emerged about the capacity of its **political institutions**, and the **political actors** that work within and across them, to produce meaningful political and policy outcomes for the nation's citizens. Australia's federal institutions remain largely unchanged since Federation, yet the world is unrecognisable to that which existed in 1901. **Liberal democracy** is seemingly under threat from a range of technological, **geo-political** and environmental challenges that are domestic and international in origin. It is therefore vital to understand not only the structure of Australian federal politics, but also how these significant and varied challenges are continually shaping and redefining Australian federal politics and are likely to do so for the foreseeable future.

'Politics', of course, is not simply what occurs in Canberra in funny-shaped buildings housing politicians and faceless public servants. Politics in Australia, as for other democracies, also includes voters, the media, political parties, citizens' groups and much more. While many Australians may feel that the political world is distant and has little impact on their everyday lives, the reality is quite the opposite. Politics, broadly defined, is everywhere. It is present in our conversations with friends and families; in our schools, universities and workplaces; in the supermarkets we shop at and in the products that we choose to purchase. While it may seem like hyperbole, for political scientists and students of politics, *everything* is political. This does not mean we should all agree on the public policies to implement, whether one leader is more effective than another or whatever else; the point is that politics is an inescapable battle of ideas and approaches, and it is upon this basis that the book begins.

In 'What is politics?', we explain the competing approaches to understanding the political world before turning to contemporary Australian politics. We consider Australian political history and discuss some of the prominent institutions, actors and ideas that shape Australian federal politics. Next, we outline how and why we study politics. This includes a discussion of power, as well as the institutional, behavioural and critical approaches to studying politics. 'Contemporary challenges in Australian politics' provides an overview of the turbulence created by recent key global and national challenges and dynamics for Australian politics. This includes the impacts of **globalisation**, **neo-liberalism**, declining party identification, the rise of single issue organisations, the battle for gender equality, leadership churn and the challenges for governments of managing **fiscal policy**. Ultimately, the chapter lays the foundations for pursuing the central question at the heart of this book: how does the Australian political system, many elements of which were conceived more than a century ago, accommodate the diverse and conflicting political interests arising in what is now a far more complex and diverse Australia? The chapter concludes by outlining the structure for the rest of the book.

WHAT IS POLITICS?

A good place to start is to examine what we mean when we refer to 'politics'. Like many concepts in the social sciences, there is no universally accepted definition of politics. This is because the social world is inherently complex involving multiple interests, values, beliefs, ideas and theoretical perspectives. As such, multiple definitions exist with each author highlighting what they see as the concept's essential features. To begin with, it is important to recognise that politics is much broader than the popular notion that restricts it to the activity in parliaments and other formal institutional settings. Further, and somewhat problematically, politics in a general sense has negative connotations for many citizens; it is instructive to examine some conventional definitions that highlight politics as a specific *arena* of social life before we tackle the more expansive *process* view of politics and extend our focus beyond a moral appraisal of its worthiness.

POLITICS AS AN ARENA

Conventional definitions of politics tend to revolve around the location or *arena* within which political activity occurs (Hay 2002). For example, the *Oxford English Dictionary* defines politics as '[t]he science and art of government, the science dealing with the form, organisation and administration of a state, or part of one, and with the regulation of its relations with other States' (cited in Ball 1988, 3). It thereby renders politics as the domain of government, its formal institutional structures, and the constitution of rules and practices to govern a **nation-state** extending into the international realm. In other words, politics is fundamentally understood as the study of **the state** and its institutions. During the 19th and 20th century, as the discipline of political science began to solidify as a field of study in its own right, various scholars developed understandings of politics that broadly aligned with the arena view: 'The meaning of the term "politics" is confined to that of the business and activity which has to do with the actual conduct of affairs of the State' (Garner 1952, 4–5). Also, political science 'is the science which is concerned with the State, which endeavours to understand and comprehend the State in its conditions' (Bluntschli 2000, 12). This view of politics as an arena therefore emphasises the institutions of the state, the world of government and those who seek to influence it. From this perspective, the scope of political activity is primarily limited to decision-making in the public sphere. This view privileges formal political activity that occurs in public arenas and institutions, which is often far removed from the day-to-day lives of ordinary citizens. The 'politics as an arena' view therefore offers rather circumscribed parameters of what counts as political practice.

POLITICS AS A SOCIAL PROCESS

In contrast to the 'politics as an arena' approach, which presents a restricted understanding of politics, we aim to demonstrate in this book that politics is in fact an omnipresent social process. Politics extends well beyond formal institutions and exists in all of our

globalisation: A process of growing inter-connectedness across the globe; in particular, the ease of movement of people, ideas and capital are cited as examples.

neo-liberalism: A set of policies that emerged in the aftermath of the oil shocks and stagflation in the mid-1970s, which aimed to reduce the role the state played in the economy. The policies focused on privatisation, deregulation and free-trade.

fiscal policy: The policies that governments can employ to alter spending and taxation. This contrasts with monetary policy that is administered by a central bank, the Reserve Bank in Australia's case, which can alter the supply of money as well as interest rates.

nation-state: A geographically defined area in which sovereignty is claimed over the area and its citizens.

the state: A political entity that exercises sovereign jurisdiction over a defined geographical area and the population residing within it via institutions that structure and organise public life.

daily interactions whether we contribute as citizens, consumers, employers, employees, family members or participants within the vast array of citizens' groups, from local neighbourhood associations to environmental, human rights or industry groups. Thus, the view of politics as a *social process* is a broader, more expansive understanding of political activity (see Hay 2002). In particular, it emphasises politics as a process through which we address societal conflict, where there are no boundaries between the public and private spheres of social life and no distinctions between formal or informal arenas.

Harold Lasswell's (1958, 96) most well-known definition of political science fits into the politics as a process view: 'Politics determines who gets what, when and how'. In other words, Lasswell contends that politics is the process of sorting out who gets access to society's scarce resources. Stoker and Marsh (2002) also define politics as a process, suggesting politics is 'a social process that can be observed in a variety of settings. It is more than what governments choose to do or not do. It is about the unseen distribution of power in society, how the struggle over power is conducted and its impact in creating and distributing resources, life chances and wellbeing' (Stoker and Marsh 2002, 9). This explanation accords with more critical analyses of politics, such as those who view social life as an inevitable power struggle between social groups (see, for example, Gramsci et al. 1971; Lukes 1974).

While the above 'politics as a social process' definitions certainly go further than the conventional 'politics as an arena' view, they only hint at the notion that politics is also fundamentally about ideas as well as interests and resources. Specifically, politics concerns the development, dissemination and contest of ideas, values, beliefs and identities. For example, the notion that citizens should be free to practise religion, endeavour to own their own homes, enjoy penalty rate wages for weekend work, marry a same-sex partner, or that the Constitution be adapted to recognise Indigenous Australians in its preamble, are all underscored by political ideas. Accordingly, the process view of politics offers an expansive understanding of political activity. Not only does it have the state and the division of society's resources as a central concern, it also encompasses contests over ideas, values, beliefs and identities that inform decision-making at all levels. As such, there are few aspects of social life that cannot be analysed using a political lens.

SHORT-ANSWER
QUESTIONS
REFLECTION
QUESTIONS

TABLE 1.1 THE 'ARENA' AND 'SOCIAL PROCESS' VIEWS OF POLITICS COMPARED

	POLITICS AS AN ARENA	POLITICS AS A SOCIAL PROCESS
Scope	Public sphere	Public and private spheres
Context	Government	Government plus decision-making in any setting
Sector	State	State and society

THE INEVITABILITY OF POLITICS

Another aspect of politics concerns the popular conception that it is an undignified, morally ambiguous, even 'grubby' business, and thus something to be avoided. One element of this is the inherent potential for conflict that politics entails. Sometimes, this conflict is indeed highly visible in the form of politicians brawling on the floor of various parliaments through to armed conflict between nation-states, or other forms of violence such as terrorist acts. More often, however, politics is less physically confrontational and involves deliberate bargaining, compromise and negotiation between groups of people in order to develop rules to govern social conduct, control access to resources, and determine the rights and responsibilities of citizens. For example, trade agreements between nation-states usually involve torturously long talks to negotiate new rules to govern cross-border trade across a number of goods and services sectors. Further examples include routine state and Commonwealth bargaining over funding for hospitals in Australia; discussions among governments, industry and environmental groups over water resources such as the Murray–Darling Basin; or the procedures developed to govern people seeking refugee status in Australia. Second, politics incorporates hidden or latent conflict and extends well beyond public life into citizens' private spheres. To illustrate, the division of chores within a household, the varying workforce participation of mothers and fathers, the selection of public or private education, the purchase of fair-trade coffee and the decision to join or abstain from trade union membership in the workplace, should all be considered worthy subjects of study for political scientists. Consequently, it is simply impossible to avoid politics or isolate politics from everyday life; politics inevitably permeates most interactions between people, whether or not those interactions appear cooperative or hostile (or somewhere along this spectrum). Politics is thus fundamental to decision-making concerning the allocation of rights, responsibilities, benefits and burdens across groups of people, regardless of a group's size or the location of the decision-making arena.

RESEARCH
QUESTION

SPOTLIGHT

Describing politics

While this book explains that there are two broad approaches to the 'what is politics' question, a number of interesting, thought-provoking, and even humorous, definitions and descriptions have been developed by a wide range of political scientists, philosophers and public figures, some of which defy simple categorisation. A selection of these include:

'Politics is the constrained use of social power' (Goodin and Klingemann 1996, 7).

Politics is '[t]he activity by which differing interests within a unit of rule are conciliated' (Bernard Crick, British political theorist 1929–2008, quoted Crick 1964).

'Power relations between men and women and whenever and wherever they occur, as much, if not more, in the bed or the kitchen, for example, as in Westminster or Whitehall' (Randall 2002, 119).

Politics is 'nothing more than a means of rising in the world. With this sole view do men engage in politicks [sic] and their whole conduct proceeds upon it' (Samuel Johnson, English writer 1709–1784, cited in Boswell 1798).

'Politics, as a practise, whatever its profession, has always been the systematic organization of hatreds' (Henry Adams, American public intellectual 1838–1918, quoted Adams and Nadel 1999).

'The personal is the political' (1960s feminist movement slogan).

Politics is the 'authoritative allocation of value' (Easton 1953).

'Political history is largely an account of mass violence and of the expenditure of vast resources to cope with mythical fears and hopes' (Edelman 1971).

'Power tends to corrupt, and absolute power corrupts absolutely. Great men are almost always bad men' (Lord Acton, English Catholic historian, politician and writer 1837–1869, quoted Acton et al. 1907).

'Politics is the art of looking for trouble, finding it, misdiagnosing it and then misapplying the wrong remedies' (Groucho Marx, American comedian, stage, film and television star 1890–1977, quoted Kannan 2013, 36).

'Man is born free, and everywhere he is in chains. One man thinks himself the master of others, but remains more of a slave than they are' (Jean-Jacques Rousseau, Francophone Genevan philosopher 1712–1778, quoted Rousseau and Cranston 1968).

QUESTION

Critically analyse the definitions and descriptions of politics presented above. Can you identify any that fit within the 'arena' or 'social process' views of politics?

KEY FEATURES OF AUSTRALIAN POLITICS

federation:
One of three common systems of government used in organising modern nation-states (unitary and confederal being the others). It involves a division of power between a central government and subnational governments. There are generally three layers of government: federal, state/provincial and local. Unitary systems, in contrast, have no division between central and subnational units, while confederal systems imply states that have come together under an overarching body, which has limited power.

It is often argued that the Australian political system contains a unique institutional architecture. While the level of exceptionalism is debatable (Dowding 2016), the Australian nation-state combines features inherited from the United Kingdom (UK) and borrowed from the United States (US) to produce one of the most stable liberal democracies in the world. These features are a product of Australia's colonial origins and the decisions taken by the men and women who were central to the **federation** of the Australian colonies into a nation-state. Understanding the way these features have been combined and the impact they have on shaping Australian politics is key in deciphering how the Australian political system functions. As Table 1.2 shows, Australia shares a number of similar features with both the UK and the US.

THE ORIGINS OF THE AUSTRALIAN POLITICAL SYSTEM

More than 115 years on from Federation, it is often easy to forget that prior to 1 January 1901, the six Australian colonies had closer relationships with the UK than they did with each other. While they were bound together by geography, inter-colonial negotiations required regular conferences to be held and even then seemingly simple negotiations, like that over the standard gauge of railway tracks, were unsuccessful (De Garis 1999). Each colony also had its own complex set of tariffs on trade from other countries, including from its sibling colonies. According to De Garis (1999, 13), 'the need to do away with barriers to trade between the colonies and to establish a common tariff policy with the rest of the world was, in the end, to prove a major force for federation'.

TABLE 1.2 KEY FEATURES OF THE AUSTRALIAN POLITICAL SYSTEM COMPARED

	SYSTEM OF GOVERNMENT	PARLIAMENTARY V PRESIDENTIAL	CONSTITUTIONAL ARRANGEMENTS	SEPARATION OF POWERS	HEAD OF GOVERNMENT	HEAD OF STATE
Australia	Federal	Parliamentary	Mixture	Partial separation (fused)	Prime Minister	Governor-General (Monarch)
United Kingdom	Unitary	Parliamentary	Uncodified	Partial separation (fused)	Prime Minister	Monarch
United States	Federal	Presidential	Codified	Full separation	President	President

Figure 1.1 The opening of Federal Parliament in Melbourne, 1901

The path to federation was long and winding. Indeed, Macintyre (1999, 140) has said that 'Australians can hardly be accused of rushing into federation'. Serious discussions about federation began in the 1870s at the same time that the British were starting to reduce their military presence in the colonies and amid increasing concern about regional security (De Garis 1999; Macintyre 1999). By the 1880s, debate within the colonies was increasing, and at conferences through the 1880s and early 1890s, each of the colonies was represented in discussions about federation. New Zealand and Fiji were frequently involved too as they considered joining any new federated entity. Eventually, after much cajoling, New South Wales, Queensland, South Australia, Victoria and Tasmania all achieved majorities in their referenda to federate. A year later, in 1900, Western Australia held their referendum, which was also successful (AEC 2011). Then, in July 1900, Australian delegates went to London with a draft of a constitution for the new federation and the British parliament passed the *Commonwealth of Australia Constitution Act 1900* (Parliamentary Education Office: The colonial parliaments of Australia.).

VIDEO

The new federated nation

VIDEO

With the birth of Australia as a nation-state, on 1 January 1901, a new set of institutions was required to complement the institutions that were present in the colonies (which would go on to become the states). But what did this actually mean in terms of the institutional structure?

SIX KEY FEATURES OF THE AUSTRALIAN POLITICAL SYSTEM

The contemporary Australian political system remains basically the same as that devised at Federation and the following six features can be seen as key to the functioning of the system. Each of these will be discussed in more detail through the rest of this book.

1. Parliamentary system of government – This means that voters elect a local representative and then the party or group of parties who form a majority in the lower house decide who will be part of the executive, including who will become the leader of the government, the prime minister.

2. Federalism – In the Australian context, federalism means a division of powers between, on the one hand, the federal government and, on the other, the states. In practice, this creates three layers of government: federal, state and territorial, and local. Figure 1.2 shows these three levels of law-making.

3. Constitutional government – Australia's system of constitutional government is unlike both the UK and the US. The reason for this is that it utilises both a codified constitution, like the US, and conventions, like the UK. As a result, Australia is often noted as having a 'mixed' constitutional arrangement.

4. Constitutional monarchy – While a representative democracy, Australia also remains a constitutional monarchy with the British crown as the Head of State who is represented by the Governor-General at the federal level and the Governors at the subnational level.

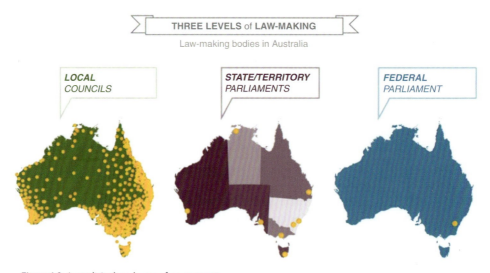

THREE LEVELS of LAW-MAKING

Law-making bodies in Australia

LOCAL COUNCILS

STATE/TERRITORY PARLIAMENTS

FEDERAL PARLIAMENT

Figure 1.2 Australia's three layers of government
Source: Parliamentary Education Office

5. Strong bicameralism – Australia has a tradition at the federal and subnational levels of strong bicameralism. This means that the legislature consists of two chambers – lower and upper houses – with relatively equal powers. At the federal level, this means the Senate has significant powers to block the passage of legislation.

6. Majoritarianism – As a result of the electoral system used in lower houses and strong party discipline, Australia historically has exhibited the features of party majoritarianism, which is consistent with that of the Westminster system. Changing voting behaviour, however, suggests that Australia's adherence to the major political parties is beginning to change.

Local government within Australia's federal system

While the attention of many Australians is focused on the federal, state and territory governments, local government also plays a vital role within the federal system. According to the Parliamentary Education Office, Australia has around 560 local councils that collect their own set of taxes and provide basic services such as rubbish collection, water and sewerage, as well as issuing licenses for pets and permits for building. The roles that local governments play in each state are determined by legislation passed by their state parliaments. In contrast to this, Section 51 of the Australian Constitution sets out the powers of the federal parliament to make laws in relation to national matters but the role of the states was never codified. The reason for this is that, similar to what has happened in the United States, the federal government was never expected to become the dominant level of government. Indeed, if many of those who supported federation knew this was likely to occur, unquestionably they would have opposed unification.

QUESTION

When would a unitary structure, like that in the UK, be an advantage over the federal model in Australia? When would it be a disadvantage?

Federal or unitary: A comparison with the unitary UK system which is in transition

The United Kingdom (UK) is frequently cited as an example of a unitary state (sometimes referred to as a unitary system of government). This is particularly relevant for students of Australian politics as the UK is often used as a comparison with our federal system, which involves an additional layer of government at the subnational level (states and territories). However, the UK is in a period of transition and change. Over the last two decades, a process of devolution has occurred within the UK. This process began in 1997 when referenda were held to establish a Scottish parliament and a National Assembly in Wales. Then, in 1998, as part of the peace agreement commonly known as the Good Friday Agreement, Northern Ireland held a similar referendum. Following these referenda, the UK parliament in Westminster passed legislation to devolve some powers to these regional legislatures. *Considering this period of devolution, then, does the UK remain a unitary state?* Yes, it does. There are a few reasons for this. First, Westminster remains sovereign. It has the capacity to overturn legislation enacted at the regional level, though this would be rare. Second, federal systems require some explanation of how powers are divided between central and subnational governments. This is usually done, like in Australia, in the constitution. However, the UK does not have a written constitution. While there are agreements between Westminster and the parliaments of Scotland, Wales and Northern Ireland, these are only Memoranda of Understanding. Third, while some powers have been devolved, they could be returned to Westminster with a vote in parliament. In a federal system, this would be far more complex and generally would require changing the constitution. While the UK remains a unitary state for now, it is clear that the amount of power that the central government in Westminster has is certainly less than it was prior to this period of devolution (UK Parliament n.d.; Gov. UK 2013).

QUESTION

Are there any regions or states in Australia that you think would prefer to manage their affairs independently of the federal government?

WHY AND HOW DO WE STUDY AUSTRALIAN POLITICS?

The Australian political system, as demonstrated above, is complex. Bringing together ideas, traditions and institutional structures from across the liberal democratic world, Australia has been, from Federation to the present day, one of the world's safest and most prosperous places to live. In recent years, Australia, like very few other countries, has successfully been able to avoid the fates of many of our allies, trading partners and regional neighbours in the Asia–Pacific. A prescient example of this is Australia's good fortune in avoiding the most damaging effects of the 2008 **Global Financial Crisis (GFC)**. The GFC was the worst global economic downturn since the Great Depression yet Australia stood almost alone in avoiding recession. Across North America and Western Europe, unemployment rose considerably, and economic growth slowed dramatically. While the inter-connectedness of the global economy meant that Australia did indeed experience the effects of this global event, our economy slowed far less and recovered much more quickly than that of almost any other country (McDonald and Morling 2011). How do we explain this miraculous recovery and incredible durability? Without understanding the Australian political system – including its history, actors and institutions – it is impossible to answer this question.

Global Financial Crisis (GFC): Also known as 'the great recession' emerging in 2008–2009 to refer to the global downturn in economic growth resulting from the collapse of several US and European financial institutions.

THE 'LUCKY COUNTRY' OR THE LUCKY FEW?

Australia is often referred to as the 'lucky country'. But what is it that makes us lucky? And just how widely dispersed is this supposed luck? While referring to Australia as the lucky country has been a national pastime for decades, it is often overlooked that according to the person widely credited with bringing this turn of phrase to popular attention, this was anything but a compliment. In his 1964 book, Donald Horne said, 'Australia is a lucky country run mainly by second rate people who share its luck. It lives on other people's ideas, and, although its ordinary people are adaptable, most of its leaders (in all fields) so lack curiosity about the events that surround them that they are often taken by surprise' (1964, 233). Written over 50 years ago, Horne's critique of the lack of innovation, intellectual life and the colonial hangover still resonates for many Australians today. For others, contemporary Australia remains a shining beacon of the best parts of the British Empire that landed here in the 18th century. These are, of course, not the only two views and a variety of perspectives on this topic are to be expected in a geographically and culturally diverse country like Australia.

Nonetheless, debates about luck and culture cannot be properly considered without reference to the relationship and history between Indigenous and non-Indigenous populations. Very few debates in Australia generate as much heat as those about the history of this relationship. Much of the controversy relates to competing ideas about who Australians are and what our role and place is on this landmass we call home. While the plight of Indigenous people waxes and wanes in importance for many Australians, the evidence clearly shows that governments of both major parties have failed to meaningfully 'close the gap' between Indigenous and non-Indigenous Australians in ways that lead to lasting improvements in Indigenous people's lives (Brennan 2016).

The reality is that while many of our citizens are wealthy, healthy and happy compared to citizens of other countries, considerable numbers of Australians still live in poverty and are socio-economically disadvantaged. According to the Australian Institute of Health and Welfare, Indigenous Australians born in 2010–12 were expected to have a life expectancy which was 10.6 years less for men and 9.5 years less for women than the non-Indigenous population (Australian Institute of Health and Welfare n.d.). Could a country which has such variation in the life expectancy of its citizens be described as 'lucky' or does this label only apply to the few?

The variation in living standards among Australian citizens also extends beyond race. Australia is not just a nation-state, it is a continent. With a landmass as large as almost the whole of Western Europe, Australia is a federation with distinct regional variation. The lived experiences for those who live in Northern Tasmania in comparison to those who live in inner-city Sydney is completely different. Considering the different employment prospects and services available to them, for example, it is unsurprising that voters in these two regions, or any others you wish to compare, have different political and policy preferences.

VIDEO
SHORT-ANSWER
QUESTIONS

THE STUDY OF AUSTRALIAN POLITICS

Theory and concepts play a critical role in how we understand the political world around us. In the Australian context, a variety of theories and concepts have been developed to help students of Australian politics unpack critical issues and events. One of the most widely debated of these theories is that of the 'Australian Settlement'. In Paul Kelly's 1992 book, *The End of Certainty,* he argued that there were five elements of the Australian nation-building project: a racially 'white Australia', industry protection, wage arbitration, state paternalism and imperial benevolence. While the idea of the 'settlement' and what this may even contain are hotly contested (Melleuish et al. 2004; Stokes 2004; Fenna 2012), Kelly's thesis remains hugely influential.

The Australian settlement

Kelly's 1992 book, *The End of Certainty*, has become one of the most influential analyses of the rise of the Australian Federation. In it, Kelly (1992, 2–11) argued that five policies were central to the growth of the nation.

1. White Australia: One of Australia's most controversial sets of policies in its history, the White Australia policy and its predecessors, aspired to a nation of racially white people primarily through immigration protections.

2. Industry protection: This was intended to assist in building a diversified economy to be implemented by imposing tariffs on imports.

3. Wage arbitration: This recognised the principle of the 'fair go' in wages and conditions and the need to find peaceful ways of resolving industrial conflict.

4. State paternalism: This described the principle of promoting 'individual happiness through government intervention'. So, in other words, it allowed for governments to intervene in markets to maintain employment.

5. Imperial benevolence: This described 'the belief that Australian prosperity and security was underwritten by the [British] Empire'.

In contrast, Stokes (2004) contends that the Australian Settlement comprises nine elements. In addition to the elements identified by Kelly, such as the White Australia policy and arbitration and conciliation, Stokes argues for the inclusion of, for example, *terra nullius*, masculinism and state secularism.

SHORT-ANSWER QUESTIONS

QUESTION

What are the defining characteristics or policies of Australian politics in the 21st century?

CONTEMPORARY CHALLENGES IN AUSTRALIAN POLITICS

Since the turn of the millennium, a number of challenges have arisen that have put various pressures on Australian political institutions and have arguably made the task of effective governance more difficult. Externally, Australia's foremost allies, the United Kingdom and the United States, are undergoing significant political change that appears, at least at face value, to be isolationist in tendency, which supposedly the growth of 'populist' movements have facilitated. Among these significant changes are the UK's exit from the European Union ('Brexit') and the Trump presidency in the US. Likewise in Australia, the re-emergence of Pauline Hanson's One Nation party and the increasing vote for minor parties and independents suggests economic and cultural challenges are re-shaping the voting behaviour of many Australians.

In regard to international trade and global finance, on which Australia's economic fortunes depend, there appears little likelihood that the 21st century's first comprehensive regional trade agreement, the Trans-Pacific Partnership (TPP), encompassing 12 nations spanning the Americas and the Asia–Pacific region will proceed as originally envisaged, despite Australia's efforts as a key broker. Concurrently, Australia's largest trading partner, China, is seeking to expand its global reach via institutions such as the Asian Infrastructure Investment Bank, which Australia has joined. On Australia's doorstep, the relationship with Indonesia is proving challenging following a series of controversies over Indonesian people smugglers, defence cooperation and multiple high profile legal sagas involving Australian citizens and the Indonesian justice system. Meanwhile, on the security front, Australia has committed to fighting Islamic extremism both domestically, in terms of the 'home-grown' threat, and abroad with military commitments to the US-led coalition's efforts to combat the Islamic State group in Iraq and Syria. The impacts of these challenges are certainly testing for Australian foreign policy officials. Indeed, previously popular narratives from the 1990s about an increasingly globalised, open and interdependent world (Giddens 1990; Rosenau 1997) are now offered with less certainty.

VIDEO

FISCAL CHALLENGES

Several of the broader global trends pinpointed above have ramifications for contemporary Australian politics. First, in regard to the nation's finances, the 2008 GFC, as well as the decline of the mining boom, has had an ongoing impact that was not widely anticipated during, or in the immediate aftermath of, the crisis. Although Australia's response to the GFC in the form of cash 'handouts' and rapid financial injections into infrastructure for education and environmental projects was lauded internationally, the medium-term outlook for the Australian budget has become a source of ongoing political conjecture. Namely, while Australia appeared to escape the worst aspects of the global downturn, Australia's budgetary position has remained weak, with the outlook for a return to a budget surplus not expected until beyond 2020. While terms such as 'debt and deficit disaster' and 'budget emergency' were promulgated by the Coalition following the GFC, both major parties, as well as independent and minor party representatives, have acknowledged the ongoing challenge to the nation's finances. In response, a variety of savings measures have been proposed by the government, the opposition and those on the crossbench. These savings measures have generally proved contentious and many measures have failed to pass through both houses of parliament. Among the key battle lines are subsidies for property investors, concessions for superannuation holders and social security payments including the age and disability pensions.

ELECTORAL CHALLENGES

A second major challenge is the growing sense that Australia's relatively stable system of majoritarian government consolidated in the second half of the 20th century is in decline. Recent federal elections have seen a significant increase in first preferences for minor parties and independents in both the House of Representatives and the Senate. In turn, the election of non-major party candidates has created additional problems in forming government after an election. Minority governments, or governments with very slim majorities, have become commonplace. This has resulted in a sense of 'gridlock' in legislative terms, with some commentators referring to Australia's politics as 'broken' (Kelly 2015). In regard to the funding of political parties and their campaigns, another challenge centres on Australia's political donations system which is increasingly criticised as non-transparent. A further electoral challenge is the revolving door that has afflicted the office of Prime Minister since 2010. Indeed, the crisis in Australian political leadership has been described as the 'corrosive coup culture in Canberra' (Murphy 2017). In summary, a number of serious institutional challenges confront Australia's political system in the 21st century.

ENVIRONMENTAL CHALLENGES

A third major set of issues for Australian policymakers is the management of the natural environment, which encompasses energy production, water governance, protection of the Great Barrier Reef and, of course, addressing global warming. Reducing greenhouse gas emissions to slow global warming is a global collective action problem that clearly transcends Australia's territorial borders but has become an ongoing flashpoint in Australian politics. While successive Australian governments have participated in international efforts to curb emissions, exactly how this should be implemented is heavily contested, particularly given Australia's large fossil fuels sector (including an export sector) that currently provides a significant portion of the nation's electricity. Relatedly, the health of Australia's Great Barrier Reef World Heritage Area is under threat from warmer ocean temperatures resulting in coral bleaching. Meanwhile, access to and the use of water, including from the Murray–Darling Basin, continues to occupy policymakers at the local, state and federal levels. While security issues may be said to have dominated 20th century politics, contests over environmental policy issues, often encompassing economic and 'new' security aspects, are now among Australia's leading challenges in navigating the 21st century.

NATIONAL IDENTITY AND CIVIL RIGHTS CHALLENGES

Finally, in addition to the fiscal, electoral and environmental challenges facing Australia, a number of ongoing, high profile contests have emerged over issues that may be termed 'national identity and civil rights' challenges. For example, while a successful referendum removed two major discriminatory references to Indigenous people from the Constitution in 1967, the issue of further constitutional recognition of Indigenous people thus far remains unachieved despite the formation of a Referendum Council in 2015. While there appears to be broad agreement for constitutional change in and of itself, the process has elicited a further debate about the possible development of a treaty between Indigenous people and the Australian state. This has proved far more contentious than the changes to the preamble of the Constitution initially proposed.

Further, the rights of aspiring Australian citizens in the form of asylum seekers, their means of travel and our treatment of them has been a simmering, seemingly intractable issue since the early 2000s. Of greatest contention in this regard is the unauthorised nature of asylum seeker boat arrivals facilitated by Indonesian people smugglers and the mandatory, and seemingly indefinite, detention of asylum seekers in offshore locations including Christmas Island, Manus Island and Nauru by successive Australian governments. The key fault line on this issue is conservative/liberal in nature with those in the liberal camp seeking an end to indefinite offshore mandatory detention and better treatment of, and increased rights for, asylum seekers. In contrast, those representing a conservative view emphasise the need to 'stop the boats' and strengthen control of Australia's maritime borders. Similarly – and more broadly – concern among some sections of the Australian community about an increasingly multicultural Australia and the impacts on community cohesion, access to welfare and economic opportunities is part of a perpetual debate about immigration in Australia that emerged even before Federation. In the late 20th and early 21st century, these currents have given rise to the establishment of a multitude of new Australian political parties and elected representatives critical of multiculturalism, notably Pauline Hanson's resurgent One Nation party as mentioned above, plus an array of other peripheral parties espousing 'Australia for Australians' rhetoric.

In contrast, a preference for government intervention in restricting citizens' right to free speech in the context of Australia's race discrimination laws somewhat reverses the liberal inclination for less of a governmental presence in public life. The 1995 addition of Section 18C to the Australian Racial Discrimination Act sought to address 'hate speech' to the extent that it results in a material disadvantage for an individual or group. Indeed, liberals typically cite the need for government intervention to protect minority groups from discriminatory speech, while conservative sections of Australian society have vehemently argued for a less restrictive approach than currently exists in Australian law. For critics, the addition of Section 18C is viewed as a broader debate in several liberal democracies in the 21st century about 'political correctness' that is said to limit Australian citizens' right to freedom of expression.

One breakthrough has been the passage of legislation which legalises same-sex marriage in Australia. The source of much debate for over a decade, Australia had been a laggard in this respect, with numerous liberal democracies legalising same-sex marriage in this period. The passage of legislation in December 2017, following a voluntary postal survey of Australian citizens over the age of 18, further highlighted the conservative/ liberal division in Australian politics whereby conservatives emphasised their view of traditional and religious values, while those promoting a more liberal view criticised the exclusionary role the state was playing in upholding what they viewed as an outdated and discriminatory set of beliefs.

The struggle for and against the broadening of access to various types of civil recognition and rights – including for Indigenous people and asylum seekers, and over marriage and freedom of speech – is thus an ongoing contest that reflects some long running divisions between conservatives and liberals forged in 20th century Australia. Together, these issues have the potential to significantly reshape Australian political institutions in the 21st century and consequently the Australian national identity.

REFLECTION QUESTIONS

OVERVIEW OF THE BOOK

Twelve chapters follow this introduction, each of which introduces and contextualises the traditional and more recent institutions of Australian politics. Through the lens of these centuries-old institutions, each chapter will present the contemporary challenges that affect them. Chapter 2, *From colony to Commonwealth: The Australian Federation*, considers the way federalism has significantly shaped Australian democracy since Federation and demonstrates how federalism is the defining feature of Australian political life. Chapter 3, *The legislature: Representative democracy*, discusses the changes in the functions of parliament in Australia, as well as the processes of making laws and the checks on executive power that the legislature provides. Chapter 4, *The executive: Functions, power and accountability*, investigates the tensions between executive power and accountability. The relationship between prime ministers, their Cabinets and the Governor-General are also canvassed. Chapter 5, *The political rulebook: The Australian Constitution and the High Court*, discusses the role that the Constitution plays in setting the 'rules of the game' as well as the requirements to change the Constitution via referendum.

The role that the public service plays in Australian political life is reflected upon in Chapter 6, *'Red tape': The bureaucracy and public policy*. This chapter also considers the shift from 'government to governance' and the subsequent implications of this change are considered. Chapter 7, *Elections, the electoral system and the Australian voter,* outlines the systems and rules used to govern elections in Australia. It includes a discussion of the role that parties play during the election process and how voters, as a collective group, can be understood in terms of the choices they make at the ballot box. This leads into the discussions in Chapters 8 and 9. The historical relationship between the major parties and different sections of the Australian community are discussed in Chapter 8, *The origins and evolution of the major parties*. The chapter considers how this has changed over time and analyses whether Australia's major parties are different to those in other comparable democracies. Chapter 9, *A growing influence: Minor parties and independents,* reflects upon the growing importance of minor parties and independents in Australia and evaluates the effect the growing role these party and non-party actors will have on Australian democracy. Chapter 10, *Follow the leader: political leadership in Australia,* argues that leadership is not simply about the leaders of the major political parties and examines the tension between leaders and the liberal democratic framework they work in. In Chapter 11, *The fourth estate: News media in the digital age,* the public sphere is introduced and the competing theories of the media are analysed in the context of contemporary Australian politics. Key units of civil society who do not directly contest elections are evaluated in Chapter 12, *Having a voice: Citizen participation and engagement*. Changing modes of participation and engagement with Australian democracy are also considered. Finally, Chapter 13, *Conclusion,* describes and evaluates the current state of contemporary Australian politics in light of the chapters that precede it, with particular focus on the key challenges that confront the Australian political system.

SUMMARY

Learning objective 1: Describe some of the approaches used to understand politics

In this chapter, two broad approaches to understanding the scope of politics as a field of study were introduced: the 'politics as an arena' and 'politics as a social process' views. The arena view is generally limited to formal decision-making and focuses on governments and public life, while the social process view is much broader, encompassing the public and private spheres of life, formal and informal institutions and power relationships among people in society at large.

Learning objective 2: Explain some key features of Australian federal politics

While there will always be some debate about what the key features of Australian politics are, there is little doubt that the parliamentary system of government is one of these. This clearly signals a difference between Australia and, for example, the United States, based on the separation of powers. Equally important is federalism and the role of the Constitution. These two features ensure that sovereignty is divided between different layers of government and set the stage for a key source of political conflict within Australia: intergovernmental relations. Moreover, while in practice the role of the monarchy in Australian federal political life may be largely limited and ceremonial, in theory Queen Elizabeth II remains Australia's monarch and her representatives, the Governor-General and the Governors, remain within the executive.

Learning objective 3: Understand how and why we study Australian politics

The Australian political system is complex. Combining a myriad of different electoral systems, with parliamentary government and within a federal structure, means the process and practice of politics in Australia can be confusing. Only through deepening our knowledge of the key actors, institutions and ideas which shape Australian politics can one hope to really appreciate power in Australia. In this chapter, students were introduced to some of these debates and these will be expanded upon further throughout the course of this text. Nonetheless, it is important to recognise that there is no one-size-fits-all approach to studying Australian politics. Not only are there different theoretical lenses that can be used, there are a variety of methods as well.

Learning objective 4: Identify some of the recent domestic and international challenges to Australian federal politics

The 21st century global political environment is proving dynamic and challenging for Australian policymakers and political institutions, particularly in regard to new security threats such as Islamic fundamentalism and economic uncertainty in the aftermath of the GFC. Within Australia, the ongoing contention about how best to return the federal budget to surplus has hit several hurdles in recent years, with prominent debates centring on welfare and entitlements relating to superannuation savings and housing investors. Further, the rise of small political parties and independent representatives in the Commonwealth and state parliaments has made the passage of legislation increasingly difficult, thereby disrupting the idea that Australia has a relatively stable two-party dominated system. In regard to leadership, Australia has witnessed a passing parade of prime ministers, with Prime Minister Turnbull as the fifth leader since 2007. In managing the natural environment, Australian policymakers have a number of significant issues to tackle including conservation of internationally significant heritage sites, the governance of water resources, and working towards a lower carbon emitting energy sector in the era of global warming. And finally, a number of simmering civil rights and national identity challenges have frequently dominated Australia's political discourse in recent years and these are likely to reverberate through, and potentially reshape, Australian political institutions into the 21st century.

DISCUSSION QUESTIONS

DISCUSSION
QUESTIONS

1. Which view of politics do you find most persuasive: the arena or process view? Justify your view.
2. Develop a list of the major external challenges for Australian politics. Can you rank these challenges according to their severity? What factors underpin your views in this regard?
3. Commentator Paul Kelly has described Australia's politics as 'broken'. What does he mean by this and do you agree with his assessment?
4. Do you think Australia is lucky or is our economic and political stability down to good management?
5. Of the six key features of the Australian political system listed, which of these would you most like to change and why?

FURTHER READING

Bolton, G. (2000). Sir Edmund Barton. In M. Grattan, ed., *Australian Prime Ministers*, Sydney: New Holland, pp. 22–36.

Kelly, P. (2004). Comment: the Australian settlement. *Australian Journal of Political Science*, **39**(1).

Manne, R.M. (ed.). (2001). *The Australian Century: Political Struggle in the Building of a Nation*, Melbourne: Text Publishing.

Megalogenis, G. (2015). *Australia's Second Chance: What Our History Tells Us About Our Future*, Melbourne: Hamish Hamilton/Penguin.

Melleuish, G. (2004). From the 'Social Laboratory' to the 'Australian Settlement'. In P. Boreham, G. Stokes and R. Hall, eds, *The Politics of Australian Society: Political Issues for the New Century*, 2nd edn, Frenchs Forest: Pearson.

Rickard, J. (1993). Loyalties. In J. Arnold, P. Spearritt and D. Walker, eds, *Out of Empire: the British Dominion of Australia*, Melbourne: Mandarin.

Stoker, G. (2016). *Why Politics Matters: Making Democracy Work*, 2nd edn, Basingstoke: Palgrave Macmillan.

Stoker, G. and Marsh, D. (2010). Introduction. In D. Marsh and G. Stoker, eds, *Theory and Methods in Political Science*, 3rd edn, Basingstoke: Palgrave Macmillan.

Stokes, G. (2007). Australian settlement. In B. Galligan and W. Roberts, eds, *The Oxford Companion to Australian Politics*, Oxford: Oxford University Press, pp. 56–7.

Walker, D. (1999). *Anxious Nation: Australia and the Rise of Asia 1850–1939*, St Lucia: University of Queensland Press.

REFERENCES

Acton, J.E.E.D.A., Figgis, J.N. and Laurence, R.V. (1907). *Historical Essays and Studies*, London: Macmillan.

Adams, H. and Nadel, I.B. (1999). The education of Henry Adams. *Oxford World's Classics* (p. 1 electronic text.). Retrieved from http://site.ebrary.com/lib/aberdeenuniv/Doc?id=10485525

Australian Electoral Commission. (2011). Federation Fact Sheet 1 – The Referendums 1898–1900. URL: http://www.aec.gov.au/about_aec/publications/fact_sheets/factsheet1.htm

Australian Institute of Health and Welfare. Life Expectancy. URL: http://www.aihw.gov.au/deaths/life-expectancy/

Ball, A.R. (1988). *Modern Politics and Government*, 4th edn, Basingstoke: Macmillan Education.

Bluntschli, J.K. (2000). *The Theory of the State*, Kitchener, Ontario: Batoche Books.

Boswell, J. (1798). *Dr. Johnson's Table-Talk: Containing Aphorisms on Literature, Life, and Manners; With Anecdotes of Distinguished Persons: Selected and Arranged from Mr. Boswell's Life of Johnson*, London: C. Dilly.

Brennan, B. (2016). Malcolm Turnbull hands down Closing the Gap report showing Indigenous life expectancy has not improved, *ABC News*, 10 February. Retrieved from http://www.abc.net.au/news/2016-02-10/indigenous-life-expectancy-has-not-improved-closing-the-gap/7154566

Crick, B. (1964). *In Defence of Politics*, Rev. Pelican edn, Baltimore: Penguin Books.

De Garis, B. (1999). Federation. In R. Manne, ed., *The Australian Century: Political Struggle in the Building of a Nation*, Melbourne: Text Publishing, pp. 11–47.

Dowding, K. (2016). Australian exceptionalism reconsidered. *Australian Journal of Political Science*, 1–18. doi:10.1080/10361146.2016.1267111

Easton, D. (1953). *The Political System: An Inquiry into the State of Political Science*, 1st edn, New York: Knopf.

Edelman, M.J. (1971). *Politics as Symbolic Action: Mass Arousal and Quiescence*, Chicago: Markham Pub. Co.

Fenna, A. (2012). Putting the 'Australian settlement' in perspective. *Labour History: A Journal of Labour and Social History*, 102, 99–118.

Garner, J.W. (1952). *Political Science and Government*, Calcutta: World Press.

Giddens, A. (1990). *The Consequences of Modernity*, Cambridge, UK: Polity Press in association with Basil Blackwell, Oxford, UK.

Goodin, R.E. and Klingemann, H.D. (1996). *A New Handbook of Political Science*, Oxford; New York: Oxford University Press.

Gov.UK. (2013). Devolution of powers to Scotland, Wales and Northern Ireland. URL: https://www.gov.uk/guidance/devolution-of-powers-to-scotland-wales-and-northern-ireland

Gramsci, A., Hoare, Q. and Nowell-Smith, G. (1971). *Selections from the Prison Notebooks of Antonio Gramsci*, London: Lawrence & Wishart.

Hay, C. (2002). *Political Analysis*, Houndmills, Basingstoke, Hampshire; New York: Palgrave.

Horne, D. (1964). *The Lucky Country*, Ringwood, Victoria: Penguin.

Kannan, O. (2013). *The Book of Quotes*, Xlibris.

Kelly, P. (1992). *The End of Certainty: Power, Politics and Business in Australia*, Sydney: Allen & Unwin.

Kelly, P. (2015). Broken system can't fix nation's problems, *The Australian*, 19 March. Retrieved from http://www.theaustralian.com.au/opinion/columnists/paul-kelly/broken-system-cant-fix-nations-problems/news-story/50f526196cb8db5bd5fb63f17e3d5d0a

Lasswell, H.D. (1958). *Politics: Who Gets What, When, How. With postscript (1958)*, New York: Meridian Books.

Lukes, S. (1974). *Power: A Radical View*, London: Macmillan.

Macintyre, S. (1999). *A Concise History of Australia*, Melbourne: Cambridge University Press.

McDonald, T. and Morling, S. (2011). The Australian economy and the global downturn, Part 1: Reasons for resilience. *Economic Roundup Issue 2*. Retrieved from http://www.treasury .gov.au/publicationsandmedia/publications/2011/economic-roundup-issue-2/report/ part-1-reasons-for-resilience

Melleuish, G., Boreham, P., Stokes, G. and Hall, R. (2004). From the 'Social Laboratory' to the 'Australian Settlement'. In *The Politics of Australian Society: Political Issues for the New Century*, 2nd edn, Frenchs Forest: Pearson.

Murphy, K. (2017). Major headache for Malcolm Turnbull as minor parties rise, *The Guardian*, 6 February. Retrieved from https://www.theguardian.com/australia-news/2017/feb/06/major-headache-for-malcolm-turnbull-as-minor-parties-rise

Parliamentary Education Office. The colonial parliaments of Australia. URL: http://www.peo.gov .au/learning/closer-look/short-history/the-colonial-parliaments-of-australia.html

Parliamentary Education Office. Three levels of law-making. URL: http://www.peo.gov.au/learning/ fact-sheets/three-levels-of-law-making.html

Randall, V. (2002). Feminism. In D. Marsh and G. Stoker, eds, *Theory and Methods in Political Science*, 2nd edn, Basingstoke, Hampshire: Palgrave Macmillan, pp. 109–30.

Rosenau, J.N. (1997). *Along the Domestic-foreign Frontier: Exploring Governance in a Turbulent World*, Cambridge, New York: Cambridge University Press.

Rousseau, J.J. and Cranston, M.W. (1968). *The Social Contract*, Harmondsworth: Penguin.

Stoker, G. and Marsh, D. (2002). Introduction. In D. Marsh and G. Stoker, eds, *Theory and Methods in Political Science*, 2nd edn, Basingstoke, Hampshire: Palgrave Macmillan.

Stokes, G. (2004). The 'Australian settlement' and Australian political thought. *Australian Journal of Political Science*, **39**(1), 5–22.

UK Parliament. Devolved Parliaments and Assemblies. URL: http://www.parliament.uk/about/ how/role/devolved/

CHAPTER 2

FROM COLONY TO COMMONWEALTH: THE AUSTRALIAN FEDERATION

LEARNING OBJECTIVES

After reading this chapter, you should be able to:

1. Explain how and why federalism divides powers

2. Analyse the Australian variant of federalism and explain how it has evolved

3. Explain how the way states are funded enlarges the role of the Commonwealth

4. Analyse COAG and its importance to contemporary politics and policy-making

5. Make an informed judgement about the need for, and prospects of, reforming the Federation

INTRODUCTION

If you Google 'federation', you will find accounts of systems of government in which sovereignty is divided between a central, national government and a series of regional, partially self-governing states. You will probably find a webpage of the Parliamentary Education Office recording that, 'in a process known as Federation' Australia 'became a nation on 1 January 1901 when six British colonies – New South Wales, Victoria, Queensland, South Australia, Western Australia and Tasmania – united to form the Commonwealth of Australia' (PEO 2017). You may also see links to various peak associations such as the National Farmers Federation, Australian Federation of Air Pilots or Football Federation Australia – the latter describing itself as the governing body of Australian football with 'a member-based organisation loosely based on Australia's federated system of government'. These search results suggest some key takeaway points for students of Australian politics.

First, a federation is a particular form of political system in which national and regional-level governments share the authority to make and administer laws. Second, when capitalised 'Federation' describes a process resulting in the creation of Australia at the dawn of the last century. Further, the term can also be a synonym for 'association' as in the case of Football Federation Australia. Often associations formed to advance the interests of their members are organised in ways which reflect their need to lobby state as well as the Commonwealth (or federal) governments. Hence, a third point to note is that Australia's federal system shapes its politics. Its federation provides a good example of how 21st century Australian politics remains in the grip of institutions established in the historical past for largely forgotten reasons. Beginning with the exploration of the theory of federalism, in this chapter we shall explore each of these points.

AUTHOR
PANEL
REFLECTION
QUESTION

WHAT IS FEDERALISM?

federalism: A political theory that sees benefit in constitutionally dividing the authority to make and administer laws between a national government and a series of regional subnational governments.

Federalism as a prescriptive political theory seeks both to divide power to prevent its abuse and to fix government in a local context, 'close to the people'. In seeking to limit the power that governments can accumulate, it falls within a centuries-old liberal tradition. Classical (or small) liberalism accepts that governments are necessary to preserve social order and a political community that can secure citizens their rights and freedoms. But liberals also fear that governments will grow to make and enforce unnecessary laws, and thus come to threaten these prized individual rights and freedoms. Various solutions have been proposed to deal with this dilemma. One is to subject governments to the 'rule of law' and to place constitutional constraints upon them, often by providing for a 'separation of powers' such that no single group can control the legislative, executive and judicial branches of government. The theory of federalism offers an alternative constitutional prescription for preventing the abuse of power by government, proposing its fragmentation and distribution in a system of multiple subnational governments.

THE DIVISION OF POWERS

Instead of providing for the constitutional separation of powers, federalism prescribes shared sovereignty and the **division of powers** between constitutionally separate national and subnational tiers of government. In short, federations are political systems that seek to prevent any single group from monopolising power by requiring that the legislative and executive responsibilities of government be shared out between a national-level government and a set of subnational governments. In Australia's Federation, the national-level government is known as the Commonwealth Government (or federal government), while the subnational tier of government comprises six states, the Australian Capital Territory and Northern Territory governments, plus 546 local (municipal and shire) governments (DIRD 2016).

Federalism is a prescription for accommodating diversity within a single, unified political system. The American political scientist W.H. Riker defined a federal system as 'a political organisation in which the activities of government are divided between regional governments and a central government in such a way that each kind of government has some activities on which it makes final decisions' (Riker 1975, 101). According to Cook, Walsh and Harwood (2009, 114), '[f]ederalism is a mechanism for sharing powers and responsibilities between members of political executives at a central and regional level. It is characterised by a division of powers, shared sovereignty and financial independence.' Hollander (2014, 316) writes that '[f]ederalism is defined by divided sovereignty, an arrangement whereby government authority is divided between different levels of government, with neither having the legal authority to intervene in areas of the others' sphere of competence'. Ratnapala (2014, 66) defines a federation as a 'political association of regions under which the regions enjoy an assured measure of autonomy' and adds that most 'are constitutionally established in the sense that regional autonomy is part of the national constitutional structure'.

DEVOLVED DECISION-MAKING

Often definitions of federal systems emphasise the role of a constitution in specifying the powers available to national and subnational governments (as well as the importance of a supreme or constitutional court able to uphold its provisions). The constitutional devolution of powers is a distinctive feature and a key point of difference with unitary systems. Some 85 per cent of United Nation member states have unitary rather than federal systems. New Zealand, Indonesia, China and Japan are all examples. In unitary systems, all executive and legislative powers that a government is entitled to exercise are constitutionally located in a single, national-level government. But even in such systems, political power is devolved to regional or municipal subnational governments.

In practice, the increasingly complex business of governing a country cannot be effectively managed from national capitals such as Beijing, Tokyo or Wellington, nor by a single government. Indeed, around the globe, and in political systems having very different institutional forms, we have seen the emergence of de facto federations and 'a revolution' involving the extensive devolution of decision-making to subnational governments (Martinez-Vazquez 2011, 1). In short, both unitary and federal systems will exhibit 'some vertical hierarchy among different levels of government' (Beramendi 2009, 753). However, in unitary systems the devolution of decision-making to subnational

division of powers: Found in federal systems, where the responsibility for some policy areas are allocated to a national government and other policy areas are reserved for subnational governments.

VIDEO

governments can be reversed by national governments: 'regional or provincial officials do not have constitutional status as effective actors in a bargaining process with the center' (Beramendi 2009, 754). This contrasts with federal systems where constitutions entrench the authority and autonomy of subnational governments.

In Australia's case, the various subnational governments within its federal system do not all enjoy the same constitutional status. Australia's Constitution establishes the range of policy areas that fall within the jurisdiction of the states. But the Australian Capital Territory and the Northern Territory are self-governing territories exercising an authority extended to them by the Commonwealth Parliament. Legislation enacted by territory parliaments can and – as in the notable case of euthanasia laws passed by the Northern Territory in 1995 – has been quashed by the Commonwealth Government. The position of territory governments is not all that different from the third tier of subnational governments comprising shire and municipal governments. These operate under state legislation with a devolved authority that can be withdrawn.

It is sometimes said that 'there are likely as many different federalisms as there are federations' (Anderson 2010, 130). The scale of the Australian Federation is a distinctive

Figure 2.1 Australia's states and territories

feature. The US has 50 states and Nigeria 36. India's federation encompasses 29 states (plus seven union territories). Switzerland has 26 cantons. Brazil also has 26 estados plus a federal district. In contrast, Australia, with six states and two self-governing territories, has relatively few subnational governments. The small scale of Australia's federation has, literally, made it possible for the state, territory and Commonwealth governments to 'sit around the table'. It has allowed collaboration between governments not so easily achieved in larger federal systems. This suggests we need not only understand federal systems as a type of government, but also investigate the particular features of the Australian Federation.

REFLECTION QUESTION

THE AUSTRALIAN VARIATION, ITS HISTORY AND EVOLUTION

'Federation' has several meanings. While it describes a political arrangement in which power is constitutionally divided between central and subnational governments, in an Australian setting, federation also refers to the process that gave birth to Australia as a nation. It is difficult to imagine now, but in the 19th century, border control measures restricted trade and travel between what are now neighbouring Australian states. Prior to 1901, Australia was a continent, not a country. New South Wales, Queensland, Western Australia, Tasmania, Victoria and South Australia were all separate entities, much as Australia and New Zealand are today. Each was a self-governing British colony. Federation describes the process whereby the six colonies agreed to form, and to share the task of governing with, a new Commonwealth government with jurisdiction over the entire country. This agreement was cemented in a Constitution drafted by a series of Conventions, meeting between 1891 and 1897; approved by voters in the various colonies at referenda elections held between 1898 and 1900; legislated as the *Commonwealth of Australia Constitution Act 1900* by the British parliament; and assented to by Queen Victoria on 9 July 1900. It took effect on 1 January 1901.

The 'federal compact' struck by the colonial politicians who negotiated the 1901 Constitution founding Australia has since shaped its politics. The Australian federal system has its critics today, even within the ranks of the Liberal Party, which long championed **'states' rights'**. The prime minister whose term bridged this and the last century (John Howard) believed that Australia would likely opt for a centralised, not a federal, system of government 'if we had our time again' (Howard 2005). Australia's Federation, with its roots in an agreement struck in the 1890s, is creaking at the seams. It is today often seen as a source of duplication and inefficiency. According to the influential Business Council of Australia, the 'poor performance of the current system of federal–state relations' explains many of the 'policy failings and reform limitations holding Australia back' (BCA 2007, 21). States depend heavily upon the Commonwealth: they are only able to fund the roads, police, hospitals and schools for which the Constitution gives them responsibility with the assistance of the Commonwealth. Another frequent cry is that Australians are 'over governed'. However, proposing reform is one thing, achieving it is quite another. For chief among the legacy we have inherited from the politics of the 1890s is a difficult-to-change Constitution that entrenches a federal system.

states' rights: In the Australian context, a political doctrine asserting the importance of protecting individual states from undue interference by the Commonwealth Government.

'THE ONLY WAY TO MAKE A NATION'

From time to time, Australia's federal system has been portrayed as an essential safeguard of individual freedom. For example, in the midst of the Second World War with national survival at stake, a Labor government proposed altering the Constitution to give the Commonwealth additional powers to facilitate Australia's defence. But the then opposition leader (and, later, Liberal Party founder) R.G. Menzies refused support, pointing to the 'necessity of divided power for liberty' and the 'unsound doctrine' holding that 'central governments should always be presumed to be wiser and more efficient than local government' (Tiver 1978, 130). In this vein, Smith (2013, 362) writes that '[t]he evolution of the Australian federation is rooted in a deep understanding of the need to limit government, while ensuring it is used to preserve a free society'. The former prime minister Tony Abbott (2008, 3) has a more prosaic view: the Constitution's authors did not set out to safeguard against government tyranny; rather federalism 'was the only way to make a nation out of six colonies'.

Like Menzies before him, Abbott served as Liberal leader. Yet his view of federalism is very different and points to a more recent shift in Liberal Party thinking. Abbott's account of Australia's Federation as a pragmatic solution to the challenge of nation building in the 1890s rather than a product of a liberal concern to entrench freedom has merit. Those involved in designing the Australian Constitution (such as Queensland premier Sir Samuel Griffith) were often colonial political leaders. Most will have seen their role as NSW premier Henry Parkes did: he told the 1891 Australasian Federation Conference 'it will be our duty to see that our respective colonies are not injured' in their joining together (Official Report 1891, 910–11).

Unsurprisingly, its authors crafted a Constitution that would allow the colonies to continue as state governments without undue loss of power and influence. The history of Federation has been extensively told and, today, the record of proceedings of the various Conventions which gathered during the 1890s are available online. This record contains no fine speeches on the 'necessity of divided power for liberty' nor a spirited advocacy of federalism as a way of securing individual freedom for Australia's citizens. Even those liberals participating (such as Alfred Deakin) had more practical concerns with how the Federation might be best organised – for example, with questions of how taxation powers might be shared between the Commonwealth and states in ways that would secure free trade between colonies.

VIDEO

COORDINATE FEDERALISM

coordinate federalism: A theory which holds that regional and national governments within a federation should be substantially independent of one another and free to exercise their allocated powers without interference.

When Deakin told the 1897 Convention that '[w]e should make the spheres of state and federal finance as distinct as they can be made' (Official Records 1897, 56) he was advancing a particular understanding of federalism. **Coordinate federalism** holds that no level of government ought to be subordinate to the other. It stresses 'the importance of national and state governments each occupying a discrete sphere of activity' in which they are 'independent, distinct and separate from each other' (Windholz 2011, 4). The theory of coordinate (or dual) federalism appears to have held sway during the drafting of the 1901 Constitution, which carefully enumerated the powers that were to be available to the Commonwealth.

The Constitution gives the Commonwealth a limited range of *exclusive* powers including the right to make laws regulating currency (Section 115), the raising of military forces (Section 114), Commonwealth public service departments, and the collection of customs and excise duties (Section 90). Section 51 lists many other areas in which the Commonwealth Parliament may legislate. These *specific* powers range from the right to make laws about trade and commerce with other countries to the regulation of lighthouses and marriage. Mostly these specified powers are *concurrent* and thus are also available to states. A constitution which hands states and the Commonwealth concurrent powers to legislate may initially appear incompatible with the theory of coordinate federalism, but this principle is ensured by Section 109. It establishes that Commonwealth legislation must prevail where laws passed by the Commonwealth and a state parliament clash. It is noteworthy that the right to pass laws pertaining to taxation was specified as a *concurrent* power, available to both the Commonwealth and the states so that neither would financially depend on the other.

While the Constitution handed the Commonwealth Parliament a range of specific powers, it made no mention of many policy responsibilities including transport, policing, education, hospitals and public health. Section 108 defined these as *residual* powers and established them as policy areas in which only the states might make laws. Many residual powers – for example, those pertaining to health – involve policy areas that directly impact the lives of citizens. In dividing legislative responsibilities between the two levels of government as they did, the Constitution's authors intended states to continue alongside the Commonwealth as separate and important political actors. As Wanna et al. (2009, 11) suggest, '[t]he Australian federation was designed on the assumption that the levels of government would operate with a high degree of independence'. But coordinate federalism is more a legalistic concept than a practical formula for government. In embracing it, the 1901 Constitution 'made little provision for integration of policy-making and implementation between the Commonwealth and the states'.

VIDEO
SHORT-ANSWER
QUESTIONS

INVENTING COOPERATIVE FEDERALISM

The practical business of governing confounds the notion that governments might operate with a high degree of independence. To take a very simple example, interstate road and rail networks cannot be built without neighbouring states first reaching an agreement. Similarly, management of the Murray–Darling river system cannot be achieved by governments acting independently of one another: it requires their interaction and agreement. Reaching agreements of this kind 'requires an architecture of cooperation' (Wanna et al. 2009, 3). The problem with the original design of the Australian Federation is that it provided few mechanisms to allow **cooperative federalism**. These had to be invented, often in an ad hoc fashion to deal with challenges as they arose.

The 1901 Constitution did establish a house of parliament in which each state is equally represented. However, although the Senate was designed to be the 'States' House' and champion their interests within the new Commonwealth, it failed in this role because of the influence parties secured within it. The Constitution also provided for an Inter-State Commission (Section 101) to administer free trade between the states, but this failed and eventually lapsed. Because the Constitution did not provide a viable architecture to enable intergovernmental cooperation, it proved necessary to build new structures outside of its provisions. For example, prior to Federation the premiers of the various colonies had

cooperative federalism: A federalism that is manifest in federations where the different levels of government consult and collaborate in developing policy solutions to their common problems.

periodically met to discuss matters of common concern. The Constitution did not provide for such a meeting but as early as 1901, state premiers found it necessary to revive this practice. Thereafter, Special Premiers' Conferences were expanded to include the prime minister and met annually for much of the last century.

The resurrection of Premiers' Conferences signalled the beginning of a 'cooperative federalism' characterised by formal agreements establishing 'joint schemes of policy and legislation' and the creation of 'new national intergovernmental bodies' (Painter 1996, 101). The River Murray Commission was another institution created as part of Australia's improvisation of cooperative federalism. It was established to give expression to the 1915 River Murray Waters Agreement and to integrate the actions of the Commonwealth, New South Wales, Victoria and South Australia, all with a stake in the river system. Like the Premiers' Conference, which ultimately morphed into the **Council of Australian Governments (COAG)** in 1992, the River Murray Commission was replaced (in 1988) by the Murray–Darling Basin Commission and then with the Murray–Darling Basin Authority (MDBA) (in 2008). COAG and the MDBA are both more recent, pragmatic expressions of cooperative federalism.

Following the path pioneered by Premiers' Conferences (and extending the emerging architecture of cooperation), state and Commonwealth ministers with similar portfolios began to meet regularly with the goal of avoiding duplication and developing uniform policy. The first such ministerial council originated in 1923 with the creation of the Loan Council as part of an informal agreement between the Commonwealth and states to act collectively to secure more favourable terms in borrowing from banks. In 1934 the Australian Agriculture Council was established to harmonise the regulation of primary industries spanning state borders. In 1936 state education ministers agreed to meet regularly as the Australian Education Council. Meetings of ministerial councils were often preceded by meetings of state and Commonwealth public servants to hammer out the details of complementary policies. During the last century, ministerial councils grew in number and progressively became an important vehicle for intergovernmental relations and thus for cooperative federalism. In the early 1990s, when the first of several attempts was made to streamline their activities, there were more than 40 different ministerial committees in place.

The development of the Loan Council took an unusual course. It evolved into a statutory body in 1927 when the Commonwealth imposed a *Financial Agreement* as a condition for taking over state debts, and its work was subsequently given a constitutional basis (by a 1928 referendum approving Section 105A). It continues today, although with a diminished brief, no longer setting borrowing limits, but instead shining light upon the extent of public sector borrowing. There is one further noteworthy part of the architecture of cooperation devised in the decades after Federation that survives today with an important role. The Commonwealth Grants Commission was established in 1933 following a series of ad hoc Royal Commissions that had advised upon federal–state financial relations. Its role was to advise the Commonwealth on how special financial assistance grants provided for in **Section 96** should be distributed between claimant states with different populations, needs and economic circumstances. The Grants Commission is a quasi-judicial statutory authority, not a ministerial council. (This is an area where federal Cabinets are keen to insulate themselves from political acrimony that inevitably attaches to decisions to support or reject pleas for assistance from claimant states.) Today the role of the Grants

Council of Australian Governments (COAG): A forum for intergovernmental collaboration, established in 1992, which brings together the leaders of state, territory and Commonwealth governments.

Section 96: Section 96 of the Constitution empowers the Commonwealth to set conditions on how states must spend any grants that it provides them.

Commission is to advise how GST revenue collected by the Commonwealth on behalf of the states should be distributed.

SHORT-ANSWER QUESTIONS

COOPERATIVE FEDERALISM IS A MISLEADING TERM

Since 1901 Australia has devised various 'pragmatic arrangements enabling governments to work together horizontally and vertically. These arrangements, sometimes called the "gossamer strands" that tie the federation together, have broadened and deepened over the years' (Wanna et al. 2009, 13). This institutional architecture includes the Premiers' Conference and COAG, which has now subsumed it; ministerial councils, which have now found a new importance under the COAG umbrella; and the more specialised Murray–Darling Basin Authority and Grants Commission. None were originally described in the Constitution. They were subsequently invented to allow Commonwealth and state governments to act collaboratively. Without the protection of the Constitution such **ad hoc intergovernmental arrangements** are vulnerable to political pressures and to alteration when there is a change in the party elected to govern.

ad hoc intergovernmental arrangements: The 1901 Australian Constitution made few provisions for intergovernmental cooperation so, of necessity, new mechanisms have since been developed for this purpose, often in an ad hoc fashion as problems requiring a joint policy response arose.

Clearly the Australian Federation has departed from the coordinate vision of the 1901 Constitution's authors. It is now better seen as a form of cooperative federalism. But cooperative federalism is a rather misleading term. It refers to an institutional architecture that allows the national and subnational units within a federal system to interact where effective policy–making requires consultation and joint action. It does *not* imply that governments within a federation will work harmoniously together. In Australia, the Labor and Liberal parties contest both state and national elections. Elections occur frequently. Often the Commonwealth Government and different state governments are controlled by rival parties. The tensions between them will permeate institutions such as COAG (where state and Commonwealth leaders sit around the same table). Cooperative federalism is also a misleading term because the pragmatic development of institutions enabling governments to work together to improve and coordinate policy–making has contributed to a centralisation of power. As Windholz (2011, 2) writes, the practice of federalism in Australia has shifted away from coordinate federalism and 'from relative equality to a system characterised by a constitutionally and fiscally dominant Commonwealth'.

FISCAL FEDERALISM

How the Commonwealth emerged as fiscally dominant is a key part of the story of Australia's evolving federal system. The 1901 Constitution established taxation as a concurrent power available to both state and the Commonwealth parliaments. In the late 19th century and immediate years after Federation, customs and excise duties provided the major source of revenue available to governments. However, with Australia's subsequent economic transformation and development, personal income and company taxation grew increasingly important. In addition to this economic change, the High Court made a series of decisions that enhanced the revenue-raising powers available to the Commonwealth.

Most notably the High Court upheld the Commonwealth Government's 1942 *Uniform Taxation Act*. Introduced during the Second World War, this Act secured control of income and company taxation for the Commonwealth while providing for tax reimbursement grants to the states. The Commonwealth subsequently acted to retain its monopoly of these increasingly important revenue streams by requiring that the states not levy income taxes as a condition for receiving tax reimbursement grants. When Victoria challenged this arrangement in 1957, in the *Second Uniform Tax* case, the High Court again ruled in favour of the Commonwealth, upholding its constitutional power to attach conditions to reimbursement grants. In other decisions, the High Court has also ruled in ways that prevented the states from imposing taxes on goods and challenging duties they had imposed on tobacco, alcohol and petrol. As a result, the states have been left with a limited capacity to raise revenue via lesser and inefficient means such as stamp duty, payroll and land taxes. As a consequence, the states are only able to deliver the health, education, transport and other services and infrastructure for which they are responsible with additional funding from the Commonwealth.

VERTICAL FISCAL IMBALANCE

vertical fiscal imbalance: A situation that arises in a federation where one tier of government lacks the revenue-raising capacity of the other and relies on grants to meet its policy commitments.

Today Australia's federation features pronounced levels of '**vertical fiscal imbalance**'. Fiscal imbalance refers to a mismatch between a government's spending responsibilities and its ability to raise the revenue needed to meet them. Vertical fiscal imbalance describes circumstances within a federation where one tier of government faces a revenue shortfall and depends upon a transfer of funding from the other to meet its commitments. Usually it is subnational governments that depend upon central government disbursements. Australia fits this pattern. Indeed '[i]n Australia, taxation power is more centralised than in other federations' (Ratnapala 2014, 76). While the states and territories are unable to raise the revenue needed to meet their recurrent spending obligations, the Commonwealth collects four of every five tax dollars paid and more revenue than it needs to fund its own policy programs.

The extent of vertical fiscal imbalance within the Australian Federation can be measured by the revenue transferred by the Commonwealth to the states as a proportion of their total revenue. Table 2.1 shows both the reduced capacity of states to raise their own revenue and the extent of their current dependence on Commonwealth transfers. Grants from the Commonwealth usually fund about half of state and territory general government spending. For example, in the 2014–15 financial year the Commonwealth provided 43.6 per cent of the total revenue of the states. Smaller states are especially dependent on

TABLE 2.1 REVENUE COLLECTED UNDER STATE LEGISLATION AND SUPPLEMENTARY COMMONWEALTH TRANSFERS

	PROPORTION COLLECTED UNDER STATE LEGISLATION	PROPORTION OF STATE REVENUE FROM COMMONWEALTH TRANSFERS
1901–02	59.0%	36.7%
1938–39	53.4%	13.9%
1946–47	15.1%	46.1%
1980–81	21.7%	62.0%
2000–01	22.2%	46.2%
2014–15	26.2%	43.6%

Source: Commonwealth Grants Commission 2016, 3

Commonwealth transfers: in 2014–15 South Australia obtained 51.5 per cent of its total revenue from the Commonwealth, and Tasmania obtained 61 per cent. Commonwealth transfers have long 'been a large part of state budgets', accounting for 'around half since World War II' (CGC 2016). That the Commonwealth financially underwrites the states helps explain the centralisation of power within the Australian Federation.

Section 96 of the Constitution authorises the Commonwealth to provide funding to the states on the terms and conditions of its choosing. It is able to provide assistance conditionally in the form of 'payments for special purposes' and unconditionally as 'general revenue assistance'. The latter category of financial assistance to the states is inflated by the transfer of the proceeds of the lucrative goods and services tax (GST). The GST was proposed in 1998 by the Howard Government, which pledged to hand over all of the monies raised as general revenue assistance (providing the states ended a number of inefficient state taxes). The automatic transfer of revenue raised by the GST commenced in 2000. It was intended to ameliorate vertical fiscal imbalance within the Federation by guaranteeing the states an efficient and expanding revenue source; however, while GST revenue is now returned to the states to spend as they choose, the Commonwealth still provides significant amounts of additional funding conditionally.

SHORT-ANSWER
QUESTION

PAYMENTS FOR SPECIAL PURPOSES

Since 2009, Commonwealth financial transfers have been made under the terms of the *Intergovernmental Agreement on Federal Financial Relations*, which acknowledges that the states have primary responsibility for service delivery across a range of areas, but also provides for collaborative policy development and service delivery and for the conditional funding of economic and social reforms of national importance. In 2014–15 the Commonwealth budgeted to provide the states with $101.1 billion, $46.3 billion in the form of payments for special purposes. Special purpose payments are sometimes described as 'tied grants' because recipient states must spend these funds on particular policy programs, pursuant to agreements struck with the Commonwealth. There is a long history of national governments providing the states with funding conditional upon their adoption of the Commonwealth's own policy priorities and settings. Using 'tied grants' in this way, the Commonwealth has been able to progressively exert influence over education, health, transport and other policy areas, which the Constitution's authors intended to be state responsibilities.

Although the Commonwealth Government operates no schools, it nonetheless has a sizeable Department of Education and holds sway in shaping national policy. On occasion, the Commonwealth Government has set quite specific conditions for special purpose payments; for example, in 2004 it 'tied school funding to flying the Australian flag. To get their slice of … Commonwealth funds, [state] schools had to have a functioning flagpole' (Ackland 2011). The NAPLAN tests that students in all states complete during their schooling is a similar example of a policy intervention to which Commonwealth Government funding is 'tied'. It is often suggested that the Commonwealth Government's capacity to impose its policy priorities through conditional funding has reduced the independence of state agencies; blurred who is responsible for policy; and limited the capacity of voters to hold governments accountable. In short, the complaint is that the manner in which taxation is raised and distributed has contributed to the centralisation of power within Australia's federal system.

HORIZONTAL FISCAL EQUALISATION

Horizontal fiscal imbalance describes an inequity that arises where the various subnational governments within a federation have different capacities to raise revenue and face different service delivery costs. This is likely to occur where, as in Australia's case, there is significant variation in economic and geographic circumstances across a federation. In such circumstances federations typically develop mechanisms for horizontal fiscal equalisation – for transferring revenue to assist poorly-placed subnational governments.

As might be expected in a federation in which half of the population resides in New South Wales and Victoria and where the states range in physical size from 68 401 square kilometres (Tasmania) to 2 529 875 square kilometres (Western Australia), state governments face different challenges in funding and delivering education, transport, health and other services to their citizens. Regional variation across Australia has meant that horizontal fiscal imbalance has long been a feature of its federation. Long-term structural causes of horizontal fiscal imbalance can be exacerbated by demographic change or by economic developments (such as the mining boom of the early 2000s from which Western Australia and Queensland especially benefitted). As we have seen, horizontal fiscal imbalance proved a problem from the beginning, leading to several judicial inquiries, and then to the establishment of the quasi-judicial Commonwealth Grants Commission to advise the Commonwealth Government on the appropriate levels of top-up special assistance funding for disadvantaged claimant states.

Australians expect the same standards of education and health care from government irrespective of the particular state or territory in which they happen to live. To achieve this egalitarian outcome across the Federation, states must be treated differently, rather as horses in the Melbourne Cup are assigned different handicap weights to give all the best chance of victory. After 1910, the Commonwealth Government fell into the practice of supporting weaker states, including Western Australia. It soon found that providing a state with special financial assistance, and thus treating some more generously than others, was fraught with political difficulty. The creation of the independent Commonwealth Grants Commission in 1933 served to distance the processing of applications for special assistance by the states from day-to-day party politics. In 1976 the work of the Commonwealth Grants Commission was extended to advise the Commonwealth Government on how it might best distribute general revenue assistance to remedy horizontal fiscal imbalance and ensure that states with different geographies, service costs and revenue-raising capacity were all able to provide the same level of education, health and other services to their citizens.

Today the Commonwealth Grants Commission investigates the 'relative fiscal capacities' of the states and territories and then dispassionately recommends how GST revenue raised by the Commonwealth Government on their behalf should be distributed among them. In this process it seeks the best available data, consults with states, and weighs their preferences against the available evidence. The process is transparent and the methodology it uses is regularly reviewed. The Commission calculates 'per capita relativities', which are updated annually. These scores (see Table 2.2) dictate the share of the GST collected by the Commonwealth Government that each state will receive; for example, in 2015–16, Western Australia's per capita relativity of 0.29999 entitled it to

TABLE 2.2 AUSTRALIAN GRANT COMMISSION PER CAPITA RELATIVITIES: 2015–16

NSW	0.94737
Victoria	0.89254
Queensland	1.12753
WA	0.29999
SA	1.35883
Tasmania	1.81906
ACT	1.10012
NT	5.57053

Source: Australian Government 2015, 80

30 per cent of its population share of the available GST pool, while Tasmania received 182 per cent of the amount it would have secured had revenue been parcelled out on a per capita basis. From time to time, state premiers do still complain about how general revenue assistance is shared. Most recently – for reasons suggested by Table 2.2 – Western Australia has been a vociferous critic, arguing that more GST monies raised within its borders ought to be returned to it. However, its critics notwithstanding, Australia's particular solution for quarantining the process of horizontal fiscal equalisation from the rough and tumble of politics has been largely successful.

REFLECTION
QUESTION
RESEARCH
QUESTION

SPOTLIGHT

Agencies that manage Commonwealth–state fiscal relations

This short review of the key agencies at the centre of Commonwealth–state fiscal relations was produced by the Queensland Treasury. Note that, in addition to COAG, it lists the Council on Federal Financial Relations, which is a ministerial council and part of the COAG framework, and the more frequent Heads of Treasury meetings, which bring together senior public servants from the various state, territory and Commonwealth treasury departments.

COMMONWEALTH–STATE FINANCIAL RELATIONS

The Intergovernmental Agreement on Federal Financial Relations provides the overarching framework for the Australian Government's financial relations with the states. It sets the foundation for collaboration on policy development and service delivery, and for the implementation of economic and social reforms in areas of national importance.

There are a number of intergovernmental forums that oversee Australia's system of Commonwealth–state financial relations. These include:

> *Council on Federal Financial Relations (CFFR), which comprises the treasurers of the Australian, state and territory governments and which oversees the operation of the Intergovernmental Agreement on Federal Financial Relations.*

> *Heads of Treasuries (HoTs) meetings, which are convened every three to four months to discuss federal financial relations issues, and which are attended by Commonwealth, state and territory under treasurers or secretaries. HoTs also provide advice to the CFFR as required.*

Council of Australian Governments (COAG), the peak intergovernmental forum in Australia, attended by the prime minister, state premiers and chief ministers, and the President of the Australian Local Government Association.

Source: Queensland Treasury, 2017

REFLECTION QUESTION

QUESTION

Why do you think that no mention is made of the Commonwealth Grants Commission here?

COAG AND CONTEMPORARY POLITICS AND POLICY

Calls to reform the Federation have long been a motif of Australian politics. During the last half-century, newly elected Coalition and Labor governments alike often came to office with – albeit different – plans for a 'New Federalism'. The Rudd Labor Government elected in 2007 had such a commitment to reforming the federal system. In late 2007 it succeeded in securing the support of the Council of Australian Governments for a significant shift in Commonwealth–state funding arrangements, and in persuading all Australian governments to embrace a wide-ranging national reform agenda.

The *Intergovernmental Agreement on Federal Financial Relations* adopted in 2008 significantly reduced Special Purpose Payment 'tied' funding to the states and territories and allowed them greater flexibility in implementing their programs and in managing their budgets. Where the Commonwealth and states and territories reached formal agreements (via COAG) setting out mutually agreed policy objectives and outcomes, as in the case of the Closing the Gap National Partnership Agreements, the Commonwealth Government would provide funding via a new category of National Partnership Payments. These reforms were predicated on the recognition that Australia faces significant environmental, economic and social policy challenges that require national policy solutions and extensive and ongoing collaboration between all levels of government.

The importance of collaboration between Australian governments in addressing economic change loomed large in the last decades of last century as Australia faced the substantial pressures brought by globalisation and the opening of its economy to free trade and international competition. These pressures were for 'microeconomic reform' or the removal of barriers to Australia operating as an efficient single market. Examples of such barriers included state legislation creating different haulage and road transport rules; setting in place different labour market regulations; fixing different food safety manufacturing and packaging requirements; or imposing different duty and other state revenue-raising measures. All were sources of economic inefficiency. Against this backdrop, COAG was established in 1992 to better manage matters of national importance requiring a concerted policy response by Australian governments.

THE COUNCIL OF AUSTRALIAN GOVERNMENTS

As a forum for the leaders of state and Commonwealth governments (and the president of the Local Government Association (LGA) representing the third tier of Australia's Federation), COAG enabled agreement upon and implementation of an extensive microeconomic reform agenda in the 1990s. In turn, the vital part COAG played established it as a far more substantial federal institution than the Special Premiers' Conference, which it had replaced. Leaders attend COAG with the 'authority to negotiate on behalf of their jurisdiction and to strike and implement agreements which are binding' (Menzies 2013, 383). In the quarter-century since its establishment, COAG has enabled various intergovernmental partnerships and policy agreements.

An early, significant agreement reached in 1994 introduced a National Competition Policy to accelerate the microeconomic reform process. Thereafter, COAG has been the vehicle through which a variety of intergovernmental agreements have been struck. These include agreements to reform Commonwealth–state financial relations; to establish a national competitive electricity market; to introduce a National Disability Insurance Scheme; to standardise credit and consumer laws; to 'close the gap' by improving the lot of Indigenous Australians; to introduce uniform counter-terrorism laws; and to manage gene technology. COAG has also been instrumental in developing collective policy responses in the areas of early childhood development, gun control, affordable housing, educational and vocational training, natural disaster relief, and climate change. Initially established to enable Australia to respond to the economic challenges posed by globalisation, COAG has since expanded its role to drive policy initiatives across a wide range of policy areas where the 'the policy capacity of both levels of government needs to be harnessed' (Menzies 2013, 386).

We have already seen that COAG is one example of those 'pragmatic' and patchwork arrangements that Australia has developed to allow intergovernmental cooperation. This has given it a flexible character. Neither 'constitutional nor statutory in origin or nature' but rather 'an administrative creation of executive will', COAG is 'constantly changing and adapting to political and other circumstances' (Blayden 2013). Political 'circumstances' and Australia's adversarial party system will clearly impact how COAG functions. Its members are state premiers, territory chief ministers and the prime minister (plus a LGA representative). Often, the members belong to rival political parties. Especially in the case of politically sensitive issues, they will likely have very different ideological convictions and policy priorities. None will want 'to give any wins to a federal leader of an opposing party' where this might confer electoral advantage (Menzies 2013, 384).

Furthermore, administrative support for COAG is provided by the Department of Prime Minister and Cabinet, and it assembles at the request of the prime minister who chairs its meetings and oversees its agenda. This puts prime ministers in the driver's seat (states and territories rarely succeed in raising matters for consideration.) Since its establishment in 1992, different prime ministers have chosen to use COAG in different ways and in pursuit of their own political agendas. Some have attached far more importance to COAG as a policy instrument than have others.

SHORT-ANSWER
QUESTION

MINISTERIAL COUNCILS AND EXECUTIVE POWER

That the role of COAG is inevitably shaped by politics is clear. Less so the further argument that COAG is an expression of 'executive will'. To unpack this claim we need to examine some of the gossamer threads that have been woven around COAG itself. COAG usually meets annually to address problems requiring collaborative, national solutions. Meetings are typically preceded by working groups of senior public servants from various governments, whose role is to settle the policy detail needed to implement decisions that political leaders will take. These have become an institutionalised feature of the COAG framework. As it has grown in importance, 'a growing network of working parties and committees of officials operating across state borders' has sprung up around COAG which Anderson (2008, 495–6) suggests can 'be characterised as a "nascent bureaucracy of federalism"'.

The framework woven around COAG meetings also extends to ministerial councils, which bring together Commonwealth, state and territory (in some cases even New Zealand) ministers with similar portfolios (such as health and education). These fora also allow intergovernmental collaboration and decision-making. Ministerial councils often also have responsibility for proposing reforms to, and for overseeing the implementation of agreements struck by, COAG itself. Within a decade of its creation in 1992, in a rather ad hoc fashion, COAG had spawned over 40 different ministerial councils. This number has since been greatly reduced, and the place of ministerial councils within the COAG framework formalised. In 2010, COAG reduced the number of ministerial councils to fewer than a dozen overseeing major policy areas of 'ongoing importance to both the Commonwealth and the states' (such as health and education). It further streamlined the system of ministerial councils in 2013.

The more than 40 ministerial councils existing in the early 2000s were replaced with just eight, each reporting to COAG via their chairperson. Each of these 'COAG councils' has considerable autonomy to develop policy and service delivery in the areas it oversees. None is a permanent institution. COAG will conduct biennial reviews to ensure that ministerial councils that report to it align with its policy priorities and is open to establishing new councils or terminating existing ones. Those in place in 2017 had responsibility, respectively, for Federal Financial Relations; Disability Reform; Transport and Infrastructure; Energy; Industry and Skills; Law, Crime and Community Safety; Education; and Health. Beyond these policy areas, the streamlined system established in 2013 permits meetings of Commonwealth and state ministers outside of the COAG council system and allows for ad hoc meetings of ministers on specific issues.

Ministerial councils that are part of the COAG framework often operate away from the media spotlight, meeting once or perhaps twice a year. As in the case of COAG meetings of the leaders, each ministerial council is supported by a secretariat (supplied by the Department of Prime Minister and Cabinet). Moreover, meetings are also associated with groups of senior public servants from the different governments represented, who work in the background on the finer details of policies. Where ministers attending council meetings reach a consensus, the COAG process obliges their governments to implement the decisions that are made. This arrangement hands ministerial councils (and the senior public servants who advise them) a considerable decision-making power. Ministers and public servants comprise the executive arm of government. Their dominance of the COAG processes of intergovernmental negotiation – along with the range and importance of policies now decided via COAG – points to the emergence of what some describe as 'executive federalism' (Anderson 2008, 496).

EXECUTIVE, COLLABORATIVE AND OTHER FEDERALISMS

It may be useful to review our account of the Australian Federation here. It was designed long ago to allow state and Commonwealth governments to operate side-by-side and largely independent of each other. But this prescription for a coordinate federalism proved impractical. It forced the pragmatic invention of institutions and processes to facilitate cooperation between governments. In short, Australia evolved an ad hoc system of cooperative federalism. The most recent steps along this path have involved the creation of COAG, its associated framework of ministerial councils, the emergence of a nascent associated bureaucracy, and the reaching of a range of economic and other intergovernmental agreements. But cooperative federalism does not imply harmony nor the absence of political tensions. It is in this context that we should consider the claim that although COAG 'began as a means of encouraging cooperative federalism', it has encouraged the centralisation of power and 'played a part in entrenching executive federalism' (Anderson 2008, 496).

Executive federalism describes 'the channelling of intergovernmental relations into transactions controlled by elected and appointed officials of the executive branch' (Sharman 1991, 25). The COAG framework strengthens the hand of executive government and political leaders. The obligation to implement agreements reached by leaders at COAG (and even by ministerial councils) diminishes both state and Commonwealth parliaments alike, reducing them to 'rubber stamping' any associated legislation. Anderson (2008, 506) suggests that the particular 'form of executive federalism that COAG has fostered is one which has supported greater centralisation within the federation'. Prime ministers who convene COAG and largely control its agenda especially benefit from this centralisation. It has been one cause of their growing power. Critics of the rise of executive federalism point to 'the "behind closed doors" character of intergovernmental decision-making' and to the resultant diminished scope for community consultation and parliamentary deliberation (Sawer 2009).

Executive federalism is but one of several concepts that political scientists have used to reframe our understanding of cooperative federalism and to explain the nature and shortcomings of the intergovernmental institutions and processes that have been devised to enable all Australian governments to liaise and to search for ways of addressing policy problems requiring a national approach. Hollander and Patapan (2007) have described the ad hoc approach to intergovernmental relations taken by Labor and Coalition Commonwealth governments since the 1950s (from which COAG framework has evolved) as 'pragmatic federalism'. Institutions such as COAG have not been developed to give expression to some 'grand theory' of federalism. Rather they have been seen as solutions to pressing problems and often (as in the case of National Competition Policy) placed greater power in the hands of the Commonwealth. Intergovernmental relations have evolved incrementally, and this process has been unencumbered by traditional arrangements or 'states' rights' or similar ideological imaginations.

Australia has also been described as having a system of 'collaborative federalism'. Painter (1998, 1) depicts the Federation this way, arguing that it 'has undergone a [recent] fundamental reshaping' with state and Commonwealth governments finding themselves 'cooperating evermore closely on joint schemes of policy and administration', albeit often 'against their immediate wishes'. COAG in particular has 'greatly accelerated this trend' and blurred the distinctiveness of the states and Commonwealth: they are less and less 'separate political actors in a federal system'.

'Coercive federalism' is a term that has also been used to describe the circumstances arising from vertical fiscal imbalance, which have allowed the Commonwealth Government to drive the COAG process and push states into accepting its direct involvement in areas (such as education) that ostensibly belong to the states (Hamill 2007, 43–56). Others argue that the COAG framework has produced not cooperative federalism but a 'cooperative centralism' that has consolidated the dominance of the national government as policy 'instigator and coordinator and frequently as a policy driver' (Anderson and Parkin 2010, 111).

The different ways in which the evolution of cooperative federalism has been represented point to the complexity of these changes (as well as to the propensity for political scientists to disagree). If there is a common thread to these different characterisations of the architecture of intergovernmental relations that has been created outside of provisions of the Constitution, it is that states have lost out as the Commonwealth Government has established its dominance. The centralisation of power within the federation has been welcomed. It has enabled Australia to develop integrated, national responses to pressing problems. But the financial dependency of states upon the Commonwealth Government and the extended role of the Commonwealth Government in developing uniform policy solutions also has its critics. Chief among those are scholars who prefer a more 'competitive federalism' in which states would adopt their own particular approach to solving policy problems and from which 'the best' solutions might ultimately be identified.

REFLECTION
QUESTION
VIDEO

CASE STUDY

Medical marijuana: A case study of federalism at work

In a federation, citizens in different regions are subject to different laws because most decision-making is devolved to the local level. This information from a 2016 ABC news story offers a case study. It reports the different approaches that states and territories were (at that time) developing to regulate the medical use of marijuana. How is such variation in policy possible? Is it desirable? Notice that as a consequence of individual states each advancing their own laws, children with epilepsy would have access to this drug treatment in some but not all parts of Australia. Would a uniform national policy be preferable?

SO, HOW DOES IT WORK STATE BY STATE?

Queensland: Legal for specialists to prescribe for some patients from March 2017. This includes certain patients who have illnesses including MS, epilepsy, cancer and HIV/AIDS. There are no age restrictions, but approval will only be provided by a doctor who needs to show evidence that medicinal cannabis could help the patient.

NSW: Available for adults with end-of-life illnesses.

Victoria: Available for children with epilepsy from early 2017.

ACT: Legislation that will include education sources for doctors still in the works for 2017.

Tasmania: Legislation for Controlled Access Scheme still in the works for 2017.

WA: Legal for doctors to prescribe from 1 November, under strict conditions. Products will only be able to be dispensed by a pharmacist. However, there is still no legal product available in Australia.

SA/NT: No information available.

Source: Timms, 2016

QUESTION

What are the impacts of having differing laws between states? What other issues can you think of that result in different life and medical opportunities for people depending on the state in which they live?

SHORT-ANSWER QUESTION

REFORMING THE FEDERATION AND THE FUTURE OF STATES

It is difficult now to imagine an Australia in which premiers of the larger states were more politically influential than prime ministers, or in which powerful Liberal state premiers might – as happened to Sir John Gorton in 1971 – force a Liberal prime minister from power for pursuing centralist policies perceived as infringing 'states' rights'. Once a shibboleth of the Liberal Party, the concept of states' rights has few adherents today. The 19th century argument that federalism limits the power of government and protects freedom by dividing power has largely lost out to a contemporary view that the Australian federal system is costly, inefficient and anachronistic. A 2010 study found many Australians viewed the Federation negatively, and that three-quarters would prefer to see a different system in place (see Windholz 2011, 1). Their number includes former state and national leaders, as well as influential interest groups such as the Business Council of Australia who have advocated fundamental reform of the Federation.

Would-be reformers offer various reasons why wholesale reform of the Federation ought to be considered. The federal system is argued to be a source of duplication and inefficiency. The Business Council of Australia calculates that inefficiencies within the Federation sees governments waste some nine billion dollars each year. A related complaint is that, with a Commonwealth parliament plus six separate state parliaments, Australia is 'over governed' and oversupplied with politicians. Yet another argument for reforming the Federation suggests that the range of economic, environmental, technological and other challenges facing Australia today all require a national or uniform policy response, something best achieved by the Commonwealth Government being formally handed control of policy areas presently conferred upon states by an antiquated Constitution. In short, the '19th Century constitutional division of powers is not capable of meeting the challenges presented by increasing globalisation, international economic competition and rapid advances in technology' (Windholz 2011, 1). From this vantage point, there is also merit in replacing ad hoc intergovernmental processes and mechanisms with a constitutionally protected, 'permanent institution' serving this role (Menzies 2013, 387).

Some reformers believe that improved intergovernmental processes ought to be matched by the reform of Commonwealth–state financial relations to correct vertical fiscal imbalance. Yet another argument for reform stems from the premise that it is often impossible for voters to hold governments accountable for policy failures because the authority of state and Commonwealth governments is not – as should be the case – clearly delineated. Both tiers of government are increasingly entangled given that states and territories are only able to fund roads, schools and hospitals with the support of the Commonwealth Government, which often makes funding available conditionally. Often the case for modernising federalism hangs on refashioning 'the role of the states' (Smith 2013, 362). But some reformers recognise that 'local government is a silent partner' (Althaus, Bridgman and Davis 2013, 92) within the Federation, whose role warrants formal protection not presently afforded by a Constitution that makes no reference to it.

SPOTLIGHT

States' rights

There are few contemporary advocates of states' rights. Furthermore, the 19th century argument that federalism limits the power of government and protects freedom by dividing power has largely lost out to a contemporary view that the federal system is costly, inefficient and anachronistic. In this century, when the nation faces environmental and economic challenges that require a concerted national policy response, some suggest that Australia would be better off if states were scrapped in favour of a strong central government; however, there are constitutional obstacles that will likely prevent this 'reform'. If unitary government is not an option, then the only practical solution is that suggested by the 2010 Senate Select Committee on the Reform of the Australian Federation: ending the pronounced gap in the revenue streams available to the Commonwealth and state governments, which it considered to be a principal source of the present dysfunction within the Australian Federation.

QUESTION

Why are there few contemporary advocates of states' rights? What are the arguments for decentralised government?

FEDERALISM AS PART OF AUSTRALIA'S POLITICAL DNA

For some, the problem is the mismatch between Australia's regions and state boundaries. For instance, in 2016 the newly installed Minister for Northern Australia, Matt Canavan, endorsed calls for a referendum on the creation of a seventh Australian state in north Queensland (to be achieved by splitting Queensland in two). It was, he said, a proposal that had 'merit' and should be put to the people (Koziol 2016). Such calls for the creation of new states have periodically punctuated Australian politics. None has sustained any real momentum. One reason is that the creation of any new state must be 'put to the people' – to all the citizens of Australia in a referendum election, not just those in the region seeking a separate future. Section 128 of the Constitution requires that any formal change to the Constitution be approved by a majority of states and by an overall majority of electors voting in a referendum election. Just eight of 44 proposals to amend the Constitution, which have been put to referenda since 1901, have succeeded.

It is not clear even that the Northern Territory will smoothly fulfil its ambition to become Australia's seventh state (or that the LGA will succeed in having the Constitution amended to formally recognise local government as a third tier of the Federation). Section 128 looms as a roadblock to anyone wishing to overhaul the Australian Federation. This may be why some suggest that the question of whether or not the Federation 'is a sensible way to organise government and democracy' is 'a bit of a non-issue' (Cook, Walsh and Harwood 2009, 114). It is a non-issue because, like it or not, the Federation is 'constitutionally embedded' (Anderson 2008, 494). It is part of Australia's political DNA. This is not to say that citizens today are passionately invested in the federal division of powers (as may have been the case in the 1950s and 1960s when premiers were able to invoke states' rights in their contests with Canberra). Today most see themselves as Australians and 'state of origin' is more celebrated on the football pitch than in political life. But the six founding states are very much a fixed feature of the Australian political system. Federalism is ingrained in all aspects of Australia's political system, which is in and of itself a substantial barrier to changing this.

A SHAPING INFLUENCE ON POLITICS

The shaping influence of the Australian Federation on its politics is little noticed but very real. The Federation serves to fragment key political institutions. We have already noted that many interest groups engaged in influencing public policy are often organised into state and Commonwealth bodies. For example, trade unions are represented at the national level by a peak association, the Australian Council of Trade Unions. But because state governments play an important role in regulating industrial relations, in each state and territory, unions also form state-level representative labour councils (such as the Queensland Council of Unions or the Victorian Trades Hall Council). In New Zealand, which has a unitary rather than federal system and where unions need deal only with the national government, there is a single peak association representing unions, the New Zealand Council of Trade Unions.

Other interest groups are similarly organised. There are Councils of Social Service giving voice to people experiencing poverty and social disadvantage in each state, and an overarching Australian Council of Social Services, which lobbies at the national level. Many professional associations are similarly organised. The Australian Institute of Architects has state and territory chapters and a National Council responsible for overarching policy. The Australian Dental Association, representing the dental profession, aspires to influence government policies affecting dentistry and oral health and 'maintains an active presence in every state and territory via its Branches' as well as a national secretariat to lobby the Commonwealth Government. There are numerous other examples of interest groups shaping their activities and organisation to mirror the federal structure of government.

The very logic of federation (which creates multiple and overlapping power centres) obliges interest groups wishing to influence policy to mirror it. This same fragmentation is apparent in the organisation of political parties. It is a curious fact that citizens cannot join the national Australian Labor Party (ALP) or Liberal Party of Australia. Rather they must join a state or territory branch or division of these federated organisations. We are accustomed to thinking of them as single entities but each of the two major parties is in fact a loose federation of separately constituted state and territory organisations. Each Liberal Division and ALP Branch has its own membership and network of local sub-branches.

Each has its own constitution and is separately registered with the Australian Electoral Commission. Each has its own parliamentary team and internal factional politics. Each provides delegates to conferences who guide the policy direction that the national-level organisation will take. The national-level Liberal and Labor parties have their own office bearers and administrative staffs. In Labor's case, the central party organisation has the constitutional authority to intervene in failing state branches; but even in the ALP, individual state branches are differently organised.

The rivalry between the two major parties plays out differently in each state and at the national level. The Liberal's coalition with the National Party, which is an entrenched feature of national politics, is not automatically reproduced at the state level. In some states, the National Party does not operate. In Western Australia, the two parties have an uneasy relationship. Indeed, at the 2017 Western Australian state election, the Liberals opted to preference One Nation candidates ahead of National Party candidates. A different set of circumstances applies in Queensland, where the Liberals and Nationals have merged to form one party in order to be electorally competitive at the state level. The creation of this Liberal National Party (LNP) has had a curious side effect: although it is formally the Queensland Division of the Liberal Party of Australia, LNP members in the Commonwealth Parliament represent either the Liberals or the Nationals! This messy arrangement underscores the different ways that politics plays out in individual states and at the national level. State Liberal Divisions and ALP Branches often get caught up by the state-level politics and priorities. Party organisations get pulled in different directions. In this way, the Federation imposes a different pattern on parties than is apparent in comparable unitary systems (such as New Zealand).

REFLECTION
QUESTION

SUMMARY

Learning objective 1: Explain how and why federalism divides powers

Federalism is a prescriptive theory holding that we ought to prevent government from accumulating excessive power by constitutionally dividing it – by allocating the authority to decide policy in certain areas to a national government while giving a series of subnational governments responsibility to make decisions in other policy areas. While federalism shares the goal of preserving freedom by constitutionally constraining government, the federal division of powers between distinct tiers of government should not be confused with the separation of powers aiming to ensure that no single group controls the legislative, executive and judicial arms of government.

Learning objective 2: Analyse the Australian variant of federalism and explain how it has evolved

Understanding the Australian Federation begins with recognising that its Constitution embraces the theory of federalism and divides the authority to make policy between the Commonwealth and state governments. Its framers intended that these governments would operate side by side and largely independent of one another. But their 19th century prescription for coordinate federalism, underestimated the need for, and failed to establish, institutions that were able to satisfactorily manage intergovernmental relations. To correct this shortcoming, it proved necessary to invent additional institutions to allow governments to consult and collaborate. The evolution of the Australian Federation into a form of cooperative federalism unfolded in an unplanned patchwork fashion. It began with the resurrection of Premiers' Conferences almost immediately in 1901 and continues today with the refinement of the COAG framework.

Learning objective 3: Explain how the way states are funded enlarges the role of the Commonwealth

The Constitution's authors intended that states would continue as an important seat of power. But this vision was dealt a blow by the High Court – most notably in the 1942 and 1957 *Uniform Tax* cases, which handed the Commonwealth Government control of income and company taxation. Its monopoly of these lucrative revenue sources enabled the Commonwealth Government to raise more revenue than it required for its own policy programs. This introduced a pronounced vertical fiscal imbalance within the Australian Federation, which successive governments have exploited to expand the role of the Commonwealth Government. Section 96 of the Constitution empowers the Commonwealth to provide the states with financial assistance on its terms and conditions. In the past half century or more, the Commonwealth Government has attached conditions to the 'tied grants' it has offered the states in order to extend its influence into areas such as education and health, which the Constitution's authors imagined would remain in state hands. The result has been a greater integration of Commonwealth and state policy-making plus a 'creeping centralisation' of power.

Learning objective 4: Analyse COAG and its importance to contemporary politics and policy-making

The Council of Australian Governments, formed in 1992, assembles government leaders – the prime minister, state premiers, territory chief ministers and a representative of local governments. Prime ministers convene and chair its meetings and COAG is administratively supported by the Department of Prime Minister and Cabinet. Since 1992, its importance has ebbed and flowed as individual prime ministers with their own political agendas have chosen to make different use of COAG. Nonetheless, COAG has been instrumental in achieving intergovernmental agreements in diverse policy areas including climate change, counter-terrorism, gene technology and management of the Murray–Darling. It has clearly widened its scope since the 1990s when it emerged as an invaluable tool for addressing the economic challenges posed by globalisation.

COAG is more than a meeting of leaders. Working parties of state and Commonwealth public servants meet to develop the details of the policy agreements that COAG meetings will decide upon. The COAG process also involves a series of ministerial councils bringing together Commonwealth and state ministers with similar portfolios. Alongside COAG they are important vehicles for securing intergovernmental agreements on matters requiring an integrated policy response from Australian governments.

Learning objective 5: Make an informed judgement about the need for, and prospects of, reforming the Federation

Some reformers of the Federation see the need to strengthen COAG by giving it constitutional protection. Their goal is to end the ad hoc approach to intergovernmental relations and to rescue COAG from dependence upon prime ministers and the temptation to place party advantage ahead of developing national policy solutions to pressing problems. Other would-be reformers have quite different aims. Some see the federal system as an anachronism. Some wish to more clearly delineate the responsibilities of states and the Commonwealth. Yet others wish to free states from the heavy hand of the Commonwealth Government by ensuring that they have taxation powers that will remove their dependency upon financial assistance provided by the Commonwealth Government.

Changing the Federation need not involve hurdling the barrier which is Section 128. Australia's federal system has, and will continue to, evolve. Some treat the 'creeping centralism' associated with the evolution of cooperative federalism as inevitable, even welcome. After all, problems that governments increasingly must grapple with require a national approach and a coordinated, consistent policy response, which is something more likely to be achieved within a federation in which the Commonwealth Government carries most weight. But a rival view holds that there are regional variations across Australia that may require state governments to adopt different solutions to environmental, economic and other such challenges as they arise. A 'one size fits all' national approach may not always be an appropriate policy response. Proponents of competitive federalism believe that, where states are not compelled to follow Commonwealth policy but free to experiment with their own solutions to problems they have in common, one will likely hit on a better policy response that others can then adopt or adapt.

Today there is little popular enthusiasm for reforming the Federation. Nowadays any push for change comes largely from within the ranks of government policymakers and hangs on questions of institutional design that do not resonate with the wider public. There is no grassroots groundswell for reform. Federation remains ingrained in Australian political life. It is taken for granted but still a central feature of a political system that mixes federal and parliamentary forms of government.

DISCUSSION QUESTIONS

1. What is the core difference between a de facto federal system and the Australian Federation?
2. What is COAG and what role does it play in contemporary Australian politics?
3. What might an understanding of Federation (or the way in which Australia was created from the six colonies which had occupied the continent) add to understanding the Australian federal system today?
4. What arguments are made in favour of federalism? Are there any countering arguments that ring true in the Australian setting?
5. Review the case study that describes the different state laws in place in 2016 regulating the medical use of marijuana. Is this a case study that can be used to illustrate the merits of 'competitive federalism' (which is an idea often now used in defence of federalism)?

FURTHER READING

Hollander, R. (2014). Federalism and Intergovernmental Relations. In C. Miller and L. Orchard, eds, *Australian Public Policy*. Chicago: Policy Press.

Kildea, P., Lynch, A. and Williams, G. (eds) (2012). *Tomorrow's Federation: Reforming Australian Government*, Annandale: Federation Press.

Tiernan, A. (2015). Reforming Australia's federal framework: Priorities and prospects. *Australian Journal of Public Administration*, **74**(4), 398–405.

Windholtz, E. (2011). Federalism in Australia: A concept in search of understanding. *Journal of Contemporary Issues in Business and Government*, **17**(2), 1–18.

Zimmerman, A. and Finlay L. (2011). Reforming Federalism: A proposal for strengthening the Australian federation. *Monash University Law Review*, **7**(2), 190–231.

REFERENCES

Abbott, T. (2008). Speech Notes. Australian Federalism: Rescue & Reform Conference, *Griffith University & Institute of Public Administration Australia*, Tenterfield, 24 October. Retrieved from https://www.griffith.edu.au/__data/assets/pdf_file/0019/206560/Abbott2008-tenterfield speech.pdf

Ackland, R. (2011). Religiously follow the rules, or catch church in bed with state, *The Sydney Morning Herald*, 4 February. Retrieved from http://www.smh.com.au/federal-politics/political-opinion/religiously-follow-the-rules-or-catch-church-in-bed-with-state-20110203-1afbf.html

Althaus, C., Bridgman, P. and Davis, G. (2013). *The Australian Policy Handbook*, 5th edn, Crows Nest, NSW: Allen & Unwin.

Anderson, G. (2008). The Council of Australian Governments: A new institution of governance for Australia's conditional federalism. *UNSW Law Journal*, **31**(2), 495–6.

Anderson, G. and Parkin, A. (2010). Federalism: A fork in the road? In C. Aulich and M. Evans, eds, *The Rudd Government: Australian Commonwealth Administration 2007–2010*, Canberra: ANU E-press.

Anderson, L.M. (2010). The paradox of federalism. In J. Erk and W. Swenden, eds, *New Directions in Federalism Studies*, London: Routledge.

Australian Government. (2015). Budget Review 2015–16. URL: http://www.aph.gov.au/About_Parliament/Parliamentary_Departments/Parliamentary_Library/pubs/rp/BudgetReview 201516/GSTDist

Beramendi, P. (2009). Federalism. In C. Boix and S.C. Stokes, eds, *The Oxford Handbook of Comparative Politics*. Oxford: Oxford University Press.

Blayden, L. (2013). COAG. Briefing Paper No 6/2013 NSW Parliamentary Research Service. URL: http://www.parliament.nsw.gov.au/researchpapers/documents/coag/coag.pdf

Business Council of Australia. (2007). *A Charter for New Federalism*. [Policy Paper] 18 December. URL: http://www.bca.com.au/publications/a-charter-for-new-federalism/view-all-related-publications

Commonwealth Grants Commission. (2016) Commonwealth–state Financial Relations. URL: https://cgc.gov.au/index.php?option=com_docman&view=document&slug=cgc-commonwealth-state-financial-relations-pdf-1&layout=default&alias=924-cgc-commonwealth-state-financial-relations-pdf-1&Itemid=471

Cook I., Walsh, M. and Harwood, J. (2009). *Government and Democracy in Australia*, 2nd edn, South Melbourne, Victoria: Oxford University Press.

Department of Infrastructure and Regional Development. (2016). Local Government. URL: http://regional.gov.au/local/

Hamill, D. (2007). W(h)ither federalism. In *Upholding the Australian Constitution*, **19**, The Samuel Griffith Society, 43–56.

Hollander, R. (2014). Federalism and intergovernmental relations. In C. Miller and L. Orchard, eds, *Australian Public Policy*, Chicago: Policy Press.

Hollander, R. and Patapan, H. (2007). Pragmatic federalism: Australian federalism from Hawke to Howard. *Australian Journal of Public Administration*, **66**(3), 280–97.

Howard, J. (2005). Reflections on Australian federalism (Speech delivered at the Menzies Research Centre, Melbourne, 11 April). Retrieved from http://www.mrcltd.org.au/research/economic-reports/australian_federalism_final.pdf

Koziol, M. (2016). Northern Australia Minister Matt Canavan backs poll plan for new North Queensland state, *The Sydney Morning Herald*, 28 March.

Martinez-Vazquez, J. (2011). *The Impact of Fiscal Decentralization: Issues in Theory and Challenges in Practice*, Asian Development Bank.

Menzies, J. (2013). Reducing tensions in Australian intergovernmental relations through institutional innovation. *Australian Journal of Public Administration*, **72**(3), 382–9.

Official Record of the Debates of the Australasian Federal Convention. Second Session. Sydney, 2nd to 24th September, 1897. URL: http://www.aph.gov.au/About_Parliament/Senate/Powers_practice_n_procedures/Records_of_the_Australasian_Federal_Conventions_of_the_1890s

Official Report of the National Australasian Convention Debates. Sydney, 2 March to 9 April, 1891. URL: http://www.aph.gov.au/About_Parliament/Senate/Powers_practice_n_procedures/Records_of_the_Australasian_Federal_Conventions_of_the_1890s

Painter, M. (1996). The Council of Australian Governments and intergovernmental relations: A case of cooperative federalism. *Publius*, **26**(2), 101–20.

Painter, M. (1998). *Collaborative Federalism. Economic Reform in Australia in the 1990*, Melbourne: Cambridge University Press.

Parliamentary Education Office. (2017). Federation. URL: http://www.peo.gov.au/learning/closer-look/federation-cl.html

Queensland Treasury. (2017). Commonwealth-state financial relations. URL: https://www.treasury.qld.gov.au/economy-and-budget/queensland-budget/commonwealth-state-financial-relations

Ratnapala, S. (2014). Fiscal federalism in Australia: Will *Williams v Commonwealth* be a pyrrhic victory? *University of Queensland Law Journal*, **31**(3), 63–82.

Riker, W.H. (1975). Federalism. In F.I. Greenstein and N.W. Polsby, eds, *Handbook of Political Science, Vol. 5 Governmental Institutions and Processes*, Reading, Mass: Addison-Wesley, pp. 93–172.

Sawer, M. (2009). The trouble with federalism, *Canberra Times*, 8 April. Retrieved from http://apo.org.au/node/6253

Sharman, C. (1991). Executive federalism. In B. Galligan, O. Hughes and C. Walsh, eds, *Inter-governmental Relations and Public Policy*, Sydney: Allen & Unwin.

Smith, D. (2013). How should we govern our big brown country? In T. Wilson, C. Carli and P. Collits, eds, *Turning Left or Right: Values in Modern Politics*, Ballarat: Connor Court Publishing.

Timms, P. (2016). Medicinal marijuana to become legal to grow in Australia – but how will it work? *abc.net.au*, 29 October. Retrieved from http://www.abc.net.au/news/2016–10–29/medicinal-marijuana-to-become-legal-explainer/7975194

Tiver, P.G. (1978). *The Liberal Party: Principles and Performance*, Milton, Queensland: Jacaranda Press.

Wanna, J., Phillimore, J., Fenna, A. and Harwood, J. (2009). *Common Cause: Strengthening Australia's Cooperative Federalism*, Final Report to the Council for the Australian Federation, May.

Windholz, E. (2011). Federalism in Australia: A concept in search of understanding. *Journal of Contemporary Issues in Business and Government*, **17**(2), 1–18.

CHAPTER 3

THE LEGISLATURE: REPRESENTATIVE DEMOCRACY

LEARNING OBJECTIVES

After reading this chapter, you should be able to:

1. Understand the historical evolution of legislatures in Australia

2. Explain for what purpose the institutions of state exist

3. Describe the key legislative functions of Australian parliaments

4. Understand the process through which laws are made

5. Identify the limits and variations of Australian legislatures

INTRODUCTION

When we think about parliaments and the legislature, we might be propelled back to consider the first 'parliaments' – whether the fora of Ancient Greece or the Althing of Norse Iceland – as being a group of people coming together to make laws. Parliaments and legislatures have developed considerably since those times to be complex bodies, but the key idea of a group coming together to make laws remains. While other chapters will discuss the way parliaments are elected – the electoral system – and who gets to choose who the candidates are – the parties or individuals – this chapter will discuss the role, purpose and operation of the Australian Parliament, as it is the legislature that citizens, members of parliament (MPs) and parties all aim to attend and control.

The early parliaments had a restricted group of people who could be a member of the legislature, just as there was a restricted group of people who could vote in elections. Originally the exclusive domain of property-owning men, the parliaments of early 21st century Australia now have remarkably few restrictions on those who can sit and serve (Parliament of Australia 2009). Where such bars to representation do exist, they are more a product of the party system (see Chapters 8 and 9) or of the vagaries of electoral representation (Chapter 7) than deliberate attempts to prescribe who might sit in parliament, or even vote in elections. The one clear exception has been Section 44 of the Constitution (Constitution of Australia 1900), which has at various times tripped up MPs who failed to comply with its provisions.

Parliaments themselves are in reality a collection of people, however chosen, who represent the broader population. They are a key element in a democracy as they allow for deliberation and debate about the decisions that affect the lives of citizens. In this, parliament exists to make laws that govern the nation, regulate its citizenry, and raise and expend money. It is an advance upon the previous feudal system, which relied on fealty and payment of taxes and rent to Lord and King but provided very few with any say in who governed them or how they were governed. We call our own democracy a 'representative democracy' in recognition of the representative nature of the parliament, but it could just as easily be called a 'parliamentary democracy' in recognition of the primacy of the role of parliament (Heywood 2000, 172–4). Either way, parliament remains a key institution and one that developed over a long period of time.

AUTHOR PANEL

SPOTLIGHT

Section 44 and Australian politics

Section 44 was in the news for much of 2017 because of its effect on the government and minor parties, with more than a dozen MPs resigning or being declared to be in violation of this section of the Constitution. Section 44 relates to disqualification of candidates for various reasons or offences. It is important because it states which citizens cannot stand for parliament because of some action on their own part.

DISQUALIFICATION

Any person who:

(i) is under any acknowledgment of allegiance, obedience, or adherence to a foreign power, or is a subject or a citizen or entitled to the rights or privileges of a subject or a citizen of a foreign power; or

(ii) is attainted of treason, or has been convicted and is under sentence, or subject to be sentenced, for any offence punishable under the law of the Commonwealth or of a State by imprisonment for one year or longer; or

(iii) is an undischarged bankrupt or insolvent; or

(iv) holds any office of profit under the Crown, or any pension payable during the pleasure of the Crown out of any of the revenues of the Commonwealth; or

(v) has any direct or indirect pecuniary interest in any agreement with the Public Service of the Commonwealth otherwise than as a member and in common with the other members of an incorporated company consisting of more than twenty-five persons;

shall be incapable of being chosen or of sitting as a senator or a member of the House of Representatives. (Constitution of Australia 1900)

The MPs disqualified in 2017 were caught by subsections (i), (ii) and (v), with five being found to have dual citizenships in a large case before the High Court sitting as the Court of Disputed Returns in 2017 (see HCA3 2017, HCA14 2017 & HCA45 2017). This has itself raised the question of who should be eligible to stand for parliament. The key question for most commentators was whether you should have to renounce all other citizenships to be an MP – which in a country such as Australia with half the population either born overseas or with a parent born overseas, raises interesting questions about what it means to be Australian.

QUESTION

Do you think that Section 44 should be amended to allow those with dual citizenship to serve in parliament?

THE EARLY AUSTRALIAN LEGISLATURE

Australia's electoral history is naturally entwined with that of the country that provided the bulk of the first white arrivals in Australia, the United Kingdom. The British parliament at Westminster provided to Australia a model for parliaments in the early colonies, and the basic principles were adopted as those colonies gradually reached a suitable size to need more formal government that was derived from a military governor. The first governments in Australia were military in nature, with Governors ruling the colony in New South Wales, initially alone and then with the aid of advisers. These advisers were appointed and served at the Governor's pleasure to assist the Governor, as the Monarch's representative, in providing good government in the newly established colonies. From 1823 these advisers formed the first Legislative Council.

Through the early part of the 19th century the colony grew considerably. The increasing need for good governance, past that which could be provided by a military Governor, meant expanding the original Legislative Council, until it numbered between 10 and 15 at any one time. The Governor met with the Council to pass Acts to regulate such things as excise and the postal system. At the same time, new colonies were being founded in Tasmania (military outpost settled in 1803, separate colony in 1825), Western Australia (military outpost settled in 1827, separate colony in 1829) and Victoria (first settled in 1835, separate colony in 1850) (see Moon and Sharman 2003).

As the colonies grew, the demands to provide law, order and effective management escalated. Although the 'Mother Parliament' in London still controlled affairs in the colonies, this was largely confined to external affairs (soldiers, navies, foreign relations and the like), even as English law was received as part of Australian law. However, the very different landscape and conditions required innovation and forethought – whether to navigate the rivers, police the town and countryside over considerable distances, or provide services to far-flung settlements.

This necessity for an expanded bureaucracy brought with it a need to manage the colonies' finances. In doing so, the colonies developed tax and excise regimes to raise the funds needed to provide the various services. This required laws and an expanded legislature. The growing colonies enabled, constructed and built colonial legislatures as they expanded from the early coastal settlements and pushed into the outback.

The first of the colonies, New South Wales, established a Legislative Council in 1823 to advise the colony's Governor, which became a **bicameral** legislature following the passage of the *1855 Constitution Act*. The creation of the colony of Victoria in 1850 allowed Victoria to implement a Westminster-style Legislative Assembly and Legislative Council, which began functioning in 1856. Tasmania created its own bicameral system in the same year. Other colonies, hived off from the original New South Wales colony, each founded their own legislative bodies, such that by 1890, each of the six colonies had a functioning legislature. So, when Australia was created as a self-governing nation in 1901, the colonial legislatures were able to continue operating as they had done so previously, only now as state parliaments.

These legislative bodies were at first wholly appointed. However, these soon gave way to elected bodies, first as Legislative Councils and then as operating Assemblies, modelled on the English House of Commons. Suffrage (the right to vote) was at first restricted to men, with a 'property' bar ensuring that only those men who owned property could be engaged in parliamentary affairs. This too passed fairly quickly into history, with first women being allowed to vote at federal elections after 1902 (in the states between 1895 and 1908), and then the property bar disappearing altogether, though a racial bar existed until the 1960s. While some restrictions on the right to vote still exist, 'universal suffrage' has largely been achieved, with the only significant restriction being the age at which a person can vote, along with some restrictions on prisoners.

> **bicameral:** A parliament that has two houses, such as a Legislative Assembly (the lower house or 'house of government') and a Legislative Council (the upper house – sometimes called a 'house of review'). The two houses of parliament are usually elected via different electoral systems.

THE STRUCTURE OF THE LEGISLATURE

As noted above, the early Australian parliaments consisted of single houses (styled as Legislative Councils), acting as advisory bodies to the Governors. However, this soon gave way to dual houses, at first with only the Legislative Assemblies being elected, and the Legislative Councils being appointed. But at the beginning of the 20th century, all Legislative Councils were elected, except in New South Wales and Queensland, with the last appointed Council in New South Wales only becoming fully elected after reforms in 1978. All legislatures in Australia are now elected, even though the manner of election varies between jurisdictions.

Legislative Councils were not, however, always popular. The Labor Government in Queensland abolished the Legislative Council in 1922, and Labor attempted to do this twice in New South Wales (failing on both occasions). For the Labor Party, Legislative

REFLECTION QUESTIONS

Councils were a conservative bulwark against progressive government, especially when fully appointed bodies. Following many reforms and the failed attempts at reform, proportionally elected Councils have now been accepted by Labor as an important part of the Australia's institutional arrangements.

The houses of parliament

Most states, and the Commonwealth, now have two houses of parliament. The original Legislative Councils continue to live on as the state upper houses in New South Wales, Victoria, Tasmania, South Australia and Western Australia. The upper house at the Commonwealth level is called the Senate. Most involve some level of proportional representation (except Tasmania), and so non-major parties have found it easier to be elected to them.

The lower house of parliament is called the Legislative Assembly (in Queensland, Victoria, New South Wales and Western Australia) or House of Assembly (South Australia and Tasmania). The Commonwealth version is called the House of Representatives. Each of these houses of parliament, with the exception of Tasmania, are elected from single member electorates.

The two territories (the Northern Territory and Australian Capital Territory) are distinctive. They were not part of the original Federation but were created by Acts of the Australian Parliament – they are therefore not 'states' as defined in the Constitution, but self-governing territories. Both have a single house of parliament, in the Australian Capital Territory a House of Assembly, and in the Northern Territory the Legislative Assembly. The Australian Capital Territory House is elected by proportional methods, and the Northern Territory Parliament with single member electorates.

TABLE 3.1 HOUSES OF PARLIAMENT – ELECTION METHODS

JURISDICTION	UNI- OR BICAMERAL	METHOD OF ELECTION	
		ASSEMBLY/ REPRESENTATIVES	COUNCIL/SENATE
Commonwealth	Bicameral	Single member	Proportional
Queensland	Unicameral	Single member	(abolished 1922)
New South Wales	Bicameral	Single member	Proportional
South Australia	Bicameral	Single member	Proportional
Tasmania	Bicameral	Proportional	Single member
Victoria	Bicameral	Single member	Proportional
Western Australia	Bicameral	Single member	Proportional
Territories			
Australian Capital Territory	Unicameral	Proportional	-
North Territory	Unicameral	Single member	-

Even within this, there is variation in methods used to elect MPs. As will be seen in Chapter 7, each state and territory has evolved in a slightly different way, and the electoral system in each of the states is different. For instance, while some elect the Assembly in single member districts, others (New South Wales and until recently Queensland) have non-compulsory allocation of preferences. While a number of Councils use a proportional method of election, some (New South Wales and South Australia) use a system where the whole state is treated as an electorate, and others (Victoria and Western Australia) use a system with a number (in Western Australian, 6; in Victoria, 8) of multi-member electorates, with each electorate electing a certain number of MPs (in Western Australia, 6; in Victoria, 5). Electorates vary in size and in the number of electors.

PARLIAMENTS IN OPERATION

Now that we have set out the differences in the various Australian parliaments, we should consider what is similar within them. Being a **Westminster system** means that there are certain common features across the various parliaments.

First, Bills are passed through both houses (except Queensland, Australian Capital Territory and Northern Territory, where there is only a single house) before becoming law as an Act. The set process for this, derived from the process used in the UK Parliament, means that a Bill has three 'readings', during the second of which amendments may be made to the Bill. The two houses must also agree on the Bill when it is passed for it to become an Act. Finally, the Governor of each state (or Governor-General for the Commonwealth) must sign the Bill – this last step being '**Royal Assent**'.

Following the Westminster precedent, the person who presides over the business of the various lower houses is called the **Speaker**. At the first sitting of parliament after an election, the initial task is to elect the Speaker, as the person who controls debate and generally manages the lower house. In the UK, the Speaker is generally considered non-partisan (although may well be a member of a party prior to election). The UK tradition is that the Speaker is not opposed by the existing opposition when he or she stands in elections, but of course after the election the Speaker may be changed. This tradition does not exist in Australia, although a number of Speakers have been well respected for their impartiality. The governing party usually nominates one of its own as Speaker.

In the upper houses, the person who presides over business is the **President**. The President is also elected after each election, in the same way as the Speaker, with the convention that the President will come from the same party as is in government. This may lead to the situation of the presiding officer of the upper house being from a party that does not have a majority in the upper house, and this has generally been the situation in the Senate since the 1980s.

In terms of seating, from the standpoint of the Speaker's chair, the government is always seated on the right, the **opposition** on the left, and minor parties and independents sit opposite the Speaker. This is mirrored in the upper house, on either side of the President. Ministers and shadow ministers sit at the front, with other government MPs arranged behind. From this arrangement derives the term the '**frontbench**', signifying the senior ministers. Opposition or shadow ministers also sit at the front (the 'opposition frontbench'), while those MPs not in the government or in the main opposition party are called the '**crossbench**', because of their position in the benches between the two main parties and opposite the Speaker. This particular seating arrangement is said to have originated at the time of the French Revolution, when the three 'Estates' were arrayed in front of the King (see Goodsell 1988, 296).

SHORT-ANSWER QUESTIONS

Westminster system: A system of government in which there are two Houses of Parliament, and the chief minister and the Cabinet are drawn from one of the Houses. The model for this form of government is the parliament of Westminster in the United Kingdom. Not all Westminster-based systems have two Houses, but all have the executive drawn from parliament.

Royal Assent: All Bills must receive Royal Assent to become Acts of Parliament. This involves the Governor-General, or their equivalent at the state and territory level, signing the Bill so that it becomes law. From this comes the phrase 'signing a Bill into law'.

Speaker: The Speaker is elected from the members of parliament to act as the 'Presiding Officer' for the House. The Speaker's role is to allow for the orderly operation of the House, and with the President of the Senate or Legislative Council is responsible for the conduct of the parliament as a whole.

VIDEO REFLECTION QUESTION

THE LEGISLATURE AS AN INSTITUTION

WESTMINSTER 'CHAIN OF RESPONSIBILITY'

Parliaments on the Westminster model, such as Australia, the United Kingdom and Canada rely on the notion of lines of **responsibility** between the Sovereign (the reigning monarch) and the citizenry. This is sometimes referred to as the 'Westminster Chain of Responsibility' and forms the basis of 'responsible government'. At its simplest form, it is the idea that the Monarch is linked to the citizens via the ministers and parliament (Marshall 1963).

However, the idea of responsible government is more complicated, as even though the ministers act as 'Ministers of the Crown' – an advisory role to the Sovereign – they are drawn from the elected parliament and remain responsible to the people. The same can be said for the prime minister, who exists as a chief minister – also known as the 'first among equals' – and although nominally the second most important person in the nation (after the Sovereign or their representative – the current Governor-General being Major General Sir Peter Cosgrove) is the person whom we would normally call the leader of the nation. So, while the Sovereign (in the form of Queen or King of Australia – currently Queen Elizabeth II) is the Head of State, for all practical purposes the Prime Minister (in 2018, Malcolm Turnbull) remains the head of government.

Tied to the discussion of the chain of responsibility is the debate around the 'reserve powers' of the Governor-General. As the Sovereign's representative, the Governor-General has the power to dismiss a government if required. It is his or her signature on election writs that dissolves parliament and begins the election process. It is the Governor-General who formally appoints the prime minister and ministers. The additional power is to dismiss governments. This power, a remnant of the days of powerful monarchs ruling their Cabinet, is generally only used on the advice of the prime minister. The dismissal of the Whitlam government in 1975, part-way through its term, is the only example at the Commonwealth level, and Governor-Generals generally avoid engagement in overtly political actions.

PARTIAL SEPARATION OF POWERS

Allied to the chain of responsibility is a partial separation of powers. Following the lead of earlier democratic theorists who proposed a separation of executive and legislative functions, the 18th century political philosopher Montesquieu formulated the notion of the 'separation of powers' to balance the various competing institutional powers against each other, as a bulwark against tyranny (see Kurland and Lerner 1987).

The notion itself is fairly straightforward and can be seen more clearly in the operation of key institutions in the United States of America. The three key powers are designated as the executive, the legislative and the judicial. They are located, respectively, in the government administration (the ministers and departments), the parliament and the judiciary. In the US, the executive is controlled by the President, who nominates cabinet members (the ministers in charge of departments). The legislative body is the Congress, and the President's appointees to the Supreme Court are ratified by the Senate representing the states of the Union. The US Supreme Court can make judgements on the constitutionality of bills passed by the Congress, which also have to be signed by the President. The idea is that the three power centres (executive, legislature, judiciary) check each other.

President (of the Senate or Legislative Council): The Senator or Legislative Councillor elected by the Senate or Legislative Council to be Presiding Officer for the upper house. Like the Speaker, the President is responsible for the orderly operation of the Senate or Council, but also has additional responsibilities as the person who welcomes foreign dignitaries and the reigning Monarch to parliament.

opposition: Generally taken as referring to the largest party not part of the government. Opposition are seated to the left of the Speaker.

frontbench: The collective term for those members of parliament (MPs) holding ministerial responsibilities. Those MPs in the opposition who 'shadow' ministers (that is, who have responsibility of covering that portfolio area) are referred to as shadow ministers and sit on the 'opposition frontbench'.

crossbench: A group of members of parliament who are not members of either the government or the opposition parties, so referred to as they sit at the bottom of the parliament facing the Speaker.

responsibility: The notion that ministers are responsible and answerable for their actions to parliament, and ultimately to the people.

REFLECTION
QUESTIONS

RELATIONSHIP TO THE EXECUTIVE AND THE JUDICIARY

Since Montesquieu wrote of the necessity of the separation of powers to prevent tyranny, there has been a debate regarding the proper relation of parliament to the executive and the judiciary. This relationship, in an Australian context, is based on precedent and convention. Some specific elements do remain. The parliament is the maker of laws but requires an administration to oversee and implement those laws. It is therefore incumbent upon the administration (through the executive and ministers) to provide for the proper functioning of government.

Parliament also retains the role of oversight of the various government departments, and generally performs this role through its various committees. Because of the partisan nature of the lower house, this generally tends to be a more limited oversight in Assemblies and the House of Representatives. However, given that most upper houses are not controlled by the government of the day, a significant committee system has developed within bodies such as the Senate. The Senate committee system allows senators to question both ministers and senior bureaucrats on what has happened in their department, whether funds have been well spent and whether policy has been implemented effectively. This can and has been used by opposition parties to probe the running of government, and at times to embarrass governments that may have wished for some policies to remain hidden or at best not discussed. The functioning of committees will be discussed in more depth in the next section, but it is important to note that probing by committees has led to changes in how departments function and can cause problems for ministers if wrongdoing or waste is uncovered.

In relation to the judiciary, parliament has a more restrained role, given that although the Attorney-General and Cabinet (all of whom are members of parliament) advise the prime minister on the nomination of High Court justices for appointment by the Governor-General, once judges are appointed, the role of parliament in oversight of their judgements and duties is very limited. The Attorney-General retains a direct relationship with the judicial system, as the portfolio holder, and controls the administration of the court system. This has led to the Attorney-General being referred to as the country's 'first law officer', as the head of the justice system, although the Commonwealth Solicitor-General is the person who leads the Commonwealth case on important issues, particularly in the High Court. Each state has control of its own court system, so the states' attorneys-general are in an analogous position.

SHORT-ANSWER
QUESTIONS

THE FUNCTIONS OF PARLIAMENT

Parliaments function on a number of levels, the most obvious being the operation of the modern nation-state. While parliament in Montesquieu's schema forms part of the three great elements of the state, parliament in a Westminster system has other discrete functions (Kurland and Lerner 1987). First, the party or faction with the largest number of seats within parliament forms government. Second, parliament passes legislation. Third, parliament allows for the views of electors to be represented. Last, parliament scrutinises the operation of government and holds government accountable for its actions. In relation to the first point, the number of parties in parliament is in part a function of the electoral system. French political scientist Maurice Duverger formulated this as three key outcomes:

1. a majority vote on one ballot is conducive to a two-party system
2. proportional representation is conducive to a multiparty system
3. a majority vote on two ballots is conducive to a multiparty system, inclined toward forming coalitions. (Duverger 1972, 23)

Duverger was noting that Westminster systems, such as Australia, where members of parliament are elected from single-member districts, tend to produce a two-party system. This is not an iron law, but certainly it tends to reduce the number of effective parties in parliament, and governments tend therefore to be made up of one or two parties. One of parliament's key functions is to determine who governs. In Australia's case this has been relatively straightforward, with the effective grouping of parties into the Australian Labor Party (ALP), Liberal Party and Country/National Party since the Second World War. In only one instance at the federal level since the Second World War has a government not formed almost immediately after an election, with the clear result being between the ALP on one side and on the other the Liberal and National Parties. In the period prior to the Second World War this was more complicated, but the strongest tendency since 1909 was for government to be formed by the ALP or a combination of non-Labor parties, to the same effect.

IMPACT OF THE ELECTORAL SYSTEM

The electoral system tends to deliver majority to either of the two main political groupings, but this is not necessarily the case. For example, after the 2010 federal election, there was no overall majority for either the ALP or the Liberal–National Party Coalition. Negotiations ensued to allow the Governor-General to have **confidence** that one side or another can pass legislation and provide for government. This is known as guaranteeing 'confidence and supply', where 'supply' is the money to pay for government services. These negotiations with minor parties and independents allowed Julia Gillard to form government, and as the Leader of the Parliamentary Labor Party to become Prime Minister. If Gillard had been unable to negotiate effectively with the minor party MPs or the independents, then Tony Abbott, as Leader of the Liberal Party (and as such, de facto head of the Coalition), would have had a chance to form government.

The formation of government involves choosing the ministry. In the Australian election system for the House of Representatives, as a preferential single-member system (see Chapter 7), the leader of the party that controls a majority of the House chooses the ministers. As noted above, this has been the Leader of the Parliamentary Labor or Liberal Party. The Leader would then become Prime Minister, after advising the Head of State (in the person of the Governor-General) that he or she has the confidence of the House and could then choose their ministry. The chosen ministers are then appointed by the Governor-General. This is the same method used for hundreds of years in the United Kingdom and similar to how many parliamentary systems operate around the world.

confidence/no confidence: If a party (or coalition) has the majority of seats in the lower house, it is usually tested by a 'no confidence' motion, which if passed means that a new government must be formed, perhaps with a new group of members of parliament or parties, or a new election being held.

Second Turnbull ministry, 20 December 2017

SPOTLIGHT

MINISTER	TITLE
Malcolm Turnbull	Prime Minister
Barnaby Joyce	Deputy Prime Minister and Minister for Infrastructure and Transport
Julie Bishop	Minister for Foreign Affairs
Scott Morrison	Treasurer
Senator Mathias Cormann	Minister for Finance Vice-President of the Executive Council Leader of the Government in the Senate Special Minister of State
Senator Marise Payne	Minister for Defence
Christopher Pyne	Minister for Defence Industry Leader of the House
Peter Dutton	Minister for Home Affairs Minister for Immigration and Border Protection
Christian Porter	Attorney-General
Senator Mitch Field	Minister for Communications Minister for the Arts Deputy Leader of the Government in the Senate
Senator Simon Birmingham	Minister for Education and Training
Josh Frydenberg	Minister for the Environment and Energy
Greg Hunt	Minister for Health
Dan Tehan	Minister for Social Services
Michael Keenan	Minister for Human Services
Senator Nigel Scullion	Minister for Indigenous Affairs
Kelly O'Dwyer	Minister for Women Minister for Revenue and Financial Services
Dr John McVeigh	Minister for Regional Development, Territories and Local Government
Steve Ciobo	Minister for Trade, Tourism and Investment
Senator Bridget McKenzie	Minister for Regional Communications Minister for Rural Health Minister for Sport
Senator Michaelia Cash	Minister for Jobs and Innovation
Senator Matthew Canavan	Minister for Resources and Northern Australia
David Littleproud	Minister for Agriculture and Water Resources

(See https://www.aph.gov.au/About_Parliament/Parliamentary_Departments/Parliamentary_Library/Parliamentary_Handbook/Current_Ministry_List for the most up-to-date full ministry list)

QUESTION

What criteria might the Prime Minister use to choose his or her ministry?

SHORT-ANSWER QUESTIONS

POLICY AND LEGISLATION

The second role of parliament, after determining who will govern, is to determine policy and legislation. Any party or faction that has the largest number of MPs, with a majority of them providing confidence to form ministries, then passes legislation. While the government, as the operator of the public service (what would be termed in the US 'the administration') can function on a day-to-day basis, it needs to formulate and pass Acts of Parliament. These Acts are devised to empower the various parts of the government to operate by paying their wages, causing actions to be undertaken or benefits to be made. Thus, an Act providing for education is required to first establish that there will be a public school system, then to build the schools, define how they will be run, and then to allow for the employment of teachers. This may be contained in one Bill (what an Act is called before it is passed), but generally all the operations may not be covered because of the intersection of different parts of the public service.

The passing of Acts is often seen as the most important function of parliament, as it is what allows many of the public services that we often take for granted to operate. In Australia, with two levels of government constructed by constitutions (the Commonwealth by the Commonwealth Constitution, the states by the various state Constitution Acts) means that state and Commonwealth governments are empowered to pass legislation. Governments use this power first to collect taxes, and then to disburse those taxes to provide services and benefits. In all states and territories, with the exception of the Australian Capital Territory, state governments also empower local governments (usually called councils) to make regulations for the management of local issues.

This leads to the broader activities of the parliament in terms of committees and public inquiries. The Australian Parliament, sitting in Canberra, can seem fairly remote from what the majority of Australians do on a daily basis. Canberra is a 'public service' town, with most people employed directly by the public service, or by organisations and businesses that support it. How then do members of parliament gain an understanding of the impact of their legislation? While some legislation may be seen as 'nation building', such as those to do with the establishment of banks, the Snowy Mountains Hydro Scheme or constructing the armed forces, most of the legislation considered within parliament is more mundane. MPs have offices in their electorates and home states, but they do not see or hear from the bulk of their constituents, and they require some way of gauging the impact of (and desire for) legislation and regulation.

COMMITTEES

committee: Delegated group of members of parliament who meet to discuss and debate Bills or matters of interest, so that parliament does not have to go through an investigatory or debate process as a whole. House committees are generally controlled by the government of the day, but upper house committees are sometimes controlled by the crossbench, so such committees often produce wide-ranging reports with more far-reaching recommendations.

This is where committees and public inquiries come in. Both Houses of Parliament, the Representatives and the Senate, have **committees**, either standing or select, that may be established by one or both houses (when both houses establish a committee it is known as a joint committee). All committees are established with terms of reference passed by the house that establishes them and with a set time to report back to parliament. The operation of committees is governed by Parliament's Standing Orders, which covers the operation and proceedings of parliament (Parliament of Australia 2017). At the calling of an election all inquiries and committee proceedings are terminated on the issue of writs, irrespective of whether they have reported or not, with select committees being disbanded. Standing committees continue after the election, although the composition may change depending on who is in government and who has kept or lost their seats.

Standing committees can gather material, take submissions, and generally can look more deeply into the impact a piece of legislation might have, or whether it is even required. Standing committees can therefore work on existing or proposed legislation, and their reports are often used as the basis for new policy that may be enacted as legislation or regulation, or simply to propose better ways of government operating (see Phillips et al. 1998, 58–62). Standing committees can also hold inquiries into matters of public interest where an issue is of such contention that parliament decides it needs more information.

Either house can also establish select committees to look into particular issues on an ad hoc basis. The issues dealt with by a select committee are usually tightly focused on a specific issue. The select committee will also be established for a relatively short period of time, and it will report back to the parliament in which it was established. Select committees are often established to deal with new, fairly straightforward and specific issues, although they may also be established to provide a report that then forms the basis for legislation (see Halligan et al. 2007).

The House of Representatives and Senate also have a small number of joint standing committees that look at critical information that effects the operation of the state. One such committee is the Joint Standing Committee on Electoral Matters, which gathers evidence after each election and provides recommendations for amendments to the electoral system (the current Committee's work can be found at https://www.aph.gov.au/Parliamentary_Business/Committees/Joint/Electoral_Matters).

Of course, much of the discussion of committees relies on the notion that executive government really wants to know or understand the outcome of committees. The work of committees has expanded considerably over the previous 30 years, especially for senators who may spend up to 20 per cent of their time on committee work (Brenton 2009, 60–1), yet may be unwelcome news for the government. When committee findings do not accord with the government or party's agendas, they may be seen as obstructive. Equally, committee members may feel that the work they do on a committee is difficult, onerous and thankless. As the former Foreign Minister Senator Gareth Evans asked early in his parliamentary career: '… is it enough that the committee … has simply created the preconditions for others to act rationally?' (1982, 83).

REFLECTION
QUESTIONS

LEGISLATION

VIDEOS

BEGINNING THE LEGISLATIVE PROCESS

Legislation is one of the key purposes of parliament, after the formation of the government. In its simplest form, legislation consists of a title, a purpose, some definitions of terms used in the Act, and then what is being legislated. In the case of simple amendments or enacting Bills, this may run to a few pages, or in the case of complex legislation, such as the various Tax or Social Security Acts, to many hundreds of pages. Each piece of legislation, whether as a primary piece of legislation or as an amendment, has to pass through both Houses of Parliament. The process of constructing legislation, once done by MPs themselves, is now done by a legal team within the Commonwealth Parliament called the Office of Parliamentary Counsel, and exists across a number of Westminster-based parliaments (Page 2009).

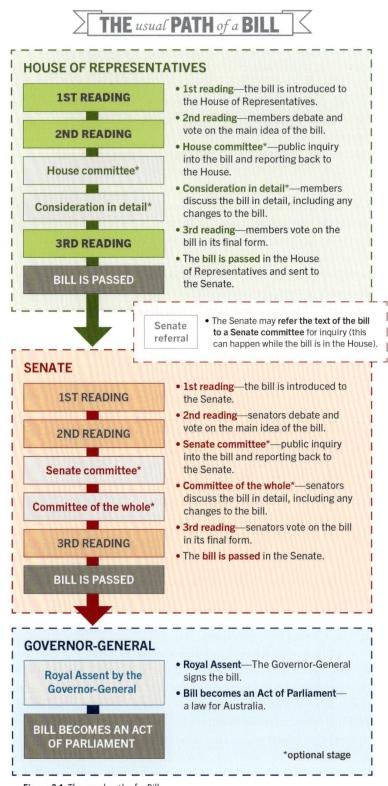

Figure 3.1 The usual path of a Bill
Source: Parliamentary Education Office

Most legislation, before it is proposed will have gone through a lengthy policy process (see Chapter 12). That policy process will have discussed the reasons for the legislation, seen some debate among the public service and any other stakeholders, and potentially an inquiry on the matter. It will then be drafted by a team either within parliament or the department from which the policy originated (in the case of complex policy instruments), whose job it is it write legislation in such a way as for it to be interpreted to actually do what it is intended to do. The team that drafts the legislation generally involves skilled lawyers, with a good understanding of the structure of law, and if necessary a good understanding of the existing legislation in the policy area. The legislation is then sent to the MP (whether the relevant minister, opposition MP, or MP from the crossbench) who asked for it.

If the relevant MP or minister is happy with the draft Bill, he or she may then decide to propose it to parliament. This is not as easy as simply standing up in parliament and requesting that the Bill be heard. Because there are many MPs who may wish to put forward Bills, and certainly a government and administration that wishes to turn policy into legislative action, the process is considerably longer. For Bills proposed by the government, the process is such that their Bills will get listed. However, prior to a government Bill being introduced to parliament, it will first have been through the Cabinet process. The relevant minister will have tabled first the policy underlying the Bill, and then the Bill itself if it is agreed to proceed. This gives the rest of the Cabinet an opportunity to debate the Bill and any objections to be dealt with. The relevant party room will also meet to discuss major Bills, although all government MPs will have been informed of the legislative agenda beforehand. For the ALP, it would go to caucus when the party is in government, or in the case of a Coalition Government, to the Joint Party Room – which is the combined party rooms of both the Liberal and National parties.

These processes are obviously the model, and contentious issues may obviate the party rooms, although there may then be significant party room debate if the issue becomes a *cause celebre* in the media.

WHIPS AND VOTING

After the Bill has been decided on, and prior to its actual introduction into parliament, there will be a meeting of the group of people who are essential communicators between parties, the 'whips'. The whips are those MPs designated by the parties in parliament to negotiate with the other parties and to communicate between their own MPs. You may have heard, in relation to the UK Parliament, the phrase, 'the three-line whip'. This is in relation to another function of the whip, which is to get MPs to vote according to the agreed party line. While 'one-line' is a guide on voting issued by the chief whip on behalf of the party leader, the 'two-line whip' refers to a directive for Westminster MPs to attend and vote. The three-line whip will be a written directive, underlined three times, to MPs from the chief whip, directing them to attend and vote, with severe consequences if they do not. A recent example was the vote on Brexit, in which Jeremy Corbyn issued a three-line whip on the vote to trigger Article 50 to begin the process of leaving the European Community. The whips' meeting involves discussion of what the parliamentary agenda will be. In the House of Representatives, this is also the place where agreements about speaking orders and the introduction of non-government Bills occurs. At this point, if there has not already been public discussion of the Bill, the MPs get to see what will be introduced into parliament. Notice will then be given that at the next sitting of parliament a Bill will be introduced.

For opposition and crossbench parties, the inclusion of any legislation they wish to put forward, or indeed in respect of questions or motions they wish to ask or move, is negotiated with the other parties at the whips' meeting. As the government has the numbers to pass legislation in lower houses, the opposition and crossbench business is usually far less regularly introduced or debated than government Bills, questions or motions, but all are allocated some time. What this does mean is that it is fairly rare that the opposition and minor parties get to introduce Bills into the lower house, and they are far more likely to introduce Bills in the upper house.

There are examples of Acts that have originated as non-government Bills, called private members' Bills, such as the Bill to allow same-sex marriage in Australia, but these are rarely passed. There are also other types of Bills where the whip is not applied as the Bill is of a contentious nature. These Bills, where party members can vote in any way they like, without fear of sanction from their party, are often called a conscience or free vote. An example of this was the debate and vote in 2016 on whether the Health Minister could regulate the drug RU486. Abortion law reform is another area where conscience votes have occurred.

INTRODUCING THE BILL

Hansard: The official record of the proceedings of each house of parliament.

Once a Bill has a timetable for introduction, it moves forward to being formally introduced into parliament, with a 'first reading'. At this point, the Bill is introduced by having its title read out by the Clerk of the House, and this is recorded in **Hansard**. Usually, a motion will then be passed for the Bill to be read a second time (the 'second reading'), and the relevant minister will give a speech about the general purpose of the Bill. Debate on the Bill is then adjourned until a later time to allow MPs a chance to see what is in the Bill and to consider the consequences of passing the Bill.

If the Bill does make it back from adjournment (which rarely happens for the opposition or crossbench Bills, but mostly for government Bills), this is called the 'second reading debate'. At this point, the opposition will respond, with the relevant shadow minister or MP stating the opposition's position. Debate then occurs, with MPs speaking for or against the Bill. At the end of the debate process, a vote is taken and so long as the Bill is agreed, the Bill passes onto the committee stage.

THE COMMITTEE STAGE

On reaching this point, the Bill may be referred to a committee for inquiry; the House may move into 'Committee of the Whole', which allows the whole chamber to discuss the Bill and agree on amendments; the Bill may then move directly to the final stage. None of these options are specifically prescribed but will have been decided upon by the government and passed by a motion in the House. They will also occur in that order, such that if a committee inquiry is required, the Bill will be sent to the relevant committee with a reporting timeframe for when it is to come back to parliament, at which time the report will highlight the findings of the committee and its suggested way to proceed. If the House moves into Committee of the Whole, the general outline of the Bill is debated, but in a more informal setting than usual. At this point, each clause of the Bill is debated in detail by the MP and parties, and amendments may be moved.

Once all committees have reported, amendments made, and debates had, the Bill will be put to a vote. The vote in the lower house is generally a formality, assuming the government has a majority of the seats, but in the Senate this may not be the case. However, assuming that the government has the numbers, the vote will be taken, the Bill passed, and the clerk then reads the title for the third time (the 'third reading').

RESOLUTION AND ROYAL ASSENT

The Bill having passed through one house, must now move onto the other house. Assuming that the Bill was a government Bill, and so originated in the lower house, it now moves to the upper house. Debate then proceeds in the same order until the Bill is finally agreed upon. At this point, the upper house may have made amendments to the Bill as it was passed by the lower house. The changes are transmitted back to the lower house. Discussion then occurs between the two houses until a resolution is made and the final form of the Bill is agreed.

At this point, the Bill makes its way to the Governor-General, from whom it receives Royal Assent and becomes law as an Act of Parliament.[1]

As a corollary to this, the legislation passed as an Act can also delegate some of the powers of parliament to the executive (as the government) to pass regulations and other statutes. These items are called delegated legislation. These regulations are formal powers of the government but must also be presented to parliament and they may be disallowed (that is, not agreed to) by either house. The term 'disallowable instrument' refers to these forms of delegated legislation.

VIDEOS
SHORT-ANSWER
QUESTIONS

NEW CHALLENGES TO AN OLD PRACTICE

It is worthwhile thinking through these processes that parliament uses. The process outlined above has been in use since Federation. While parliament itself has a set of standing orders on the actual process, and can vary those orders as it desires, the general form of how parliament works has remained largely the same since the beginning of the 18th century. The question might then be asked whether these processes, developed in the English Parliament, are still appropriate or useful in the 21st century. The development of parties, disdained by the writers of the Australian Constitution, has changed the process of debates. Developments in communication and travel have changed the way citizens can interact with their representatives, committees and even the government of the day. Governing in a globalised world has seen the number of Bills being passed each year from less than 100 in the mid-18th century to over 200 in 2016, but with Bills being increasingly complex and supported by regulation (Department of the House of Representatives 2016).

At the same time, the sitting hours of parliament have remained largely the same, even while constituency demands have increased immeasurably. Even if seats are not quite as big as whole states, the number of electors living in each electorate – well over 100 000 – means that MPs have many more constituents to meet, discuss, debate and interact with. The complexities of international trade, unthought of in the time of the British Empire, require large bureaucracies managed by ministers in the executive, still reporting and answerable to parliament.

REFLECTION
QUESTIONS

---

1   This process is covered in detail by the Australian Parliament House website: http://www.aph.gov.au/About_Parliament/House_of_Representatives/Powers_practice_and_procedure/00_-_Infosheets/Infosheet_7_-_Making_laws

VARIATIONS BETWEEN STATES AND TERRITORIES

There are nine legislatures covering the nine Commonwealth, state and territory jurisdictions. They are different in size, structure and operation. For instance, the fact that Queensland, the Australian Capital Territory and the Northern Territory do not have upper houses means that the role and operation of the single chamber takes on a different importance from the other bicameral parliaments.

Table 3.2 indicates that as the population of a state increases so does the number of MPs in the lower house. This is because the key functions of government are assigned to elected ministers, and these ministers are preferably but not entirely drawn from the lower house. In the case of the three smallest parliaments, they are drawn almost exclusively from one house (in Tasmania, MPs elected to the Legislative Council are generally elected as independents). The number of seats required to govern – 13 – is considered the minimum required to form a cabinet, where there are enough MPs so that ministers are not allocated too many responsibilities. The minimum size of parliaments is in reality constrained by the necessities of government.

TABLE 3.2 POPULATION AND SEATS BY JURISDICTION

JURISDICTION	POPULATION	LOWER HOUSE MPS	UPPER HOUSE MPS
Commonwealth	24 386 000	151*	76
New South Wales	7 798 000	93	42
Victoria	6 244 000	88	40
Queensland	4 884 000	89	-
Western Australia	2 568 000	59	36
South Australia	1 717 000	47	22
Tasmania	519 000	25	15
ACT	406 000	25	-
Northern Territory	245 000	25	-

* Commonwealth Parliament increased to 151 following 2017 redistribution

Source: Adapted from ABS (2017)

There is also no requirement for a set number of citizens per MP, so the representatives for some House of Representatives seats have electorates in excess of one million square kilometres. The seats of Durack (1.7 million /km^2) and Lingiari (1.4 million /km^2) are currently the largest seats, but the former seat of Kalgoorlie (abolished in 2008) was 2.3 million /km^2, and encompassed some 90 per cent of the land area of Western Australia. If we consider that most inner-city seats are less than 50 km^2, the size disparity is extreme. This also brings difficulties for representatives from the largest districts as servicing constituent complaints – or even just visiting the various towns in the electorate – can be a major undertaking. Nonetheless, parliaments have resisted setting maximum sizes (or populations) for electorates, even as Western Australia and Queensland have used Large District Allowance[2] calculations as partial compensation for the lack of electors in the largest electorates.

---

2 http://www.boundaries.wa.gov.au/electoral-boundaries/electoral-enrolment-statistics

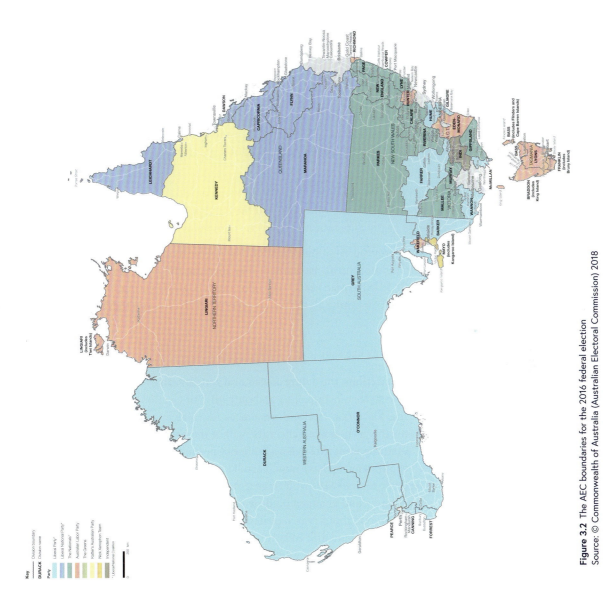

Figure 3.2 The AEC boundaries for the 2016 federal election

Source: © Commonwealth of Australia (Australian Electoral Commission) 2018

During periods of electoral experimentation, seat sizes, district magnitudes and parliament sizes have all fluctuated. For instance, the Tasmanian Parliament has had as many as 37 seats (towards the end of the 19th century) and between 1959 and 1998 had 35. New South Wales Legislative Assembly elections between 1919 and 1926 were conducted in multi-member electorates. In respect of different chambers, Queensland itself had an upper house between the establishment of self-government in 1860 to its abolition in 1922 (Parliament of Queensland 2011). Single member upper houses, present when both Western Australia and Victoria had dual-member seats where only one was elected at each election, have largely disappeared, and where there are two houses they remain composed differently. Tasmania might be considered an exception, but with the Tasmanian Legislative Assembly being elected using a proportional system, the two houses remain differently elected.

Finally, the size of the Australian Parliament has grown from 75 to 151 members in the House of Representatives and from 36 to 76 Senators. The ratio of members of the House of Representatives to Senators is guaranteed by Section 24 of the Constitution of Australia (1900):

> The House of Representatives shall be composed of members directly chosen by the people of the Commonwealth, and the number of such members shall be, as nearly as practicable, twice the number of the senators.

REFLECTION QUESTIONS

The Constitution also makes provision that states may or may not be divided into divisions (electorates), and that the Commonwealth Parliament may increase the number of seats in parliament. Indeed, until 1948, Senate seats were allocated via block voting, not via proportional means, with a party winning all the Senate seats in a state if it won the largest vote in that state.

THE IMPACT OF ELECTORAL SYSTEMS

As we will see in Chapter 7 on elections, the nature of electoral systems, district magnitude and seat size can all affect the styles of campaigns and outcomes of elections. If we take Andrew Inglis Clark's desire for a fair electoral system at face value, and agree that parliaments should, as reasonably as possible, reflect the will of the people, then we need to consider how and why Australia went through a number of permutations, and why we have apparently settled on the systems we have now (Farrell and McAllister 2005).

The earliest English legislatures had MPs who represented town and city boroughs in the parliament. As boroughs grew and changed (and in some cases declined), it became clear that a solid basis for representations was required. The Reform Act of 1832 (first applied to England and then to Scotland and Ireland), began the long process of reform and enfranchisement of adults within the UK (Reform Bills were enacted in 1867, 1884 and 1918) (Phillips and Wetherall 1995). The Australian Constitution in some respects reflected the debates within the United Kingdom, but in other ways reflected a broader consideration of the liberal ideas of writers like John Stuart Mill. The changes in the understanding of who should be able to vote, once the province of landholders but now extending to business owners, renters and other social groups, meant there were increasing pressures on parliaments to implement policies that reflected these groups.

This was perhaps most aptly seen in the development of the first Labour parties in Australia, an outgrowth of the early union movement, representing working people. This pushed other social groupings to organise themselves, the idea being that a group of parliamentarians should represent the collective interests of social groups, which was a shift for former colonial politicians. The liberal idea of individual freedom, which might have been seen as being abridged in the collective organisation of unions and parties, could also find expression in the activities of those who chose to be part of these new organisations, and this could extend past just working men to women (especially as part of the suffragette movement) and to other groups. The old English system of allocation of MPs by boroughs was replaced with even-sized electorates, use of the secret ballot, and from 1924 compulsory voting in Commonwealth elections. However, different states still adopted different rules over time, including South Australia being the last to adopt compulsory voting in 1942.

While parties were quite fluid in the immediate years after Federation, and for a variety of reasons throughout the inter-war period, the impact of different electoral systems in the different states was not particularly marked in the post-Second World War period of party stability. There were long stretches of single party domination, such as that which allowed Sir Robert Menzies to remain Prime Minister from 1949 to his retirement in 1967 (Brett 2003). At times, this single party domination was due to gerrymandering (such as in the case in Queensland for much of the 20th century), but the good economic conditions in the long post-war boom meant that while there were occasional changes in government this was not generally the result of dramatic shifts in public opinion. Even when pressure to change the electoral system became overwhelming – as in the case of the Queensland gerrymander and Victorian and Western Australian province systems, all of which sought to entrench conservative majorities either in government or in upper houses – these did not necessarily indicate a desire by the public for wholesale change. However, this period of relative stability began to break down with the arrival of significant minor parties in the 1980s and 1990s.

SUMMARY

Learning objective 1: Understand the historical evolution of legislatures in Australia

Parliaments do not generally spring to life fully formed – they have a historical base for their existence, and a rationale for the way they are constructed. This chapter briefly covers the historical formation of Australian parliaments and the path to the structures we are familiar with today. That also extends to the potential for ongoing change to how legislatures are elected and constituted, and possible paths leading forward.

Learning objective 2: Explain for what purpose the institutions of state exist

The institutions covered in this chapter sit at the heart of Australian constitutional life, as they are part of what we consider to be 'civic' life. They are critically important and are often considered the pivot (and veto) points for grand schemes and new ideas. The parliament is important in itself as the law-making vehicle, but then so are the courts as law interpreters and enforcers. Also we need to recognise that systems are not static, and the history of Australian parliamentary politics is also a story of change, adaptation and experimentation.

Learning objective 3: Describe the key legislative functions of Australian parliaments

While Australia has a rich parliamentary history, it can also be confusing, and this chapter delineates those areas that can be most difficult in terms of understanding. In particular, attention is paid to the rationale of legislative control, as well as the processes of governing through parliament.

Learning objective 4: Understand the process through which laws are made

Laws do not magically appear – they have to be carefully constructed. The parliamentary process is at the end of a longer process of policy-making that extends into evaluation and future legislative changes. This process is iterative, and should involve debates, discussions and inquiry into what is best in terms of the Australian population and individual citizens.

Learning objective 5: Identify the limits and variations of Australian legislatures

That the state does have limits might seem self-evident – in so far that it has borders. However, the Constitution sits at the apex of the laws that govern Australian life, and so needs to be recognised as a guiding instrument that also limits what each element of the state can pursue. The variation between states – in size, electoral systems and policy processes – is itself both a response to and a test of those limits, and is a challenge to governing Australia as a whole. Equally, the challenges that started in 2017 to MPs' eligibility to sit in parliament should be a warning that the Constitution covers all citizens, and that those at the heart of politics are perhaps doubly constrained in their ability to control the state.

DISCUSSION QUESTIONS

DISCUSSION QUESTIONS

1. At various times, there are calls to make members of parliament (MPs) more accountable between elections – how might this be achieved, and what effect would it have on the operation of parliament?

2. If MPs are independent representatives, as in the Westminster conception of representative democracy, why is party cohesion and discipline so high, to the point of single parties being able to control the legislature?
3. Do parties all have similar policies? Is there genuine deliberation and debate over issues? Or is parliamentary business primarily a process of consensus and coalition building?
4. How is a parliament 'relevant' to most people – what makes any of the current parliaments in Australia work? Is it that parties have just grown stronger and are in control?
5. What is the potential effect of a more rigid role for the executive (the prime minister and the Cabinet) on the role of parliament, in the context of the Westminster system of responsible government, cabinet solidarity, and the role of the Senate as a House of Review?

FURTHER READING

Clune, D. and Smith, R. (eds). (2012). *From Carr to Keneally: Labor in Office in NSW 1995–2011*, Crows Nest: Allen & Unwin.

Dryzek, J. and Dunleavy, P. (2009). *Theories of the Democratic State*, Basingstoke: Palgrave Macmillan.

Galligan, B., McAllister, I. and Ravenhill, J. (eds). (1997). *New Developments in Australian Politics*, South Melbourne: Macmillan.

Moon, J. and Sharman, C. (eds). (2003). *Australian Politics and Government: The Commonwealth, the States and the Territories*, Melbourne: Cambridge University Press.

Smith, R., Vromen, A. and Cook, I. (2006). *Keywords in Australian Politics*, Melbourne: Cambridge University Press.

REFERENCES

Australian Bureau of Statistics (ABS). (2017). *3101.0 – Australian Demographic Statistics, Dec 2016*. Canberra: Australian Bureau of Statistics. URL: http://www.abs.gov.au/AUSSTATS/abs@.nsf/mf/3101.0

Brenton, S. (2009). *What Lies Beneath: The Work of Senators and Members in the Australian Parliament*, Canberra: Department of Parliamentary Services.

Brett, J. (2003). *Australian Liberals and the Moral Middle Class: From Alfred Deakin to John Howard*, Melbourne: Cambridge University Press.

Commonwealth of Australia Constitution Act [Constitution of Australia]. (1900). URL: http://www.austlii.edu.au/cgi-bin/viewdoc/au/legis/cth/consol_act/coaca430/s24.html

Department of the House of Representatives. (2016). Work of the Session. Canberra: Department of the House of Representatives. URL: https://www.aph.gov.au/About_Parliament/House_of_Representatives/Powers_practice_and_procedure/Work_of_the_Session#43P

Duverger, M. (1972). Factors in a two–party and multiparty system. In M. Duverger, ed., *Party Politics and Pressure Groups*, New York: Thomas Y. Crowell, pp. 23–32.

Evans, G. (1982). Scrutiny of the executive by parliamentary committees. In J. Nethercote, ed., *Parliament and Democracy*, Marrickville: Hale and Iremonger.

Farrell, D.M. and McAllister, I. (2005). 1902 and the origins of preferential electoral systems in Australia. *Australian Journal of Politics and History*, **51**(2), 155–67.

Goodsell, C.T. (1988). The architecture of parliament: legislative houses and political culture. *British Journal of Political Science*, **18**(3), 287–302.

Halligan, J., Miller, R. and Power, J. (2007). *Parliament in the Twenty-first Century: Institutional Reform and Emerging Roles*, Carlton: Melbourne University Press.

Heywood, A. (2000). *Key Concepts in Politics*, Basingstoke: Palgrave Macmillan.

Kurland, P.B. and Lerner, R. (1987). The separation of powers. In P. Kurland and R. Lerner, eds, *The Founders' Constitution*, Chicago: University of Chicago Press. URL: http://press-pubs.uchicago .edu/founders/documents/v1ch10I.html

Marshall, G. (1963). Ministerial responsibility. *The Political Quarterly*, **34**(3), 256–68. URL: http:// onlinelibrary.wiley.com/doi/10.1111/j.1467-923X.1963.tb01946.x/full

Moon, J. and Sharman, C. (eds). (2003). *Australian Politics and Government: The Commonwealth, the States and the Territories*, Melbourne: Cambridge University Press.

Page, E. (2009). Their word is law: Parliamentary Counsel and creative policy analysis. *Public Law*, **4**, 790–811.

Parliament of Australia. (2009). *The first federal election*. Website exhibition 'For peace, order and good government'. URL: http://exhibitions.senate.gov.au/pogg/election/first_election.htm

Parliament of Australia. (2017). *Annotated standing orders of the Australian Senate Chapter 5 – Standing and Select Committees*. URL: http://www.aph.gov.au/About_Parliament/Senate/ Powers_practice_n_procedures/aso/so025

Parliament of Queensland. (2011). Legislative Council Chamber. URL: https://www.parliament .qld.gov.au/explore/history/parliament-house/inside-parliament-house/legislative-council-chamber

Phillips, H., Black, D., Bott, B. and Fischer, T. (1998). *Representing the People: Parliamentary Government in Western Australia*, Fremantle: Fremantle Arts Press.

Phillips, J.A. and Wetherall, C. (1995). The Great Reform Act of 1832 and the political modernisation of England. *American Historical Review*, **100**(2), 411–36. Retrieved from https://www.jstor.org/ stable/2169005?seq=1#page_scan_tab_contents

CHAPTER 4

THE EXECUTIVE: FUNCTIONS, POWER AND ACCOUNTABILITY

LEARNING OBJECTIVES

After reading this chapter, you should be able to:

1. Explain what executive power is and distinguish between the political and administrative wings of the executive

2. Describe the main functions that political executives perform

3. Understand the key features of the role of the prime minister and the Cabinet and explain the relationship between them

4. Describe the tensions between executive power and accountability, and how they are manifested in Australia's system of government

INTRODUCTION

In Australia, executive power is concentrated in the roles of the prime minister and the Cabinet – the body of senior ministers who provide leadership for the government and departments of state. Executive power is the capacity to 'execute' or implement political decisions and legislation. Although the Australian Constitution formally vests executive power in the Queen, which is then 'exercisable by the Governor-General as the Queen's representative' (Australian Constitution, Chapter 2, article 61), this executive power is chiefly symbolic. Real executive power resides in the elected government of the day, led by the prime minister and the Cabinet. When political scientists and journalists refer to *The Executive*, it is this government leadership to which they are referring. The legitimacy of the prime minister and the Cabinet's executive function derives from the fact of being elected to parliament as part of a party or coalition who can command a majority in the House of Representatives. Yet in recent years this legitimacy, and Australia's executive government stability, has been called into question.

In the period between 2010 and 2015, for example, Australia had a change of prime minister four times, despite there being only two federal elections. The replacement of Kevin Rudd by Julia Gillard, and then Gillard by Rudd, was later followed by elected Prime Minister Tony Abbott's ousting by Malcolm Turnbull. All of these political executions were met with a degree of public irritation and hostility. How could it be that an elected prime minister, with a mandate to govern, is deposed outside of a new election? Is it not voters who choose an executive government led by a particular prime minister, rather than that prime minister's parliamentary colleagues? The frequency with which these sorts of questions are asked speaks to the degree to which Australia's prime ministers have become the focus of the public's political attention and preferences (Weller 2005, 35). This trend is sometimes identified with a growing 'presidentialisation', which is often viewed as a key challenge to Australia's parliamentary form of executive government. While there is undoubtedly much truth to such claims, they can sometimes underestimate the extent to which Australia's prime ministers are beholden to their party, parliamentary party room/ caucus (all of their MPs) and the Cabinet. Between elections, it is the latter that ultimately determines if a prime minister remains in the top job.

In this chapter, we examine these issues in more detail. We begin with defining executive power and distinguishing between the political and administrative wings of executive government. We continue with a consideration of the functions that the executive government serves. The chapter then delves deeper into the heart of Australia's executive government, examining the key features of the roles of the prime minister and the Cabinet, and the relationship between them. We end by considering the tensions between executive power and accountability.

AUTHOR
PANEL

THE POLITICAL AND ADMINISTRATIVE EXECUTIVE: WHAT IS THE DIFFERENCE?

In discussing the executive in modern systems of government, it is helpful to make a distinction between its political and administrative arms. The former refers to that branch of the executive that has responsibility for making decisions about policy and, at the federal level, responding to national challenges as they arise. In Australia and other parliamentary systems, this is the **prime minister** and the **Cabinet** (in each Australian state, it is the premier and the Cabinet). In addition to the Cabinet, there is also an outer ministry composed of ministerial portfolios deemed to be of lesser importance, and whose ministers only attend Cabinet meetings when needed and invited. The **administrative executive**, by contrast, refers to the various branches of the state that have responsibility for administering policy and law in particular spheres. The public service or bureaucracy, as it is sometimes called, and its various subdivisions into health, education, finance, defence, trade, foreign affairs, police and justice and so on, constitutes the administrative wing of the executive. While there is a degree of overlap between the two wings – in that senior civil servants often play a substantial role in policy formation – formal power resides in the elected **political executive**.

THE POLITICAL EXECUTIVE

As a constitutional monarchy, executive political power in Australia is formally vested in the Queen, who is also our Head of State. The monarchy's formal **executive power** is 'exercisable by the Governor-General as the Queen's representative' (Australian Constitution, Chapter 2, article 61). The **Governor-General** acts on advice from his or her ministers, organised into a Federal Executive Council (FEC), which typically meets fortnightly to formalise or ratify decisions taken by the government. As the legal personality of the government of the day, and more specifically Cabinet, the FEC gives legal expression to the decisions governments make (Boyce 2007, 195). This is an institutional residue of the colonial governments prior to Federation, and before that the Westminster system in the UK as it had developed from the second half of the 17th century. At that time, executive power had shifted decisively from the Monarch to parliament and its ministers. Increasingly, real executive power came to reside with parliament, while the Monarch played a chiefly symbolic role as the personification of state unity.

THE GOVERNOR-GENERAL

A superficial reading of Australia's written Constitution can give the impression that it is the Governor-General, on behalf of the Queen, who exercises real executive power, rather than the prime minister and the Cabinet – a body that is not even mentioned in the Constitution. But this is not the case. Constitutional convention, which is no less a part of Australia's constitutional order than is the written Constitution, dictates that the Governor-General's role is chiefly symbolic, signifying unity of the nation and presiding over various ceremonial tasks such as swearing in ministers (Maddox 1996, 480–2). The Crown, whose local representative is the Governor-General, is above politics. Moreover, convention dictates that the Governor-General must take advice from his or her ministers – the elected government of the day, enjoying the confidence of a majority in the House of Representatives. This is why, among many other reasons, the 1975 dissolving of Gough Whitlam's democratically elected Labor Government by the unelected representative of a European hereditary monarch was so controversial (Sexton 2005, 239–62). In taking the decision to terminate Gough Whitlam's commission to form a government, while inviting Malcolm Fraser to be the interim prime minister despite leading a party/coalition that was in a minority in the House of Representatives, the Governor-General Sir John Kerr seemed to usurp executive powers that more properly belonged to the prime minister and the Cabinet. He did so without the advice of ministers from the party still enjoying a majority in the House of Representatives.

prime minister: The head of the political executive and government, by virtue of the fact that the party that they lead has the confidence of a majority of members in the House of Representatives.

SHORT-ANSWER QUESTIONS

Cabinet: The government's central leadership and decision-making body that includes ministers responsible for government departments, and which is chaired by the prime minister.

administrative executive: The public service wing of the executive branch of government, which is responsible for the administration of the machinery of state.

political executive: The wing of the executive that provides political leadership for the political community, which is distinguishable from the administrative executive.

executive power: The capacity to execute or implement political decisions on behalf of a given political community.

Governor-General: Australia's Monarch is represented in her absence by a Governor-General who has extensive, constitutionally given executive powers. Convention requires these be used only as the prime minister advises.

VIDEO

THE CABINET AND THE PRIME MINISTER

If the executive role of the Governor-General is chiefly symbolic and ceremonial, in parliamentary democracies like Australia real executive power resides with the Cabinet and the prime minister. The Cabinet, as already intimated, is a body composed of senior ministers who make the most important decisions about overall government policy. Each minister stands at the head of a government department (such as finance, education, human services), and has responsibility for the effective functioning of that department and its implementation of government policy. Cabinet ministers are always elected members of parliament and are ultimately responsible to parliament. This is unlike some presidential systems such as in the United States, where Cabinet secretaries are unelected officials appointed by and serving the President. That said, the prime minister powerfully shapes the composition of Cabinet in Australia's system of government. Liberal Party prime ministers, for example, have always chosen their own Cabinet, which gives them tremendous powers of patronage – the capacity to distribute the spoils of power, to promote or demote, and thereby influence careers and political outcomes. By contrast, Labor's parliamentary caucus (all Labor members in the House of Representatives and Senate) has typically elected its Cabinet members, with the leader then distributing portfolios, making it a process much more subject to factional negotiation and bargaining. This changed in 2007 when Kevin Rudd insisted that he choose his own Cabinet. Yet it was key figures in that same Cabinet that moved against him in 2010, which speaks to the constraints of prime ministerial power.

The prime minister stands at the summit of executive power in Australia and is the head of government. Their power derives from being the leader of the party, or a Coalition of parties in the case of the Liberal–National Party Coalition, enjoying the confidence of a majority in the House of Representatives. This being so, the prime minister exercises both executive and legislative power, reflecting the fact that these functions are fused in the Australian system. In exercising these powers, the prime minister's key relationship and managerial challenge is with their own Cabinet and political party. Here the prime minister has historically been understood as first among equals (*primus inter pares*), though many have suggested that this has changed as recent prime ministers have concentrated greater power in their hands, often at the expense of the Cabinets that they lead (Kefford 2013; Weller 1985). This vexed issue is discussed below. But first, we need to further elaborate on the other main arm of executive government – the administrative executive, or public service bureaucracy as it is sometimes called.

REFLECTION
QUESTIONS

THE ADMINISTRATIVE EXECUTIVE

The administrative executive is constituted by a public service organised into government departments that mirror the organisation of portfolios in the Cabinet and the outer ministry (a minister may have responsibility for more than one portfolio). Sitting within, or sometimes alongside, these departments are additional government agencies (for example, the Australian Federal Police, the Australian Security Intelligence Organisation, Centrelink) that are ultimately answerable to their political masters, in the form of ministers. Thus, there is a chain of responsibility and accountability, organised in a bureaucratic hierarchy where appointments are ostensibly made according to merit, which stops with a minister who is responsible to parliament and ultimately the electorate. This is why Australia, following its Westminster forebears, has what is known as a system of 'responsible' government. Public servants serve the public by serving the political executive that the public has elected to govern.

Is the public service apolitical?

As part of responsible government, the public service is supposedly apolitical. Indeed, public servants sign up to the Public Service Code of Conduct that requires them to be apolitical (Maley 2012, 238). In other words, employees within the public service are meant to be neutral with respect to political parties when discharging their duties. This does not mean that public servants do not or should not have political opinions and preferences, but merely that they should not bring them to their work. Rather, they should conscientiously implement policy while, at the senior levels of the public service, offering 'frank and fearless' advice to their masters in the political executive, regardless of the latter's political complexion (Mulgan 2007, 570). The measure of professionalism for public servants is the extent to which they are able to personify this neutrality, even when dealing with policies and politicians that they might find morally reprehensible and acting outside the public interest. This understanding of professionalism raises the thorny question of whether or not a public servant's ultimate loyalty is to the government of the day or to the public?

To whom is a public servant responsible? The Wilkie Affair

SPOTLIGHT

The question as to a public servant's principle loyalty was brought into sharp relief in 2003, around what has become known as the Wilkie Affair. At that time, Andrew Wilkie was an analyst with the Office of National Assessments (ONA), a government agency that filtered and analysed raw intelligence that had a bearing on national security. In late 2002 and early 2003, the Australian Government of John Howard was becoming increasingly vocal in its support of the United States' warnings about the dangers of Iraq's President Saddam Hussein and the state that he led. The essential argument was over whether the intelligence showed that Iraq possessed weapons of mass destruction (WMDs – chemical, biological and nuclear weapons), or if Saddam had links with terrorists. The danger, President Bush and his Australian allies asserted, was that Iraq might arm terrorists with WMDs, which could have catastrophic consequences for the US and its allies. As Prime Minister Howard argued in a speech to the National Press Club on 13 March 2003, this constituted a 'lethal threat to Australia and its people' (Howard 2003), which could only be avoided by military action to disarm Iraq.

Yet as Australia geared up for war, ONA analyst Andrew Wilkie, who had access to much of the intelligence that Howard was basing his case on, approached the media with startling revelations. In a clear transgression of the norms of public service neutrality, he suggested that the government was misleadingly presenting intelligence, in order to justify a decision for war in Iraq that had already been made. Wilkie resigned from his post and was derided by many conservative politicians and other public servants for a lack of loyalty and professionalism. Others viewed his whistleblowing as a heroic and selfless act of public service (see Kingston 2003, for arguments from both sides). Either way, the entire affair shone a light on the sometimes fraught relationship between public servants and the executive politicians under whom they serve.

QUESTION

Was Andrew Wilkie right to blow the whistle on the Howard Government's misleading use of intelligence? Do public servants ultimately serve the government or the broader public?

VIDEOS

Historically, political neutrality within the public service has been promoted by security of tenure and promotion according to merit (Singleton et al. 2003, 196). A public servant can do their job more effectively if they do not have to worry about offending either side of politics, which in the absence of tenure could jeopardise their continued employment. This is particularly important in the Senior Executive Service – the top echelon to the public service – whose employees provide advice to ministers. Put bluntly, it is easier to tell a minister what they don't want to hear, but what they perhaps need to hear, when one is secure in one's job. But this ideal, as with the broader ideal of the public service being apolitical, is discrepant with some important political realities that have been sharpened in recent decades (MacDermott 2008).

The first discrepancy to note is between the *ideal* of political neutrality and the *reality* of partisanship, albeit manifested in differing degrees and in different forms. It has often been observed, for example, that much of the federal public service was an obstacle to Whitlam's Labor Government realising its program (Whitlam 1985). After 23 years serving the Liberal–Country Party Coalition, many senior public servants had become habituated to conservative rule and were deeply suspicious of the novel economic and social agenda being pursued by Labor. Strong personal links with conservative politicians, built up over a generation, along with superior knowledge of and a willingness to use bureaucratic measures to defend the status quo, meant that at least part of the public service was an impediment to, rather than an enabler of, Labor's political executive.

The public service and ideology

Partisanship within the public service can also take subtler ideological forms. In his classic account *Economic Rationalism in Canberra* (1991), Michael Pusey sites a wealth of evidence to show that during the Hawke governments of the 1980s, senior bureaucrats in the core departments of Treasury, Finance, and Prime Minister and Cabinet, were overwhelmingly committed to free market solutions to national problems. Ideological assumptions about the desirability of deregulation, corporatisation and privatisation masqueraded as impartial, technical advice to ministers who were often out of their depth when it came to debating the finer points of economic policy. This dry economic advice was a part of a broader neo-liberal political project. While it would be exaggerated to say that bureaucrats instead of politicians were making policy, they certainly played a bigger hand in Australia's economic reorientation than a politically neutral public service would have.

Outsourcing public service

Another development that has impacted the relationship between the administrative and political arms of the executive is the outsourcing of roles previously performed by the public service. In particular, the growth in the private employment of ministerial advisers since the 1970s has often been at the expense of advice derived from senior bureaucrats in the public service. All ministers and most opposition figures in the shadow Cabinet now have 'political staff'. While some defend this development as providing more diverse sources of advice and therefore more informed final decisions, others say that it shields ministers from advice they may not want to hear but need to hear. Walter and Strangio, for instance, argue that ministerial advisers mediate between the administrative and executive arms of government, and in so doing 'drive, sieve and skew advice; and they insist on what the minister wants as opposed to the public interest or the integrity of the policy process' (2007, 54). In other words, the advice from ministerial advisers is political rather than neutral.

The new public management

A final development that has transformed the administrative executive since the 1980s has been the rise of a new paradigm of public sector management (see Christensen and Laegreid 2007; MacDermott 2008; Pollitt and Bouchaert 2011). The 'New Public Management', as it is called, put the public service on a more business-like footing, with economic efficiency becoming a primary goal. It advocates a management model borrowed from the corporate sector, in which the performance of managers is continually audited against quantitative criteria and subject to monetary incentives. Among the senior ranks of the public service, tenure is replaced by short-term contracts, the renewal of which is subject to meeting key performance indicators. Critics suggest that this has been a negative development in the relationship between the administrative and political wings of Australian executive government. On the one hand, performance as measured against quantitative criteria – like budget savings or customer satisfaction surveys – is an overly narrow way of assessing the value of a senior public servant's contribution. On the other hand, the absence of tenure makes public servants more susceptible to political pressure, which can lead to a politicisation of the advice that they give (Mulgan 1998).

We have shown in this section that the prime minister and the Cabinet and the public service bureaucracy fulfil the functions of executive power. But what exactly are the more specific functions that they fill? The following section, 'Executive power and its functions', answers this question.

REFLECTION
QUESTION

EXECUTIVE POWER AND ITS FUNCTIONS

Executive power can be defined, in narrow formal terms, as the capacity to execute or implement law and policy (Heywood 2007, 358). But in reality, the powers of modern executives extend far beyond what this formal definition suggests. Political executives do not just execute or give effect to laws passed in the legislature, they also initiate changes to the law, develop policy, craft communication strategies, navigate national crises, conduct diplomacy with other states, make decisions about war and peace, and much else besides. If governance is about 'steering the ship of state', executive power is about who, or what, controls the rudder of that ship.

KEY FUNCTIONS

The key function of the political executive is, as we have already seen, leadership. It stands at the summit of state power, and shapes the political, social and economic direction of a given country. It does so by *executing* law and policy, as its name implies, but also by initiating and refining law and policy, and navigating the many challenges that a country and its citizens face over a government's term in office. The political executive functions as a leader for the government of the day and also for the machinery of state more broadly conceived. Beyond this general leadership function, the political executive fulfils a number of more specific functions. These include: symbolic and ceremonial functions; public leadership functions, including managing crises and national emergencies; policy-making functions; regulating Australia's interaction with its external, international environment; and providing leadership for the public service.

SYMBOL OF NATIONAL UNITY

One key function of political executives is to provide a symbolic personification of a national community's unity, which is periodically reaffirmed in public rituals and ceremonies. Presidents, Monarchs, Governor-Generals and other heads of state represent the nation personally. They are central to the reproduction of what Benedict Anderson famously referred to as the 'imagined community' that is the nation (Anderson 1991). Because citizens in modern nation-states can only ever personally know a handful of their fellow citizens, mechanisms are necessary for producing a sense of national community and solidarity in the minds of those who are otherwise remote from each other. Such mechanisms include symbols, rituals and ceremonies that emphasise the continuity of the nation through time. Our political leaders often participate in these events, and indeed cultivate them for their own political purposes, which provide a focus for our national imaginings.

SHORT-ANSWER
QUESTIONS

SPOTLIGHT

ANZAC Day and the political executive

ANZAC Day has undergone a reinvigoration over the past three decades. Dwindling numbers of ex-servicemen and women have been more than replaced by new generations of Australians attending dawn remembrance services here and overseas. Liberal Prime Minister John Howard (1996–2007) was at least partly responsible for this reinvigoration, as he actively promoted war and the ANZAC legend as central to Australian national identity. Regardless of the partisan political purposes to which remembrance services and other such events can be put, it is essential that the political executive attend. The Governor-General and the prime minister are always present. Their sombre laying of wreaths and recounting of a national narrative with war, sacrifice and mateship at its heart, provides a public focus for national commemoration and the reaffirmation of Australian identity, albeit one understood in a particular masculine and military light (Garton 1998, 86–7; Seal 2004, 4–6). Members of the political executive attend these ceremonies not as private individuals, but as representatives of the state and symbols of national unity and continuity. In so doing, they fulfil an important function in symbolically tying the national present to the past and the future, and legitimising the institutions of state and government. But ANZAC Day has not been without its critics. For some it is viewed as glorifying the horrors of war and sacralising the secular (Inglis 1998), while feminist scholars have rightly pointed out that it celebrates and therefore perpetuates a masculine national identity where female achievements and sacrifices are largely ignored (Lake 1992; Lake and Reynolds 2010).

QUESTION

Can a prime minister, who is a party political figure, adequately represent the unity of the national community in the way that the non-party, above politics Governor-General can?

LEADERSHIP TO THE PUBLIC

Another function of political executives is to provide leadership to the public, particularly in times of national crisis. Prime ministers, and to a lesser extent their senior Cabinet ministers, present themselves as providers of solutions to national problems, no matter how acute. This involves not just advancing pragmatic policy solutions, but also fashioning particular images of leadership appropriate to the circumstances being confronted.

In times of war, for instance, a prime minister, irrespective of gender, seeks to appear strong, stoic and resolute, in the way that Margaret Thatcher did during the Falklands War (1982), and Labor Prime Minister John Curtin did in the darkest days of the Second World War (Day 1999). Similarly, in the wake of the Port Arthur massacre in 1996, and again after the Bali bombing of 2002 in which 88 Australians were killed, prime ministerial leadership demanded that John Howard act in ways that expressed the emotions of his public. In the first case, Howard channelled national grief and harnessed it to bolster political support for a government gun buyback scheme, which was widely applauded as showing resolute leadership. The second case encompassed expressions of anger at the perpetrators, grief at the loss of life, and a quiet determination to take action to ensure that it could never happen again. In his Bali memorial speech, Howard said he spoke for '19 and a half million Australians who are trying however inadequately to feel for you and to support you at this time of unbearable grief and pain'. He continued, 'I can on behalf of all the people of Australia declare to you that we will do everything in our power to bring to justice those who were responsible for this foul deed' (Howard 2002, 1). Irrespective of whether or not John Howard the man was personally experiencing these emotions, his role as prime minister demanded that he express them. He was, essentially, channelling the emotions of the public, and in so doing providing a focus for Australians' grief and anger and their determination that these events should never occur again. Trauma was thereby transformed into a catalyst for national identification (Hutchison 2010, 65–8). At the same time, such crises are opportunities for political executives to concentrate greater powers in their hands, as was the case after both of these episodes. Crisis management often involves and invokes security anxieties. These in turn are readily translated into greater executive power – through means such as emergency legislation that suspends usual judicial protections for citizens – to meet real or imagined threats.

POLICY AND LEGISLATIVE LEADERSHIP

Political executives also, crucially, function to provide leadership in the policy and law-making process. They formulate broad political, economic and social programs (policy 'platforms') within which specific policies are developed. In Australia, the prime minister and the Cabinet are central in navigating the passage of these policies through both their party room and the legislature, though often having to make compromises along the way. Compromises are particularly necessary when the government does not have a majority in the Senate, or when there is significant opposition from within the prime minister's own party ranks. Nevertheless, generally speaking the executive has a firm hold over the legislature in Australian policy-making. This is because it sits within a parliament where its party usually (not always – sometimes minority governments are formed with independents' support, as with Julia Gillard's Government from 2010–13) enjoys a majority in the House of Representatives.

In most liberal democracies, this legislative function of the executive expanded over the course of the 20th century, in response to the greater complexity of modern societies and economies, and under the whip of stronger party discipline. It would be mistaken to think, however, that all policy is exclusively a function of the political executive. Senior civil servants play an important role in the development of much government policy, as their expertise and experience are often greater than that of their supposed political masters in the Cabinet. Furthermore, much policy is also initiated by interest groups and their lobbyists, and then embraced and sold to the public by executive politicians (see Chapter 12). The latter present policy as being in the universal, national interest, when in fact they often serve the narrow sectional interests of those groups and industries that promote them.

LEADERSHIP ON THE WORLD STAGE

An increasingly important function of the modern executive is managing a state's interactions with its external economic and political environment. As a country that has always been reliant on trade, the importation of capital for investment, and the security umbrella of powerful allies, Australia was, from its very inception, deeply involved in international politics and the global capitalist economy. With the acceleration of globalisation in the second half of the 20th century, this involvement deepened. Consequently, the function of managing Australia's bilateral relationships with other countries, fulfilling its obligations under international treaties, and overseeing its security alliances and trade relationships, has become increasingly important for the modern executive. The political executive also makes decisions about taking the country to war, a prerogative that both Bob Hawke (Labor Prime Minister 1983–91) and John Howard (Liberal Prime Minister 1996–2007) energetically defended when they mobilised the Australian military in the first and second Gulf Wars, respectively. In fulfilling the function of leading Australia on the world stage, the political executive is hugely dependent on a vast array of public servants – ranging from ambassadors and other embassy staff, through trade officials and military officers, to scientific personnel and various international emissaries – who, formally led by the foreign minister, collectively constitute an administrative arm of the executive in the international field.

LEADING THE PUBLIC SERVICE

This brings us to the final function of the political executive, which is providing leadership to the administrative bureaucracy. In Australia's system of 'responsible government', the executive branch is organised into different departments, each with a minister at its head. That minister, as part of the political executive, has the responsibility for leading their department in accordance with the demands of law and the government's policy priorities. In discharging this responsibility, they play a key role in overall policy coordination, and are ultimately accountable for departmental failings. The buck stops with the minister. Or at least that is the ideal.

In reality, the 'buck' often does not stop with the minister, but instead stops with their staff and senior bureaucrats. But ministers do not have it all their own way. Ministers are politicians who come and go. They are heavily reliant on their departmental secretaries and other senior bureaucratic staff who frequently have greater competence and experience than they do. In addition to greater experience in particular portfolios, these senior staff often also have superior skills in navigating the many pitfalls that bedevil all bureaucratic forms of organisation. Despite this, it is the political executive that ostensibly fulfils the function of leadership.

To better understand this and the other functions outlined, it is necessary to deepen our understanding of the roles of the prime minister and the Cabinet, and especially the relationship between them.

REFLECTION
QUESTIONS

PRIME MINISTER AND THE CABINET GOVERNMENT

A political executive composed of a prime minister and the Cabinet that they lead, we have already noted, dominates Australia's system of government. But we have not yet explored these roles in detail or examined the relationship between them. In this section we deepen the analysis of the roles of the prime minister and the Cabinet, and explore the sources of possible discord between them, and what this can mean when the relationship breaks down.

THE PRIME MINISTER AND PRESIDENTIALISATION?

Australian prime ministers are at the heart of our political executive (Weller 2013). They lead the party who can secure majority support in the House of Representatives and thus dominate parliament. They shape the composition and policy agenda of Cabinet, chair Cabinet meetings, and have tremendous powers of patronage that can be deployed as leverage in bringing their party room and Cabinet to heel. Prime ministers have the massive resources of the Commonwealth state bureaucracy at their disposal, and they can use the Department of Prime Minister and Cabinet to oversee, and thus control, the performance of other ministers. They are the government's chief political communicator and the main focus of media attention. Voters may or may not recognise members of the Cabinet, but they are almost certainly familiar with the prime minister of the day. This is no surprise. The prime minister, after all, wields the largest microphone in the land, with ready access to a media enthralled by the leader's every utterance. Prime ministers can call snap elections at times that maximise their chances of victory, and then campaign from a position of prime ministerial authority, with all of the advantages that this confers. They claim to speak on behalf of the nation, a claim that is at least tacitly accepted by millions. In times of national crisis, it is the prime minister who is the public face of the government's response. They salve national wounds and channel the emotions of their public, becoming the repository of both hopes and grievances. The prime minister is, in every sense of the word, the *chief* executive of the political executive.

Prime ministers as political agents

The manner in which different politicians have occupied the position of prime minister, however, has been very different (Grattan 2000; Weller 1992). These differences are shaped partly by personality, partly by the circumstances under which prime ministers have secured and kept power, and partly by the institutional constraints that they confront at any point in time. Prime ministers are political agents of change and/or continuity, and their choices and leadership matter, even if they are constrained by institutions and structures. Prime ministerial leadership makes a difference.

Some prime ministers, such as Robert Menzies (United Australia Party 1939–41 and Liberal 1949–66), Bob Hawke (Labor 1983–91) and John Howard (Liberal 1996–2007), accumulated authority and power over their Cabinets and parliament that other prime ministers could only dream of. Much of this authority was derived from their success in leading their parties to successive election victories. Even where a prime minister is not especially loved and admired by his or her colleagues, as was the case with Malcolm Fraser (1975–83), delivering election victory, and thus electoral seats to party candidates, ensures a solid core of party and Cabinet backing that is only diluted when electoral support wanes (Maddox 1996, 207–8).

Some prime ministers have also been brilliant performers in the cut and thrust of parliamentary theatre. Paul Keating (Labor 1991–96) was certainly in this category, and Malcolm Turnbull (Liberal 2015–) is also building a reputation as a strong parliamentary performer, while others were underwhelming at best and embarrassing at worst. Liberal Prime Minister William McMahon (1971–72) was one who was widely viewed as a poor parliamentary performer.

Prime ministers also differ with respect to their approach to the Cabinet and Cabinet business. Julia Gillard (2010–13) and especially Bob Hawke (1983–91), for example, were well known for their 'Chair of the Board' style of leadership, in which they sought consensus and were comfortable with delegating authority to others. Kevin Rudd (Labor 2007–10 and 2013) and Tony Abbott (Liberal 2013–15), by contrast, gained a reputation for micro-managing and political centralisation, which contributed to their respective downfalls. John Howard's (1996–2007) approach to leadership and the Cabinet fell somewhere between these two poles. He was a 'Cabinet traditionalist' for whom all of the big issues had to be discussed by the Cabinet, although over time 'he increasingly worked with an inner circle' to make decisions (Bennister 2012, 41).

VIDEO

Presidentialisation?

The propensity to work with a trusted inner circle to make decisions implies a political centralisation around the prime minister, which some view as symptomatic of a broader 'presidentialisation' of Australian politics (Kefford 2013). The presidentialisation thesis argues that prime ministers in parliamentary systems increasingly exhibit features that have long been associated with executive Presidents (Poguntke & Webb 2005). Executive Presidents claim an indivisible personal mandate to govern, and secure that mandate on the basis of an electoral process that is highly personalised and focused on the particular qualities of presidential candidates. They appeal to voters directly, rather than through the mediation of their party. They construct a political 'brand' around themselves and gather an army of political and media advisers who are only loyal to the President.

Similarly, it is argued, prime ministers are now the supreme focus of electoral campaigns in countries with parliamentary systems. The modern media is preoccupied with, and almost exclusively focused on, the qualities of the respective leaders vying for power (also see Chapter 10). Consequently, these leaders often claim a personal mandate to lead the country if elected and gather around them hand-picked advisers who may have more sway over the prime minister than Cabinet ministers or departmental secretaries (Prime Minister Tony Abbott's former Chief of Staff Peta Credlin is a good example). Moreover, in most circumstances, prime ministers are increasingly able to dominate their

Cabinets and the broader political agenda because as the leader of their party they are the focus of a preponderance of media attention.

Clearly, the presidentialisation thesis illuminates important developments in Australian politics. Few would disagree that prime ministers, and their opposition counterparts, are the main focus of media in and between modern elections, and that they are the chief political communicators for their parties. Moreover, voters may formally be electing a local member, but for most it is the party and the party's leader that is paramount when making their electoral choice. If a federal election were held tomorrow, the choice for most voters would be about whether Malcolm Turnbull or Bill Shorten should be prime minister, not who should be their local member.

Given all this, we can agree with some of the central propositions of the presidentialisation thesis, though with a couple of important qualifications. First, prime ministers have in some ways always been as powerful, or perhaps even more powerful, than Presidents, especially with respect to the former's dominance of the legislature. After all, they lead the party enjoying the confidence of a majority in the House of Representatives. Second, prime ministers, for all of the political advantages that they enjoy, vis-à-vis their Cabinet colleagues, are still vulnerable to being removed by their own party, in a way that Presidents are not. It is this relationship between the prime minister and the Cabinet, then, that is fundamental to Australia's executive government.

REFLECTION
QUESTIONS

CABINET GOVERNMENT

Australian Government is often described as Cabinet government (Weller 2007). It is perhaps more precise to describe the Australian system as prime minister and Cabinet government, given the centrality of leaders. Nevertheless, the importance of the Cabinet – the executive leadership team constituted by ministers at the head of key departments, plus the prime minister – cannot be underestimated. Generally meeting weekly, sometimes more, it is the political body that steers the ship of state. It shapes policy, determines priorities, provides leadership to government departments, and discusses and provides solutions to the most pressing issues facing government. Taking its inspiration from the Westminster model, Cabinet and Cabinet ministers – and their shadow Cabinet counterparts, who act to hold governments accountable and present themselves as an alternative government – are governed by a set of principles that are absolutely central to effective governance. These are confidentiality or secrecy, solidarity and collective responsibility (Maddox 1996, 212).

Confidentiality

Confidentiality simply means that given information should not be circulated or discussed beyond the person or group of persons who are legitimate parties to that information. When we *confide* in another person, we entrust them with private information that we do not expect they will share with others. Our reasons for doing so may vary, but typically involve the sensitivity of the information to ourselves and/or those around us. Similarly, Cabinet deliberations are conducted on the assumption of confidentiality, and colleagues are entrusted with information that it is presumed will not go beyond Cabinet.

This is not because of the naïve belief that devious politicians always have something to hide (although they may and often do have something to hide), but because it allows for the fullest and most open debate possible in a body that is always composed of strong personalities and diverse opinions. The absence of such confidentiality would mean that ministers would always have to be mindful of the political fallout of anything that they might say in Cabinet. This is especially so if a minister holds a position that is contrary to present government policy, which the media and political opposition could present as evidence of divided and incohesive government. The leaking of Cabinet differences to the media, we will see below, provides a negative proof of the importance of the confidentiality principle and the practice that it justifies. The breakdown of Cabinet confidentiality signals an erosion of trust and collegiality and is often a prelude to a larger government crisis. Confidentiality goes hand in hand with Cabinet solidarity and collective responsibility.

Solidarity

Solidarity refers to the unity of interest and purpose among a given group, and the group acting collectively on this basis. When we act in solidarity with a person or group, we act in ways that demonstrate our loyalty, identification and shared interests with them. In Cabinet, solidarity means acting as one and promoting government policy with a unified voice. Ministers are obliged to publicly defend Cabinet decisions even if they disagree with them and argued against them in Cabinet deliberations. If they are unable to do this, the convention is that they should resign and move to the backbench.

Clearly this does not always happen. Breaking Cabinet confidentiality necessarily entails breaking Cabinet solidarity. But Cabinet leakers rarely identify themselves or offer up their resignation. Rather, leaking to the media is a sure-fire way of corroding Cabinet solidarity and destabilising the very foundations of executive government, often with a view to changing its leadership. Hence, as with confidentiality, Cabinet solidarity is essential for the maintenance of stable and effective government.

Collective responsibility

The final principle and practice animating our system of prime ministerial and Cabinet government is that of collective responsibility. Closely linked to the notion of Cabinet solidarity, collective responsibility means that everyone in Cabinet takes responsibility for the decisions of government, and for its successes and, more importantly, its failings. Collective Cabinet decision-making implies collective Cabinet accountability. Where decisions are made they must be executed and defended with vigour by all ministers of Cabinet, and all ministers must take responsibility for those decisions. This is a core ideal of what was earlier described as responsible government. But it is an ideal that is often at odds with the contemporary political realities of Cabinet disunity and dysfunction.

SHORT-ANSWER
QUESTIONS

SPOTLIGHT

Buying ministerial access?

In May 2014, the Fairfax media published articles with the provocative headline 'Treasurer for sale: Joe Hockey offers privileged access'. Among other things, the articles argued that the then Treasurer, Joe Hockey, was offering privileged access to business people and lobbyists in return for tens of thousands of dollars in donations to the Liberal Party (Nicholls 2014). The donors were members of a campaign fundraising group called the North Sydney Forum, which was run by Mr Hockey's North Shore Federal Election Conference (FEC), an incorporated entity of the Liberal Party. The articles observed that in return for annual fees of up to $22000, members were rewarded with 'VIP' meetings with the Treasurer. In other words, money could buy access to a minister, with the implication being that perhaps it could also buy influence.

When Prime Minister Tony Abbott was queried about these fundraising activities, he responded that 'all political parties have to raise money. Typically, you raise money by having events where senior members of the party go and obviously they meet people at the events' (cited in Nicholls 2014). The alternative, he suggested, would be that taxpayers would have to fund party election campaigns, an alternative that was clearly not appealing to Mr Abbott or those sharing his small government ethos.

Mr Hockey subsequently made a defamation case against Fairfax media, which was upheld in the Federal Court and he was awarded $200000 in damages. Interestingly, the judgment of defamation related only to the headlines on advertising posters and tweets, which Justice Richard White found defamed Hockey by implying that he was corrupt. But the judge dismissed all of Mr Hockey's other claims, finding that the article's content was well researched and factually correct. Given those facts, we can conclude that the article had shone a light on the murky world of political donations in return for access to ministers or their shadow cabinet counterparts.

QUESTION

Is it legitimate in a democracy to elicit campaign donations in return for access to members of the political executive?

THE PERILS OF CABINET DISUNITY

The sources of Cabinet discord are many and varied. All Cabinets are composed of strong-willed and ambitious individuals, with at least some who have prime ministerial aspirations. Although in Australia these individuals all come from the same side of politics, many will hold differing views on a range of issues, which will reveal themselves in Cabinet discussions.

This can often reflect political differences in the constituencies that ministers represent. Those who represent more conservative, rural electorates, for example, are more likely to adopt conservative positions within Cabinet than are their urban-based colleagues. Yet sometimes these differences arise from deeper philosophical commitments that are a continual source of friction between ministers, or blocs of ministers, holding equally strongly held positions. In these cases, ministers routinely line up with like-minded ministers when it comes to arguing for particular positions.

These differences can harden over time and be a source of considerable conflict, which prime ministers must skilfully manage if they are to maintain control over their Cabinets. Such divisions have often been noted between conservatives and social liberals within Coalition governments, and between left and right factions within Labor governments. But a more important source of Cabinet disunity, especially in recent years, has been when ministers are dissatisfied with their leader's performance. This is exacerbated when Cabinet colleagues feel themselves to be taken for granted by a prime minister being insufficiently consultative. In such circumstances, anonymous ministers might leak politically sensitive

Cabinet information to the media, which undermines the appearance of unity and, in extreme cases, may undermine the prime minister's hold on power.

Cabinet rolls a prime minister

In May 2015, for example, ministerial leaks to the Fairfax media revealed that Cabinet had rolled Prime Minister Tony Abbott on a proposal that he and his immigration minister, Peter Dutton, had belatedly brought to a Cabinet meeting. The proposal would allow the immigration minister to strip Australian citizenship from those he suspected of being or having links to terrorists, without that proposition needing to be tested in a court against the usual standards of evidence.

The leaks were extraordinary in terms of the level of detail of Cabinet discussions. They revealed that senior ministers including Malcolm Turnbull, Barnaby Joyce, Christopher Pyne, George Brandis and Julie Bishop had all strongly spoken out against the proposal. One unnamed minister pointed out that, 'We are talking about executive detention without limit. It's an extremely dangerous proposal' (cited in Hartcher 2015a). Another questioned the propriety of stripping someone of citizenship, thereby making them stateless, when terrorism was suspected but not proven. This contradicted the rule of law and the principle that one is innocent until proven guilty. It also transgressed centuries of political and judicial development that protected citizens from the arbitrary exercise of executive power, by separating executive and judicial functions and thereby creating checks and balances against tyranny. By contrast, the Abbott/Dutton proposal, if successful, would concentrate in the hands of a single executive minister the functions of judge, jury and executioner.

As important as these issues of substance were, the fact that they were leaked was prompted more by Abbott's cavalier treatment of his Cabinet colleagues and his disregard for long-settled Cabinet conventions. The proposal was not presented to Cabinet in a written submission, and nor was it on the official agenda of the Cabinet meeting where it was raised. And yet the following morning Tony Abbott's messenger of choice, the *Daily Telegraph*, carried a report stating that the proposal had already been passed in Cabinet. This was despite the Prime Minister denying to his Cabinet colleagues that that media source had been briefed. As one minister complained, 'Ministers were genuinely shocked that something this important would be attempted to be put through without due process' (cited in Hartcher 2015b).

All of this manifested in broader tensions between Prime Minister Abbott and his Cabinet. The Prime Minister's propensity for micro-management and the making of what he called 'captain's calls', without Cabinet consultation, was symptomatic of an over-centralisation of decision-making in his own office. His Chief of Staff, Peta Credlin, became a particular source of irritation among those who viewed her as behaving in a high-handed way towards some Cabinet ministers, and generally acting beyond her proper role as a staffer. Such tensions were compounded when Abbott reacted to the leaks by making barely veiled threats that there would be 'personal and political consequences' for the leakers. But the leaks continued, Abbott's poll numbers dropped further, and we can now see in retrospect that this was the beginning of the end of his prime ministership. Three months later, on 14 September 2015, colleagues informed him that he no longer enjoyed the confidence of a majority of his Cabinet. That night he lost a leadership ballot to Malcolm Turnbull by 54 to 44 votes. Tellingly, Prime Minister Turnbull's first promise was to lead a 'thoroughly traditional Cabinet government that ensures we make decisions in a collaborative manner' (cited in Bourke 2015).

This entire episode illustrates much that is central to discussions of prime ministerial and Cabinet government today. It highlights issues around presidentialisation in Australian politics, while also underlining the limitations of prime ministerial powers when confronted with Cabinet opposition; it highlights the norms of Cabinet government including confidentiality, solidarity and collective responsibility, by illuminating an instance of their egregious violation; and, above all, it exemplifies the destructive impact of Cabinet disunity for executive government. Cabinet disunity and frictions with the prime minister are often prompted by falling public support for the government, which is then exacerbated by the appearance of disunity, which drives public support even lower. The prime minister's tenure can enter into a death spiral that only ends with their replacement. Such are the perils of Cabinet disunity for the political executive in general, and the prime minister in particular.

REFLECTION QUESTIONS

Prime Minister Rudd and his Cabinet

SPOTLIGHT

Interestingly, the dynamics between Prime Minister Tony Abbott and his Cabinet, and the eventual destruction of the former by the latter, had played out in a similar way, five years previously. Kevin Rudd had been elected in the so-called 'Rudd slide' of 2007, vanquishing an opponent who had been Prime Minister for 11 years. This success emboldened Rudd to demand he choose his own Cabinet, which broke with the usual Labor protocol of the caucus electing Cabinet and the leader distributing portfolios. After an initial period of popularity – in which Rudd made his famous parliamentary apology to the Stolen Generations and successfully navigated the global financial crisis – the political landscape shifted in 2009–10. Prime Minister Rudd's poll numbers deteriorated, and he became the subject of dissatisfaction among Cabinet colleagues, who viewed his leadership as beset by the same micro-managerial and overly centralised style as Abbott's leadership would later exhibit. Lack of consultation with Cabinet, plus condescension and a perceived lack of respect from Rudd's personal advisers created frictions with Cabinet that would eventually doom Rudd, who had little factional backing (Evans 2011). With the numbers clearly stacked against him, he did not contest the leadership spill engineered by his colleagues. Australia's first female Prime Minister, Julia Gillard, replaced him uncontested. While the personality foibles of Rudd, and later Abbott, were at play in the dynamics that eventually led to their downfall, political centralisation, and the Cabinet frictions to which it gave rise, might also be understood as a structural feature of a system undergoing presidentialisation. These cases also show that prime ministers are vulnerable to Cabinet machinations in a way that executive Presidents are not.

QUESTION

Given that Kevin Rudd had been elected with such a significant mandate from the electorate, was it appropriate for his Cabinet and broader caucus to insist that the prime ministership be subject to a caucus vote?

EXECUTIVE POWER AND ACCOUNTABILITY

Australia's political system, it is often pointed out, incorporates elements of both the Westminster system of responsible government and the US system of federalism (Thompson 1980). For all of their differences, key elements of both the British and US systems were a response to and a way of placing limits on executive power, and making it more accountable to the governed. Expressed differently, both systems of government developed in the shadow of executive power that was viewed as threatening to civil liberty (in both cases, as it turns out, the British Crown – though at different times and for different reasons). They both developed institutions and conventions, therefore, that would check executive power and make it accountable to the legislature and ultimately citizens. Australia is an heir to these institutional arrangements, and they continue to provide protections against the abuse of executive power, albeit imperfect ones. And yet they are arrangements that are often in tension with each other, with democratic governance and accountability.

RESPONSIBLE GOVERNMENT, FEDERALISM AND ACCOUNTABILITY

As we have seen, responsible government implies a chain of responsibility and therefore accountability, which ties the government to the governed. The political executive is responsible for the successes and failings of their policies, and they are accountable to the parliament and to voters, who will ultimately choose whether or not the existing government will be re-elected. The problem is that this *ideal* of responsible government frequently comes into conflict with political *realities* that derive from federalism.

In addition to Australia's main two tiers of government, federalism intrudes directly into the Commonwealth Parliament in the form of the Senate, which is of course elected on the basis of state representation. This 'unrepresentative swill', as Labor Prime Minister Paul Keating once colourfully referred to the Senate (cited in Watson 2002, 271), violates the principle of one person/one vote, as all states have 12 Senators irrespective of their population size (the Australian Capital Territory and Northern Territory get two Senators each). Historically, governments have infrequently had a majority in the Senate, and have thus typically relied on the support of minor parties and/or independents to get their legislation passed and, even then, often in modified form. The problem in terms of accountability, is that governments can plausibly argue that Senate recalcitrance, rather than government incompetence, accounts for policy failures. If a problem needs fixing, but the Senate blocs or even waters down the political executive's preferred solution, how can the government be held accountable for the continuation of the problem? This argument is particularly persuasive when minor parties exaggeratedly claim that they also have been elected with a mandate to block legislation.

A similar logic can be applied to the responsibility of ministers for their departments. Where ministers are unable to advance solutions to problems that their department encounters because of impediments in the Senate, they are able to deflect criticisms and evade being held to account. Whether rightly or wrongly, they are able to lay responsibility for departmental failings at the feet of others, including political opponents with no access to the levers of executive power. Ministerial accountability, then, along with the accountability of the political executive more generally, is a very slippery thing where the institutions of federalism are married with those of responsible government.

We can see, therefore, that federalist checks and balances that were designed to stop all-powerful executives from behaving badly can also stop them from doing what is necessary and desirable. The paradox is that what was designed to make political executives more accountable can enable them to evade accountability.

But this is not the only or even the main area where there is a question mark over the accountability of the modern executive. In recent years, the '**securitisation**' of a number of policy areas has restricted scrutiny of particular measures taken by the executive, and thus limited its accountability.

SECURITISATION AND ACCOUNTABILITY

In the middle of 2001, John Howard's Liberal Government had been trailing the Labor opposition by a wide margin in opinion polling and looked destined to lose the upcoming election. Then, in the space of less than a month, two events occurred that shook the very foundations of Australian politics, resurrected Howard's fortunes and strengthened the hand of the political executive in ways that are still being felt today.

First, in late August a Norwegian shipping vessel, the *M.V. Tampa*, responded to a distress signal from a sinking vessel carrying asylum seekers. It picked up 438 survivors and asked for permission to disembark them on the Australian territory of Christmas Island. The Howard Government refused, and instead ordered special service military personnel to board the ship and take control. In the days that followed, the so-called 'Pacific solution' was born (Marr and Wilkinson 2003), in which asylum seekers were placed in mandatory detention on Nauru and on Manus Island in Papua New Guinea. The second event occurred two weeks later. The attacks on the World Trade Center and the Pentagon in September 2001, represented a watershed moment for Australian politics. Prime Minister John Howard was in the United States at the time, and immediately assured his US political counterparts that 'Australia will provide all support that might be requested of us by the United States in any action that might be taken' (cited in Summers 2007). He was good to his word. Australia joined the US in its invasions of Afghanistan and Iraq and provided strong diplomatic support for George W. Bush's Global War on Terror.

Both of these events and their aftermath provided the impetus for what political scientists refer to as 'securitisation'. This refers to the process whereby particular issues are constructed as central to state security, and thus become the subject of extraordinary government measures that dilute civil liberties and judicial protections (Buzan et al. 1998, 25). Such measures often occur behind a veil of secrecy and executive privilege that is said to be necessary for both state security and the safety of those implementing the measures. Once successfully securitised, a policy area will attract disproportionate media attention and state resources, with the latter often being itself subject to secrecy. This in turn amplifies its gravity in the eyes of the public, and thus perpetuates its usefulness to the political executive, which claims to be the most resolute public protector against the perceived security threat.

In this country, terrorism and maritime asylum seekers, and the frequent conjoining of the two, are the most obvious examples of securitisation at work. Since John Howard provided the political template for how these issues could be successfully exploited for political gain, wedging the Labor opposition in the process, Coalition *and* Labor governments have been at pains to continue highlighting the security aspects of these issues. With this, has gone an empowerment of the various security agencies (Federal

SHORT-ANSWER
QUESTIONS

securitisation:
The process of constructing particular issues as central to state security, which then become the subject of extraordinary government measures that often erode civil liberties.

Police, ASIO, Border Force, the Australian Defence Force), with an attendant diminution of civil liberties once thought to be sacrosanct.

For example, in all states except South Australia, terrorism suspects can be held in detention for up to seven days without any charges being laid against them. At the time of writing (November 2017), Prime Minister Turnbull is seeking to have this increased to 14 days. Interestingly enough, Attorney-General George Brandis was once mindful of the dangers of this: 'Detention without charge ... for an unreasonably long period, could be seen to be a form of executive detention' he told the ABC's AM Program in 2015 (cited in Connifer 2007). By executive detention he means detention at the behest of the executive, without judicial due process. Such detention is, by definition, without the executive accountability that we would normally associate with democracies governed by the rule of law, and by a separation of powers between the judiciary and the executive. That is why it is so dangerous.

Thankfully, there are other bodies and institutions that provide important oversight and scrutiny of the political executive. These include Ombudsmen who investigate citizen complaints at various levels of government, a Human Rights Commission, and parliament itself. The latter includes the political opposition who, as well as presenting itself as an alternative government, is tasked with scrutinising government policy and legislation. There are also various parliamentary committees, which are useful watchdogs over executive power, even when they are chaired and controlled by members of the government. Finally, the media and investigative journalism remain crucial for shining a light on the darkest recesses of executive government, and thereby providing some measure of executive accountability.

VIDEO
RESEARCH
QUESTION

SUMMARY

Learning objective 1: Explain what executive power is and distinguish between the political and administrative wings of the executive

Executive power is the capacity to make political decisions and to put them into effect. This implies a political and administrative component of any executive. In Australia, the public service constitutes the administrative executive, clearly distinguishable from the political executive – composed of the prime minister and the Cabinet. While Australia's Constitution formally vests executive power in the Queen, with that power being exercisable by her representative the Governor-General, this power is in fact only nominal and symbolic. Notwithstanding the extraordinary events of 1975, constitutional convention dictates that the Governor-General acts only on the advice of ministers (prime minister and Cabinet), who are elected representatives of the citizenry.

Learning objective 2: Describe the main functions that political executives perform

The main function of the executive is to provide political leadership. In doing so, it also functions as a symbol of national unity, a leader to the public, a body for making policy and providing legislative leadership, and a provider of national leadership on the world stage. Finally, it serves the important function of leading the public service, which is organised into departments that broadly mirror the portfolios of Cabinet ministers and junior ministers in the outer ministry.

Learning objective 3: Understand the key features of the role of the prime minister and the Cabinet and explain the relationship between them

The prime minister and the Cabinet constitute the real political executive and are responsible for making the most important decisions of government. The prime minister is at the apex of executive power and wields formidable powers in respect of the party, the Cabinet, the electoral process, the media and political opposition. This has contributed to what some have referred to as a presidentialisation of Australian politics. Despite this accumulation of powers, prime ministers are still vulnerable to being replaced by a majority vote of their parliamentary colleagues, should they falter in the polls and/or become subject to hostile action by influential Cabinet ministers. Cabinet refers to the collective leadership body, with the prime minister at its head, which ideally makes the most important government decisions. It ostensibly operates according to the principles of confidentiality, solidarity and collective responsibility. In reality, it often departs from these principles, which manifests a degree of disunity that can be very damaging for governments and prime ministers.

Learning objective 4: Describe the tensions between executive power and accountability, and how they are manifested in Australia's system of government

Finally, Australia's system of executive government has often been embroiled in concerns about a lack of accountability. This stems partly from tensions arising from the political traditions from which it has developed – responsible government on the one hand and federalism on the other. But it is also a function of the securitisation of particular areas of policy and law making, which by their very nature dilute the accountability of the political executive. This is perhaps the most worrying development in contemporary Australian politics.

DISCUSSION
QUESTIONS

DISCUSSION QUESTIONS

1. Has Australia's political executive accumulated greater powers since the turn of the century?
2. If Australia was to become a republic, would the political executive be strengthened or weakened or remain unchanged?
3. Has Australia's federal public service become increasingly politicised in recent years?
4. Is federalism incompatible with the norms and conventions of responsible government?
5. What consequences does securitisation have for executive accountability and therefore democracy?

FURTHER READING

Brett, J. (2007). *Robert Menzies: Forgotten People*, new edn, Melbourne: Melbourne University Press.

Hamilton, C. and Maddison, S. (eds) (2007). *Silencing Dissent*, Sydney: Allen & Unwin.

Neustadt, R. (1990). *Presidential Powers and the Modern Presidents*, New York: Free Press.

Manne, R. (ed.) (2004). *The Howard Years*, Melbourne: Black Inc.

Rhodes, R.A.W. and Dunleavy, P. (eds) (1995). *Prime Minister, Cabinet and Core Executive*, Basingstoke: Macmillan.

Tiernan, A. (2007). *Power Without Responsibility*, Sydney: UNSW Press.

Weller, P. (1985). *First Among Equals*, Hemel Hempstead: Allen & Unwin.

REFERENCES

Anderson, B. (1991). *Imagined Communities: Reflections of the Origins and Spread of Nationalism*, London: Verso.

Bennister, M. (2012). *Prime Ministers in Power*, Basingstoke: Palgrave Macmillan.

Bourke, L. (2015). Malcolm Turnbull defeats Tony Abbott in Liberal leadership spill to become Prime Minister, *The Sydney Morning Herald*, 15 September. Retrieved from http://www.smh.com.au/federal-politics/political-news/malcolm-turnbull-defeats-tony-abbott-in-liberal-leadership-spill-to-become-prime-minister-20150914- gjmhiu.html

Boyce, P. (2007). Executive Council. In B. Galligan and W. Roberts, eds, *The Oxford Companion to Australian Politics*, South Melbourne: Oxford University Press.

Buzan, B., Wæver, O. and de Wilde, J. (1998). *Security: A New Framework for Analysis*, Boulder: Lynne Rienner.

Christensen, T. and Laegreid, P. (eds) (2007). *Transcending New Public Management: The Transformation of Public Sector Reforms*, Aldershot: Ashgate.

Connifer, D. (2017). Terrorism laws: Renewed push for suspects to be held for a fortnight without charges. Retrieved from: http://www.abc.net.au/news/2017–10-04/renewed-push-for-terrorism-suspects-to-be-held-for-a-fortnight/9012588

Day, D. (1999). *John Curtin – A Life*, Sydney: Harper Collins.

Evans, M. (2011). The rise and fall of the magic kingdom: Understanding Kevin Rudd's domestic statecraft. In C. Aulich and M. Evans, eds, *The Rudd Government: Australian Commonwealth Administration 2007–2010*, Canberra: ANU Press.

Garton, S. (1998). War and masculinity in twentieth century Australia, *Journal of Australian Studies*, **22**(5b), 86–95.

Grattan, M. (ed.). (2000). *Australian Prime Ministers*, Sydney: New Holland.

Hartcher, P. (2015a). Tony Abbott rolled by his own ministry over stripping terrorists of citizenship, *The Sydney Morning Herald*, 29 May 2015. Retrieved from http://www.smh.com.au/comment/tony-abbott-rolled-by-his-own-ministers-over-stripping-terrorists-of-citizenship-20150529-ghcuxf.html

Hartcher, P. (2015b). Abbott only has himself to blame for Cabinet leaks over citizenship stripping proposal, *The Sydney Morning Herald*, 5 June 2015. Retrieved from http://www.smh.com.au/comment/tony-abbott-only-has-himself-to-blame-for-cabinet-leaks-over-citizenshipstripping-proposals-20150605-ghhv0i.html

Heywood, A. (2007). *Politics*, 3rd edn, Houndmills, Basingstoke: Palgrave Macmillan.

Howard, J.W. (2002). John Howard's Bali Memorial Speech, *The Sydney Morning Herald*, 18 October 2002. Retrieved from http://www.smh.com.au/articles/2002/10/18/1034561270521.html

Howard, J.W. (2003). Address to the National Press Club, 13 May 2003. Retrieved from http://www.theage.com.au/articles/2003/03/13/1047431139664.html

Hutchinson, E. (2010). Trauma and the politics of emotions: Constituting identity, security and community after the Bali bombing. *International Relations*, **24**(1), 65–86.

Inglis, K. (1998). Anzac and the Australian military tradition. In J. Lack, ed., *ANZAC Remembered: Selected Writings by K.S. Inglis*. Melbourne: Melbourne University, Department of History Monograph.

Kefford, G. (2013). The presidentialisation of Australian politics? Kevin Rudd's leadership of the Australian Labor Party. *Australian Journal of Political Science*, **48**(2), 135–46.

Kingston, M. (2003). Wilkie-v-Howard: who's the villain, who's the hero? Retrieved from http://www.smh.com.au/articles/2003/09/14/1063478071549.html

Lake, M. (1992). Mission impossible: How men gave birth to the nation – nationalism, gender and other seminal acts. *Gender and History*, **4**(3), 305–22.

Lake, M. and Reynolds, H. with McKenna, M. and Damousi, J. (2010). *What's Wrong with Anzac? The Militarisation of Australian History*, Sydney: UNSW Press.

MacDermott, K. (2008). *Whatever Happened to 'Frank and Fearless'? The Impact of New Public Management on the Australian Public Service*, Canberra: ANU Press.

Maddox, G. (1996). *Australian Democracy in Theory and Practice*, 3rd edn, South Melbourne: Longman.

Maley, M. (2012). Politicisation and the executive. In R. Smith, A. Vromen and I. Cook, eds, *Contemporary Politics in Australia*, Melbourne: Cambridge University Press.

Marr, D. and Wilkinson, M. (2003). *Dark Victory*, Crows Nest: Allen & Unwin.

Mulgan, R. (1998). Politicising the Australian Public Service? Parliamentary Library Research Paper 3, 1998–99.

Mulgan, R. (2007). Truth in government and politicisation of public sector advice. *Public Administration*, **85**(3), 569–86.

Nicholls, S. (2014). Treasurer for sale: Joe Hockey offers privileged access, *The Sydney Morning Herald*, 5 May. Retrieved from http://www.smh.com.au/federal-politics/political- news/treasurer-for-sale-joe-hockey-offers-privileged-access-20140504-zr06v.html

Poguntke, T. and Webb, P. (2005). *The Presidentialization of Politics: A Comparative Study of Modern Democracies*, Oxford: Oxford University Press.

Pollitt, C. and Bouchaert, G. (2011). *Public Management Reform: A Comparative Analysis – New Public Management, Governance and the Neo-Weberian State*, 3rd edn, Oxford: Oxford University Press.

Pusey, M. (1991). *Economic Rationalism in Canberra: A Nation Building State Changes its Mind*, Cambridge: Cambridge University Press.

Seal, G. (2004). *Inventing Anzac: The Digger and National Mythology*, Lt Lucia: University of Queensland Press.

Sexton, M. (2005). *The Great Crash: The Short Life and Sudden Death of the Whitlam Government*, Carlton North, Vic: Scribe Publications.

Singleton, G., Aitkin, D., Jinks, B. and Warhurst, J. (2003). *Australian Political Institutions*, Melbourne: Pearson.

Summers, A. (2007). The day that shook Howard's world, *The Age*, 17 February. Retrieved from http://www.smh.com.au/news/opinion/the-day-that-shook-howards-world/2007/02/16/1171405438845.html

Thompson, E. (1980). The Washminster mutation. In P. Weller and D. Jaensch, eds, *Responsible Government in Australia*, Melbourne: Drummond.

Walter, J. and Strangio, P. (2007). *No Prime Minister: Reclaiming Politics from Leaders*, Sydney: UNSW Press.

Watson, D. (2002). *Recollections of a Bleeding Heart: A Portrait of Paul Keating*, Sydney: Knopf.

Weller, P. (1985). *First Among Equals*, Hemel Hempstead: Allen & Unwin.

Weller, P. (ed.) (1992). *Menzies to Keating: The Development of the Australian Prime Ministership*, Melbourne: Melbourne University Press.

Weller, P. (2005). Investigating power at the centre of government: Surveying research on the Australian executive. *Australian Journal of Public Administration*, **61**(1), 35–42.

Weller, P. (2007). *Cabinet Government in Australia 1901–2006*, Sydney: UNSW Press.

Weller, P. (2013). *The Prime Ministerial Condition: Prime Ministers in Westminster Systems*, Oxford: Oxford University Press.

Whitlam, G. (1985). *The Whitlam Government 1972–1975*, Ringwood: Penguin.

CHAPTER 5

THE POLITICAL RULEBOOK: THE AUSTRALIAN CONSTITUTION AND THE HIGH COURT

LEARNING OBJECTIVES

After reading this chapter, you should be able to:

1. Explain why a constitution can be broadly defined as the 'rules governing government'
2. Understand why the Australian Constitution makes no mention of the prime minister or the Cabinet
3. Describe judicial review and the role of the High Court as the constitutional umpire
4. Explain why the High Court is a political as well as a legal institution
5. Understand judicial activism and the conservative case against a Bill of Rights
6. Analyse the referendum process and the obstacles to formal constitutional change

INTRODUCTION

Governments (it is said) are failing – failing to address climate change, to prevent growing inequality, to secure affordable housing and jobs, to engage citizens and to manage the challenges of globalisation. The list is long. The inevitable conclusion: government is 'broken'. The challenge of fixing government begins with understanding constitutions. For constitutions comprise 'the collection of rules which establish and regulate or govern the government' (Wheare 1966, 1) and 'form the legal basis of states' (Grimm 1995, 282). Each Australian state retains its own constitution. But it is *The Constitution of Australia* that distributes legislative and executive powers between the Commonwealth and states. It is the political rulebook that establishes the parliamentary and federal institutions and processes that are available to Australians today as they address the many challenges they face.

The Australian Constitution was originally drafted by colonial politicians in the 1890s; approved by a series of referenda elections; and legislated by the British Parliament as part of Australia's creation. It took effect in 1901 and is imbued with values typical of that era. By design it is difficult to change (in keeping with an underlying purpose of a constitution, which is to prevent politicians in power from changing the rules of the game to suit themselves). If Australians were free to construct their constitution anew, it would likely be a very different document. Today Australia is an advanced and multicultural society. But in the 1890s Australians saw themselves as a white outpost of the British Empire and as Queen Victoria's loyal subjects.

As might be expected of a settler society, which imagined that Australia was uninhabited until British settlement, the 1901 Constitution denied Indigenous peoples constitutional recognition. It created Australia as a monarchy, embraced British forms of parliamentary government, and established Australia as a federation, intending states to have a prominent role. Despite the reputation that Australian colonies had acquired for extending adult suffrage, pioneering the secret ballot, and giving women the right to vote, the 1901 Constitution did not expressly guarantee free speech, equality for women, or even the right to vote. Without such a 'Bill of Rights', the written Constitution appears dated, even ill-suited to Australia's contemporary needs.

Rules invariably require umpires to interpret them. The Constitution establishes the High Court of Australia as that umpire. Since its inception in 1903, the High Court has re-interpreted some elements of the Constitution. Much of its work as a constitutional court has involved clarifying the federal division of powers. We will see that the High Court has progressively enlarged the authority of the Commonwealth well beyond what the Constitution's authors intended and stamped its mark on Australian politics.

AUTHOR
PANEL
REFLECTION
QUESTION

THE 'RULES GOVERNING GOVERNMENT'

Constitutions establish the authority that governments exercise in making, administering and enforcing laws. Therefore, the US document begins 'We the People of the United States … do ordain and establish this Constitution'. Australia's Constitution establishes a monarchy. Although Australia is a democracy, the authority that its government possesses legally derives from the Crown, not the people. While the authors of Australia's

Constitution borrowed from the US, they did not establish a US-style **republic**. The Americans had rebelled against British authority; Australia was created by combining six separate, self-governing British colonies at a time when Australians considered themselves British antipodeans.

A MIX OF US FEDERALISM AND WESTMINSTER PARLIAMENTARY GOVERNMENT

Federation had the blessing of the British Colonial Office. The Constitution that established the new nation of Australia in 1901 may have been written by colonial leaders and approved by voters in referenda held in all six colonies, but it was finalised by the *Commonwealth of Australia Constitution Act 1900 (UK)* passed by the British Parliament in Westminster. Federation was always a process that would see Australia reproduce a form of parliamentary government; but the Constitution that, with great symbolism, took effect on the first day of 1901, also established a US-style federation.

As we will see in Chapter 7, Australia is said to have a '**Washminster**' system because it draws both from British parliamentary and US federal traditions. Its constitutional marriage of federalism with parliamentary government involves 'a compromise between two fundamental political concepts that inherently conflict'. In 'drawing from the British system, the framers of the Australian Constitution created a system in which the Ministers of the Crown were to be responsible to the lower house only'. At the same time, they created a US-style Senate – a distinct, powerful upper house 'designed to represent the states in the national legislature on an equal basis' irrespective of population size (Chordia and Lynch 2014, 85).

The essence of responsible parliamentary government is that prime ministers and cabinets come from and answer to a parliament chosen by voters. This Westminster model works best in 'unicameral' systems (as in NZ) where there is just one house of parliament, and in 'bicameral' systems (such as the UK) where the powers of the second upper house are limited. It is less well-suited to Australia. Parties with a majority in the popularly elected House of Representatives do form government. But having a lower house majority does not ensure that a prime minister and the Cabinet can implement the policies for which they were elected. The Senate can reject most proposed legislation. Section 53 of the Constitution gives it the same powers as the House of Representatives except the authority to initiate or amend money bills.

WHAT IS A CONSTITUTION?

Contemporary understanding of constitutions as the basic legal framework for national governments traces back to the French and American revolutions of the 18th century. Constitutions typically 'designate the key branches of government such as the legislature, the executive and the judiciary; lay down the methods of determining their composition; prescribe procedures for their exercise; set out, where relevant, the constitutionally protected rights and freedoms of the citizen; and state the manner in which the constitution itself may be changed (Ratnapala 1999, 3).

Constitutions outline how governments are to be organised. They can also have a symbolic importance, signalling a nation's democratic, liberal or other aspirations.

republic: A political system in which the power that government wields derives from the citizenry, and in which citizens choose who governs them. The term derives from the Latin '*res public*', meaning a 'public matter'.

Washminster: Washminster blends 'Washington' and 'Westminster'. It flags the fusion of US-style of federalism and Westminster parliamentary government, which is a feature of Australia's political system and sometimes a source of tension.

VIDEOS

constitution: Sets out rules for the organisation and conduct of government.

Some scholars think of constitutions as a social contract that provides citizens with confidence in government institutions and processes. Constitutions can also confer political identity or cultural self-awareness in addition to legitimacy. From a legal perspective, constitutions are **superior law**. The provisions of a constitution prevail, should executive decisions or ordinary legislation clash with it. In keeping with this idea, they are often more difficult to amend than ordinary legislation. This is the case with the Australian Constitution.

The Parliamentary Education Office (2017) says that, since 1901, the Constitution 'has been an important document' because it sets out 'rules by which Australia is run'. A contrary view is that the 'Constitution is an anachronistic, dusty old book, with no relevance today' (CEFA 2016). Each of these different claims describes Australia's Constitution as a document. A more nuanced view would be that the 'rules by which Australia is run' exist in the written document as it has been amended since 1901; in the many cases in which the High Court has interpreted or even extended its meaning; in supplementary legislation such as the Electoral Act (dictating how elections are conducted); and in conventions. This is what Ratnapala (1999, 3) describes as a 'living' rather than a 'paper' constitution.

Australia's 'paper' Constitution describes the composition, role and powers of the Commonwealth Parliament. It provides for an elected Senate and a House of Representatives, from which governments are formed. It sets out how the Commonwealth and state parliaments share the power to make laws. It also details the role of executive government and the High Court, and defines certain rights of Australian citizens, such as religious freedom. What the Constitution fails to mention is also important. A key word search returns no mention of prime minister, nor of Cabinet. It does seem odd that the Constitution does not provide for what are today two key Australian political institutions. But this was originally a deliberate design feature, not an oversight.

Mostly national constitutions are found in a document or charter. But neither NZ nor the UK have an equivalent of the 'written' Australian Constitution. Their constitutions comprise a mix of ordinary legislation, precedent, custom, common law and conventions. Even where written constitutions formally set out rules for the organisation and conduct of government, there must always be additional 'everyday non-constitutional law, written and unwritten, that structures … government and society' (Sachs 2013, 1797). The business of government is too complex. No written constitution can provide rules for all contingencies. This suggests the folly of thinking of the Australian Constitution as just an 'old book'.

If we understand constitutions as the rule book governing government itself, then the wider Australian constitution comprises the 'paper' Constitution in the first instance, but also that mix of everyday law, precedent, judicial interpretation, common law, custom and constitutional conventions, which all set down rules regulating the organisation and conduct of government. Whereas the 'paper' Constitution is dated and difficult to amend, there are many elements of the 'living' constitution that have been adapted or remain open to adaptation and development as Australian society and politics evolve.

CONSTITUTIONAL CONVENTIONS

Jennings (1959, 50) writes that 'constitutional conventions provide the flesh which clothe the dry bones of the law; they make the legal constitution work; they keep in touch with the growth

superior law: Superior (or paramount) law overrides ordinary legislation where there is a clash. As superior law constitutions are often unchangeable by ordinary legislative means.

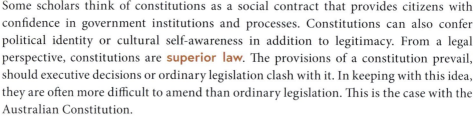

SHORT-ANSWER QUESTION

REFLECTION QUESTION
SHORT-ANSWER QUESTIONS

of ideas'. **Conventions** are non-legal rules that impose expectations on how political actors should properly act, the 'breach or violation of which will give rise to legitimate criticism' and accusations of 'unconstitutional conduct' (Barnett 2011, 38). Because they are not laws, conventions are not legally enforceable. Their enforcement relies upon the weight of public opinion, critical media commentary or other informal sanctions that can be brought to bear.

Britain is unusual because convention plays a large part in organising its parliamentary system. Key political institutions such as the prime minister and the Cabinet, the power of parliament, and even the role of the monarch, are substantially defined by precedent and convention. This had consequences for Australia. In the 1890s the authors of Australia's Constitution blended elements of the Westminster and federal systems. In drafting the Constitution, they allowed that Australian prime ministers and Cabinets would be governed by convention, just as in Westminster. Hence, the Constitution makes no mention and provides no express rules for the operation of the Cabinet and the prime minister.

Convention rather than the Constitution itself dictates that an Australian prime minister who loses the confidence of the House of Representatives should either tender his or her resignation to the Governor-General or advise that parliament be dissolved, and fresh elections held. It is a convention that imposes collective ministerial responsibility by obliging all ministers to support decisions taken by the Cabinet irrespective of their personal views. In the realm of politics where so much is argued about and disagreement is rife, the operation of the Cabinet or the powers exercised by an Australian prime minister are circumscribed by conventions or agreed rules. Further what counts as agreement about a constitutional convention is frequently unclear. Oppositions and governments may form different views, say as to whether a minister has acted in accordance with the rules. Often the rules governing government are not clearly defined, but are fuzzy, contested and fought over.

> **conventions:**
> Constitutional conventions are agreed, non-legal rules that impose expectations on how political actors should act, that, when violated, give rise to public and media criticism, which are the chief means by which conventions are enforced.

How are conventions 'agreed'?

SPOTLIGHT

A benefit of political institutions being governed by convention rather than law is that conventions can be adapted to suit changing circumstances. 'Individual ministerial responsibility' illustrates this point. It is the expectation that ministers be accountable to parliament for their own conduct and that of their departments. In the 19th century, this Westminster convention obliged ministers to answer to parliament and to resign from the ministry should public servants for whom they were responsible bungle the administration of public policy. A century ago it may have been feasible to require ministers to take responsibility for the actions of public servants.

In 1905, Treasury had 41 employees, and the bigger department of Trade and Customs, 1100. Today the public service is far larger. Ministers can no longer be asked to closely supervise and be accountable for the actions of public servants. Last century saw 'a change in the perceptions of both ministers and informed commentators as to what is required by the convention of individual ministerial responsibility. The real practical limitations on strict adherence to the convention as it was traditionally conceived are now openly acknowledged' (Wright and Fowler 2012, 51). Today, ministers are still asked to account to parliament for the administration of policy by departments they supervise; however, they do not 'bear the blame for all the fault'. They are not 'bound to resign or suffer dismissal' unless a failing arises directly from their own actions (Wright and Fowler 2012, 50). But even this is an ambiguous rule, open to different interpretations.

Ministerial responsibility cannot be precisely defined. It is not decided and enforced by courts. Rather its meaning is largely established by political circumstance and the 'court of public opinion'. As conventions are, it is enforced by practitioners. Using parliament and the media as platforms, oppositions will demand that ministers resign where they have overseen policy failure or maladministration. But resignation (or removal) 'on these grounds is rare' (Mulgan 2012, 179). Governing parties, loath to pay the political cost of removing or losing a minister, incline toward more modest interpretations of any penalties that responsible ministers should pay. Hence, what this convention means and requires of ministers is renegotiated and established in the hurly burly of such political brawls, when they arise.

QUESTION

What are the advantages and disadvantages of having political institutions governed by convention rather than law?

THE GOVERNOR-GENERAL, THE CABINET AND THE PRIME MINISTER

Governor-General: Australia's Monarch is represented in her absence by a Governor-General who has extensive, constitutionally given executive powers. Convention requires these be used only as the prime minister advises.

Australia is a monarchy. Its Monarch resides elsewhere and is represented by a **Governor-General** in her absence. A literal reading of the Constitution might suggest that the Governor-General is politically powerful. All executive authority embodied in the Crown is attached to the office. The Governor-General may determine when parliament sits 'as he thinks fit' and dissolve parliament ahead of issuing election writs (Section 5). Laws passed by parliament only take effect when the Governor-General, 'according to his discretion', assents. It is the Governor-General who appoints ministers to oversee public service departments and who can terminate their appointment (Section 64). The Governor-General is also commander-in-chief of Australia's navy and military (Section 68) and appoints members of the High Court (Section 72).

The office has symbolic and legal importance; however, Governor-Generals do not wield political power. The Constitution that gives them extensive power needs to be read alongside a longstanding Westminster constitutional convention that requires, in almost all circumstances, that the executive powers belonging to the Crown be exercised only upon the advice of prime ministers and the Cabinet, while they retain the confidence of parliament. This convention derives directly from Britain where, after a centuries-long struggle, powers once exercised by kings devolved to their advisers and to parliament. Its effect is to transfer powers that the paper Constitution hands to the Governor-General to the prime minister and the ministry. Since the prime minister and their ministers answer to parliament in the first instance, and ultimately to voters who choose the party that will govern, this convention allows Australia to function as a parliamentary democracy.

Cabinet goes unmentioned. But the Constitution does establish a Federal Executive Council of ministers to 'advise the Governor-General in the government of the Commonwealth' (Section 62). This is not Cabinet by another name. It has formal functions (such as signing legislation into law), which Cabinet does not. It meets with the permission of, or is chaired by, the Governor-General and is an inappropriate forum for ministers to pursue political agendas. Ministers meet separately as the Cabinet. The Constitution's authors clearly intended – in keeping with Westminster convention – that executive powers formally given to the Governor-General would be exercised as advised by a prime minister and the Cabinet selected from within, and answerable to, the Commonwealth Parliament.

Governor-Generals, as representatives of Australia's Monarch, do have certain reserve powers and need not always act as prime ministers advise. Westminster convention establishes the Monarch's right to be consulted about and to encourage or warn against a proposed policy. In Australia, it is generally agreed that a Governor-General's reserve powers include a discretion to act independently where a prime minister acts illegally or loses the confidence of parliament. A wider view of reserve powers will emphasise that the Governor-General is duty-bound to protect the Constitution and Australia's system of responsible parliamentary government. Indeed, the suggestion that a Governor-General, armed with reserve powers, can safeguard the public interest is central to the argument that modern-day monarchists make in rejecting proposals to transform Australia into a republic.

Along with the written (or paper) Constitution and augmenting legislation such as the Electoral Act, conventions count among the rules governing the process of government. They do often lack precision and are argued about. From a legal perspective, conventions are inferior to constitutional elements, which are open to clarification by courts. But 'constitutional systems together with their component conventions and legal systems are political arrangements' (Galligan and Brenton 2015). Constitutional conventions illustrate how rules governing government are often themselves the very object of, and are decided by, political struggle. In politics, victory over a rival can involve establishing what the rules will allow or prevent. Such contests may be fought out in parliament, in news and social media, and even in the courts via judicial review.

SHORT-ANSWER
QUESTIONS

THE HIGH COURT OF AUSTRALIA

EVERY SET OF RULES REQUIRES AN UMPIRE

The High Court is not usually considered a political institution. It is Australia's supreme court and a central legal institution. Furthermore, Australia's Westminster-derived system imposes a **separation of powers** that isolates the judicial branch of government from the (overlapping) executive and legislative branches. This separation is symbolised by the High Court building, located near but discreetly removed from Parliament House. It is reinforced by several conventions including the requirement that appointees to the Court sever their political connections and – should the Court come under political attack – leave any public defence to the Attorney-General.

Yet for political scientists, the High Court is not just a legal institution. It is an important political actor. As the umpire charged with interpreting and applying the Constitution, the Court is often called to decide in favour of one or another rival political interests. In many instances it has been asked to referee disputes between states and the Commonwealth. Claims that the High Court is a political, not purely legal, institution often flow from observations that its decisions since the 1920s have transformed Australia's Federation by expanding the scope of Commonwealth authority.

separation of powers:
A constitutional arrangement intended to constrain the power of government by placing the legislative, executive and judicial branches of government each in different hands.

AUSTRALIA'S SUPERIOR COURT

The High Court comprises seven justices including a Chief Justice, all having tenure until the age of 70. In 1903 the first High Court comprised three judges. Today the Court is housed in an impressive Canberra building designed to convey its importance. Its Australia.gov.au (2017) entry describes it as 'the highest court in the Australian judicial system' and adds that: 'Its functions are to interpret and apply the law of Australia; to decide cases of special federal significance including challenges to the constitutional validity of laws and to hear appeals, by special leave, from Federal, State and Territory courts.' There is no recognition in this official account of the Court's political significance.

The High Court, as the Court of Disputed Returns, is occasionally asked to decide whether elections have been properly conducted and candidates properly elected. But this is a minor part of its role. It is not simply a constitutional court. It sits at the apex of the legal system with broad responsibilities. Although it has an original jurisdiction, much of its work nowadays is as Australia's superior court. Simply put, when it considers that there are legal or constitutional issues to be clarified, it hears cases on appeal from subordinate courts on whom its decisions are binding. Much of the Court's work involves settling the meaning of commercial and other areas of general law. About 10 per cent of cases it hears, raise constitutional questions. For much of last century the High Court's decisions could be appealed to the British Privy Council. But passage of the 1975 Privy Councils Appeals Abolition Act and, in 1986, of the Australia Acts by the British and Australian parliaments, severed residual links between the British and Australian legal systems. Today the High Court has an unfettered authority to decide the application and meaning of Australian law, including the Constitution, where this is in dispute.

That judges interpret and apply the law is widely understood. Less well-understood is that the meaning of the law – even the Constitution – is not fixed. As the then Chief Justice Robert French noted in a 2009 speech: 'The meanings of legislative words are not like rocks lying around on the ground waiting to be picked up' (French 2009). In 2005 Justice Kirby was even more forthright: he said clarifying the law is 'inescapably a process shaped by values'. Judges with 'a vision of the Constitution and of society' will often place a different emphasis upon the protection of human rights and freedoms. Kirby J concluded that: 'Governments of all persuasions know this', which invariably 'influences their judicial appointments' (Kirby 2005).

HOW APPOINTMENTS TO THE HIGH COURT ARE MADE

Opportunities to shape the Court rarely present. Up to and including the appointment of Edelman J in 2017, there have been just 42 Justices and 13 Chief Justices. The Constitution originally permitted judges to serve until their voluntary retirement or death. This was altered by a 1977 referendum amending Section 72 to mandate retirement of High Court judges upon reaching the age of 70. Once appointed, judges can only be removed in extraordinary circumstances. None ever have been. Therefore, it is only by carefully choosing appointees that governments can influence the High Court.

In the US making appointments to the Supreme Court is visibly politicised: the President nominates and the Senate must approve appointees. Filling vacancies on the High Court of Australia is less transparent, but still a political process. This does not mean that judges are appointed because of their party allegiance and political experience.

In 1903 the very first High Court comprised three ex-politicians – including Australia's first prime minister (Edward Barton). However, there are no recent examples of similar appointments. The last politician elevated to the Court was the Labor Senator and Attorney-General, Lionel Murphy, and his 1974 appointment proved highly controversial.

The High Court of Australia Act passed in 1979 obliges the Commonwealth to consult state Attorneys-General and requires that appointees be suitably qualified. There is also practical need to nominate accomplished lawyers because the Court's substantial appellate role requires expertise extending beyond constitutional law. Nonetheless subtle political judgements are involved when High Court vacancies are filled. In 1997 an acting prime minister acknowledged this: Tim Fischer said that his Coalition government should, when it could, appoint a 'capital-C conservative' to the Court. He was not suggesting a Liberal or National Party member, but a judge who would steer the Court away from 'judicial activism' (Savva 1997, 6).

Governments have proceeded to appoint justices in different ways. Early on, in 1913, A.B. Piddington was appointed to the High Court. But he never took his seat because of scandal caused by public disclosure of the behind-the-scenes efforts of the Fisher government to ensure that he did not favour 'states' rights' – its political test for making an appointment. In this century, Attorneys-General have been accused of informally interviewing candidates to explore their views. Usually Attorneys-General seek advice from bar associations, professional bodies such as the Law Council of Australia, from other judges, and from state governments. In 2008 a Labor government formalised this process, seeking to inject transparency and foster a judiciary better reflecting 'the rich diversity of the Australian community' (Attorney-General's Department 2010).

This 2008 reform obliged the Attorney-General to consult designated stakeholders to identify meritorious candidates. It was abandoned by the Coalition government elected in 2013, which reverted to an ad hoc, more opaque approach to filling High Court vacancies (JCA 2015, 3). But even the 2008 initiative fell short of matching ways judges are appointed to comparable courts. For example, in Britain the decision is not left, as in Australia, 'entirely in the hands of a small group in the executive' (Williams 2008, 166). Rather an independent Judicial Appointments Committee of laypersons, judicial and legal professionals provides a shortlist of eligible candidates from which Cabinet must choose. Adopting a similar process might lessen the temptation (and opportunity) to 'stack' the High Court. It would seem a necessary step to update this aspect of Australia's Constitution.

The way the Court is appointed is mirrored in the kinds of people who have served as justices. Many have been barristers from New South Wales and Victoria, from the heights of a predominantly conservative profession. In the 1970s, High Court judges were typically male, white, protestant, and from Sydney or Melbourne (Neumann 1973, 105–6). This made for a substantially conservative Court. More recent appointees have come from a somewhat wider pool, some from less privileged backgrounds. In 2017 the Court had a record of three female justices (including a female Chief Justice). However, the first woman was not appointed until 1987, and the next not until 2005. There has never been an Indigenous appointee, nor has there been a South Australian High Court judge. That the Commonwealth decides appointments has long encouraged states to believe that this is why justices have favoured centralising power in the hands of the national government.

REFLECTION
QUESTION

JUDICIAL REVIEW AND THE HIGH COURT AS A POLITICAL ACTOR

The High Court makes as well as applies the law. Because Australia was created from six British colonies, its courts inherited (and have since refined) a body of customary or common law that emerged in English common-law courts from the Middle Ages onwards. (Habeas corpus establishing the right of Australians held in custody to be brought before a court is a well-known example.) Common law is found in precedents set by previously decided cases. Therefore, it is judge-made. This is not a controversial claim, but the idea that judicial review gives judges a further capacity to make law is.

MAKING THE LAW

It is frequently argued that elected parliaments must make laws and that unelected courts ought not usurp their legislative function. Yet courts do engage in making law and policy. This is 'most evident when powerful national supreme courts … exercise their power of judicial review to hold laws or major government actions unconstitutional' (Tate 2008). Like the US Supreme Court, the High Court of Australia 'exercises the power of judicial review to determine the constitutionality of laws'. Consequently, it 'inevitably intervenes in the political arena' (Patapan 2000, 3). As Galligan (1995, 164) writes, 'in its adjudicatory role the court has had the determining say in a range of major policy questions throughout Australian political history'. The Court is where disputes between rival political interests are often decided.

The High Court does not (as its Canadian counterpart will) offer advisory opinions. It will not advise governments whether proposed legislation is constitutionally valid. It confines its role to **judicial review** – to determining, when it comes into question, whether executive action or legislation passed by Commonwealth and state parliaments falls within the powers given that tier of government by the Constitution. The authority that the Commonwealth has to regulate television and the internet provides a case study of how judicial review involves the Court in making law and shaping policy.

Television broadcasting commenced in Australia in 1956. There was no referendum to alter the Constitution to assign responsibility for its regulation. But Section 51(v), drafted well before the advent of radio and television broadcasting, gives the national government power to make laws regulating 'postal, telegraphic, telephonic, and other like services'. The High Court first determined that this authorised the Commonwealth to legislate for radio in 1935 (in *R v Brislan*), and then to regulate television (in *Jones v Commonwealth (No 2)* in 1965). More recently the Commonwealth has relied on Section 51(v) in seeking to regulate the internet. These cases illustrate how judicial review can involve law-making: it was the Court, not parliament that decided the Commonwealth (not the states) should regulate broadcasting.

Section 128

Where the High Court interprets an Act in ways that a government disapproves, parliament can pass correcting legislation. But where the Court imposes an unwelcome interpretation of the Constitution, the only remedy is to alter the Constitution. Under the terms of Section 128 this requires a **referendum election** in which both a majority of

judicial review: Courts engage in judicial review when they determine whether legislation passed by Commonwealth and state parliaments is a proper exercise of their constitutionally given powers.

referendum election: An election in which citizens vote to approve or reject a proposed alteration of the Constitution. Section 128 requires proposed amendments to be supported by both a majority of Australians and by a majority of states.

SHORT-ANSWER QUESTIONS

states and an overall majority of voters must vote in favour. In practice, this has proved a substantial obstacle. Just eight of 44 attempts to amend the Constitution have succeeded. It was last successfully amended in 1977. Hence, for all practical purposes, the Constitution means what the High Court decides it does. Its interpretation of the Constitution has been one of the chief ways that changes have been made to the way the Constitution operates.

RESEARCH QUESTIONS

REINVENTING FEDERALISM

Much of the High Court's constitutional work has involved settling disputes as to whether laws enacted by a state or the Commonwealth come within their constitutional jurisdiction. This is unsurprising. The Constitution was intended to cement a federal 'compact' by setting out the powers that the Commonwealth holds exclusively; by enumerating those it shares with the states; and by establishing the states' right to exercise residual powers. Umpiring this Constitution invariably involves the High Court in clarifying the division of powers between the states and the Commonwealth.

It may be entirely coincidental that the Commonwealth appoints justices. But in umpiring the federal system, the Court has long shown bias toward the national government. It has arguably done 'the real work' to modernise a Federation conceived in 'the age of the horse and buggy'. The Court's interpretation of the Constitution over the past century has 'generally favoured the Commonwealth' such that the states are no longer 'dominant players' (Williams 2006). The suggestion that the High Court has modernised Australia's federal division of powers further underlines its political importance.

Between 1903 and 1920, the Court contained judges whose previous political careers had included drafting the Constitution. When cases arose requiring clarification of the federal division of powers, they narrowly interpreted the Commonwealth's powers, seeking to preserve the autonomy of states and to secure the coordinate federalism that the Constitution's authors had intended. But after some change in its membership, beginning with the 1920 Engineers case, the Court was persuaded to abandon reading a theory of federalism into it and, instead, to read the Constitution 'according to its own terms, finding the intention from the words of the compact' (Knox CJ, Isaacs, Rich and Starke JJ 1920, 142).

SHORT-ANSWER QUESTION

Widening the Commonwealth's powers

To see why 'judicial review is by its very nature political' and has shaped the Australian Federation (Galligan 1995, 164) we need to further delve into history. In the several decades that followed the Engineers case, the High Court umpired the federal compact in ways advantaging the Commonwealth, refusing to consider the framers' intentions, instead preferring 'textual' readings of the Commonwealth heads of power in the Constitution. Lasting to the mid-century, this second distinct phase of judicial review saw Commonwealth powers 'read broadly and without any overt consideration of federalism issues' (Selway and Williams 2005, 467). *R v Brislan* 1935 is an example of the Court expanding the Commonwealth's reach. The best known, most significant example, is the 1942 Uniform Tax case in which the Court ruled that the Commonwealth had acted within its constitutional powers in legislating to end the practice of the states collecting income tax.

Not all High Court decisions in this period favoured the Commonwealth. Notably the Court overturned legislation by the Chifley Labor Government seeking to control the private banking system (in the 1948 Bank Nationalisation case). Legislation to nationalise interstate airlines met a similar fate in the 1945 Airlines case. Moreover, Chifley's 1944 Pharmaceutical Benefits Act, opposed by the medical profession as nationalised healthcare, was found to exceed the Commonwealth's appropriation powers (in the 1945 First Pharmaceutical Benefits case). These rulings blocked the Chifley Labor Government's democratic socialist policy agenda – and provided Labor partisans with grounds to argue that the High Court represents a conservative political force.

Selway and Williams (2005, 467) identify a further, third phase of judicial review from mid-last century onward during which the Court 'provided a framework for the development of the Australian Federation', reaching decisions in a range of cases that increased the relative importance of the Commonwealth. They are, though, reluctant to see the Court as driving change. Rather their view is that the Court reflected rather than caused 'changes and developments in the federation'. There is scope here to mention just a few of the landmark cases in which the High Court permitted the Commonwealth to expand its importance at the expense of the states.

REFLECTION QUESTION

'True power' given to Canberra

In the much-cited 1983 Tasmanian Dam case, the High Court ruled that Tasmania lacked the constitutional authority to build a dam in the Wild Rivers National Park. It found Commonwealth legislation prohibiting its construction valid: the external affairs power given to the national government in Section 51(xxix) entitled it to protect the World Heritage-listed park (as required by the UNESCO Convention to which Australia is a signatory). In short, the Court found that the Commonwealth could override the states wherever this was necessary to uphold international conventions to which it had agreed. Since Australia is signatory to a wide range of international agreements, this decision handed the Commonwealth power to legislate in a variety of policy areas. The more recent 2006 WorkChoices case had a similar effect.

The Sydney Morning Herald headlined the Court's WorkChoices decision as 'The day true power went to Canberra' (Dick, O'Malley and Garnaut 2006, 1). The nub of this case was whether the Commonwealth could rely upon the corporations' power given in Section 51(xx) to regulate industrial relations across Australia. The High Court determined that it could, significantly extending the national government's power to regulate industrial relations matters. Moreover, because corporations are a ubiquitous organisational form, this decision appeared to give the Commonwealth scope to use the corporations head of power to regulate in areas such as transport, education, health and local government, all policy areas ostensibly within the purview of the states.

In the last half of last century, the Court also diminished the financial autonomy of the states. Upon losing the ability to collect income taxes in the Uniform Tax cases of 1942 and 1957, the states turned to forms of indirect taxation, which they argued were neither excises nor duties as defined by Section 90 (which hands 'duties of customs and excise' exclusively to the Commonwealth). However, the High Court then took a series of decisions that narrowed the ability of the states to raise indirect taxes in this way (by expanding the definition of an excise covered by Section 90). Then in *Ha v NSW* 1997 the Court 'removed an anomalous situation that had allowed the states to levy significant taxes on alcohol, tobacco, and petrol'. This blow to their finances forced a 'major restructuring of the Australian taxation system' and the introduction of a new tax on goods and services to be collected by the Commonwealth and returned to the states (Selway and Williams 2005, 486).

Some welcome the High Court's reshaping of the Australian Federation. Some suggest that it did the real work to drag the Federation from the horse and buggy era when parliament and the referenda process could not. Their argument is that, by enlarging the Commonwealth's role beyond that originally envisaged by the Constitution's authors, the High Court has better-equipped Australia to deal with economic, environmental and other contemporary challenges requiring national policy solutions. However, others lament the Court's role in the transforming 'a highly de-centralised federation into a highly centralised quasi-federation' (Craven 1999, 250). These differences turn upon whether the federal division of powers, which the authors of the Constitution intended, is seen as intrinsically desirable or an obstacle to good policy outcomes. Where both sides agree is that the 'High Court has consistently upheld the capacity of the Commonwealth to dominate the States financially' and has frequently read the heads of power in the Constitution in ways that have allowed 'the Commonwealth to enter almost any imaginable field of public regulation' (Allan and Aroney 2008, 259). It has 'sanctioned substantial increases of central power' and thereby shaped the political system Australia has today (Galligan 1995, 164).

SHORT-ANSWER QUESTIONS

THE CONSERVATIVE CASE AGAINST A BILL OF RIGHTS

Australia may be a democracy, but its paper Constitution does not expressly guarantee the right to freely engage in political debate or protest. Indeed, it secures few rights. Section 116 does provide for religious freedom. Section 80 secures a right to trial by jury and Section 117 protects against discrimination based on state residence. Australia is a signatory to, and in 1948 had a prominent role in drafting, the UN Universal Declaration on Human Rights. But its Constitution does not expressly safeguard those civil and political rights (like the right to life, liberty, free speech and privacy), which the Declaration requires ratifying nations to protect. It does not expressly protect the right to vote. It does not expressly safeguard against discrimination on gender or racial grounds. We use the word 'expressly' here advisedly.

The Constitution's authors imagined that the rights of citizens would be protected by common law (e.g. habeas corpus) and by parliament itself. They rejected a US-style Bill of Rights. However, a century later, the High Court appeared to reach a different conclusion about the wisdom of constitutionally entrenching political freedoms. During the 1990s, Australia 'experienced significant judicial development of civil rights and liberties' (Galligan and Morton 2006, 17). The High Court identified certain political rights that are implied by the way the Constitution is constructed although not specifically protected by its written passages. To find implied rights within the Constitution, the Court had to abandon the 'textual' judicial method (legalism) it had adopted in, and used since, the Engineers Case.

CASE STUDY

A civilised country needs a Bill of Rights BUT …

Extract from a lecture by Scott Reid in the Department of the Senate Occasional Lecture Series at Parliament House on 23 October 1998:

> It seems to me that even in as civilised a country as Australia, Canada, or the United States, there are a number of vital services that can be performed by a well-written, well-interpreted Bill of Rights. These are functions that cannot be performed by any other institution of which I am aware.
>
> This being said, however, I freely confess that I am a great deal less optimistic about either the willingness or the ability of courts to always serve as absolutely neutral defenders of the law and of the public interest. If Australia adopts a Bill of Rights, whether constitutionally as in Canada and the U.S. or by means of legislation as in New Zealand, it will be placing enormous potential power in the hands of the judiciary.
>
> The manner in which the judges choose to exercise this power will be entirely their own decision; Parliament will have lost the power to rein in the High Court, should the justices choose to begin the process of striking down legislation. As Gil Remillard, a Canadian cabinet minister, warned shortly after the 1982 adoption of the *Canadian Charter of Rights and Freedoms*, 'The Charter will be whatever the Supreme Court chooses to make it, because only a constitutional amendment … may alter a Supreme Court decision.'
>
> This would not be problematic, if:
>
> * judges could be counted upon to always enact decisions that are entirely impartial and entirely free of arbitrary content; and
> * impartial judgments always promoted justice, equity and other socially important goals.
>
> Sadly, neither of these two propositions is valid.
>
> … In the course of this talk, I hope to outline some of the dangers that can result from unchecked judicial supremacy, and also to suggest some potential solutions to these dangers. Intelligent observers have long recognized the concerns that I will be raising today. Ninety-one years ago, U.S. Chief Justice Charles Evans Hughes warned, 'We are under a Constitution, but the Constitution is what the judges say it is.'
>
> Source: Reid (1998)

QUESTION

Do you think that Australia should have a Bill of Rights? Why? Why not?

1990S HIGH COURT 'ACTIVISM'

In 1952 Dixon CJ observed that: 'Close adherence to legal reasoning is the only way to maintain the confidence of all parties in Federal conflicts … There is no other safe guide to judicial decisions in great conflicts than a strict and complete legalism' [(1952) 85 CLR xi, xiv]. This celebration of the textual method the High Court had adopted in 1920 hinted at its political utility. As Dixon CJ intimates, legalism protected the Court from being seen as having a dog in any fight between the Commonwealth and the states or between left and right. As Galligan (1987) argues, 'strict legalism' allowed the Court to cloak its essentially political reasoning in, say, the Bank Nationalisation case.

Proof of Galligan's thesis emerged in the 1990s when the Court abandoned legalism, adopted a new 'activist' judicial method, and promptly suffered a sustained barrage from conservatives who complained that it had strayed into the political domain. In the 1992 Mabo case, the High Court addressed an injustice that parliament had not remedied. It reversed 150 years of property law founded on an assumption that the Australian continent was unoccupied when settled by the British, instead ruling that, where it had not been lawfully extinguished, native title persisted. Mabo signalled that a majority of the Court had embraced an 'activist' method, one in which judges feel bound to interpret legislation (and the Constitution itself) in ways which correct injustices in contemporary society.

The High Court set about rectifying what some justices saw as the inability of an executive-dominated parliament to protect individual rights. In the 1992 Political Broadcasting case, television broadcasters challenged the validity of legislation that proscribed paid political advertising during elections. The Court took this opportunity to identify a hitherto unrecognised right to free and open political communication, which is implied by the Constitution's explicit provision for a system of representative government. In several subsequent cases (e.g. *Theophanous v Herald & Weekly Times* 1994), the High Court refined its finding that certain freedoms can be implied from the Constitution.

The conservative response to both Mabo and the Court's discovery of implied rights asserted that parliament, not the courts, should make law. As one West Australian politician said of Mabo: 'No amount of legal nicety … alters the fact that the High Court has moved from the area of judicial interpretation … to legislative creation' (Hassell 1993). Similar complaints were levelled at the Court's discovery of implied rights. In 1997 the then Attorney-General Daryl Williams (1997) argued that 'each arm of government has its distinct place in the constitutional framework' and that, 'to act legitimately', judges must 'refrain from trespassing on the proper role of the legislature'. Protest spilled into the media. In *The Australian*, a conservative columnist wrote: 'Arrogant activist judges are damaging the rule of law … A war on democracy is … being launched by activist judges trying to overturn the will of the people' (Allbrechtsen 2003, 11).

VIDEO

Rights regimes and rule by judges?

The High Court's experiment with activism dissipated early this century. A Coalition government elected in 1996 lasted until 2007 and, during this period, appointed six new justices to reshape the Court. This experiment underlined the Court's political significance. Furthermore, it sharpened fears that social policies might be legislated by 'meddling, unelected judges' instead of 'democratically elected politicians' should Australia introduce a Bill of Rights (Albrechtsen 2017). This fear underpins the conservative case against constitutionally entrenching rights and freedoms.

Several decades of advocacy having failed, Australia still has no bill or charter of rights and remains the exception among comparable parliamentary and common law countries. Parliament has passed various laws (e.g. the Disability Discrimination Act) which proscribe discrimination on the grounds of gender, race and disability. But this is ordinary law, which can be varied by governments. Section 128 – a much larger hurdle – would stand in the way of altering rights entrenched in the Constitution. Those who advocate adding a Bill of Rights to the Australian Constitution see this as an advantage. Opponents see it as a problem. Short of initiating a referendum – a difficult political process unlikely to succeed – there would be no way of correcting an expansive interpretation of constitutionally given rights by any future 'activist' Court. Adding a Bill of Rights would expand the temptation for unelected, unaccountable courts to interpret legislation and the Constitution in ways which change its intended meaning.

SUMMARY

Learning objective 1: Explain why a constitution can be broadly defined as the 'rules governing government'

The 'point of a constitution is to organise politics and society in particular ways' (Hardin 2013, 52). Constitutions are rule books that shape how nations are governed – and ultimately how their governments can respond to the contemporary policy challenges they face. Lawyers view constitutions as superior law. Political scientists are wont to stretch the definition to encompass all rules that, directly and indirectly, govern the authority and operation of governments. Some of these are found in 'dusty old books'. Some are found in ordinary legislation (say the Electoral Act), and yet others in precedent and agreed ways of proceeding (or conventions), which cannot be tested in court.

Learning objective 2: Understand why the Australian Constitution makes no mention of the prime minister or the Cabinet

Australia's paper Constitution was drafted by colonial politicians in the 1890s. They took as their model the British parliamentary system, which is not described in a 'written' charter. Rather it owes much to precedent and convention. In laying out rules for responsible parliamentary government in Australia, the Constitution's framers followed suit. Therefore, the Constitution fails to describe and, as in Britain, leaves to convention, the operation of key political institutions – most notably the prime minister and the Cabinet. Instead of defining their powers and function, the Constitution formally assigns executive power to the Governor-General. But the politics are very different. Convention dictates that the Governor-General only exercise executive powers as advised by a prime minister who has the support of the House of Representatives. This transfers executive power to the governments that Australians elect and hold accountable at regular elections.

Learning objective 3: Describe judicial review and the role of the High Court as the constitutional umpire

The Constitution makes the High Court Australia's 'federal supreme court' and constitutional umpire. It has an original jurisdiction. Today much of its work entails hearing appeals from subordinate federal and state courts in cases where it believes that a law or the Constitution itself requires clarification. The Court engages in judicial review where it is asked to determine whether executive actions or legislation passed by parliament comply with the Constitution. When the Court has been asked to hear cases raising concerns about the proper application of the Constitution, often a question relating to the division of powers between the Commonwealth and the states has been involved. After all, the 1901 Constitution is substantially concerned with establishing Australia as a federation and contains no 'Bill of Rights' (which might otherwise engage the Court in judicial review). In umpiring the federal compact, the High Court, over many decades and in many cases, has enlarged the authority of the Commonwealth at the expense of the states.

Learning objective 4: Explain why the High Court is a political as well as a legal institution

The High Court's role in reshaping Australia's federation points to its political importance. Claims that the High Court is a political institution do run counter to its own account of its purpose, namely to interpret and apply the law of Australia. If the Court is a political body, it is clearly an unusual one, having just seven members none of whom is elected and all of whom eschew membership of parties and other political groupings. Yet political considerations often permeate the process of appointing judges. Moreover, the Court is sometimes asked to resolve conflicts between rival political interests – often the Commonwealth and the states but occasionally interest groups. Judicial review may see the High Court making, rather than applying, the law. As with its 1992 Mabo decision to recognise native title, the Court has sometimes substantially shaped public policy. These are all reasons why political scientists view the High Court as political, not purely a legal institution.

Learning objective 5: Understand judicial activism and the conservative case against a Bill of Rights

For six decades after the Engineers case, the High Court employed a method which relied on close textual analysis to determine the law (rather than reading the Constitution in the light of coordinate federalism or other political theories). In the 1980s and 1990s it showed a newfound willingness to interpret the Constitution in the light of community values, finding implied political freedoms required by modern democracy within, but not explicitly described in the Constitution. This retreat from legalism was controversial. Critics condemned the Court's attempt to supplement and modernise the Constitution as unwarranted 'judicial activism'. Its willingness during this short-lived activist period to extend freedoms where the parliament had failed to do so (and where the Constitution is silent) underpins the conservative case against adding a US-style 'Bill of Rights' to the Australian Constitution. Such an addition might grow the opportunity for unelected, unaccountable 'activist' judges to usurp the law-making role of parliament.

Learning objective 6: Analyse the referendum process and the obstacles to formal constitutional change

In the 21st century, Australia still has a Constitution that is largely silent on rights and freedoms that define liberal democracies and that entrenches a mix of federalism and responsible government that many argue ill-suits the challenge of governing a nation caught up in rapid technological, social and economic change. But updating the Constitution is no easy thing. Although Section 128 allows its amendment via a referendum process, changes have been difficult to achieve. Change first requires parliament to pass initiating legislation, and then that amendments be approved by a majority of voters and of the states.

Since Federation only eight amendments have been successfully prosecuted. This does not mean the wider constitution has not evolved. The High Court is able to change how the Constitution is interpreted, even if it cannot change the words on the page. And some rules governing government are open to alteration. Parliament can amend the *Electoral Act*. Conventions are ultimately decided in the court of public opinion and open to reinterpretation. But altering the formal Constitution is another matter. Often political obstacles stand in the way. This reminds us that constitutions are not only rules governing how political actors should behave. They are themselves the object of political struggle since they ultimately dictate who wins and loses in contests for political power.

DISCUSSION QUESTIONS

1. What is a constitution?
2. Is Australia's Constitution an 'anachronistic, dusty old book'?
3. Australian state constitutions can be changed without holding referenda elections. Should the Commonwealth Parliament be able to similarly amend the Australian Constitution?
4. Should the High Court 'make law'?
5. What are the arguments for and against adding a Bill of Rights to the Australian Constitution?

DISCUSSION
QUESTIONS

FURTHER READING

Australian politics explainer: the writing of our Constitution. URL: https://theconversation.com/australian-politics-explainer-the-writing-of-our-constitution-74518

Fenna, A. (2013). The Australian system of government, especially, in A. Fenna, J. Robbins and J. Summers, eds, *Government and Politics in Australia*, Frenchs Forest: Pearson Australia, pp. 23–8.

Galligan, B. and Morton, F.L. (2006). Australian exceptionalism: Rights protection without a Bill of Rights. In T. Campbell, J. Goldsworthy and A. Stone, eds, *Protecting Rights Without a Bill of Rights: Institutional Performance and Reform in Australia*, Burlington: Ashgate Publishing Ltd.

Patapan, H. (2001). *Judging Democracy: The New Politics of the High Court of Australia*, Melbourne: Cambridge University Press.

REFERENCES

Allan, J. and Aroney, N. (2008). An uncommon court: How the High Court of Australia has undermined Australian federalism. *Sydney Law Review*, **30**(2), 245–94.

Albrechtsen, J. (2003). Death to democracy, *The Australian*, 23 July, p. 11.

Albrechsten, J. (2017). Politics, judiciary need to remain separate, *Weekend Australian*, 4 February.

Attorney-General's Department. (2010). *Judicial Appointments: Ensuring a strong, independent and diverse judiciary through a transparent process.* Commonwealth of Australia, Canberra. URL: https://www.ag.gov.au/LegalSystem/Courts/Documents/JudicialApptsEnsuringastrongandindependentjudiciarythroughatransparentprocess.pdf

Australia.gov.au. (2017). The High Court of Australia. URL: http://www.australia.gov.au/search/site/high%2520court%2520of%2520australia

Barnett, H. (2011). *Constitutional and Administrative Law*, 9th edn, Oxford: Routledge.

Chordia, S. and Lynch, A. (2014). Federalism in Australian constitutional interpretation: Signs of reinvigoration? *University of Queensland Law Journal*, **33**(1).

Constitution Education Fund Australia. (2016). Constitutional crisis or is the system working as it was designed? 8th July 2016. URL: http://www.cefa.org.au/ccf/constitutional-crisis-or-system-working-it-was-designed

Craven, G. 1999. Australian constitutional battlegrounds of the twenty-first century. *University of Queensland Law Journal*, **20**(2), 250–61.

Dick, T., O'Malley, N. and Garnaut, J. (2006). The day true power went to Canberra, *The Sydney Morning Herald*, 15 November, p. 1.

French CJ (2009). Judicial activism. The boundaries of the judicial role, LAWASIA Conference, Ho Chi Minh City, 10 November. Retrieved from http://www.hcourt.gov.au/assets/publications/speeches/current-justices/frenchcj/frenchcj10Nov09.pdf

Galligan, B. (1987). *Politics of the High Court*, St Lucia: University of Queensland Press.

Galligan, B. (1995). *A Federal Republic: Australia's Constitutional System of Government*, Melbourne: Cambridge University Press.

Galligan, B. and Brenton, S. (2015). Constitutional conventions. In B. Galligan and S. Brenton, eds, *Constitutional Conventions in Westminster Systems*, Cambridge: Cambridge University Press.

Galligan, B. and Morton, F.L. (2006). Australian exceptionalism: Rights protection without a Bill of Rights. In T. Campbell, J. Goldsworthy and A. Stone, eds, *Protecting Rights Without a Bill of Rights: Institutional Performance and Reform in Australia*, Burlington: Ashgate Publishing.

Grimm, D. (1995). Does Europe need a constitution? *European Law Journal*, **1**(3), 282–302.

Hardin, R. (2013). Why a constitution? In D.J. Galligan and M. Versteeg, eds, *Social and Political Foundations of Constitutions*, New York: Cambridge University Press.

Hassell, B. (1993). Mabo and federalism: The prospect of an Indigenous people's treaty. Proceedings of the Second Conference of The Samuel Griffith Society, The Windsor Hotel, Melbourne, 30 July–1 August.

Jennings, Sir I. (1959). *The Law and the Constitution*, 5th edn, London: University of London Press.

Judicial Conference of Australia. (2015). *Judicial appointments: A comparative study.* Judicial Conference of Australia, Sydney. URL: http://www.jca.asn.au/wp-content/uploads/2013/10/P17_02_42-RESEARCH-PAPER-final.pdf

Kirby J (2005). Judicial dissent. Address delivered to the Law Students' Society of James Cook University at Cairns, Saturday 26 February. Retrieved from http://www.hcourt.gov.au/assets/publications/speeches/former-justices/kirbyj/kirbyj_feb05.html

Knox CJ, Isaacs, R. and Starke JJ (1920). *Amalgamated Society of Engineers v The Adelaide Steamship Company Limited and Others* (Engineers Case) (1920) 28 CLR 129.

Mulgan, R. (2012). Assessing ministerial responsibility in Australia. In K. Dowding and C. Lewis, eds, *Ministerial Careers and Accountability in the Australian Commonwealth Government*, Canberra: ANU E-Press.

Neumann, E. (1973). *The High Court of Australia: A Collective Portrait 1903–1972*, 2nd edn, Dept. of Government and Public Administration, University of Sydney.

Parliamentary Education Office. (2017). The Australian Constitution. URL: http://www.peo.gov.au/learning/fact-sheets/australian-constitution.html

Patapan, H. (2000). *Judging democracy: The New Politics of the High Court of Australia*, Melbourne: Cambridge University Press.

Ratnapala, S. (1999–2000). The idea of a constitution and why constitutions matter. *Policy: A Journal of Public Policy and Ideas*, **15**(4), 3–10.

Reid, S. (1998). Curbing judicial activism: The High Court, the people and a bill of rights. Lecture in the Department of the Senate Occasional Lecture Series at Parliament House on 23 October. Retrieved from https://www.aph.gov.au/binaries/senate/pubs/pops/pop33/reid.pdf

Sachs, S.E. (2013). The 'unwritten constitution' and unwritten law. *University of Illinois Law Review*, **2013**(5), 1797–846.

Savva, N. (1997). Fischer seeks a more conservative court, *The Age*, 5 March, p. 6.

Selway, B. and Williams, J. (2005). The High Court and Australian federalism. *Publius: The Journal of Federalism*, **35**(3), 467–88.

Tate, C.N. (2008). Judiciary, *The Encyclopaedia Britannica*. Retrieved from https://www.britannica.com/topic/judiciary

Wheare, K.C. (1966). *Modern Constitutions*, Oxford: Oxford University Press.

Williams, D. (1997). Judicial independence, the courts and the community: [Press Release.] Speech to the SA Chapter of the Australian Institute of Judicial Administration, Adelaide, 7 February.

Williams, G. (2006). There's no denying the old buggy has lost a wheel. *The Sydney Morning Herald*, 5 July.

Williams, G. (2008). High Court appointments: The need for reform. *Sydney Law Review*, **30**(1), 163–9.

Wright, B.C. and Fowler, P.E. (2012). *House of Representatives Practice*, 6th edn, Department of the House of Representatives.

CHAPTER 6

'RED TAPE': BUREAUCRACY AND PUBLIC POLICY

LEARNING OBJECTIVES

After reading this chapter, you should be able to:

1. Explain the origins and use of the term bureaucracy

2. Provide an overview of the Australian Public Service

3. Outline the key 21st century challenges for the public service

4. Define public policy and describe the policy process

5. Understand the shift from 'government' to 'governance'

INTRODUCTION

This chapter examines the role of the administrative arm of government known as the **bureaucracy**, public service or civil service. Political scientists focus on bureaucracies because they are central components of government activity and the means by which governments put public policies into action. The first section of the chapter charts the origins and development of bureaucracy as a model of organisation, which contrasts with the popular, and largely negative, understanding of the term. Turning to the Australian context, the chapter provides an overview of the Australian federal bureaucracy, the Australian Public Service (APS), from its embryonic status at the time of Australia's Federation through to its development into a large, complex and multifaceted institution in the 21st century. It discusses the significance of the **New Public Management** (NPM) reforms that the public service was subjected to during the 1980s and 1990s. In the contemporary post-NPM era, the public service faces key challenges including the ongoing controversy over the sector's size and efficiency, the use and regulation of digital technology, and its status as the pre-eminent source of policy advice to governments.

In explaining the bureaucracy's role in Australia, the chapter outlines a key activity: policy-making. In doing so, it examines definitions of **public policy** and the main stages of the policy process. In practice, however, these stages represent an idealised understanding of the policy work of the bureaucracy. In reality, the world of policy-making is often chaotic, ad hoc and subject to opportunities and political leadership. The chapter concludes with a discussion of the discursive shift from government to **governance** that has taken place in the late 20th and early 21st centuries in the context of public sector organisations and their policy-making roles. The term governance is now frequently employed to denote contemporary governing activity inclusive and beyond the sphere of government whereby a complex array of public, civil society and business organisations contribute to the policy process. The degree to which state institutions including bureaucracies are strengthened or compromised by contemporary governance arrangements is a source of active debate among political scientists.

WHAT IS BUREAUCRACY?

The term 'bureaucracy' has French and Greek origins. It is derived from the French word bureau to denote an item of furniture comprising a writing desk with multiple filing compartments. The second part of the term is derived from the Greek word kratos meaning 'a pattern of rule' or governing. Bureaucracy can thus be extrapolated as a workplace where officials collectively administer public affairs. It was first employed in this way by 18th century economist Vincent de Gourney who described it as 'a form of government in which officials dominate' (Bevir 2010, 143).

While the term bureaucracy is only a few hundred years old, the concept is said to have originated with early empires seeking to exert rule over expanded territories (Crooks and Parsons 2016). Bureaucracy was utilised in the Qin and Han dynasties in China, the Inca Empire, and the Ottoman Empire to name just a few, for a number of administrative tasks such as determining and collecting taxes, governing trade and providing early forms of policing.

bureaucracy: A mode of administration common in large organisations, but particularly associated with public sector agencies, based on hierarchical structures and adherence to processes, rules and routines.

New Public Management: A reform program applied to most public sector organisations in developed countries during the 1980s and 1990s based upon private sector management techniques and market logic.

public policy: A core aspect of government activity involving governments committing resources to address public problems and issues.

governance: The broad process of governing comprising various strategies, processes and relationships and involving governments and/or a range of societal groups and institutions.

AUTHOR PANEL

In the contemporary context, bureaucracy has been defined in a number of ways: as 'a hierarchical organisation of officials appointed to carry out certain public objectives' (Etzioni-Halevy 2010, 85); 'organisation characterised by hierarchy, fixed rules, impersonal relationships, strict adherence to impartial procedures, and specialisation based on function' (Bevir 2009, 37); or simply as behaviour that rigidly applies general rules to particular cases. A central aspect of bureaucracy is that it is a form of organisation that prioritises rules and processes as an approach to administering human activity.

Inevitably, as its imperial use suggests, some degree of bureaucracy is essential for managing large numbers of people effectively or developing plans involving several elements where there is a need to establish authority, order and systems. However, contemporary government bureaucracies do not involve the dominance of government by public officials, but rather that full-time professional officials administer the everyday affairs of governments. While elected politicians are responsible for decision-making, the role of government bureaucracies is to formulate policy options and implement government decisions. Bureaucracies are therefore the institutional machinery for providing policy advice and putting decisions into effect.

In the contemporary Australian political system, there is a permanent layer of bureaucracy associated with each tier of government at the local, state and territory, and federal levels. In broad terms, the bureaucracy is active across three general policy arenas: (1) law and order, national defence and foreign affairs; (2) economic management including regulation of the private sector; and (3) social welfare spanning health, education, arts, culture, heritage, aged care and disability services. At the municipal level of Australian government, local government bureaucracies undertake activity associated with town planning and development, roads maintenance and waste collection. At the state and territory level, bureaucracies deliver health services, education, and manage infrastructure, water resources and electricity generation, to name just a few policy areas. And at the national level, the APS is the bureaucracy supporting the federal government and is most active in national policy areas including economic management, social security, overseeing inter-governmental relations, and defence and foreign affairs.

BUREAUCRACY AS A MODEL OF ORGANISATION

In establishing the notion of bureaucracy as an organisational model, the scholarly work of German sociologist Max Weber has been most influential, particularly his foundational book *Economy and Society*, first published in 1922. According to Weber, bureaucracy is the institutional form of rational-legal authority whereby power is exercised on the basis of expert knowledge, rather than on the basis of patronage, lineage, kinship or some other arbitrary preference (Weber and Andreski 1983). Indeed, bureaucracy was viewed in the early 20th century as an efficient, rational and modern form of organisation that would inevitably replace these more traditional governing approaches. During the 20th century, bureaucracies in most industrialised countries were modelled on bureaucratic principles derived from Weber's work. These principles include the dominance of hierarchy, specialisation, processes and rules; a permanent and merit-based staff; and the separation of administration from politics. These principles are elaborated in the box below. It should be noted that although Weber was instrumental in developing the 'ideal-type' bureaucratic model, he was decidedly not enamoured with its implications. Instead he saw bureaucracy as ultimately constituting an 'iron cage' antithetical to personal individuality and creativity (see Mitzman 1970).

'Principles of bureaucracy'

Drawing upon Weber, Gerth and Mills (1998), Max Weber's principles of the ideal-type bureaucratic model include:

Hierarchy and functional specialisation: organisations should be structured as hierarchies with lower levels of an organisation reporting upwards and higher levels of an organisation accepting responsibility for lower level activity. Further, organisations should be functionally specialised in two ways: first, they should specialise in a particular policy area or portfolio, and second, there should be functional separation of core activities internally. In Australia, and elsewhere, these ideas resulted in departmental secretaries overseeing government departments and the minister/s in charge of that portfolio ultimately accepting responsibility for departmental activities.

The dominance of process, rules and procedures: these are a cornerstone of bureaucracies and are enshrined in comprehensive manuals and document templates. All actions and communications are recorded in file management systems. This is said to make for certainty in decision-making and ease of review.

Permanent and merit-based staffing: public administration is considered a special kind of activity warranting bureaucracies staffed by professional, permanent, merit-based, and anonymous employees with the ability to serve governments effectively and equally. In Australia, in return for their 'frank and fearless' advice, the recruitment of outsiders above base level was discouraged, and staff enjoyed regular promotions, protection against arbitrary dismissal and generous retirement pensions.

The separation of administration from politics: government bureaucracies should be politically neutral, simply undertaking policy functions regardless of the government in power. Strategy and policy decisions are the domain of elected representatives and public servants are to provide advice and carry out instructions only. They are therefore not personally responsible for results.

QUESTION

Develop a list of the organisations that you interact with regularly. In your experience of these organisations, to what extent are Weber's principles of bureaucracy evident?

BUREAUCRACY AS A PEJORATIVE TERM

From the 19th century onwards, with the rise of modern industrial and political systems, government bureaucracies flourished. By the mid to late 20th century, it was common to equate bureaucracy with any large-scale organisation, public or private. It was not an exaggeration to say that during this period, bureaucracy was a defining characteristic of modern life; people who lived in developed countries spent most of their lives in bureaucracies – they were born, educated, employed, and spent their leisure time in them. In the scholarly realm, the Weberian model of bureaucracy dominated social science thinking about the way organisations, particularly public ones, should be structured.

As bureaucracy became pervasive, it was increasingly viewed in negative terms. By the 1970s, when criticisms of big government and the **welfare state** rose to prominence, bureaucracy, which privileged process and rules over results and innovation, was often portrayed as monolithic, uncontrollable, invasive, costly and compromising individual

welfare state: A manifestation of the state during the 20th century whereby governments play chief roles in promoting the social security of citizens via a range of health, education and economic wellbeing programs.

freedoms. In this regard, bureaucracy was associated with 'red tape', meaning a rigid or obstructive official routine or procedure, a notion derived from the red coloured tape used to bind government documents in the United Kingdom (Bozeman 2000). In essence, bureaucracy became associated with an obsessive focus on processes, rules and regulations. Bureaucrats were parodied as a 'fragmented set of individuals so bound with red tape and rules books that they don't know what they are about at any one time, sending television sets to people who lack electricity and doing research on the optimal shape of toilet seats' (Peters 1989, 251). In the 21st century, bureaucracy continues to be employed as a pejorative term.

SHORT-ANSWER QUESTIONS VIDEO

THE AUSTRALIAN PUBLIC SERVICE (APS)

In Australia, as for other developed nations, the bureaucracy has grown substantially over the course of the 20th century. However, Australia is somewhat unique in that bureaucracy has been a central component of its governance since the arrival of the British in 1788. Australia's status as a British outpost and penal colony required governing authorities on behalf of the British Government to administer the convict system, provide law and order, allocate property rights, establish trade, and build early systems of transport and other infrastructure. The vast size of the Australian continent and the small population meant that government was the sole provider of many important services that private enterprise was unable or unwilling to provide but which private enterprise historically provided elsewhere (Bell and Hindmoor 2009). In this respect, Australians have long relied on governments and their bureaucracies.

On 1 January 1901, on Australia's Federation, the Commonwealth Public Service was established consisting of seven departments with staff drawn from the ranks of the former colonial administrations (Spann 1959). These included the following departments: Postmaster-General, Trade and Customs, Defence, External Affairs, Home Affairs, Attorney-General and Treasury. Of these, the Postmaster-General's Department was the largest comprising 6000 offices around Australia and several thousand employees (*The Canberra Times* 1926). In contrast, the Commonwealth Treasury was the smallest department with an initial staff of five bookkeepers (The Treasury).

GROWTH OF THE APS

Keynesian economic management: An approach to managing a nation's economic prosperity via active government intervention through monetary and/or fiscal (taxing and spending) policies to lessen the extreme tendencies of unmitigated capitalism.

Over the 20th century, Australia adopted a similar pattern of bureaucratic expansion to that in other industrialised nations. The most intense period of growth occurred between the 1930s and 1970s. During this era, governments required large bureaucracies in order to manage the national economy through taxing and spending programs that accorded with **Keynesian economic management** principles (Keynes 1957). These principles became paradigmatic following the Great Depression of the 1930s that resulted in severe hardship for much of the population. Keynesian principles dictate that governments should actively intervene in the economy in order to smooth out the tendency for freely operating market forces to create 'booms' and 'busts', such as the Great Depression. The theory postulates that governments should deliver 'counter-cyclical budgets', whereby governments should spend, even if they go into deficit, in times of economic downturn in order to stimulate demand. And in the good economic times, governments should collect more tax and spend less in order to prevent an economy from overheating (Keynes 1957).

From Federation onwards, the size, scope, and organisational complexity of the Commonwealth bureaucracy grew dramatically. While it initially dealt with the logistical requirements of the unified colonies, it went on to acquire new functions as the Australian nation consolidated and the demands of the Second World War (1939–1945) took hold. Indeed, the Second World War prompted the growth of a government-led 'war economy', which required the building of national institutions, significant centralised planning, and the mobilisation of citizens' towards the war effort. In the post-war period, as Australia's population increased, technology advanced, international trade expanded, and national development became a key objective, the number of Commonwealth departments and public servants proliferated further.

The adoption of Keynesian economic principles over the 20th century aligned with and legitimised social democratic objectives resulting in a greater role for bureaucracies in citizens' lives. Australia developed a generous array of social policy provisions in the areas of education, health, housing and income support, which required large, specialised and professional bureaucracies to administer them. Further, the Keynesian approach justified the establishment of specialist bodies to facilitate industry development in areas such as railway infrastructure, hydroelectricity, commodity exports such as wheat and wool, and scientific research (Ward and Stewart 2010, 68). Hierarchical or bureaucratic governance consequently became a dominant aspect of Australian public life and governments were viewed as the answer to many of society's problems.

PUBLIC SECTOR REFORM

In the 1970s, the model of traditional public administration outlined above was subjected to criticism in line with the broader discontent with 'big government' that emerged in this period. This was facilitated by the challenging economic context of the 1970s, which included energy price spikes (the 'oil shocks'), rising unemployment, high inflation and, as a result, declining tax revenues. The critique of 'big government' was informed by those espousing **public choice theory**, which holds that governmental actors seek to maximise their own self-interests over serving in the public's interest (Buchanan and Tullock 1965). In this view, bureaucrats will naturally attempt to enlarge their departments and the scope of their work for private gain at the expense of citizens. By the 1970s, it was increasingly argued that public sector agencies had become bloated, inefficient, unaffordable, difficult for governments to steer, and were crowding out private sector activity (see Sawer 1982).

In response, governments in most industrialised nations initiated what proved to be controversial reforms to streamline and modernise their bureaucracies. A core assumption underpinning the reforms was that market principles allocate resources more efficiently, encourage greater innovation and promote overall economic welfare to a greater degree than bureaucratic principles. Consequently, the reforms were labelled 'New Public Management' (Hood 1991) and in Australia, 'economic rationalism' (Pusey 1991). A central aim was to adopt market-based strategies to guide both the internal operation of government departments and their programs. Instruments employed included the privatisation of public utilities, contracting out the delivery of government services to

public choice theory: An economic approach to political phenomena emphasising the self-interested and utility-maximising behaviour of individuals.

the private sector, introducing 'user-pays' systems to allocate public services, developing public–private partnerships to fund and deliver infrastructure and other projects, and introducing performance management systems to assess public servant's productivity. The reforms sought to improve government efficiency through the introduction of competition; shift the focus from process to outcomes; encourage innovation; and improve the accountability and transparency of government bureaucracies to elected representatives. The reforms however were highly contentious as they sought to shift the existing balance between 'market' and 'state' in favour of market-based approaches. Indeed, this was viewed as ushering out an era of governmental benevolence to citizens to make way for the brave new globalised world and the pursuit of economic growth over economic equality.

From managerialism to marketisation

The NPM reform agenda was part of a broader paradigm shift away from Keynesian economic principles to a more liberal approach to managing markets and an embrace of private sector management techniques. The Royal Commission into Australian Government Administration (the 'Coombs Commission') was established by the Whitlam Government in 1973 to review the nation's approach to public administration, while similar reviews were conducted at the state level. Many of the Commission's recommendations were implemented by the Whitlam, Fraser, and Hawke governments during the 1970s and 1980s. The initial wave of reform included new administrative law to provide greater oversight of public servants' activity, offset administrative complexity, and improve transparency and accountability. New institutions were created including the Office of Ombudsman; the Administrative Appeals Tribunal; the Administrative Review Council; and the *Freedom of Information Act 1982*. From the mid-1980s, new procedures were developed to make public sector employment more equitable for women, migrants, and Indigenous people. Overly complex employment structures and divisions were abolished to allow greater mobility within the public service.

While the initial wave of reforms did not necessarily reduce the size of the bureaucracy, the 'managerial' and 'marketisation' reforms that followed were more significant. As Prime Minister Hawke stated in a media release announcing his government's reforms, '[a]lthough the primary impetus for these fundamental changes is efficiency and the better delivery of government services, there will be substantial savings arising from amalgamations, through economies of scale and the removal of duplication' (Hawke 1987). The managerial reforms included:

» the reorganisation and reduction of the number of departments
» the formalisation of political advisers to support ministers in exercising control over agencies
» the creation of a Senior Executive Service employed on a fixed-term basis to provide professional management skills
» rules to allow for greater employment flexibility and offering redundancies
» strategic management and corporate planning techniques from the private sector
» a new budgeting and accountability framework to demonstrate cost effectiveness and provide forward estimates of expenditures.

In further reforming Australian bureaucracy, the marketisation reforms included the privatisation of public enterprises such as Qantas, Telecom and the Commonwealth Bank;

the introduction of National Competition Policy to expose public utility monopolies to market conditions; user-charges for previously free services such as university education and dental services; and engaging external consultants via contracts to deliver public services.

In short, Australia experienced the NPM reforms as a reorganisation, rather than radical overhaul, of the public sector. In broad terms, the reforms resulted in governments extracting their institutional machinery from 'rowing' (providing public services in their entirety) in order to concentrate on 'steering' (determining overall goals, strategies and directions) (Osborne and Gaebler 1992).

SHORT-ANSWER QUESTIONS
REFLECTION QUESTIONS

THE CONTEMPORARY AUSTRALIAN PUBLIC SECTOR

In the 21st century, the public sector reform agenda in Australia relaxed with a period of consolidation rather than experimentation. Today, the APS refers to all Commonwealth departments and agencies that draw on the Commonwealth public account and are staffed under the 1999 Public Service Act. The Act outlines the responsibilities and powers of agency heads, provides the legal framework for employing APS employees, and details employees' rights and obligations. In 2016, the overall public sector workforce (including the local and state and territory level bureaucracies) comprised approximately 1.924 million employees, although this figure includes those employed within public corporations, universities, non-profit institutions controlled by government, government marketing boards, and legislative courts (ABS 2016a). This figure equates to approximately 13 per cent of all employed Australian people (ABS 2015).

TABLE 6.1 AUSTRALIAN PUBLIC SECTOR EMPLOYMENT, 2015–2016

LEVEL OF GOVERNMENT	EMPLOYEES (JUNE 2016)
Commonwealth	243 300
State and territory	1 495 100
Local	186 500
Total Public Sector	1 924 800

Source: Adapted from ABS (2016a)

It is interesting to note that many workers not immediately considered public servants undertake a range of roles that extend beyond simply the provision of policy advice. For example, police officers, the staff of public hospitals, public schools, the Australian Broadcasting Commission (ABC), local government planning, heritage and waste collection officers are all technically public servants. Table 6.2 lists the main government portfolios at the Commonwealth level, and while these are frequently re-structured according to the government of the day's requirements, it indicates how the Australian federal bureaucracy is organised. Within each portfolio, there are numerous specialist agencies (too numerous to list here) that ultimately report to the minister/s in charge of that portfolio. The table also provides the average staffing level within that portfolio over the 2016–17 period.

TABLE 6.2 LIST OF AUSTRALIAN GOVERNMENT PORTFOLIOS AND AVERAGE STAFFING LEVELS, 2016–2017

PORTFOLIO	STAFF
Agriculture and Water Resources	5384
Attorney-General	14 631
Communications and the Arts	7815
Defence	99 035
Departments of the Parliament	1185
Education and Training	2676
Employment	3757
Environment	4350
Finance	2759
Foreign Affairs and Trade	7064
Health	6441
Immigration and Border Protection	13 445
Industry, Innovation and Science	10 889
Infrastructure and Regional Development	2535
Prime Minister and Cabinet	4841
Social Services	33 158
Treasury	25 508
Total 2016–17	245 474

Source: Adapted from The Commonwealth of Australia (2017)

SPOTLIGHT

APS values

Because public servants undertake important work on behalf of governments and the broader public, the APS operates on the basis of a set of values detailed in Section 10 of the *Public Service Act 1999*. The APS Values outline expectations of public sector employees in terms of performance and standards of behaviour, which are derived from the traditional model of public administration. As outlined on the Australian Public Service Commission's website (2016), these values are:

Impartiality: the public service operates in an apolitical manner and provides advice to governments that is 'frank, honest, timely and based on the best available evidence'

Commitment to service: the public service is 'professional, objective, innovative and efficient' and works in a collaborative manner to deliver results for the government and Australian public

Accountability: the public service operates transparently and is accountable to both ministers (via the framework of responsible government) and the public under the law

Respectful behaviour: the public service 'respects all people, including their rights and their heritage'

Ethical conduct: the public service 'demonstrates leadership, is trustworthy, and acts with integrity, in all that it does'.

21ST CENTURY CHALLENGES FOR THE APS

In the 21st century, public sector organisations face a number of criticisms and challenges, despite the zeal for more radical reform subsiding. First, the appropriate size and efficiency of the public service is an ongoing point of contention. Second, the speed of technological change and the bureaucracy's use of digital technology in service delivery is challenging the regulatory and data safety capacity of government agencies. Third, the exclusivity of the public sector as the pre-eminent source of policy advice to governments is vulnerable to alternative sources of advice from political advisers and external consultants.

Size, cost and efficiency?

There is a long running debate in Australia about the appropriate size, cost and efficiency of the public sector. This is a residual issue stemming from the criticisms of big government that surfaced in the 1970s. The crux of the contention is that the public sector consumes too great a share of taxpayers' money and uses its resources inefficiently. As Carr (2015) explains, 'citizens need to ask whether the bureaucrats we employ are working at maximum efficiency and whether the country is getting maximum bang for its buck'. The series of budget deficits following the Global Financial Crisis (GFC) reinvigorated these criticisms. The cost of the Rudd Government's Building the Education Revolution program, for example, which formed part of the set of measures to avert an economic recession in Australia, has been criticised as an exercise in waste, red tape and inefficiency. Currently, it is estimated that the federal bureaucracy accounts for 14 per cent of total government spending (Carr 2015). However, the proportion of Australian employees residing in the public sector workforce has dropped significantly since 2000, with the ABS reporting a decline from 20 per cent of the total workforce in 2000 to 13 per cent in 2015 (ABS 2015).

In 2013, in the context of 'budget repair' following the GFC, the Abbott Government announced the establishment of a review into the performance, functions and roles of the Commonwealth level of government by the National Commission of Audit. The resulting report, Towards Responsible Government, generated 86 recommendations across a range of public sector activities in line with achieving a surplus of one per cent of GDP by year 2023–24. Among the proposals for radical spending cuts in health, education, welfare and industry assistance, the Commission's recommendations included a reduction in the number of boards, committees and councils that the Commonwealth supports, the privatisation of a range of public sector bodies in the short to medium term, harnessing 'the benefits of outsourcing' to a greater extent, and increasing reliance on 'user-pays' systems in health services and university education (National Commission of Audit 2014). As O'Flynn (2014) summarises, '[m]uch faith is placed in the ability of the market to allocate resources and citizens to do things for themselves. Less faith is placed in government's ability, in particular the public service'. While the Abbott Government did not embrace the Commission's recommendations in their entirety, the 2014 Federal Budget did incorporate

Figure 6.1 The 2014 Federal Budget: Treasurer Joe Hockey at a press conference at Parliament House on 13 May 2014 in Canberra.

the advice to cut government spending on the age pension, health, unemployment benefits and higher education. However, many of the proposed measures were abandoned in the face of widespread public discontent and opposition in the Senate. In other areas of government bureaucracy, however, budget considerations have been less prominent. The Department of Defence and intelligence agencies in particular have received greater resources for responding to the security threats posed by global terrorism and Islamic extremism.

Another remnant of the NPM reforms is the continual pressure for efficiency within the public service. Since 1987, successive governments have actively monitored the size and performance of the public sector workforce through the application of annual 'efficiency dividends'. These savings measures are applied to agencies' operating budgets whereby budgets are reduced across the board by a small percentage each year, typically in the range of 1 to 4 per cent, but usually spanning a range of 1 to 1.25 per cent (Hamilton 2015). The rationale of efficiency dividends is to encourage public sector managers to be innovative in carrying out government business and enable governments to redirect savings to high priority areas. The Department of Finance and the Australian Public Service Commission are additionally tasked with closely monitoring staffing levels across the entire APS.

Despite the immutable rhetoric about public sector inefficiency, the international evidence shows that Australia's government bureaucracies compare favourably with similar developed nations. For example, the World Bank's Worldwide Governance Indicators list Australia's level of government effectiveness as greater than the OECD average for 2015, ahead of the United States, France, Belgium and Ireland, but trailing Canada, Denmark, Germany, Japan and the United Kingdom (World Bank Group 2017).

Digital technology

The development and speed of digital technology has proved challenging for public sector agencies to utilise and regulate in the 21st century, not just in Australia, but worldwide. While successive Australian governments have driven the provision of infrastructure for Australian citizens to access the internet via the National Broadband Network, government agencies have proved less adept in employing digital technology. This is despite 86 per cent of all Australian households possessing home internet access (ABS 2016b). The key aspects of this challenge relate to the delivery of public services online and the complex task of regulating online activity.

e-government

Delivering public services via digital or mobile technology is known as e-government or digital government and it is becoming increasingly prevalent. It offers a potentially lower cost, more efficient method for government agencies to conduct their business as well as a greater level of transparency. Currently, the myGov service is the main online platform for citizens to access public services including Medicare, the Australian Taxation Office and Centrelink. In 2015, the government established the Digital Transformation Agency to facilitate the use and provide oversight of digital technology across government agencies (see the Agency's website www.dta.gov.au). Despite these developments, progress in e-government in Australia has been slower than anticipated. As of 2016, Australia ranked 8th internationally in the provision of online services (World Bank Group 2016, 155).

In its high-profile report discussed above, the National Commission of Audit (2014) recommends that the APS speed up the transition to online service delivery via the appointment of a Chief Digital Officer, the championing of the digital agenda across the APS, and a 'digital by default' approach. Further, the Commission recommends 'cloud computing' and the creation of a whole-of-government cloud computing provider panel permitting computer services to be leased and shared over a network thereby reducing costs (National Commission of Audit 2014).

While it offers a host of efficiency benefits, the Australian Government has encountered some high-profile problems stemming from the use of digital technology. In 2016, the Australian national census overseen by the Australian Bureau of Statistics (ABS) was largely conducted online but was criticised over privacy concerns and ultimately taken offline when security problems emerged. These issues compromised the census itself when millions of citizens were then unable to complete the forms. The episode highlights the difficulties involved in ensuring online data safety, particularly relating to citizens' private details. It also demonstrates the need for government agencies to adequately communicate with the public in the transition to online service delivery, as well as effectively manage relationships with private online technology providers.

In another example of recent e-government maladministration, the human services portfolio, Centrelink, the nation's welfare agency, came under fire in 2017 for using a new automated debt raising and recovery system to assess overpayment of benefits, resulting in the issue of thousands of letters incorrectly requiring welfare recipients to repay benefits. According to the Ombudsman's investigation, the 'implementation problems could have been mitigated through better project planning and risk management at the outset. This includes more rigorous user testing with customers and service delivery staff, a more incremental rollout, and better communication to staff and stakeholders' (Glenn 2017, 3). Clearly, the use of digital technology offers efficiencies, but the cost of failure is also high in terms of damaging the reputation of, and public trust in, government and public sector agencies.

Regulating the online environment

A second major aspect of digital technology as it relates to public administration is the need for government agencies to regulate new types of commercial and illegal activity facilitated by the online environment. The advent of commercial models based on digital technology platforms in the areas of passenger transport (e.g. Uber) and accommodation services (e.g. Airbnb) to name just two, has confounded existing government regulations. It has required governments to rethink regulatory settings to account for changes in the consumption of services and the impacts on existing industries. Law enforcement in the area of online crime is another challenging aspect of advancing digital technology. Australians' penchant for illegally downloading games, television programs and films has attracted governments' attention and resulted in a national discussion about the possibilities for curbing such activity.

In 2017, the Australian Government established a data retention scheme whereby the metadata of citizens' mobile and online activity is collected and stored for two years and subjected to scrutiny by national security agencies. Government oversight of Australians' online activity however has been controversial in regard to compromising citizens' privacy. Another example of online crime relates to the policing of the 'dark web', which comprises websites for trading in illegal goods and services, child pornography, whistleblowing and evading censorship. While governments around the world periodically succeed in shutting down such websites, seemingly little time passes before new platforms are established.

Competition in the provision of policy advice

While government agencies were considered the primary source of policy advice for governments prior to the NPM reforms, in the 21st century, the exclusivity of this status is under threat. The challenge is often intensified by changes in government, in particular with 'governments believing that officials are resisting change or insufficiently skilled and knowledgeable, and officials believing that political leaders are ignoring sound advice to executive preconceived or ill-thought out ideas' (Lindquist and Tiernan 2012, 445). There are two alternative sources of advice that governments increasingly utilise: their own political advisers and consultants from the private and non-profit sectors.

Political advisers and external consultants

Political advisers or 'staffers' are employed directly by politicians as personal staff and aim to provide comprehensive advice spanning the policy, political and media landscapes. Advisers are drawn from the ranks of senior public servants and increasingly from the political parties themselves, with many aspiring to become politicians in their own right. Australia's political system is unique in that it leads the world with the largest cohort of political advisers (Creighton 2014). In the 1970s, the Whitlam Labor Government paved the way for personal staff for politicians as a method to exert greater control over the public service that had served Liberal–Country Coalition governments for 23 years. The role of political advisers was consolidated by the Hawke Government with a separate *Members of Parliament (Staff) Act 1984*. Between 1984 and 2014, the number of advisers more than doubled and the figure currently hovers around 900 (Ng 2016). This represents a sizeable cohort of influential political operators in the Australian system of government sitting between elected representatives and the public service. Political advisers frequently produce their own policy research and serve as gatekeepers to ministers thereby posing a source of frustration and policy competition for public servants. Currently, political advisers are not obliged to serve in the public interest and are not accountable to the parliament.

Contracting for private and non-profit sector consultants by the APS has similarly become an increasing occurrence in the realm of public administration. In the 21st century, both Coalition and Labor governments have engaged consultants extensively. Over the course of the Howard Government years (1996–2007), several thousand APS staff were made redundant only to be subsequently re-engaged as consultants when it was realised that the in-house capacity of the APS had declined (Lundy 2008, quoted in Whelan 2011, 25). Similarly, the Rudd Government spent almost $800 million on 6534 external consultancies in its first 18 months (Whelan 2011, 11). More recently, in the period 2014–15, $10 billion was spent on consultants' fees at the same time as several thousand APS jobs were lost (Towell 2015). Consequently, the occupation of 'management and organisation analyst' has grown steadily in recent years to 60 000 individuals across Australia (Creighton 2017).

The growing ranks of political advisers and external consultants pose a considerable challenge for the public service. As Creighton (2017) explains 'public spending on consultants creates a shadow public sector that doesn't show up in government budgets'. But in addition to the budgetary, transparency and accountability implications, the growing reliance on alternative sources of policy advice competes with the existing public service in potentially offering more politicised, rather than 'frank and fearless', advice. This shifting institutional landscape, as it continues, is likely to engender a hollowing out of robust policy capacity in the public service into the future.

REFLECTION
QUESTIONS
VIDEOS

PUBLIC POLICY AND THE POLICY PROCESS

Public policy is a core activity of governments and their bureaucracies. The study of public policy, as a sub-discipline of political science, aims to improve understanding of critical areas of government activity, particularly bureaucracies, the governmental process, and the skills and tools required for improving policy-making over time. However, like many concepts in the social sciences, including 'politics' (as discussed in Chapter 1), the definition of public policy is contested: there is no single agreed-upon meaning. In general terms, however, public policy comprises a relationship or interaction between governments, problems, resources and values. Public policy has thus been variously defined as:

» '[a] course of action or inaction chosen by public authorities to address a given problem or interrelated set of problems' (Pal 1992, 3)

» 'what governments do, why they do it, and what difference it makes' (Dye 1972, 2)

» 'an action which employs governmental authority to commit resources in support of a preferred value (Considine 1994, 2)

» 'the process by which a society makes and enforces decisions on what behavior is acceptable and what is not' (Wheelan 2011, 7).

Policy work by the bureaucracy in Australia and elsewhere is consequently a complex affair encompassing a range of activities including the formulation of policy advice, designing policy instruments, policy coordination across agencies, consulting with stakeholders, policy implementation, evaluation and service delivery, to name a few key areas.

THE POLICY PROCESS

One of the more influential ways in which public policy is understood is as a process involving a series of steps or phases. In this regard, policy-making has been compared to applied problem-solving. Scholarly attempts to generate a working model of the policy process have their roots in the theory of **behaviouralism** in political science, which became prominent in the mid-20th century. Harold Lasswell was the first to propose a seven stage model of the policy process comprising the following elements: (1) intelligence gathering; (2) promotion of particular options; (3) prescription of a course of action; (4) the

Behaviouralism:
An approach to political science that emphasises objectivity and quantification to explain and predict political behaviour.

invocation of the prescribed option; (5) application of the policy through legislation and bureaucracy; (6) termination once it had run its course; and (7) appraisal and evaluation against original goal/s (Lerner and Lasswell 1951).

In Australia, the most influential version of the staged approach to understanding the policy process is Bridgman and Davis's 'policy cycle', first proposed in 1998, which 'brings a system and a rhythm to a world that might otherwise appear chaotic and unordered' (Althaus, Bridgman and Davis 2013, 32). Originally designed for new public servants in the Queensland Government, the model divides the policy process into nine steps comparable with Lasswell's approach.

As Althaus et al. (2013) argue, the policy cycle is an idealised sequence of activities and a tool for policy development and analysis rather than an exact accurate description of policy-making in action. A key strength of a cyclical staged approach to understanding and appraising public policy include that it portrays the process as dynamic whereby a policy may go through several iterations. In doing so, it recognises policy-making as a process that is rarely complete; following implementation and evaluation, the process often restarts with the discovery of new problems, issues and ideas for refinements.

Despite their practical benefits, policy process models are criticised on a number of fronts that are insightful for aiding understanding of the complexity of policy-making and the nature of public sector work. In reality, it is difficult to map the approach of public servants to policy work onto the policy cycle model. Ministers, advisers and bureaucrats often develop policy 'on the run' and, as indicated above, policy ideas and advice frequently emanate from sources external to government bureaucracies. Second, the point at which to move from one component of the cycle to the next is not clear from the model and some steps might be compressed or ignored altogether (Everett 2003). Third, the policy cycle portrays a rather 'top down' approach whereby decision-makers are assumed to exert control over those who will ultimately implement the policy without factoring in the interpretations and discretion exercised by public servants and private contractors engaged in service delivery. Finally, the model does not fully consider the added complexity of inter-governmental relations, which is a prominent part of the federal policy context in Australia. Indeed, the interaction between local, state and Commonwealth bureaucracies is, for many policy areas, crucial, particularly given the financial dominance of the Commonwealth. In this respect, power dynamics and the complex value-laden nature of policy-making involving deeply entrenched interests, values and beliefs are not part of the more straightforward picture represented by the Australian policy cycle. Ultimately, the policy cycle model offers a somewhat rationalistic, one-dimensional view of the work of government bureaucracies. Nevertheless, it is a useful tool for initiating students to the field of public policy.

VIDEO

CASE STUDY

Dr Ken Henry: Reflections on policy-making in Australia

The APS attracts many talented people with an interest in good public policy; economic, social and environmental. A lot of policy commentary seems to assume that policy advisers operating across these various domains are in constant battle with political leaders forced into difficult trade-offs among competing policy goals: having to trade off conservation against development; and social equity against economic efficiency. I can recall some such battles in my 28 years in the APS; but by the mid-1990s APS policy advisers, for the most part, were keen to work cooperatively to develop ideas that offered progress simultaneously, in all three dimensions.

During the 1980s and 1990s, the role of the APS in the development of policy advice became increasingly contested, with economic consultancies emerging to offer their services directly to politicians, especially those in opposition. The ranks of advisers sitting in offices in Parliament House also grew strongly, as did the numbers employed by special interest advocacy groups and think tanks. All of these added to the more traditional contributions from academics and media commentators. In response, government departments were required by their ministers to develop capabilities in 'issues management'; perversely, in some cases this function was outsourced. Most of the economic consultancies offered policy perspectives similar to those to be found within departments. Differences were usually confined to second-order matters of detail, though these tended to be amplified in the media, and almost always manipulated to somebody's political advantage.

The manipulation of policy to political advantage has been the dominant theme of the period since the mid-1980s. Throughout that entire period, the most significant determinant of the success of a policy reform proposal has been the quality of political leadership, and not just within government.

The late 1980s and 1990s were characterised by audacious politicians making careers out of disproving conventional political wisdom. Reform options provided vehicles for journeys in political leadership that seemed to prove that good policy is also good politics.

But there have always been easier ways to achieve political success, and they have been much less favourable to the cause of good policy. In the 21st century, several significant politicians have realised their personal ambition by undermining sensible reforms championed by their opponents, often within their own parties; in some cases, even by attacking policies championed by their former selves.

Political leadership of optimism and policy ambition has been replaced by negativism, fear-mongering and policy choices that generally wouldn't be considered even second-best by the public servants tasked with their implementation. In the 21st century, the political contest, thus far at least, has been largely destructive of good policy.

Dr Ken Henry AC was Secretary, Department of the Treasury (2001–11) and Special Advisor to the Prime Minister (2011–12).

QUESTION

Why has it become more difficult in the 21st century to align 'good policy' with 'good politics'?

SHORT-ANSWER
QUESTIONS

FROM GOVERNMENT TO GOVERNANCE?

For much of the 20th century, political scientists saw their field of study as centred on the formal state and government including its various components such as the bureaucracy. Yet, towards the end of the 20th century, coinciding with the widespread reform of government bureaucracies across much of the developed world, political scientists began to speak increasingly of 'governance' to describe contemporary public administration. The reason for the hitherto focus on government bureaucracies was due to the formal legal authority and legitimacy of the state, its role as the major actor in international relations and, as outlined in this chapter, post-war optimism about modern bureaucracy and the welfare state. However, from the 1970s, the decline of Keynesian economic management, the associated reform of public sector bureaucracies, and the challenges of an increasingly globalised world, brought about a conceptual, if not practical, rethinking of the role of governments, and with it, a process of 'decentering' the state among a growing cohort of political scientists. Consequently, the new term 'governance' grew in popularity to describe contemporary public administration and policy-making in its entirety.

WHAT IS GOVERNANCE?

The meaning of the term governance is disputed, and it is sometimes used in a very specific sense to refer to the NPM reforms. At the broadest level, however, governance has been understood as 'the tools, strategies and relationships used by governments to help govern' (Bell and Hindmoor 2009, 2), or in longer form: 'the exercise of economic, political and administrative authority to manage a country's affairs at all levels. It comprises mechanisms, processes, and institutions, through which citizens and groups articulate their interests, exercise their legal rights, meet their legal obligations, and mediate their differences' (United Nations Development Programme 1997, 9). Governance therefore incorporates and transcends the associated concepts of the state, government and public policy. In this respect, governance is not so much the eclipse of governments but a revised logic for governing involving a wider group of actors, processes and methods beyond simply the bureaucracy. This is evident in Mark Bevir's definition of governance as 'all processes of governing, whether undertaken by a government, market or network, whether over a family, tribe, formal or informal organization or territory and whether through laws, norms, power or language' (Bevir 2013, 1). As such, use of the term governance often indicates the shifting boundaries between the public, private and community sectors in contemporary policy-making (Rhodes 2017, 166).

There are three core elements of governance. First, governance is broader than simply a focus on formal government and its components. In fact, governance is usually defined by contrasting it with what is thought of as the traditional pattern of public power in which authority is centralised and exercised hierarchically, often called the 'command and control' model exemplified by the traditional model of public administration. Second, governance centrally concerns the rules and management of society's common affairs, and the processes for developing these rules. It thus involves the organisation, development and application of processes for solving public problems and allocating society's resources by governments and/or other actors. Third, governance not only takes into account non-state actors, institutions, processes and structures within the political system that exercises authority, legitimacy, influence and control in public life, but focuses attention on the nature of relationships between governments and these actors. Relevant governing actors may include business associations, firms, trade unions, professional associations, private consultants, non-profit charity groups, grassroots community groups, lobbyists, wealthy individuals and activist organisations.

If governance is understood in this broad sense, much contemporary policy-making is thus illustrative of governance in action. For example, public–private partnerships, routine relationships between business and trade unions and government, contracting non-profit groups to deliver public services, certification systems for product labelling (e.g. fair trade or organic certified goods), the creation of markets by governments to alleviate public problems (e.g. emissions trading systems) may all be described as governance because they involve governments working in concert with other actors to address policy problems.

Governance strategies in action: Road safety and infrastructure

In recognition of the broad array of political arrangements and relationships that make up contemporary governance, scholarship has emerged around four broad strategies that are commonly employed: (1) bureaucratic or hierarchical governance; (2) market-based governance; (3) community-based governance; and (4) collaborative network governance. These governance strategies are summarised in Table 6.3 along with examples from the area of road safety and infrastructure.

TABLE 6.3 GOVERNANCE: STRATEGIES, MODES AND EXAMPLES

GOVERNANCE STRATEGY	MODE OF ACTION	ROAD SAFETY AND INFRASTRUCTURE POLICY EXAMPLES
Bureaucratic	Law, regulation, hierarchy, command and control	Imposition of speed limits, seatbelts, licences, fines
Market-based	Competition, prices, supply and demand	Use of public–private partnerships to fund new roads, user charges such as tolls
Community-based	Shared ideas, common goals and beliefs	Rotary Youth Driver Awareness programs educating new drivers about road safety
Collaborative networks	Trust, diplomacy, reciprocity and resource exchange	Partnerships between local and state governments, tourism associations, and businesses to distribute coffee cups with road safety messages

Source: Adapted from Rhodes (2017, 75)

QUESTION

Can you think of examples of public policies in the area of environmental management that appear bureaucratic, market-based, community-based and network-based?

GOVERNANCE IMPLICATIONS

Increasingly, the term governance is generally used to describe the process of governing in all its complexity, but there are a number of implications arising from this notion that are worth considering. First, the term implies that the formal power of governments is limited and therefore inadequate for addressing difficult and intractable policy problems ranging from homelessness, child poverty, Indigenous disadvantage, terrorism and global climate change. The second implication is that rather than being considered as separate, stand-alone entities, governments are in fact embedded in society. Indeed, members of parliament are drawn from the community and governments must respond to community expectations. In contrast, the traditional view sees government as above and somewhat detached from the realm of society. The term governance instead implies that government is part of the social fabric and is one of many social actors with influence over public policy. Because governments are dependent on the social environment, and many other actors, in delivering public policies, much of the new governance scholarship focuses on the interdependencies between governments and other actors. The demand for these interdependencies has been interpreted by some as resulting in a diminished, 'hollowed out' state (Rhodes 1994). Others, meanwhile, have contended that governments have not been weakened by governance, but instead must approach the task of policy-making differently. Effective governance is now more dependent on governments developing policy networks, market-based strategies and community collaboration alongside the traditional, hierarchical approach to governing favoured for much of the 20th century (Bell and Hindmoor 2009).

RESEARCH QUESTION

SUMMARY

Learning objective 1: Explain the origins and use of the term bureaucracy

This chapter introduced the idea of bureaucracy as an organising principle for public administration. It charted the origins of the concept, Max Weber's ideal-type model and the proliferation of government bureaucracies over the course of the 20th century. Indeed, by the latter half of the century, bureaucracy had become a pervasive feature of modern industrialised nations, and Australia was no exception.

Learning objective 2: Provide an overview of the Australian Public Service

The second part of the chapter examined the development and contemporary roles of the Australian federal bureaucracy or APS. While bureaucracy was employed by colonial administrators from the time of British arrival, the size, scope and complexity of Australian government agencies grew dramatically from the 1930s to the 1970s. From the 1970s onwards, however, criticism of big government emerged prompting the reform of government agencies in most developed countries over the 1980s and 1990s.

Learning objective 3: Outline the key 21st century challenges for the public service

In the 21st century, debate about the size and efficiency of the public service continues as governments seek to implement various measures to boost the performance of government agencies. The challenges of advancing digital technology have brought Australian government agencies into unchartered waters providing both new opportunities and challenges in terms of the skillsets required to both utilise and regulate the online environment and manage the associated security issues. The enlarged cohort of political advisers and increasing reliance on external consultants for policy advice is an ongoing source of competition for the Australian public sector.

Learning objective 4: Define public policy and describe the policy process

The next part of the chapter unpacked the concept of public policy as comprising interactions between governments, problems, resources and values. One popular way in which policy-making is understood is as a process or cycle consisting of a number of stages. While this is a good introductory approach to the world of policy-making, this area of government activity is often significantly more complex, value-laden and irrational than policy process models suggest.

Learning objective 5: Understand the shift from 'government' to 'governance'

Towards the end of the 20th century, the concept of governance came into vogue among political scientists and policy practitioners. It implies the rise of new strategies in public administration, including market, community and network modes of governance, additional to the previously favoured bureaucratic approaches. The broader impact of these newer governance strategies on the capacity and role of governments in the 21st century remains contested.

DISCUSSION QUESTIONS

DISCUSSION QUESTIONS

1. How does the scholarly definition of bureaucracy differ from its use in the contemporary media?
2. How did the APS develop over the course of the 20th century and why was it reformed in the 1980s and 1990s?
3. What significant challenges does the Australian Public Service (APS) face in the 21st century?
4. What is public policy and what do process models of policy-making reveal?
5. Why is the contemporary term 'governance' increasingly employed by policy practitioners and political scientists?

FURTHER READING

Althaus, C., Bridgman, P. and Davis, G. (2013). *The Australian Policy Handbook*, 5th edn, Crows Nest, NSW: Allen & Unwin.

Bell, S. and Hindmoor, A. (2009). *Rethinking Governance: The Centrality of the State in Modern Society*, Melbourne: Cambridge University Press.

Belot, H. and Mannheim, M. (2016). Consultants boom, bureaucrats bust: the hidden cost of public service cuts, *The Canberra Times*, 26 August. Retrieved from http://www.canberratimes.com .au/national/public-service/consultants-boom-bureaucrats-bust-the-hidden-cost-of-public-service-cuts-20160825-gr1mi9.html

Blacher, Y. (2012). Dealing with ministerial advisers: a practical guide for public servants, *The Conversation*, 15 October. Retrieved from http://theconversation.com/dealing-with-ministerial-advisers-a-practical-guide-for-public-servants-10031

Nethercote, J.R. (2015). *Australian experience of public sector reform*. Australian Public Service Commission. Retrieved from http://www.apsc.gov.au/publications-and-media/archive/publica tions-archive/history-of-reform

Peters, B.G. (1989). *The Politics of Bureaucracy*, 3rd edn, New York: Longman.

Whelan, J. (2011). *The state of the Australian Public Service: an alternative report*. Centre for Policy Development. Retrieved from https://cpd.org.au/wp-content/uploads/2011/08/CPD_ OP12_2011_State_of_APS_Whelan.pdf

REFERENCES

ABS. (2015). 6291.0.55.003: Labour force, Australia, detailed, quarterly, Nov 2015. URL: http://www .abs.gov.au/AUSSTATS/abs@.nsf/Previousproducts/6291.0.55.003Main Features 10 Nov 2015

ABS. (2016a). 6248.0.55.002: Employment and earnings, public sector, Australia, 2015–16. URL: http://www.abs.gov.au/ausstats/abs@.nsf/mf/6248.0.55.002

ABS. (2016b). 8146.0: Household use of information technology, Australia, 2014–15, 18 February. URL: http://www.abs.gov.au/ausstats/abs@.nsf/mf/8146.0

Althaus, C., Bridgman, P. and Davis, G. (2013). *The Australian Policy Handbook*, 5th edn, Crows Nest, NSW: Allen & Unwin.

Australian Public Service Commission. (2016). APS Values. URL: http://www.apsc.gov.au/working-in-the-aps/your-rights-and-responsibilities-as-an-aps-employee/aps-values

Bell, S. and Hindmoor, A. (2009). *Rethinking Governance: The Centrality of the State in Modern Society*, Melbourne: Cambridge University Press.

Bevir, M. (2009). *Key Concepts in Governance*, Los Angeles; London: Sage.

Bevir, M. (2010). *Encyclopedia of Political Theory*, Thousand Oaks, Calif.: Sage Publications.

Bevir, M. (2013). *Governance: A Very Short Introduction*, 1st edn, Oxford: Oxford University Press.

Bozeman, B. (2000). *Bureaucracy and Red Tape*, Upper Saddle River, New Jersey: Prentice Hall.

Bridgman, P. and Davis, G. (2000). *Australian Policy Handbook*, 2nd edn, St Leonards, NSW: Allen & Unwin.

Buchanan, J.M. and Tullock, G. (1965). *The Calculus of Consent: Logical Foundations of Constitutional Democracy*, Ann Arbor, Mich.: University of Michigan Press.

Carr, A. (2015). The cost of a bloated bureaucracy, *The Australian*. Retrieved from http://www.theaustralian.com.au/business/business-spectator/the-cost-of-a-bloated-bureaucracy/news-story/81859a3c1e89f18f00ddbce75140a4f8

Considine, M. (1994). *Public Policy: A Critical Approach*, South Melbourne: Macmillan Education Australia.

Creighton, A. (2014). How many staff members does it take to change the country? *The Australian*. Retrieved from http://www.theaustralian.com.au/business/opinion/how-many-staff-members-does-it-take-to-change-the-country/news-story/e4d9bf4c90d73a521648d57f1c18747a

Creighton, A. (2017). Paying consultants to do public servants' jobs is waste of money, *The Australian*. Retrieved from http://www.theaustralian.com.au/business/opinion/adam-creighton/paying-consultants-to-do-public-servants-jobs-is-waste-of-money/news-story/64a4c794e7fac3aa02242999e89158a3

Crooks, P. and Parsons, T.H. (2016). *Empires and Bureaucracy in World History: From Late Antiquity to the Twentieth Century*, Cambridge: Cambridge University Press.

Dye, T.R. (1972). *Understanding Public Policy*, Englewood Cliffs, N.J.: Prentice-Hall.

Etzioni-Halevy, E. (2010). *Bureaucracy and Democracy: A Political Dilemma*, 3rd edn, Abingdon, Oxon; New York: Routledge.

Everett, S. (2003). The policy cycle: Democratic process or rational paradigm revisited? *Australian Journal of Public Administration*, **62**(2), 56–70.

Glenn, R. (2017). *Centrelink's automated debt raising and recovery system: a report about the Department of Human Services' online compliance intervention system for debt raising and recovery*. Retrieved from http://www.ombudsman.gov.au/__data/assets/pdf_file/0022/43528/Report-Centrelinks-automated-debt-raising-and-recovery-system-April-2017.pdf

Hamilton, P. (2015). Australian Public Service staffing and efficiencies: Budget Review 2015–16 Index. Retrieved from http://www.aph.gov.au/About_Parliament/Parliamentary_Departments/Parliamentary_Library/pubs/rp/BudgetReview201516/APS

Hawke, R. (1987). Prime Minister: For media [Press release]. Retrieved from http://pmtranscripts.pmc.gov.au/release/transcript-7197

Hood, C.C. (1991). A public management for all seasons? *Public Administration*, **69**(1), 3–19.

Keynes, J.M. (1957). *The General Theory of Employment, Interest, and Money*, London; New York: Macmillan; St. Martin's.

Lerner, D. and Lasswell, H. D. (1951). *The Policy Sciences: Recent Developments in Scope and Method*, Stanford: Stanford University Press.

Lindquist, E. and Tiernan, A. (2012). The Australian Public Service and policy advising: Meeting the challenges of 21st century governance. *The Australian Journal of Public Administration*, **70**(4), 437–50.

Mitzman, A. (1970). *The Iron Cage: An Historical Interpretation of Max Weber*, New York: Knopf.

National Commission of Audit (2014). Towards responsible government: the report of the National Commission of Audit phase one. URL: http://www.ncoa.gov.au/report/docs/phase_one_report.pdf

Ng, Y.F. (2016). *Ministerial Advisers in Australia: The Modern Legal Context*, Sydney: The Federation Press.

O'Flynn, J. (2014). Commission of Audit report released: experts respond, *The Conversation*, 1 May. Retrieved from http://theconversation.com/commission-of-audit-report-released-experts-respond-26177

Osborne, D. and Gaebler, T. (1992). *Reinventing Government: How the Entrepreneurial Spirit is Transforming the Public Sector*, Reading, Mass.: Addison-Wesley Pub. Co.

Pal, L.A. (1992). *Public Policy Analysis: An Introduction*, 2nd edn, Scarborough, Ont.: Nelson Canada.

Peters, B.G. (1989). *The Politics of Bureaucracy*, 3rd edn, New York: Longman.

Pusey, M. (1991). *Economic Rationalism in Canberra: A Nation-building State Changes Its Mind*, Melbourne: Cambridge University Press.

Rhodes, R.A.W. (1994). The hollowing out of the state: The changing nature of the public service in Britain. *The Political Quarterly*, **65**(2), 138–51.

Rhodes, R.A.W. (2017). *Network Governance and the Differentiated Polity: Selected Essays, Volume 1*, Oxford: Oxford University Press.

Sawer, M. (1982). *Australia and the New Right*, Sydney: Allen & Unwin.

Spann, R.N. (1959). *Public Administration in Australia*, Sydney: Govt. Printer.

The Canberra Times. (1926). Federation – 25 years' achievements reviewed: Commonwealth problems, *The Canberra Times*, p. 8.

The Commonwealth of Australia. (2017). Budget papers 2016–2017, Budget Paper No. 4, Part 2: staffing of agencies. URL: http://www.budget.gov.au/2016–17/content/bp4/html/09_staff.htm

The Treasury. Our department. URL: http://www.treasury.gov.au/the-department/about-treasury

Towell, N. (2015). Australian Public Service spends $10 billion on consultants. Retrieved from http://www.canberratimes.com.au/national/public-service/australian-public-service-spends-10b-on-consultants-20151214-gln4lj.html

United Nations Development Programme. (1997). *Governance for sustainable human development*. URL: http://www.pogar.org/publications/other/undp/governance/undppolicydoc97-e.pdf

Ward, I. and Stewart, R.G. (2010). *Politics One*, 4th edn, South Yarra: Palgrave Macmillan.

Weber, M. and Andreski, S. (1983). *Max Weber on Capitalism, Bureaucracy and Religion: A Selection of Texts*, London: Allen & Unwin.

Weber, M., Gerth, H. and Mills, C.W. (1998). *From Max Weber: Essays in Sociology*, Abingdon: Routledge.

Wheelan, C.J. (2011). *Introduction to Public Policy*, 1st edn, New York: W. W. Norton & Co.

Whelan, J. (2011). The state of the Australian Public Service: An alternative report. Retrieved from https://cpd.org.au/wp-content/uploads/2011/08/CPD_OP12_2011_State_of_APS_Whelan.pdf

World Bank Group. (2016). *World Development Report 2016: Digital Dividends*, Washington, D.C.: International Bank for Reconstruction and Development.

World Bank Group. (2017). Worldwide governance indicators. URL: http://info.worldbank.org/governance/wgi/#reports

CHAPTER 7

ELECTIONS, THE ELECTORAL SYSTEM AND THE AUSTRALIAN VOTER

LEARNING OBJECTIVES

After reading this chapter, you should be able to:

1. Understand the history of elections in Australia

2. Describe the key electoral elements of Australian democracy

3. Identify the basic differences between state and Commonwealth electoral systems

4. Explain the context for Australian electoral experimentation

INTRODUCTION

As a western, liberal democracy, and one that operates with a **Westminster system**, Australia has periodic elections at all three levels of government. Elections in and of themselves do not guarantee a democracy, but they are certainly seen as a key element, without which any regime will have a hard time calling itself a democracy. While democracies can conceivably have forms of decision-making other than elections (through such mechanisms as choosing by lot or with deliberative processes), elections as we know them are certainly the easiest way to gauge opinion on who should head the formal administration of the state. There are a number of key elements to democratic elections, notably that there are a range of candidates and parties; that a maximum number of people can vote (and can vote freely); that there are a wide range of policies being debated in the public arena; and, that there is a potential for a change in government. These elements are often considered the baseline requirements for a democratic election.

We should, of course, also remember that Australia is firstly a constitutional monarchy. This means that the Head of State (which in some other systems would be a president) is the Queen of England, styled as 'the Queen of Australia'. This is a historical position, and the last effort to change the situation, in 1999, failed to gain a majority of votes to change the Constitution. So, we must first acknowledge that the Head of State is not elected. However, as discussed in Chapter 4, the Queen as Head of State exercises no real power. Her representative, the Governor-General, is the one who signs and receives the writ to call an election, heads the Federal Executive Council, and provides Royal Assent to Acts, but still only acts primarily in a ceremonial role.

Thus, when we talk of elections in Australia, we are talking about the elections for the Commonwealth Parliament in Canberra, the state and territory parliaments, and at a local level for the councils and shires. Each of these jurisdictions has an elected body overseeing the administration of government (the operations of the various parliaments being covered in Chapter 3). For each of these elected bodies there must therefore also be elections. This chapter will explore the nature of those elections, and some of the challenges facing the systems we use.

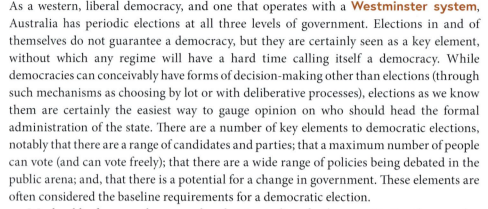

AUTHOR
PANEL

AUSTRALIAN ELECTORAL SYSTEMS

WHO GETS TO VOTE?

The first thing we need to do, before an election is held, is determine who can vote. At the time of the first General Election those who had the right to vote (known as the '**franchise**') were all men over the age of 21 and women over 21 in South Australia and Western Australia. The peculiarity of women being able to vote in the Commonwealth election of 1901 only in these two states was because the Constitution deferred to state law in this respect, and only these two states had enfranchised women (Parliament of Australia 2009). This situation changed with the passing of the Commonwealth Franchise Act in 1902, with the franchise being granted to all women for Commonwealth elections. By 1908 all jurisdictions had passed similar laws and women could vote in all Australian states and territories, although it would be many years before a woman was elected to the federal parliament.

Figure 7.1 The Womanhood Suffrage League of NSW
Source: Wikimedia Commons, State Library of New South Wales

While women gained the vote across Australia by 1908, this was not the case in the United Kingdom nor the United States. The UK did not pass amendments granting the right to vote for women until 1918, and the US Nineteenth Amendment was not ratified until 1920, after a long process at the state level, with many states providing then revoking the right of women through the 19th century. The Nineteenth Amendment itself failed at the first attempt to pass it in 1918 by two votes, but the momentum continued to the eventual ratification in 1920.

The situation for Indigenous people was worse in Australia, however, as even though some Aboriginal people had the right to vote in 1901 (through having the right to vote in their state), this was terminated by the 1902 Act. Indigenous people in the United States gained the vote in 1924 (when they were granted citizenship), but Aboriginal Australians did not receive the vote until 1962, when amendments were finally passed to the *Commonwealth Electoral Act 1918*, which had replaced the *Commonwealth Franchise Act 1902*. This was somewhat analogous to the situation of First Nations people in Canada, who could vote from 1867, but only if they gave up any treaty rights and Indian status – essentially becoming assimilated into the white population.

But does the franchise extend to everyone, including people convicted of crimes? The question around whether prisoners in jails should have the right to vote is a vexed one. Arguments range from the need to provide for universal suffrage for all people, irrespective of their status as people who are part of a society, to one of restricted franchise, based on the notion that only citizens can vote, and even then only citizens who meet certain criteria (Orr 2011). Thus while some would argue for the voting age to be lowered to 16, for prisoners to have the vote, and even the accepted notion that a person should only be able to exercise one vote ('**one vote, one value**'), the counter arguments exist and at various times are debated.

one vote, one value: Where a person's vote is equal to another. This means that within a given state or nation all electorates are as close as possible to having the same number of electors. Where this is not the case this is called 'malapportionment'.

This issue of voting rights for prisoners was last argued in the High Court when the Howard Government attempted to restrict the right to vote for prisoners to those serving sentences for crimes that had a maximum sentence of one year or more. This would have been a change to the previous three-year maximum sentence. In *Vicki Lee Roach v Electoral Commissioner and Commonwealth of Australia* (2007) HCA 43, the High Court ruled that the change was unconstitutional, but also significantly did not rule on the existing restriction. The case for 16 year olds to vote has been raised previously in various examinations of the conduct of elections (and during inquiries into electoral reform such as *Electoral Distribution Repeal Bill 2001* and the *Electoral Amendment Bill 2001 (Electoral Reform Bills) – Report 8* by the Western Australian Legislative Council (Legislative Council 2001, 163–4), but at present 16 and 17-year-old people may only pre-register to vote (and then be able to vote as soon as they turn 18). This momentarily became an issue again during the 2017 national survey on same-sex marriage, when the original directions for the survey to allow 16 and 17-year-old people on the roll to take part, required some rapid changes by government ministers (Koziol and Whitbourn 2017).

The right to vote in elections therefore remains a vexed question, and not just in Australia. While the right to vote is covered by Article 25 of the International Covenant on Civil and Political Rights (General Assembly of the United Nations 1948) this does not mean that its application is universal. Just as other human rights can be abridged, so to can the right to vote. Nonetheless, for those who do have that right to vote, as do the vast majority of Australian citizens over the age of 18, this is exercised in elections. This chapter will therefore explore these elections and election systems in use in Australia.

STRUCTURE AND VARIATION IN AUSTRALIA

To begin with, we need to recognise that Australia has a variety of electoral systems – in fact there are nine electoral systems. This is one for each of the states, the two territories and the Commonwealth. Having said that, it's not as if each system is entirely different, as each of the systems shares some common features. However, there is considerable difference in the structures and operation of each of the systems used, to the extent that they can appear quite dissimilar.

We also need to distinguish between two important system features used in Australia – the use of both **proportional** and single member **preferential** voting to elect members of parliament (MPs) to seats in parliament. The first, proportional, describes the system used in most of the states' (NSW, SA, Victoria, WA) upper houses and the Commonwealth Senate, as well as the Tasmanian lower house and the Australian Capital Territory Assembly. The second describes the system used in most of the lower houses (NSW, NT, Queensland, SA, Victoria, WA), the Tasmanian upper house and the Commonwealth House of Representatives. We then have to remember that Queensland and the two territories have no upper houses. If we were then to consider local council elections, we would have to consider even further variation. So already we can see that there are very mixed and different electoral systems being used across Australia.

You might ask why this is the case, and wouldn't it be easier to simply legislate for just one system? Indeed, it would be easier to simply have one system in place, except that electoral systems are designed for more than just electing someone to sit in a parliament. For that we have to consider what the purpose of the electoral system actually is. If we

VIDEO

SHORT-ANSWER QUESTIONS

proportional: A system of voting where multiple members of parliament (MPs) are elected for the same electorate, and the number of MPs a party or group wins is based on the party's share of the vote. Thus, a party getting 40% of the vote would get 40% of the seats. The way this is determined depends on how many MPs are to be elected, but the intent is to more clearly represent voters as an aggregate.

preferential: A system of voting where voters number a square against each candidate in the order of their preference for the candidates or parties contesting the election. Votes are then counted in the order they are numbered until one is declared the winner.

TABLE 7.1 STATE AND COMMONWEALTH HOUSES COMPARED

STATE/COMMONWEALTH	LOWER HOUSE	UPPER HOUSE
Commonwealth	Single Member	Proportional
Australian Capital Territory	Proportional	[no house]
New South Wales	Single Member	Proportional
Northern Territory	Single Member	[no house]
Queensland	Single Member	[no house]
South Australia	Single Member	Proportional
Tasmania	Proportional	Single Member
Victoria	Single Member	Proportional
Western Australia	Single Member	Proportional

are to think about the purpose of the system, we might want equally to think about the purpose of democratic systems more broadly; but for now we will restrict ourselves to discussing how do the Australian set of systems operate and why they were chosen.

One last point before we discuss the electoral systems for the Commonwealth and states. Australia has, since 1926, had **compulsory voting**. This means that it is compulsory to register to vote once a citizen turns 18, and then it is compulsory to cast a vote at elections. This is relatively unique around the globe, with only six countries having compulsory voting. Also, votes are cast at polling places in a polling booth. These are really just small booths where a person can mark their ballot paper in favour of particular candidates in secret, before placing their ballot paper in the ballot box. Now, most countries have secret voting, but this was once called 'the Australian ballot' – in that it was only done in Australia – because voting was done openly in town halls and in caucuses, or by handing a pre-printed ballot paper to the election official. A person's vote might then be known – and voters could be intimidated into not attending or not voting. The first places to use the secret ballot were the then-colonies of Victoria and South Australia, from 1856 onwards, with other states following suit shortly after, and the secret ballot was enshrined in the Australian Constitution.

Yet we might also consider that 'compulsory voting' is not really compulsory – you have to attend and have your name marked off, but there is actually nothing stopping you from not marking the ballot paper and voting informally. This seeming contradiction has been addressed by the Australian Electoral Commission, but it still remains the case that as the ballot is secret it is not possible to physically ensure a correct vote is made (Evans 2006). This hasn't stopped people advocating at times not to vote correctly, arguing that a compulsion to vote is undemocratic.

The Commonwealth

The Commonwealth electoral system is defined in the Australian Constitution, in so far as there are seats allocated to both the House of Representatives and the Senate. The designation of certain numbers of seats to each of the states for the House of Representatives is based on population, the number of seats representing the proportion of the population that the state has compared to the whole of Australia. There is an exception that states are not to have fewer than five seats, which is applied to Tasmania due to its continued small

compulsory voting: In Australia, this refers to the requirement to first register to vote once you are 18 years old and then, having registered, to vote in all elections after that. Only about 10 per cent of countries globally have compulsory voting.

RESEARCH QUESTIONS

population, but other than that the calculation is applied after every election to check if changes need to be made. The reservation of five seats does not apply to the territories, but they are allocated seats on a population basis. Originally there were 75 seats in the House of Representatives, but this has been expanded to the current 150 seats. The Senate, on the other hand, has a set number of Senators per state, irrespective of the state's population. The territories are allocated two Senators each as they are not classed as states, so do not enjoy the full allocation of Senators. Currently there are 76 Senators, 12 from each state, and 2 each from the two territories.

The way each seat is elected, however, differs between the House of Representatives and the Senate. The House of Representatives seats return one member each – that is, one person represents the electorate. The electorates themselves are divided such that each seat has roughly the same number of people in it, while respecting the state boundaries. The exception is, of course, Tasmania, which retains five House of Representatives seats irrespective of the population of the state. It therefore takes fewer individual votes to elect a person in Tasmania than in other states. Each registered elector gets a single vote and is required to cast that vote – although this extends only as far as attending the polling place and placing the ballot paper into a ballot box, as the vote is secret and so what exactly a person marks on their ballot paper is known only to that individual.

Commonwealth elections are held according to the Constitution, which stipulates that House of Representatives elections must be held three years after the first sitting of the last parliament. It does not specify a minimum time, but equally it takes time to organise, so this has to be taken into account. The Senate has a more fixed timetable, with Senators being elected for six years, with a fixed starting date (1 July) for terms, although the terms themselves depend on whether an election is held before or after that date. There is nothing to say that House of Representatives and Senate elections have to be held at the same time – and indeed up until the 1970s were often not – but given the cost of elections it has been deemed prudent to do so. The timing of an election is actually governed by the government of the day, and so does not fall on a specific date like in the US. The prime minister sets in train the election by visiting the Governor-General and asking for parliament to be dissolved. The Governor-General then issues the writs for the election, which authorises the Australian Election Commission (AEC) to conduct an election. Elections can then potentially be called quite quickly if a government wishes (often called a 'snap election'). Once an election is called, the AEC has to run to a set timetable.

In the election itself, the requirement for voters in House of Representatives elections is to number all the boxes opposite candidate names in ascending order (1, 2, 3, 4 etc), until all the boxes are filled, starting with a '1' next to the most preferred candidate. This is where the name 'preferential voting' comes from, and it affects the way a vote is counted. Essentially, the candidate with the least number of 1s next to their name is eliminated, and the vote transfers to the candidate marked next (i.e. with a '2') on the ballot paper. If there are still three or more candidates in the count, the same process is used again, with the candidate with the least total votes being eliminated, and their votes being transferred – in the order the voter has marked the ballot paper – to the remaining candidates. This continues, with votes being allocated from eliminated candidates, until only two candidates are left and the one with the most votes is declared elected.

Counting the vote

When the Australian Electoral Commission (AEC) conducts an election, it does so using a set of rules and regulations, and it publishes the processes it uses along with the results. The first thing that occurs on election day is that the doors of the polling place are closed at 6pm sharp. There are no more voters allowed into a polling place after 6pm, although those people inside may still cast their vote before leaving. Representatives of candidates may also be present (although not the candidates themselves), and these people are called 'scrutineers'. Scrutineers can observe, challenge ballot papers or process where they think an error has occurred, but cannot under any circumstances touch the ballot papers.

Once the doors are shut and the last voter has left, polling officials are able to begin their job for the night, which consists of three key tasks:

- count all the House of Representatives first preferences
- conduct a two-candidate-preferred count for House of Representatives
- count all the Senate first preferences.

The only votes counted here are the votes cast on the day for the electorate in which the polling place sits.

THE PROCESS

1. The polling officials open and empty the House of Representatives ballot boxes. Inside are the green ballot papers used for the House of Representatives, and these are all emptied out (usually onto tables). They are sorted into separate piles, with the number '1' votes (first preferences) for each candidate put together and counted. Once this is done the result is phoned through to the polling official for the whole electorate and the result appears on the AEC Tally Room site.

2. The same process is conducted, but with there only being two piles of candidates predetermined by the AEC as the likely winners – which is usually the ALP or one of Liberal or National parties – with the votes sorted by who has the lowest number marked on the ballot paper (the likely winner of the contest). This is also phoned through to the Tally Room. This is not the same as the 'two-party-preferred' vote sometimes referred to, as that is solely between the ALP and LNP – the two-candidate-preferred count may have (as in the seat of Melbourne) the contest between the ALP and Greens.

3. Finally, the Senate first preferences are counted and phoned through.

This completes the activity on the night, and often a good idea of who has won will emerge. Nonetheless, this is not the end: the ballot papers are next transported to the divisional office, where the votes are checked again, before heading into a central counting centre (usually in a warehouse) and the process is conducted in full, with all preferences being distributed for the House of Representatives, and all preferences being entered into computers for the Senate. The Senate counting can take up to two weeks to finalise, but the entering of the votes means that the process is both quicker and more accurate.

For further information, visit the AEC website: www.aec.gov.au

two-party-preferred: A system of representing the vote after it is counted that allocates all votes to the two major parties (the ALP and the Liberal/National Party Coalition). This may be different to the 'two-candidate-preferred' vote, which represents the final result in an electorate (i.e. the winner and the last person left who has not been elected).

QUESTION

How much did you know about the counting of the vote before reading this section? Were you surprised by its complexity?

proportional preferential: A system of voting where multiple members of parliament (MPs) are elected for the same electorate but where the elector allocates a preference for candidates, and that preference determines in what order MPs may be elected.

The Senate elects half of its Senators at any one time, the exception being a double dissolution when all seats are declared vacant and elected as one lot. The state in which the Senate seats are elected is considered to be one electorate. Again, each registered voter has one vote, and marks the ballot paper preferentially, but when the votes are counted six people are to be elected. The total number of votes cast is divided by seven (the number of seats to be elected (6) + 1). The resulting number is the quota, which is the number of votes that must be reached to be elected. Counting is considerably more complicated than in the House of Representatives, but the seats won will mostly end up being more proportional to the actual percentage of votes that a candidate or group of candidates receives (Farrell and McAllister 2003). If, as in many European countries, the voter just has to mark a '1' for the group or party of their choice this form of voting is called proportional voting, but in Australia, where we allocate preferences, it is '**proportional preferential**' voting.

The states and territories

States each have their own systems for electing MPs, with considerable variation in counting, optional or compulsory preference distribution, multi- or single-member electorates, and fixed or variable timing of elections. Table 7.2 shows the distribution of seats and electorates between the various Legislative Assemblies and Legislative Councils. One further difference that might be noted here is the system of counting the votes. The description above for the House of Representatives holds true for those states with single member electorates, although unlike the Commonwealth, not all states use compulsory preferential voting. In New South Wales from 1981, and in Queensland from 1992 to 2016, the marking of preferences for candidates past '1' is optional. In Tasmania and the Australian Capital Territory, five preferences need to be marked for a vote to be valid, but no more if an elector does not wish to.

TABLE 7.2 SEATS, ELECTORATES AND TERMS

| STATE OR TERRITORY | ASSEMBLY | | | COUNCIL | TERMS | |
	SEATS	ELECTORATES	YEARS	SEATS	ELECTORATES	YEARS
Australian Capital Territory	25	5	4	[no house]	25	5
New South Wales	93	93	4	42	1*	8
Northern Territory	25	25	4	[no house]		
Queensland	93	93	3	[no house]		
South Australia	47	47	4	22	1*	8
Tasmania	25	5	4	15	15	6
Victoria	88	88	4	40	8	4
Western Australia	59	59	4	36	6	4

* Both South Australia and New South Wales elections for the Legislative Councils are every four years, with half the Council elected at each election. Both Councils are whole-of-state electorates.

The method of counting the votes also varies. While single-member electorates are quite straightforward, multi-member electorates pose some problems. The Western Australian Legislative Council uses a complicated 'Weighted Inclusive Gregory' method (see Miragliotta 2002), while the Tasmanian and the Australian Capital Territory Legislative Assemblies use the 'Hare-Clark' method. The South Australian Legislative

Council and the Commonwealth Senate use identical systems for allocating votes, while the Victorian and Western Australian Legislative Councils still use Group Voting Tickets (abolished in the Senate in 2016 and South Australia in 2017). The use of Group Voting Tickets is a source of quite a bit of argument, focused on whether you should force people to number an increasingly large number of candidate boxes, or allow the party to do this. The argument goes 'Does the voter choose or does the party?'

This maze of variation might seem like a very confusing way to run elections. **'First-past-the-post'** elections (where electors only have to mark a 1 on the ballot paper, and the person with the most votes wins) in the UK and the USA are very easy to administer and count, so the question might be asked, why don't we use these kinds of systems? Simply put, electoral administrators and state parliaments (when not looking for particular political advantage) have tended to consider which system would be the fairest to use to properly represent the wishes of electors. This is an important point to understand as representation is key to the kinds of systems you might wish to use. This explains why Andrew Inglis Clark, Tasmanian barrister, Attorney-General, and principal author of the Australian Constitution, modified an earlier proportional system designed by Sir Thomas Hare to come up with the eponymous Hare-Clark system in the late 19th century. The aim of this method of counting votes was to provide a fair system of electing members of parliament. That this system of electing MPs isn't used more widely has as much to do with what we might want or expect from our MPs, as it does about the fairness of the system.

Today we mostly see MPs as representing constituents in an electorate, based on a geographical area. This owes a considerable amount to the Westminster system of government, and it also relies on a perceived connection between people who live in a place being directly represented in parliament by a single person. Yet it is entirely possible for a system to be conceived that represents particular groups of people *not* based on geography but on another basis – perhaps class, ethnicity or religion. These **social cleavages** are at least partly the basis of many European political parties that are represented in parliaments through proportional systems.

first-past-the-post: A system of voting (also called 'plurality voting') where the person with most first preference votes wins the election, even if they did not win 50% of all votes.

Social cleavages: Division in society that reflects core divisions, such as ethnicity, class, language and religion/belief. This is different from ideologies based on particular guiding principles.

VIDEO
SHORT-ANSWER QUESTIONS
REFLECTION QUESTIONS

AUSTRALIAN ELECTIONS

The question of representation is important when we come to view the post-Second World War stability in the Australian political system. What we might otherwise take for granted – stable elections, mostly two parties battling it out, with occasional other parties winning seats – was not the norm prior to 1945. In the colonial period, MPs were elected to represent particular groups of people, originally landed and male. As the franchise grew, so did the demands for wider representation. By the time of Federation in 1901, the Australian Labor Party (ALP) had been formed and could win seats. It had 'the Pledge' where members of the party pledged to follow the party's policies irrespective of their own feelings, on pain of losing the endorsement of the party, and thus potentially their seat in parliament. The question of larger, national issues, which motivated democracy campaigners and theorists such as Edmund Burke were less the concern of the ordinary ALP MP as were issues of the wages and conditions of the ordinary worker (McKinlay 1981, 20).

On the other side of the political divide there were a variety of MPs and groups. In the Colonial period, these were often grouped around individuals, but could equally represent themselves as 'Ministerialists' or 'Nationalists', to demonstrate what they thought should be the key issues of representation. In the first federal parliaments, the two key non-Labor groupings were the 'Free Traders' and 'Protectionists', who argued over trade policy. These were not hard and fast parties, however, with people moving in and out of these and other groupings. The 1909 formation of the first Liberal Party (following the earlier 'Fusion' group) brought together a core of these people around free trade, with protectionists drifting towards the ALP, and also to the Country Party, formed in 1919 (Weller and Fleming 2003).

The First World War brought its own problems with the ALP Prime Minister of the day, Fisher, arguing for conscription. The defeat of conscription plebiscites led to the first split in the ALP, and the formation of a **coalition** of parties to take Government. This coalition collapsed in 1928 with the defeat of the Bruce government, and the first instance of a Prime Minister (Stanley Bruce) losing his seat – the second was John Howard in 2007. The short-lived Scullin government allowed a number of disillusioned ALP MPs and the remains of the previous conservative coalition to coalesce into the United Australia Party, with dissident ALP MP Joseph Lyons as Prime Minister. This new formation lasted up to 1941, when, due to the rejection of the United Australia Party's budget in the House, Labor was returned to the ministerial benches under John Curtin.

coalition: A group of two or more parties who agree to a common leader and platform for government. Coalitions may be formed prior to or after elections, but when in Government all MPs of the parties agree to be bound by decisions of the Cabinet.

POST-WAR STABILITY, CONTEMPORARY VOLATILITY?

The Second World War marked a turning point in the Australian political culture. Sir Robert Menzies brought the many disparate right of centre groupings together again as the second Liberal Party, building 'a great movement of Liberal deliverance in Australia' (Brett 2003, 17), a party which has continued to flourish through to today. Out of government after the 1949 federal election, the ALP continued on, only to split again in 1955 over the perceived internal threat from the Communist Party, yet still remained the dominant left of centre party.

Electoral stability under the Liberal–Country Party coalition lasted from the 1949 election through to the election of Gough Whitlam in 1972. This period covered the formation of the Democratic Labor Party following the 1955 split in the ALP, much of the Vietnam War, and a long period of economic prosperity. The oil crisis of 1974 ended the long period of post-war economic growth, and the formation of the Australian Democrats in 1977, from dissident Liberals allying with minor parties, ended the effective two-party duopoly. Yet the Australian post-Second World War electoral system is still often characterised as a 'two-party' system, as the two dominant groupings have proved the only two political groupings governing Australia consistently.

Even while the history of Australian governments, portrayed as between the Liberal and Labor parties, is seen as being about a stable two-party system, we equally have to keep in mind that most governments in Australian history have been coalitions of two or more parties. While the Liberal Party and Country Party (later National Party) were often seen as one grouping, the two parties have remained separate entities, in organisational terms, in most states.

What we might then consider is that the period from the mid-1990s to today has seen a rapid and destabilising growth in parties of the left, centre and right, each vying for some form of electoral and political relevance. The former stability of the party system

TABLE 7.3 ELECTION RESULTS 1946–2016

ELECTION	ALP	COALITION	FORMED GOVT
28.09.46	54.1	45.9	ALP
10.12.49	49	51	Coalition
28.04.51	49.3	50.7	Coalition
29.05.54	50.7	49.3	Coalition
10.12.55	45.8	54.2	Coalition
22.11.58	45.9	54.1	Coalition
09.12.61	50.5	49.5	Coalition
30.11.63	47.4	52.6	Coalition
26.11.66	43.1	56.9	Coalition
25.10.69	50.2	49.8	Coalition
02.12.72	52.7	47.3	ALP
18.05.74	51.7	48.3	ALP
13.12.75	44.3	55.7	Coalition
10.12.77	45.4	54.6	Coalition
18.10.80	49.6	50.4	Coalition
05.03.83	53.23	46.77	ALP
01.12.84	51.77	48.23	ALP
11.07.87	50.83	49.17	ALP
24.03.90	49.9	50.1	ALP
13.03.93	51.44	48.56	ALP
02.03.96	46.37	53.63	Coalition
03.10.98	50.98	49.02	Coalition
10.11.01	49.05	50.95	Coalition
09.10.04	47.26	52.74	Coalition
24.11.07	52.7	47.3	ALP
21.08.10	50.12	49.88	ALP
07.09.13	46.51	53.49	Coalition
02.07.16	49.64	50.36	Coalition

Source: Results drawn from AEC (2017)

has shifted in the period leading up to the 2016 federal election, although signs since then suggest that the two-party system is alive and well and not in immediate danger of breaking down. This has been aided in part by the attempts of various state and federal governments limiting the impact of minor parties (although not directly eliminating them) upon the operation of parliaments. What is equally important to note is that the major parties are still capable of creating the conditions, either in government or in opposition, of large and significant wins in elections.

VIDEO
REFLECTION
QUESTIONS

THE DEVELOPMENT AND ROLE OF POLITICAL PARTIES

Parties are seen by most Australians as key to the functioning of parliaments, and indeed politics in general. That said, they are also widely despised, or at least distrusted, by the same population. The many and widespread scandals and mis-steps by prime ministers and MPs alike lead citizens to consider politicians and their parties fairly lowly, with trust in MPs being similar to talk-back radio announcers, journalists and union leaders, all trusted by between 14–17 per cent of Australians. In contrast, nurses are trusted by 94 per cent of Australians, but used-car salespeople by just 4 per cent (Roy Morgan 2017). Yet political parties have not only survived, they have proliferated, as vehicles for individuals and groups, and essential to political campaigning.

Dean Jaensch (1989) once suggested that 'Politics in Australia is party politics'. This sums up the idea that parties are intrinsically linked to the functioning of both parliamentary politics and the functioning of government. However, while we might take political parties for granted, they were not always revered organisations. In the early debates about the Constitution they were considered but also disregarded. That the Labor Party had formed and was operating at the time of the formation of the Commonwealth of Australia, and that the UK had a long history of essentially 'cadre' parties, did not endear them to the original framers of the Constitution. As Dahl (1998, 86) notes, early political 'factions' were 'generally viewed as dangerous, divisive, subversive of public order and stability, and injurious to the public good'. This extended to them not even being included within the Constitution – they were essentially seen as private organisations, and not key to the functioning of parliament or government.

We should then consider the evolution of parties in Australia to be a pragmatic development, as much to do with the organisation of class and social interests as with the organisation of parliament and elections. We can see this in the development of political parties across Europe and in other liberal democracies. Parties had their origins in bodies seen as key elements in organising not just political but also social life – as Duverger notes (1959), many organisations are responsible for the birth of parties, including philosophical, religious, labour groups and clubs. Once potentially a normalised part of social life, many now see them as something of a necessary evil, tolerated as part of the operation of parliamentary politics, declining in social power and importance, yet still seen as a key institution to manage an increasingly complex political problem (Rose 2014). We might say that this is an interesting time in the life of parties.

One point that we must consider is the changing nature of what we consider a political party to be. There is a considerable number of descriptions of what parties are, or do, from Edmund Burke's (1770) description of them being 'a body of men united, for promoting by their joint endeavours the national interest, upon some particular principle in which they are all agreed', through to Joseph Schumpeter (1942/2013), who in dismissing Burke's philosophical description instead suggested a more pragmatic purpose for a party, being 'a group whose members propose to act in concert in the competitive struggle for political power', to Giovanni Sartori (1976, 64), 'a party is any political group that presents at elections, and is capable of placing through elections, candidates for public office'. Between these descriptions there are a myriad more, some more descriptive than others. However,

Figure 7.2 Edmund Burke

one that might be most suitable in describing Australian parties is from Rodney Smith: 'political parties are organisations which aim to influence public policy in favour of an ideology or set of interests, primarily by attempting to gain control of public office' (1997).

Political parties

SPOTLIGHT

As we have already noted there are many definitions of what a political party is or what it should do. Some more are listed below:

- Robert Michels (1911/1968): 'The modern party is a fighting organisation in the political sense of the term, and as such must conform to the laws of tactics.'

- Max Weber: 'Parties live in a house of "power", their action is oriented toward the acquisition of social "power", that is to say toward influencing communal action no matter what its content may be' cited in Gerth and Mills 1948.

- John Aldrich (1995): 'Political parties can be seen as coalitions of elites to capture and use political office. [But] a political party is more than a coalition. A political party is an institutionalized coalition, one that has adopted rules, norms and procedures.'

One of the key elements most theorists agree on is that parties have to have members, and that those members have to be active for the party to be able to get elected. Although some parties rely on charismatic figures to lead them (think of Nick Xenophon or Pauline Hanson), most parties still need members to be active, distribute material and campaign for elections. This leads us to realise that party members are important to the electoral success of political parties.

QUESTION

Thinking about the various definitions provided here (and any you can think of), how important do you think party members are to electoral success?

Dependent on your answer to what a political party is, some further questions exist regarding the party's nature, structure and purpose. We might, for instance, ask if parties need to be united, which depends on whether to gain government and divide the parliamentary spoils requires strict discipline. The US example is instructive in providing a government under a president that does not always require a disciplined party system. Yet the post-Second World War experience in Australia is one of high levels of party discipline.

Equally, we might ask ourselves if political parties need 'principles'? This is not such an idle question as it may first seem. When we talk of principles in politics we need to consider the reasons that individuals and groups engage in political activity. It may be to win benefits for a particular social group or class, or it may be to win concessions for industries; it may be to gain certain freedoms from the state or it may be to restrict some freedoms based on safety, social activities or religious behaviours. What may appear as principled to one group may be an outrageous affront to another. Thus, debates over issues such as abortion and same-sex marriage have agitated political parties and groups for decades. What we might hope for is that parties have a set of guiding or organising principles under which they operate, and that they stick relatively close to those. This includes how parties might organise themselves, and what the appropriate and most effective 'norms, rules and procedures' are to achieve the party's goals.

As we know from previous discussion, one of the key elements of democracy is open competition between political parties and candidates. Arguments and debates around policy and social outcomes become the norm as parties compete, and the elector's choice is then represented within the state and national parliaments. This points to a further relationship between parties and the state, but that relationship is far more dependent on the political and legal structures around parties. For some parties in Europe, those structures embedded parties within the state, and in doing so lessened the impact of unfavourable electoral outcomes. *Partitocracy* describes where the state structures and laws enable the key parties to govern, usually in coalition, without necessarily having to deliver key election promises, but at the same time drawing on state resources to fund and organise the party and providing positions on key state institutions for important party members. At the same time the state defines and regulates the parties, describing their activities in statutes as if they were an institution of the state. Australia does not have a system that provides benefits in that way, and still does not regulate parties' behaviour other than how it directly relates to elections.

We also need to consider the normative aspirations of political parties as part of the democratic process – that parties see themselves as important to the process and seek to control and direct how politics in Australia operates. We can then describe those aspirations and activities that parties might engage in, in terms of the nature of the state:

» Parties are institutions (potentially regulated by the state) that bring citizens together for the purpose of exercising power within the state.

» Parties seek and use legitimate means for pursuing their ends.

» Parties will contest elections in the state whenever they are able to.

» Parties are institutions that seek to represent more than a single, narrow interest in society.

» Parties are groups of citizens with similar beliefs, attitudes and values.

Do parties really do this? We normally see parties acting as a link between citizens and the state, whether that linkage derives from other non-government organisations such as business and social groups, or more formalised bodies such as unions. So, the ALP has its strong links to the union movement, the Liberal Party to business organisations such as the Business Council of Australia, the National Party to groups representing rural interests such as the National Farmers Federation, and the Greens to the many environmental non-government organisations. In each party, we can see elements of one of the key purposes of parties as interest aggregators and articulators. These may be embedded within the party's ideology or policies but act to allow multiple ideas to be formulated into single demands upon government – and thus also act to assist in the functioning of parliament by providing focused points of policy debate around specific Bills.

Parties also play the role of recruiting suitable people to politics. While much is made at times of the 'pay peanuts, get monkeys' analogy as to why politicians seem unable to work together or fail to govern effectively, parties do bring citizens with excellent creativity and ability to the forefront of governance. These particular people, whether a self-educated man such as former prime minister Paul Keating or the well-educated and erudite Edward Gough Whitlam, are able to act in what they see as the best interests of the nation (and people). This ability doesn't exist solely on one side of politics, but more generally across parties.

A further important role of parties generally is that they facilitate political participation. This can be done through the party's activities or organisation – such as attending meetings, rallies and events, or by engaging with non-members in everyday life. These particular functions are mainly seen as the purpose of party members and activists – to be the front line of the party, whether dealing with people outside the party, engaging and bringing people to the party, or communicating with them before, during and after elections. As part of that broader community engagement function (and intrinsically linked to the function of the party), the party undertakes a political communication and education role, building up the knowledge of its own members on issues of civics and the political system, acculturating them to both the party and the democratic system, and then passing this information on to non-members outside the party. This role is often overlooked in thinking about parties, but much of our political knowledge comes from family, friends and colleagues, as much as it does from school, television or the internet.

We can use these functions of political parties to analyse different types and structures of political parties according to their priorities, and to assess their strength and effectiveness. And last but not least, we should not forget that parties are campaign vehicles for the political aspirations of individuals and groups in Australian society.

VIDEO
REFLECTION
QUESTIONS

THE IMPACT OF PARTIES ON PARLIAMENT

WESTMINSTER INTACT

The impact parties have had on Australian democracy is quite profound. Although the Founding Fathers who wrote the original Australian Constitution knew of, and understood, political parties, they sought to distance the new Commonwealth from them by not formalising them in the Constitution. This follows a long tradition within the Westminster system of using convention and common law to maintain particular rights and activities. Just as the Australian Constitution contains no provisions guaranteeing rights, such as the US Constitution contains, no provision was made for either political parties or even a prime minister. All could, and were, covered by both convention and common law. In this, the idea that parliament was the primary source of all authority, derived directly from the Crown, meant that Acts of Parliament enacted as laws could define all those roles.

For the early years of the new Commonwealth's existence this worked quite well, with there being only one organised party actively campaigning as a relatively unified body – the Australian Labor Party. However, its unity soon caused other parties to emerge to defend the interests of other groups within Australian society. Thus, the first Liberal Party emerged in 1909 (replacing an earlier 'Fusion' party), followed by the Country Party (now National Party) in 1919. The inter-war period saw a variety of splits and re-formulations of the major parties, and it was not until the conclusion of the Second World War that the main parties in Australia today had taken on the recognisably contemporary form. Although there have been splits and defections since, the strength of the party system has meant that the three main parties – the ALP, Liberal and National Parties – have maintained a grip on the House of Representatives.

The Senate as a filter

The Senate voting system itself, originally a 'block' voting system where the winner of the Senate ballot in the state collected all the Senators for the state, allowed for unbalanced control of the Senate and the unimpeded passing of legislation, almost as a rubber stamp to the government of the day. This changed in 1948, with the adoption of proportional representation, but this effectively divided the Senate between the major parties. The role of parties in this period was to be disciplined and provide the numbers for the passage of legislation. This was particularly the case in the Senate, with fragile majorities, whereas the House of Representatives could be relied upon to pass government legislation.

However, the late 20th century, particularly after a number of alterations to the Electoral Act in 1984 in which Parliament was expanded and the manner of counting in the Senate reformed, saw a growth in the number of effective parties competing for seats. While the ALP and Coalition maintained their grip on the House of Representatives, the Senate became a place where minor parties could have a significant influence. Beginning with the Democratic Labor Party in the 1950s and 1960s, the Australian Democrats in the 1980s and 1990s and the Australian Greens in the 2000s, a series of parties have been able to wield considerable power over government legislation. And this doesn't count the other minor parties that have been able to elect Senators and impact the flow of legislation (see Weller and Fleming 2003, 27–34).

What the early impact of parties amounted to, though, was the influencing of the passage of legislation, but not necessarily the halting or undermining of government. Arguably the most successful of the minor parties in this period was the Australian Democrats, who for the whole of the Hawke and Keating ALP governments, from 1983 to 1996, controlled the flow of legislation through the Senate. While the ALP would naturally have preferred to be able to pass legislation without it being impeded, much legislation was passed, with or without amendment. The Democrats' lasting contribution during this period was not that they saw themselves as honest brokers, to 'keep the bastards honest' as their famous catchcry stated, but in building the Senate Committee system to inquire and scrutinise legislation that came before the Senate.

WESTMINSTER IN THE 21ST CENTURY

The key role of parties in the Westminster system – to allow the formation of a governing party and the passage of government legislation through the parliament – remained relatively intact until the 21st century. The splintering of cohesive vote blocks and the declining identification by voters with the major parties (driven at least in part by the changing nature of the Australian workforce) led to the creation of multiple small parties. Enterprising electoral entrepreneurs noticed how the Senate voting system, similar in design to a number of state upper houses, could be 'gamed' to produce a win for a minor party from a very small percentage of the vote.

The proliferation of minor parties has appeared to destabilise the major parties, at least as far as upper house votes are concerned. The sheer number of seats and necessary resources required to contest all the House of Representatives electorates has proven largely prohibitive for many of the smallest parties, with only parties that can call upon a sizable percentage of the vote seriously contesting mainland lower house seats. This clearly limits the possibilities for most of the smaller parties, who tend to confine themselves to campaigning for the upper house and to gain some exposure for their policy prescriptions.

Parties with clearly defined ideologies, causes or constituencies are then able to contest seats with a vague sense that it may improve their upper house vote, or even give them a chance of winning the seat. The Greens' ability to first win the lower house seat of Cunningham in a 2002 by-election, and then win and hold the seat of Melbourne in 2013 and 2016, has demonstrated that a concentrated vote can allow a minor party to succeed – and this has borne fruit at the state level in New South Wales and Victoria in recent elections. The capacity of another minor party – the Shooters, Fishers and Farmers Party – to win not just upper house seats, but also the New South Wales lower house seat of Orange in a 2016 by-election, equally demonstrates that major parties ignore key voting groups and issues at their electoral peril.

In the midst of this, the 2010 federal election generated a 'hung' parliament, where neither the ALP nor Coalition had the majority. Although this situation had arisen after state elections on a number of occasions, this was the first time since the 1940s that this had occurred at the Commonwealth level. The crossbench, four Independents, one Green and one Western Australian National Party MP deliberated, with three of the Independents and the Greens eventually siding with the ALP. This allowed Julia Gillard to form a new ministry, although it also required Gillard to make concessions that she explicitly ruled out during the election campaign – specifically that there would be a price on carbon, which was the price for the Greens' support. While Gillard was able to govern for the next

RESEARCH
QUESTION

three years, the promise haunted her through the next election, with Tony Abbot leading the Coalition to a massive victory in 2013.

Voting and the internet

In all this discussion of the system, the parties and who gets to vote, we have to also consider one of the most significant changes of the 21st century – the internet. While books have been written on the impact of the internet on life in the new century, in respect of elections three elements are important: (1) the impact for parties on targeting voters through various media (this will be covered in Chapter 11); (2) how citizens engage in electoral politics (Chapter 13); and, (3) how the electoral system itself has adapted to the internet.

This last element, the impact on the electoral system, represents perhaps the greatest challenge to electoral politics in Australia. Parties have turned to the internet as they would to any other communication tool, and citizens have seen it as a liberating vehicle (although perhaps without considering the full ramifications). However, the electoral system is still struggling with how to use the internet without compromising the integrity (and some would say *sanctity*) of the vote. Some change has been inevitable, such as using the internet to allow people who are sight impaired to vote through braille keyboards from home, but broadly, internet or electronic voting has not been adopted in anywhere near the volume that it has in the United States, and confidence in electronic voting is still lower than in the paper-based voting system (Smith 2016). The implication of this is that it may be some time before internet or electronic voting is more widely used in Australia, even as it improves the ease of voting and communicating issues and concerns.

THEORISING THE AUSTRALIAN VOTER

To properly understand why elections have the kinds of outcomes that they do, some understanding of why people vote the way they do is important. People who study why people act the way they do are known as **behaviouralists**, and they look for patterns in the way electors vote for some parties and not others. The key motivation for many voters was thought to be socialisation; that is, how they grew up, what they learned from their parents, friends and from school. Thus, people who grew up in conservative households, went to elite private schools, and lived and worked in circles of conservative occupations such as the legal profession were more likely to vote for a conservative party such as the Liberal Party. Equally, people who grew up on farms, went to school and socialised with friends who also lived on farms were more likely to vote for a party like the National Party.

behaviouralists:
Political scientists who examine the actions and behaviours of individual actors, as opposed to the actions of institutions such as legislatures and executives.

WHY DO PEOPLE VOTE THE WAY THEY DO?

Yet socialisation does not explain the many people who are apparently NOT voting the way their parents or friends may be voting. If we consider the high level of stability in the vote for the major parties through the 1950s and 1960s, what caused this to decline in the 1980s and 1990s, particularly in the Senate. Once upon a time, we might have tried linking this to class-based voting – that is, that workers voted for Labor, business and the middle classes voted for the Liberals. Yet, John Howard's wins across Western Sydney in the late 1990s suggests that many 'workers' were no longer identifying with the 'workers' party'. The classic social cleavages of Europe have been, and perhaps still remain, ethnicity, language, class and religion (Elff 2007), yet none of these appear to have much traction in Australia in the 21st century, even while it can be argued there is still a residue of class-based voting.

In part, this non-cleavage voting has to do with Australia's demographic makeup. The census of 2016 pointed to the fact that a quarter of the Australian population was born overseas, with a further quarter having parents born overseas (Phillips and Simon-Davies 2017). This suggests that a significant proportion of Australians do not necessarily fit the white, Christian vision of Australia that existed at Federation and was prevalent in politics and culture through to the early post-war period. On top of this, many Australians do not have strongly held religious beliefs. While the Indigenous population may be growing, it is still less than 3 per cent of the population so does not account for any race-based voting, even while some Australian politicians and commentators have made claims of 'ghettos' and 'no-go areas' (Morri 2016).

The American political scientist Ronald Inglehart, in the 1970s, identified what he called '**post-materialists**' – people who were not motivated to vote by traditional material concerns of jobs, wages and conditions (and the corollary of health and education). The group of young people growing up in the 1950s and 1960s (particularly the late 'baby boomers') grew up in a period of relative abundance, with those material concerns being relatively well taken care of for most. While pockets of poverty and deprivation certainly existed in Australia and other Western nations (especially among the Indigenous populations of North American and Australia), for most Australians this period was relatively affluent. Drawing on the work of psychologist Abraham Maselow and his 'hierarchy of needs', Inglehart (1977) proposed that with material conditions now being fulfilled, there was a growing group of citizens who were looking past these material needs to issues of identity, social self-awareness and social collectivity.

Inglehart's post-materialism thesis certainly goes some way to explain why the Labor, Liberal, and National parties began to see their core votes being eroded, as voters began to ask for more than material benefits. However, other social and political scientists, including Inglehart, noticed that rather than post-materialists overwhelming 'materialists', most citizens became mixed in their views, looking for ongoing, stable material certainty, even while pushing increasingly for change around social and environmental concerns.

At the same time as these shifts in what voters had begun to seek from society, and with growing levels of education broadening many Australian's social and political horizons, institutional shifts within parties and the electoral administration opened up opportunities for new parties and political groupings. The delinking of politics from specifically material concerns also saw Australians turn away from existing social organisations such as unions, churches and charity organisations. These shifts both within society and institutions allowed voters to express their concerns around a range of issues.

However, being able to express your views on a significant range of issues is not the same as parties being able to act in their role as **policy aggregators**. Parties such as the ALP or Liberal Party act to collect and synthesise a range of views on topics as diverse as industrial relations, health, education and the environment. Their political remit is to have policies across all these areas, but policies that broadly reflect their voter base. The Liberal Party can therefore be expected to have policies that would benefit people engaged in business and small enterprise, but also people who are concerned about large government, civil liberties and personal freedom. The advent of parties such as the Greens or Pauline Hanson's One Nation, however, do not act as a broadly aggregated set of policies, but as a more tightly focused set of issues and concerns around the environment (for the Greens) or immigration and social cohesion (in the case of One Nation).

post-materialists: People who consider that their material conditions are such that their vote is determined by other factors, such as the environment or whether other groups in society have rights. This is different to materialists, who are concerned primarily with their own material conditions of life. Most people now identify as 'mixed' meaning they wish to balance both material and post-material concerns.

policy aggregators: The idea that parties bring together many ideas, and in sifting through them find the ones that the majority of members within the party can agree on.

Equally, the ability of many smaller parties, sometimes referred to as 'micro' parties on account of their very small membership and voter base, have arisen, representing groups as diverse as sporting shooters, recreational fishers, bicyclists, and the arts community. While the issue of Australian parties and their formation is dealt with more extensively in Chapters 9 and 10, the fact these parties exist within an institutional framework, run at elections, and collectively attract a significant vote means that the policy aggregation function, relied upon to give coherence to parliament and allow government to work more efficiently has declined.

Getting back to the voter, we need to recognise that their choices have expanded when it comes to who they vote for. Equally, we need to see that voters themselves have changed in respect of their motivations for voting in elections and for particular issues. In recognising this we might then want to consider how citizens engage in politics more generally, in so far as it impacts their voting choices. We know that Australians have a declining view of their 'democracy', especially those engaged in protest activity (Jackson and Chen 2015), and a low opinion of the political institutions of parliament and parties (Brenton 2008), so how does this affect their voting choices, and indeed the way they engage in politics and political life more generally?

VIDEO

SPOTLIGHT

Are we all Everyday Makers?

Political theorist Henrik Bang (2004) has argued that political actors, outside of those engaged at the core of political life in the institutions of parliament and parties, can be divided into two broad groups: Everyday Makers and Expert Citizens. Expert Citizens are an interesting group in themselves, as they are those elite individuals travelling between non-government organisations, policy bureaus and political institutions, operating generally without partisan affiliation, even while driven by a desire for particular social and political outcomes. Expert Citizens are not ordinary citizens, but an elite group, with specific expertise and knowledge. Everyday Makers, on the other hand, are that broad raft of people who might consider themselves 'apolitical', in so far as their engagement with formal politics and institutions is concerned, but who do hold views on a range of social and political issues. They are also generally engaged in the general workforce, not the specialised and politicised workforce of the Expert Citizen. The Everyday Maker dips in and out of politics and political campaigns, engaging in those that are of interest and disengaging from the organisations or issues that are of less interest to them.

In this way, Everyday Makers are able to fulfil some of those desires noted by Inglehart, of identity and self-awareness, but also maintain their engagement in their general social life. Of course, they are unreliable partisans for parties and political groups, but they are certainly more typical of how citizens engage in political activity than the existing idea of the active part member – and go some way to explaining why voters may shift from catch-all major parties, and instead vote for single issue or 'lifestyle' parties.

QUESTION

REFLECTION QUESTIONS

Now that you understand the term 'everyday makers', reflect on the title of this spotlight. Are we all everyday makers? Why or why not?

SUMMARY

Learning objective 1: Understand the history of elections in Australia

This chapter outlines the broad movement from pre- to post-Colonial electoral structures, up to the current structures and processes. This covers the two main political party groupings – the ALP and Coalition, and their respective electoral trajectories. Importantly the key contests for government have all been between the ALP and the Coalition parties, and this defines Australian post-Second World War politics.

Learning objective 2: Describe the key electoral elements of Australian democracy

The Australian electoral system is complicated by nine different systems, and understanding their evolution requires some knowledge of the evolution of Australian democratic practices. This chapter covers the evolution of the Australian vote, the use of proportional and preferential electoral systems, and the methods of counting the votes.

Learning objective 3: Identify the basic differences between state and Commonwealth electoral systems

While the nine Australian electoral systems are quite broad, the key elements of the various legislature structures that necessitate elections, and the numbers of MPs elected in each state or territory are delineated. The outlining of these elements provides some understanding of the broader panoply of Australian politics as it applies to electoral democracy, and the connection between the manner of election of an MP and their responsibility to groups of electors.

Learning objective 4: Explain the context for Australian electoral experimentation

The nine electoral jurisdictions all have different histories of development, whether first as penal colonies, free settler colonies or created territories. Each of the different histories provided a different impetus for Colonial and then Australian politicians to build particular systems of government. The necessity of having a defined franchise (and who could be included) means considering who might or might not be able to vote, and this allows for consideration of different groups within Australian society and how they might be better represented.

DISCUSSION QUESTIONS

DISCUSSION QUESTIONS

1. When elections are described in the media it is often using 'horse-race' analogy, of a contest between two parties, the ALP and the Coalition. How realistic is this analogy, given the range of parties contesting elections, and given the ability of minor parties to influence the formation of government or even be part of government?

2. When we think of how elections are run in Australia, we often consider them as being efficiently and securely run by independent bodies such as the Australian Electoral Commission or their state equivalents, yet other countries have had significant problems with elections. What does it mean for an election to have 'integrity' or to be trusted, and what are the various issues that need to be considered if we are to trust organisations entrusted to run elections?

3. Today we consider parties to be an integral part of elections and government, but what if there were no parties? How would elections be run under those circumstances, and what does this mean for government formation? Can you find examples of this situation?

4. Many different groups and organisations have an interest in who governs Australia. These organisations include churches, unions, environmental groups and business associations. Should these groups be able to try to influence the outcomes of elections?

5. Australia has compulsory voting, which means that if you are over 18 and an Australian citizen you are required to register to vote, and then when elections occur go to vote. However, most other countries do not. Should Australia have compulsory voting and why/why not?

FURTHER READING

Dalton, R.J. (1984). Cognitive mobilization and partisan dealignment in advanced industrial democracies. *Journal of Politics*, **46**(1),264–84.

Hay, C. (2007). *Why We Hate Politics*, Cambridge: Polity Press.

Katz, R.S. and Mair, P. (1995). Changing models of party organization and party democracy: the emergence of the cartel party. *Party Politics*, **1**(1), 5–28.

Kriesi, H., Koopmans, R, Duyvendak, J.W. and Giugni, M.J. (eds). (1995). *New Social Movements in Western Europe: A Comparative Analysis*, (Vol. 5). Minneapolis: University of Minnesota Press.

Lipset, S.M. (1981). *Political Man: The Social Basis of Politics*, Expanded edn, Baltimore: John Hopkins University Press.

Marsh, D. (2011). Late modernity and the changing nature of politics: two cheers for Henrik Bang. *Critical Policy Studies*, **5**(1), 73–89.

Marsh, I. (1995). *Beyond the Two Party System: Political Representation, Economic Competitiveness and Australian Politics*, Cambridge: Cambridge University Press.

Ware, A. (1996). *Political Parties and Party Systems*, Oxford: Oxford University Press.

REFERENCES

Aldrich, J. (1995). *Why Parties? The Origins and Transformation of Political Parties in America*, Chicago: University of Chicago Press.

Australian Electoral Commission. (2017). Australian Electoral Commission. URL: http://www.aec .gov.au/

Bang, H.P. (2004). Everyday makers and expert citizens: Building political not social capital. Discussion Paper, ANU School of Social Sciences. Retrieved from https://openresearch-repository.anu.edu.au/handle/1885/42117

Brenton, S. (2008). *Public Confidence in Australian Democracy*. Democratic Audit of Australia, Canberra: Australian National University.

Brett, J. (2003). *Australian Liberals and the Moral Middle Class*, Melbourne: Cambridge University Press.

Burke, E. (1770). Thoughts on cause of the present discontents. In *The Works of the Right Honourable Sir Edmund Burke*, London: John C Nimmo. Retrieved from: http://www.gutenberg.org/ files/15043/15043-h/15043-h.htm#Page_433

Dahl, R.A. (1998). *On Democracy*, New Haven: Yale University Press.

Duverger, M. (1959). *Political Parties*, 2nd edn, (Trans. B & R North). New York: Science Editions.

Elff, M. (2007). Social structure and electoral behavior in comparative perspective: The decline of social cleavages in Western Europe revisited. *Perspectives on Politics*, **5**(2), 277–94.

Evans, T. (2006). *Compulsory Voting in Australia*, Australian Electoral Commission. Retrieved from: http://www.aec.gov.au/About_AEC/Publications/voting/files/compulsory-voting.pdf

Farrell, D.M. and McAllister, I. (2003). The 1983 change in surplus vote transfer procedures for the Australian Senate and its consequences for the Single Transferable Vote. *Australian Journal of Political Science*, **38**(3), 479–91.

General Assembly of the United Nations. (1948). *The Universal Declaration of Human Rights*. New York: General Assembly of the United Nations. URL: http://www.un.org/en/documents/udhr/

Gerth, H. and Mills, C. (1948). *From Max Weber: Essays in Sociology*, New York: Oxford University Press.

Inglehart, R. (1977). *The Silent Revolution: Changing Values and Political Styles in Western Publics*, Princeton: Princeton University Press.

Jackson, S. and Chen, P.J. (2015). Rapid mobilisation of demonstrators in March Australia. *Interface*, **7**(1), 98–116.

Jaensch, D. (1989). *Power Politics: Australia's Party System*, 2nd edn, Sydney: Allen & Unwin.

Koziol, M. and Whitbourn, M (2017). Government unsure if marriage survey will exclude 100,000 voters, rules out 16-year-olds loophole. *The Sydney Morning Herald*, 11 August.

Legislative Council. (2001). Report of the Standing Committee on Legislation in relation to the Electoral Distribution Repeal Bill 2001 and the Electoral Amendment Bill 2001 (Electoral Reform Bills). Report 8. Hon John Ford MLC, Chair. Presented 26 November 2001. URL: http://www.parliament.wa.gov.au/parliament/commit.nsf/all/F39F41917D6860BB48257831003B0396?opendocument&tab=tab3

McKinlay, B. (1981). *The ALP: A Short History of the Australian Labor Party*, Richmond: Drummond/ Heineman.

Michels, R. (1911/1968). *Political Parties: A Sociological Study of the Oligarchical Tendencies of Modern Democracy*. (Trans E. and C. Paul). New York: The Free Press.

Miragliotta, N. (2002). *Determining the Result: Transferring Surplus Votes in the Western Australian Legislative Council*, Perth: Western Australian Electoral Commission.

Morri, M. (2016). Terror in Sydney: The no-go areas without big guns, *The Daily Telegraph*, 26 March. Retrieved from: http://www.dailytelegraph.com.au/news/nsw/terror-in-sydney-the-nogo-areas-without-big-guns/news-story/88ad5f306ba062e07d564f52d7a1c551

Orr, G. (2011). The voting rights ratchet: Rowe v Electoral Commissioner, University of Queensland, TC Beirne School of Law Research Paper No. 12–3. URL: https://ssrn.com/abstract=1926493 or http://dx.doi.org/10.2139/ssrn.1926493

Parliament of Australia. (2009). *The first federal election*. Website exhibition 'For peace, order and good government'. URL: http://exhibitions.senate.gov.au/pogg/election/first_election.htm

Phillips, J. and Simon-Davies, J. (2017). *Migration to Australia: A quick guide to the statistics*. Research Paper Series 2016–17. Canberra: Department of the Parliamentary Library. Retrieved from: http://parlinfo.aph.gov.au/parlInfo/download/library/prspub/3165114/upload_binary/3165114.pdf

Rose, R. (2014). Responsible party government in a world of interdependence. *West European Politics*, **37**(2), 253–69.

Roy Morgan Research. (2017). *Health professionals continue domination with Nurses most highly regarded again; followed by Doctors and Pharmacists*. Roy Morgan Image of Professions Survey

2017, Finding no. 7244, 7 June 2017. URL: http://www.roymorgan.com/findings/7244-roy-morgan-image-of-professions-may-2017–201706051543

Sartori, G. (1976). *Party and Party Systems: A Framework for Analysis*, Cambridge: Cambridge University Press.

Schumpeter, J. (1942/2013). *Capitalism, Socialism and Democracy*, Abingdon: Routledge.

Smith, R. (1997). The party system. In R. Smith, ed., *Politics in Australia*, St Leonards: Allen & Unwin.

Smith, R. (2016). Confidence in paper-based and electronic voting channels: Evidence from Australia. *Australian Journal of Political Science*, **51**(1), 68–85.

Weller, P. and Fleming, J. (2003). The Commonwealth. In J. Moon and C. Sharman, eds, *Australian Politics and Government*, Cambridge: Cambridge University Press, pp. 12–40.

CHAPTER 8

THE ORIGINS AND EVOLUTION OF THE MAJOR PARTIES

LEARNING OBJECTIVES

After reading this chapter, you should be able to:

1. Understand where Australia's major parties came from and why they emerged

2. Recognise some of the ways that the major parties have been theorised

3. Explain how the relationship between the major parties and voters has changed

4. Describe how Australia's major parties are different to major parties in other comparable advanced democracies

INTRODUCTION

The Australian Labor Party (ALP) and the Liberal Party of Australia (LPA) (who, at the federal level, are in a formal Coalition with the National Party) dominate Australian politics. In its modern guise this dominance extends back to the 1940s, though with Labor/non-Labor party electoral competition extending right back to Federation. Despite recent evidence of falling support for the two main parties, they will remain the dominant electoral forces in federal and state politics for the foreseeable future. It is important, then, to understand where exactly these parties came from, how they have changed, and the contemporary political and organisational challenges that they confront.

Despite their ritualistic claims to represent all Australians, the origins of both the ALP and LPA were decidedly *sectional*. That is, they arose from and represented the interests of certain sections of the population. To simplify greatly, the ALP grew out of and represented the interests of organised labour, while the LPA represented the interests of employers and the middle class. This picture of a crude, binary structural division was always somewhat simplistic, but has become much more so in recent decades. Voting patterns have changed, and some suggest that there has been a degree of policy convergence between the ALP and the LPA. It is also asserted that these parties frequently work together to prevent competitors from disrupting their dominance of the Australian political landscape. This idea, commonly associated with the 'cartel thesis', suggests that these parties are prepared to put their competition with one another to one side, so that they can continue to rotate between government and opposition like they have for decades. Debates like these go to a larger issue: whether the relationship between voters and these parties has changed, where trust in the major parties, like many other institutions, is on the decline. These problems are, of course, not unique to Australia. Our major parties face challenges – technological, social, cultural and political – that many other major parties face in advanced industrial democracies.

The first section of this chapter examines the history and evolution of the major parties. In doing so, we explore their organisation and ideology and then consider how, if at all, the relationship between the major parties and voters has changed. The chapter concludes by examining the ways that Australia's major parties have been classified, and how they differ from those in other advanced democracies such as the UK and the US.

AUTHOR
PANEL

AUSTRALIA'S MAJOR PARTIES: HISTORY AND EVOLUTION

The history of institutions and organisations always continues to live in the present. To fully understand the present, and alternative futures, we need some understanding of the past. This is certainly the case with political parties. Without some understanding of Australia's major parties and their history, it is nearly impossible to understand Australian politics. They are influential in the politics of the nation at every level of government – local, state and territory, and federal – and the ALP and LPA brands appear ubiquitous. Whether this dominance is in the public good and can be sustained is a matter of great importance. Major party dominance is due in part to the electoral systems employed in lower houses across Australia, but their dominance is also a product of our socialisation into politics. In part this is driven by the relationship that the parties have with different units of civil society, but it is also driven by partisanship and the effect that colleagues, families, schools and workplaces have on how we perceive the world around us, including the political parties contesting for power. To better understand the major parties, then, it is important to consider the origins and evolution of these parties.

THE ALP

Labor's election defeat in 2013, and the six turbulent years in government that preceded that loss, exemplified many of the issues that have punctuated its history. These include the role of factions, the relationship between the parliamentary and non-parliamentary wings of the party, the extent to which Labor is or should be a workers' party, and the related issue of union involvement in shaping party policies. These issues can be condensed into two questions that confront all ALP members and leaders, past and present: What is the ALP, and what does it stand for? The varying answers given to these questions have been shaped by the party's history.

The early years: from unions to party

The ALP was a creation of the union movement that developed in the Australian colonies in the 1880s and 1890s. The labour movement grew from small beginnings earlier in the 19th century, and it represented a collective effort to improve workers' lives in a context where the economy and politics were dominated by big pastoralists and urban business interests. Despite many successes, the limitations of purely union activity were starkly illuminated during the economic crisis that shook the colonies in the early 1890s. Deteriorating economic conditions contributed to social hardship and a spate of industrial conflicts. These ultimately ended in humiliating defeats for unions involved in shipping, the wharves, the mines and shearing (Macintyre 2001, 25). Colonial governments, in which workers had little or no representation, sided decisively with employers to crush worker resistance. This bitter lesson was the catalyst for the formation of various labour political organisations in the different colonies. Their purpose was the pursuit of parliamentary representation to advance the interests of workers, chiefly by gaining concessions in return for their support of non-labour politicians. By the end of the century, all the mainland eastern colonies had realised this objective. A short-lived Labor ministry had even formed in the Queensland parliament in 1899 – a world first.

In the early years after formation, Labor was an ideological amalgam of socialist and radical liberal ideas. It was committed to notions of equality, solidarity and social justice, but also constitutionalism and personal freedom. Its socialism was, from the outset, of the incremental, reformist variety. Far from fighting for the revolutionary overthrow of the existing system, the party sought parliamentary representation to affect gradual social change that could mitigate the worst excesses of capitalism, by providing industrial and social protections for workers and the elderly. Members and parliamentarians pledged themselves to 'Democratic socialization of industry, production, distribution and exchange', but only 'to the extent necessary to eliminate exploitation and other anti-social features of these fields' (ALP 2011). This pragmatic socialism was coupled with ideas drawn from the liberal tradition. These included a commitment to the rule of law and constitutionalism, a defence of freedom of thought and expression, and a strong belief in the separation of church and state. This enmeshment with liberalism did not end at the level of abstract ideas. Labor cooperated with liberal politicians around tariffs and the racist white Australia policy, which protected the privileges of white workers against coloured, imported labour (Castles 1988; Bongiorno 2001). The newly formed ALP was, then, a workers' party – with its social base firmly entrenched in the unions – but one with a deeply liberal complexion. It was a party of the working class, though it is a matter of some controversy whether it was, and still is, a party for the working class.

The early years of the ALP also brought into sharp focus organisational issues, which ultimately are also political issues – ones that continue to be sources of intra-party controversy to this day. Central here were the related questions of: (1) how to ensure that Labor parliamentarians would continue to advance the interests of, and policies endorsed by, the broader membership and their unions, and (2) how to balance the personal beliefs and judgements of members with the need to act collectively in a disciplined, centralised, and politically effective fashion?

The answer to the first of these questions involved organising the party in such a way that power and legitimacy emanated from below, at least formally (Warhurst and Parkin 2000). As Australia's first mass party, Labor organised branches within each state and federal electoral area. Members in these branches had the right to vote on but also to initiate policy proposals, and to nominate as delegates to higher bodies. If they secured the necessary votes, they could represent their branches and electoral areas in higher party bodies, up to and including state and federal conferences. These conferences, now held biennially, were where the supreme decision-making of the party took place. Importantly, these state and national conferences also reserved a certain percentage of delegates and therefore votes to member unions of the ALP (today unions have 50 per cent representation at National Conference). In this way, party structures were and are a transmission belt for union influence on the party and on its parliamentarians.

The answer to the second of the questions complements the first. The mechanism for balancing the preferences of individual members with the political necessity of acting in unison entails members accepting the obligation of party discipline, in return for the right of democratic participation in decision-making. Members have the right to argue for their position and to vote on important decisions, but once a decision is taken by a majority vote all members are bound by the decision, whether they agree with it or not. They are obliged to implement the decision and to defend it in public. This is assumed to create a unity of purpose and thus a maximisation of political efficacy. Future Labor Prime Minister Billy Hughes eloquently summed up the principle in 1908 when he wrote that:

> Nothing can more conform to the principles and ideals of Democracy and at the same time more effectively promote the interests and secure the objects for which a party contends than an institution which, enabling all to be heard, ensures that after due deliberation the party should speak with one voice (quoted in Lloyd and Weller 1975, 5).

That the party *should* speak with one voice, however, does not mean that the party *does* speak with one voice. Hughes himself prompted a split in the Labor Government in 1916, when he supported military conscription despite broader opposition in his parliamentary caucus and among the ALP rank and file (Bongiorno and Dyrenfurth 2011, 61–6). A Labor government would again split in 1931 over Depression era austerity, which portended the deeper and more damaging split of the 1950s.

SHORT-ANSWER QUESTIONS

From split to modernisation

Between the post-war period and the 21st century, three key developments have shaped the ALP's evolution: the split in 1954–55; the Party's modernisation under Gough Whitlam's leadership in the late 1960s; and the dramatic change in policy direction during the Hawke and Keating years (1983–96), which followed and was influenced by the 1975 dismissal of Whitlam's government. The first of these, the split, was a manifestation of deep divisions within the ALP, which were exacerbated by the Cold War and anti-communist hysteria (Costar and Strangio 2005; Bongiorno and Dyrenfurth 2011, 107–19). An undeclared conservative faction had crystallised in the 1940s and early 1950s, alarmed by what it viewed as growing communist influence within the labour movement. Largely Catholic in origin, it organised itself into so-called 'industrial groups' (or 'groupers') to combat alleged communist influence in the unions. It severely disrupted Labor's own union work and plunged the party into a state of almost permanent civil war with itself. This led to the expulsion of groupers and their fellow travellers in 1954–55, and the subsequent creation of the conservative Democratic Labor Party (DLP) in 1957. The latter would win enough votes away from the ALP to help keep it from federal government for the next decade and a half.

In the latter years of that period, the ALP underwent a significant modernisation. The transition of the Labor leadership from Arthur Calwell to Gough Whitlam in 1967, symbolised a shift from the working class, blue collar, masculine and largely Anglo-Celtic party that Labor had been, to a more middle class, white collar, feminised and ethnically diverse party that it was to become (Warhurst 1996). Modernisation was intimately linked to combatting the perception that unions and shadowy backroom numbers men controlled Labor parliamentarians, which had frequently been used against the party (Kefford 2015, 52–4). Before the ALP would return to government in 1972, Whitlam (and others) would go on to wage an internal struggle to modernise the party by diluting the power of unions within the National Conference and the ALP more generally, by breaking the resistance of those still hostile to the Australia–US alliance, and by ensuring that the parliamentary leadership was represented on the ALP's Federal Executive. Whitlam and his supporters would eventually succeed, professionalising the party and broadening its electoral appeal. This was based on more sophisticated use of research, marketing and media techniques that had been pioneered in the United States. Labor increasingly became a **'catch-all' party**, fighting for the support of middle class and other swing voters (voters who swing between parties from one election to the next, rather than being consistent ALP or LPA supporters) who determine election outcomes.

catch-all party: Parties which lack a clear ideological direction and, instead, promote an eclectic set of policy preferences from across the ideological spectrum are often referred as catch-all.

Labor and the dismissal

SPOTLIGHT

The dismissal of the Whitlam Government on 11 November 1975 by the Governor-General, Sir John Kerr, is without question the most controversial day in the history of Australian federal politics (Sexton 2005). At the time, the Australian economy was experiencing the same stresses and strains that were sweeping the rest of the developed world. Economic stagnation and rising unemployment were coupled with sharply higher inflation and increased industrial conflict. The opposition and conservative media presented these developments as the chaotic outcomes of misplaced Labor policies. This came to a head with the notorious 'loans affair', where Labor Minister Rex Connor misled parliament about having ended the unconventional channels through which he had explored securing an international loan. This would become part of the pretext for the Senate withholding supply (the money needed to run government) and demanding that Whitlam call an early election. Whitlam refused, presenting both the Senate and its demands as being illegitimate and unconstitutional (Whitlam 1979). A crisis ensued, and eventually the Governor-General intervened, sacked Whitlam and replaced him with the leader of the opposition, Malcolm Fraser. An election was held in December, as Fraser demanded, and Labor lost in a landslide. The entire episode seemed to exemplify the axiom that Labor could be in government but not necessarily in power. The dismissal, along with further election defeats in 1977 and 1980, chastened the ALP and made its leaders more circumspect about advancing policies that could be construed as radical. Thus, when Labor swept back into government in March 1983 it was with a very different agenda to that of its predecessors. It was an agenda that ultimately transformed the party and, many would argue, made it more remote from those it claimed to represent.

QUESTION

VIDEO

How did the ALP of 1983 differ to that of the Whitlam era? Why do some argue that this shift moved the party further from those they claim to represent?

The Labor administrations of Bob Hawke (1983–91) and Paul Keating (1991–96) are often presented as governments of neo-liberalism or, in the more Australian vernacular, 'economic rationalism' (Pusey 1991). By this, commentators mean that the Hawke and Keating Labor governments had shifted from state interventionism and market regulation that had previously characterised Labor, to a free market, small government orientated administration. There is much truth to this observation. Treasurer Paul Keating had commented in 1985 that Australia had to become more internationally competitive if it was to avoid becoming a 'Banana Republic' (Langman 1992, 75–90). To do so, the Australian Government had to learn to 'steer the boat not row the boat.' The 'rowing' would be done by a private sector liberated from the shackles of government regulation, bureaucracy, and high corporate taxes. 'Sound economic management', which became a euphemism for fiscal conservatism, became the new mantra of Labor leaders. Consequently, in its 13 years in office, Labor comprehensively restructured the Australian economy. It deregulated financial markets, replaced centralised wage fixing with enterprise bargaining, lowered tariffs, privatised many state-owned industries and floated the Australian dollar, thereby exposing the country to the constraining judgements of global financial markets. Much of this was accomplished with the acquiescence, if not the active support, of union leaders.

The instrument through which union cooperation was secured by the Labor Party and its government was a series of agreements called the **Prices and Incomes Accord** (Stilwell 1986). Critics claimed that the accords tethered the unions to the parliamentary party's right-wing agenda, to the detriment of members (Beilharz 1994). Union leaders agreed to wage restraint, limitations on industrial action, and the restructuring of the economy, in return for a place at the negotiating table and the maintenance of the 'social wage'. The social wage refers to those socialised services that benefit workers but which they do not pay for directly. These include healthcare, education and welfare, the

Prices and Incomes Accord: The accord, as it is commonly known, was a series of agreements, between trade unions and the Hawke and Keating Labor government's which led to the union movement reducing their wage demands in return for increased social provisions such as health and education entitlements.

foundations of which were largely maintained, albeit with some reductions in certain areas (such as tertiary education, where users now had to pay a certain proportion of their fees). From a political perspective, this strategy was tremendously successful. Labor won five consecutive elections while undertaking transformative change and preserving its union support. But the very success of the strategy sowed the seeds of longer-term problems for Labor, expressed in and compounded by Labor's 11 years in opposition (1996–2007). The party is still grappling with these problems.

Contemporary challenges for Labor

Labor was resoundingly defeated in the September 2013 federal election, after six tumultuous years in power. Kevin Rudd had led the party to a compelling victory in 2007, but soon faced an economic and political storm that ultimately led to his replacement by Julia Gillard. The way Gillard became Australia's first female Prime Minister in June 2010 placed a cloud over her leadership, with many viewing it as a perfidious act that betrayed not only a sitting prime minister, but also the electorate that had voted him into power. Nevertheless, it is doubtful that a male politician would have faced the same criticism in similar circumstances. Indeed, when Malcolm Turnbull replaced Tony Abbott as prime minister in 2015, there was barely a ripple of condemnation, other than from staunch Abbott supporters. It would seem, therefore, that the denunciations of Gillard had more to do with her gender than her leadership. Regardless, the ALP limped back into government after the 2010 federal election under Gillard's leadership, with the three independents and the Greens. But she would lose the leadership back to Rudd just months before the 2013 election loss. This loss ended a political era for Labor that exemplified many of the challenges the contemporary ALP faces. These include the loss of electoral support on both their left and right, changes in the labour market that dilute its traditional support base in the unions, and damaging factionalism.

While Labor maintains the support of its union base, its embrace of the market from the 1980s has strained its credentials as a party of the left and alienated some of its traditional supporters. This has manifested in a long-term decline of Labor's primary vote at federal elections. On the left, many progressive urban voters who would once have been expected to vote for Labor have become disenchanted – on cultural as much as economic issues – and drifted towards the Greens, who can now count on receiving close to one in every ten votes at federal elections. On the right, some of Labor's traditional working-class support has leaked to the Coalition, apparently attracted by its more conservative message on same-sex marriage, national security, asylum seekers and multiculturalism. Liberal Party Prime Minister John Howard accelerated this development in the late 1990s and early 2000s, through his politically adroit appeals to suburban 'battlers' (Brett 2004, 81–2). The effect was to wedge the Labor opposition and magnify internal divisions, particularly around national security and refugees arriving in Australia by boat. Under Julia Gillard's and Bill Shorten's leadership, Labor has tried to neutralise the issue by sticking close to the Coalition's political playbook. But in doing so they risk further alienating some of their progressive support. This is a political challenge that Labor will have to manage for the foreseeable future.

Another challenge for Labor has been the precipitous decline in workers' union membership. In the early 1950s around 65 per cent of the workforce was unionised. Even as late as 1980, union density was still over half. Today the figure is less than 20 per cent, but with less than 10 per cent of workers in the private sector being in a union. Structural changes to the Labor market mean that this trend is likely to continue and even deepen. The growth of the service work 'gig' economy and automation, along with a more general casualisation of the workforce, make it more difficult than ever to unionise workers. The problem for the ALP is two-fold. On the one hand, a decline of unionism represents a decline of Labor's traditional base – a base that provides funds, members and talent. On the other hand, Labor's parliamentary wing continues to be dominated by former union figures, while union members are a smaller and smaller proportion of Australia's population. This makes Labor vulnerable to the charge – which is often levelled at them – that they do not reflect the full diversity of Australian society and that they are a party of sectional interests rather than a party representative of the entire community.

Another challenge for Labor is destructive factionalism. A faction refers to a smaller organised group of like-minded individuals within a political party that organises to win influence, offices and positions of power. There is nothing wrong with factions per se. In some ways, they are effective for managing conflicts that invariably arise within political parties. For example, factions were formalised in the ALP in the mid-1980s (left faction, unity [right] faction and the centre-left faction) but this did not cause undue harm to Labor's cause. In fact, some suggest that they enhanced Labor's position because conflict was largely managed out of the public spotlight and power was shared in Labor's parliamentary caucus, with the distribution of portfolios largely a function of factional bargaining (Faulkner 2001, 216). But these undoubted benefits also have costs, which came to the fore during Labor's period in opposition (1996–2007).

The frustrations of being in opposition during the 11 years of the Howard Government exacerbated factional division and conflicts, with widespread allegations of faction-led branch stacking at state and federal level (Jaensch 2006, 39–41). The allegation was that large groups of new members would be recruited at short notice for no other reason than to provide the numbers for factional power plays, especially around pre-selections (choosing candidates to run in state and federal elections). This was particularly notable in the NSW state branch, where the manoeuvrings of factional power brokers led to the making and unmaking of a series of state premiers (Cavalier 2010). This had disastrous consequences for the public image of the state branch, ultimately being realised in a landslide electoral defeat. This exemplified the problems that arise when factions become ends in themselves, exclusively pursuing the spoils of power within the party, at the expense of the party's main objective of winning or keeping government. The success of one's faction is placed before the success of one's party.

After the faction-engineered replacement of Prime Minister Rudd by Julia Gillard, and her own demise just months before the 2013 election defeat, a powerful factional figure emerged as the new parliamentary Labor leader. Since becoming leader and consolidating his position with an unexpectedly good showing at the 2016 election, Bill Shorten has enjoyed a period of leadership stability. The lessons of disunity during the Rudd–Gillard–Rudd years appear to have been learned and rule changes that proscribe leadership challenges between elections appear to have had an impact too. Yet while this has settled one problem it may have created another. It is now extremely difficult, if not impossible, to oust a leader mid-term, even if they are under-performing. Yet for now, Shorten has successfully repositioned the party to take advantage of the growing public disillusionment with economic inequality, which has helped strengthen his leadership position.

VIDEO
SHORT-ANSWER
QUESTIONS

THE LIBERAL PARTY

In September 2015, Malcolm Turnbull replaced incumbent Liberal Prime Minister Tony Abbott. Turnbull would go on to win the 2016 election, but only by the slimmest of margins. A single seat majority in the lower house made his leadership more precarious than ever and re-energised conservative opposition within the Liberal Party. Tony Abbott's frequent interventions in the media criticising the direction of the Turnbull Government became the focus of this opposition in 2017, often with a barely concealed personal hostility being expressed towards the Prime Minister. But as important as the personal differences between Turnbull and Abbott are, they manifest a deeper political truth about the Liberal Party of Australia (LPA) and its historical forebears. This is that the various post-federation anti-Labor parties have always exhibited a degree of tension between social liberalism and social conservatism, which continues to be felt today.

Anti-socialism and liberalism: the early years

Since 1909, interparty competition in Australia has been structured around a core Labor/non-Labor divide. The first Liberal Party – not to be confused with the modern LPA, which only came into existence in 1944 – was a fusion of free trade and protectionist non-labor politicians, who came together in 1909 to combat Labor's socialist leanings and its capacity to dominate the federal sphere (Brett 2003, 20–7). This pattern continued after 1944 though with the LPA always being in a coalition with the Country Party, which in 1981 became the National Party. While the Liberals and Nationals maintain separate party organisations and identities in all states excluding Queensland, they form united cabinets and shadow cabinets, make binding agreements on the distribution of ministerial portfolios, and have mutually agreed policy platforms on major issues. The LPA is clearly the senior partner, though, and always has been.

In the decades of colonial self-government before the 1890s, politics was a highly personalised affair. Fluid alliances of individuals and factions rather than parties dominated parliaments (Loveday and Martin 1977). Colonial legislatures were filled by (almost exclusively) men of ambition drawn largely from landed and commercial interests and from the professions (especially law). Commentators at the time would attempt to politically locate and label these early politicians by drawing on British experiences. 'Liberals' were those who typically supported universal male suffrage, land reform, state sponsored compulsory secular education, the separation of church and state, and limits on the power of upper houses. Moreover, they championed a significant role for government in advancing economic development, which was a key issue in all the colonies. Men drawn from the professions and commercial classes, especially manufacturers, were over-represented among Liberals and their supporters. 'Conservatives', on the other hand, sought to preserve existing power and privilege. They resisted liberal causes, were hostile to the democratic ideal of one vote one value, favoured religious education, and sought to preserve the veto powers of legislative councils over legislative assemblies (lower or popular houses). They were over-represented among wealthy landowners, but also included among their numbers men drawn from trade and commerce.

This Liberal/Conservative divide partly overlapped with one of the most contentious economic issues of the period: tariffs versus free trade (Starr 1980). Nascent manufacturers, especially in Victoria under the leadership of Alfred Deakin, favoured government-imposed protectionist measures to help incubate emerging industries from foreign competition.

They cooperated closely with Labor on this and related issues. This was fiercely opposed by farmers and some merchant interests who viewed such measures as artificially raising their costs and thus undermining profits and being anathema to a free society. Consequently, the non-Labor forces in Australia's first three parliaments were evenly divided between Protectionists and Free Traders. Yet as deep as these divisions were, they proved not to be as fundamental as the threat that both Liberals and Conservatives, protectionists and free traders, perceived in the rise of organised labour. The leader of the Free Traders, George Reid, summed up the danger when campaigning for the 1906 federal election:

> I have not manufactured an election cry, but have discovered a real and increasing national danger, which must some day compel all liberals, whether in one camp or the other, to bury their differences and rally their forces to free parliament from the determination of the secret caucus, and to defend the industrial and political liberty of Australia from the attack of socialism (quoted in Starr 1980, 6).

Hence, it was in response to the success of the ALP in the early years of Federation that these anti-Labor politicians came together in the 'fusion' of 1909 and contested (unsuccessfully) the federal election of the following year under the banner of the Liberal Party.

From the outset, then, the Liberal Party was defined as much by its opposition to Labor and socialism, as by any common ideological platform. While all Liberal Party politicians could agree on abstract commitments to constitutionalism, the rule of law and the primacy of the individual and personal responsibility, they would remain divided over various social questions (religion, education, welfare and industrial arbitration) and over the extent to which the state should be active in protecting and shaping the economy. These divisions would remain an irritant in the conservative Nationalist governments of the 1920s, into which Liberals dissolved themselves after 1917. They also periodically resurfaced in the United Australia Party (UAP) governments of the 1930s, the immediate precursor to the modern LPA. It was the weaknesses and limitations of the latter that led one of its leading lights, Robert Menzies, to conclude that a new Liberal Party was needed.

SHORT-ANSWER
QUESTIONS

The Liberal Party of Australia and the 'forgotten people'

The LPA was formed in December 1944, after a conference had been called in October of that year to rally support for a new non-Labor Party. The UAP had fallen into disarray after losing government in October 1941, and then being crushed in the election of 1943. But the UAP's problems were not only political; they were also organisational. Any new party would need a strong and authoritative federal executive and greater organisational capacities at the level of individual electorates, which the UAP lacked (Starr 1980, 24). A central figure in the formation of such a new party – though by no means the only important player, which is the impression sometimes given by Liberal Party mythologising – was the then former prime minister, Robert Menzies.

Menzies had previously assumed the role of prime minister in 1939, after UAP leader Joe Lyons had died in office. This first tenure as prime minister, on the eve of the Second World War, had not been particularly successful or inspiring. He had earned the epithet 'Pig Iron Bob', when he clashed with waterside workers over his insistence that pig iron continued to be shipped to Japan, just months before the outbreak of the Pacific War. Moreover, his government's preparations for war had been haphazard, and many viewed him as being aloof, arrogant and overly subservient to Britain. He would later resign the leadership of his government in favour of Country Party leader Arthur Fadden, who quickly lost the government's majority in the House of Representatives when it could no longer depend on the votes of two independents (Maddox 1996, 333). Labor was invited to form government, which it did, consolidating its majority in the 1943 election.

During this period, Menzies turned his mind to clarifying his own political philosophy. In a series of radio broadcasts in 1942, he set out his vision for Australia, including most famously a speech on what he referred to as the nation's 'forgotten people' (Brett 2007). The speech is more than a political manifesto. It is a moral vision of the good society and, at the same time, a polemic against those on the left for whom social class is the organising principle of modern politics. In Australia, unlike Britain, 'the class war must always be a false war', Menzies says. Yet he continues by acknowledging the existence of social classes, and clarifying the class that he, and later the LPA that he led for more than two decades, claimed to represent:

> But if we are to talk of classes, then the time has come to say something of the forgotten class – *The Middle Class* – those people who are constantly in danger of being ground between the upper and the nether millstones of the false class war; the middle class who, properly regarded, represent the backbone of this country (Menzies cited in Brett 2007, 21).

It was this constituency to which the LPA would orient itself right from its inception. Previously, the UAP had been, and was perceived to have been, closely aligned with the interests of big business, to the detriment of the middle class. Menzies was clear that if the new party was to be electorally appealing to a broad layer of the population – if it was to be a truly *national* party rather than a party of sectional interests as the ALP was assumed to be – it would need to avoid such a perception. This was reflected in the very name *Liberal* Party, which was adopted 'because we were determined to be a progressive party …' (Menzies cited in Starr 1980, 79). But the LPA's progressive credentials, especially in respect of civil rights, would be put to the test in the period immediately after winning office for the first time in December 1949.

In those years, the early years of the Cold War, the Liberal Party energetically set about trying to undermine the civil rights of those on the political left. In 1950, the Menzies Government introduced the Communist Party Dissolution Bill. This legislation aimed to ban the Communist Party of Australia, and the freedoms of speech, assembly and association of its members, which Liberals rhetorically uphold as sacrosanct. The law would later be rejected as unconstitutional by Australia's High Court, but the damage had been done. Lives were disrupted, and reputations destroyed, and Labor was hopelessly split over the issue of communism and civil rights, eventually leading to their split in 1955.

The split in Labor helped prolong the Liberal government for another 17 years, and for that reason Menzies' willingness to play the red scare card was effective politics, if not good policy. It also underlines the profound ambivalence that LPA leaders have with liberal principles, when the temptations of political opportunity are periodically aroused around national security issues. Similar questions would later be directed at John Howard, Tony Abbott and Malcolm Turnbull's commitments to liberal principles in the context of national security challenges. It would be wrong, however, to think that it was only political opportunism that accounts for the LPA's 23 years in power till 1972. The Liberals also enjoyed, and some would argue were the architects of, an unprecedented period of economic prosperity that would see the national economic pie grow, employment expand, real wages increase and educational opportunities, especially in universities, multiply (Starr 1980). Coalition governments accomplished all of this while maintaining most elements of the welfare state, and while being broadly committed to the post-war, Keynesian economic consensus.

After the retirement of Menzies in 1966, the Liberal Party went through a period of leadership instability, with Harold Holt, John Gorton, William McMahon and Billy Snedden filling the leadership in relatively quick succession. This instability underlined the importance for the LPA of a strong parliamentary leader, who could provide focus and political cohesion for a party room that frequently encompasses diverse political tendencies. As the distribution of ministerial or shadow-ministerial portfolios is not beholden to factions, with the leader being free to choose their cabinet and shadow cabinet, LPA leaders theoretically wield more power within their party than do their Labor counterparts. It is no coincidence, therefore, that the party's most successful periods have all been under strong and authoritative leaders – Menzies (1949–66), Fraser (1975–83) and Howard (1996–2007).

SHORT-ANSWER
QUESTIONS

The Liberal Party in transition

Malcolm Fraser became Prime Minister in 1975 under the most controversial of circumstances, but he consolidated and legitimised his hold on power in subsequent elections. The Fraser Government embodied the contradictions between social liberalism and conservatism evident in the LPA from its founding (Weller 1989). On the one hand, his government will be remembered for accepting refugees arriving by boat from Vietnam and for advancing multiculturalism. On the other hand, Fraser and his ministers were harsh critics of unions and welfare recipients, with the latter being vilified as the authors of their own misfortunes. These contradictory impulses also found expression on the economic front, in the division between so-called 'wets' and 'dries'. The former were those ministers who accepted a significant role for government in regulating the economy – a position that was in keeping with the long years of Menzies' leadership. The latter advanced a starker free market ideology, focused on the alleged necessity of economic deregulation, corporatisation, privatisation and industrial relations reform, to tackle the intractable economic problems that the country faced in the form of high unemployment and inflation. Fraser was criticised by the 'dries' for not using his control of government, including periods with a Senate majority, to advance market-oriented economic reform. These divisions were starkly exposed in the years after the Coalition lost power in 1983.

It is no exaggeration to say that the long years in opposition (1983–96) created something of an identity crisis for the LPA. The Labor governments of Hawke and Keating adopted policies of economic reform more typically associated with the Liberal side of politics, leading some to speak of a 'convergence' in party politics. Regardless of the merits of this thesis – and it certainly needs to be qualified (Goot 2004) – the shift in Labor policy did create difficulties for Liberal leaders in terms of distinguishing themselves from Labor who seemed to have stolen their ideological clothes. As a result, the tensions between social liberals and conservatives, and economic wets and dries, intensified, giving rise to fierce LPA leadership battles through the 1980s and early 1990s. It was not until after the

1990 election, when John Hewson became the leader of the LPA, that the party embarked on a concerted effort to position itself for government. The result was *'Fightback'* – a turgid document whose hundreds of pages outlined a neo-liberal blueprint for transforming the Australian economy (Simms 1994). At its heart was a regressive 15 per cent goods and services tax, which would be offset by income tax cuts. These would favour high-income earners and disadvantage those on more modest incomes. Prime Minister Paul Keating exploited this fact mercilessly and ended up winning the apparently unwinnable election of 1993.

That election loss taught the Liberal Party a valuable lesson in electoral politics: that a 'small target' campaign, consisting of very modest and non-threatening proposals for change, are electorally preferable to the type of expansive, ideologically charged program represented by *Fightback*. Consequently, after winning back the Liberal leadership in 1995, the great political survivor John Howard took the Coalition to victory in 1996 on a promise to make us 'relaxed and comfortable' (Manne 2004). This was the start of 11 unbroken years of Coalition rule that again revealed tensions within the LPA between its conservative and socially liberal wings.

Although a pragmatist, when it came to issues that could electorally damage the Coalition, John Howard essentially governed as a cultural conservative, once boasting that he was the most conservative leader that the Liberal Party had ever had. The effect was to marginalise liberal voices within his caucus and the Cabinet, and drag the Coalition further to the right (Barns 2003). Howard dismissed those who acknowledged the white invasion of Australia, and the dispossession of Indigenous people, as proffering a 'black arm band' view of Australian history. He articulated a traditional, conservative view of family and gender relations. He refused to receive more than 400 asylum seekers who had been rescued at sea by a Norwegian ship (the *Tampa*), which was the first act in the so-called 'Pacific solution'. Finally, Howard's government skilfully exploited understandable concerns around national security after the terrorist attacks on the World Trade Center and the Pentagon in September 2001 and the Bali terrorist attacks in 2002. Along with mistaken intelligence about Saddam Hussein's supposed weapons of mass destruction and his support for terrorists – which Howard still insists was the best intelligence at the time, even though it would later be shown to be false – these became pretexts for Australia's support of American military aggression in Iraq (Kelton 2008, 131–5; Bamford 2004, 333–65)

On the domestic front, the Howard Government undertook welfare reforms that raised the threshold for receiving many forms of welfare for Australia's most disadvantaged (Disney 2004). At the same time, his government was also criticised for its enthusiastic support of middle-class welfare – government programs and handouts that disproportionately flowed to middle and high-income earners. These were accompanied by significant income tax cuts, which were paid for by the billions of dollars that were rolling into Australia's Treasury courtesy of the mining boom. The Coalition Government also sought to transform Australia's industrial relations landscape through its introduction of *WorkChoices* – legislation that was successfully portrayed by its critics as further dis-empowering unions and workers, and tilting the Australian workplace playing field even more in favour of employers (Peetz 2006). It was this policy, more than any other, that destroyed the Coalition's chances at the 2007 election. It embodied one of the challenges that the Coalition has faced historically, and that it continues to face today.

REFLECTION
QUESTIONS

Contemporary challenges for the LPA

In 2014, the Abbott Government brought down a budget that was widely perceived as being harsh and unfair to many sectors of the community – particularly those on welfare and low incomes. In the year that followed there was a public backlash against his leadership and government, expressed in falling poll numbers, which ultimately led to his replacement by Malcolm Turnbull in 2015. Turnbull sought to soften the party's image, while also trying to manage and, in some instances, placate conservative resentment in his party room. But this satisfied neither conservatives nor moderates in his party, and the ensuing controversies around same-sex marriage, energy, banking and climate policy left Turnbull looking weak and indecisive. These developments well illustrate the challenges that the contemporary LPA and its leaders face. These include reconciling the interests of its base constituency with those of the broader electorate, overcoming the deep divisions between its conservative and socially liberal wings, and managing more general issues of factionalism within the party.

VIDEO

As we have seen, the LPA has historically been a party that has championed the interests of the business community and middle to high-income earners in the Australian community. The underlying premise is that supporting business encourages investment, employs more workers, increases wages and grows the overall economic pie in a way that benefits all Australians. In recent years, this argument is becoming more difficult to sustain. Despite 26 years of unbroken economic growth (1991–2017), and an investment environment that is advantageous to employers, underemployment remains stubbornly high, income growth is the slowest on record, and there is a crisis of housing affordability. Moreover, economic inequality has grown since the 1970s, as it has in other wealthy developed countries. The political consequence has been an emerging backlash against policies viewed as exacerbating inequalities: policies that the LPA has long championed and that its core supporter base still demands. The problem for the LPA however, is that its base may well be out of step with what is electorally popular. When the party moves in the direction of more centrist policies that have wider electoral appeal – as it did when it made changes to superannuation in 2016 – it has drawn criticism from its own base, and accusations that it is 'Labor light'.

This is intimately related to a second challenge: managing the political and ideological gulf between the LPA's socially liberal and socially conservative wings. For much of the past quarter century, it has been the conservatives who have been ascendant, dominating the parliamentary party and the federal executive. Yet the loss of the 2007 election saw a reassertion of the more moderate social liberals, with first Brendon Nelson and then Malcolm Turnbull assuming the leadership. Turnbull would lose that leadership to Abbott by a single vote in 2009, when he was vilified by many in his own party for cooperating with Labor around climate change policy. This anticipated the shape of things to come after Turnbull regained the leadership and became Prime Minister in 2015. His efforts to reposition the party in a more moderate direction angered many conservatives in his party room, whose hostilities were intensified when the 2016 election was a close-run affair. The Prime Minister now faced the unenviable task of having to placate conservatives to shore up his own leadership, while trying to sell compromise policies to an electorate that was increasingly sceptical about the authenticity of the Liberal leader.

REFLECTION
QUESTIONS
VIDEO
SHORT-ANSWER
QUESTIONS

Liberal divisions and same-sex marriage

Nowhere was this balancing act between social liberals and social conservatives more on show than in the debate around same-sex marriage. Despite being a long-time supporter of same-sex marriage, Prime Minister Turnbull, under pressure from the right of his party, refused to bring the issue to a parliamentary vote. Instead, he advocated a plebiscite and then – when the Senate blocked that – a non-binding postal vote. The latter was widely viewed as a cynical ploy by conservatives in his party to delay the seemingly inevitable. It satisfied the desires of conservatives, led by Tony Abbott, to buy time in which they could agitate to sow doubts in the minds of a populace that polls suggested supported same-sex marriage by a considerable margin. Supporters of same-sex marriage viewed such a postal vote as being not only unnecessary, but as being positively dangerous. It would be making a discomforting public judgement about people's sexuality and could unleash hate speech against the LGBTQI community under the guise of open debate and freedom of expression. This is in fact what did happen, though it was largely downplayed in media reporting. As events transpired, the yes-vote for marriage equality did get up by a decisive margin that was very close to what the polls predicted. As Prime Minister Turnbull sought to take credit for the result, however, many conservatives in his own party tried to place further obstacles in the path of marriage equality. Under the pretext of protecting religious freedoms, they sought amendments that would allow discrimination against same-sex couples seeking to marry. These were largely unsuccessful, but they did highlight the deep divisions within the LPA, and the challenges that this poses for any potential Liberal leader. At the time of writing (December 2017), Prime Minister Turnbull clings to power as he seeks to corral support and limit an increasingly fractious internal opposition to his leadership. While this division is often portrayed as being principally about the personalities involved, it is important to remember the deeper political truth that it reveals: that the LPA encompasses, and always has, centrifugal liberal and conservative tendencies that periodically shake the party to its very foundations.

QUESTION

How can a party with members holding a wide range of views avoid this kind of intra-party conflict?

AUSTRALIA'S MAJOR PARTIES AND VOTERS

When considering the relationship that Australia's major parties have with voters, it is important to recognise the crucial role that electoral systems play. The use of the Alternative Vote system for the House of Representatives ensures that the major parties are in a very strong position to win the overwhelming majority of seats in the 150-seat chamber. In contrast, the use of the Single Transferable Vote system in the Senate generally means the government of the day – which is the largest party or group of parties in the House of Representatives – is rarely in control of the Senate. This dynamic has a critical effect on the relationship that voters have with the major parties, as the failure of governments to

crossbench: A group of members of parliament who are not members of either the government or the opposition parties, so referred to as they sit at the bottom of the parliament facing the Speaker.

negotiate the passage of their legislation through what can frequently be a challenging and complex Senate **crossbench**, ultimately falls at their feet rather than those opposing the government's proposals. The flipside to this story is that governments are rarely rewarded for negotiating the passage of legislation; this is merely seen as the task at hand. Hence, the major parties, especially when they are in government, are held to a high standard and are expected to 'get on with the job', no matter the political circumstances they find themselves in.

PARTIES, ELECTIONS AND VOTERS

The relationship between particular constituencies and the major parties can be usefully understood through the lens of processes that shape voter behaviour and perceptions. In particular, the concepts of 'Socialization', 'Immunization' and Party Identification are critical. All three emerged from research originally published in 1960 in the ground-breaking book *The American Voter*. In it, and a number of related books, political scientists started to theorise the relationships between voters and political parties standing for elected office. Socialisation is 'the mechanism by which most norms and values are acquired' (Van der Eijk and Franklin 2009, 49). What this means for the relationship between voters and the major parties is that during early life, we learn certain behaviour patterns which become habitual. These patterns come from a variety of socialising agents around us: our family, friends, people we go to school or work with, play sport with or even go to church with. As Van der Eijk and Franklin (2009, 49) suggest, 'if these influences reinforce each other, then young adults are virtually certain to enter the electorate with a partisanship consistent with those influences'.

Once the voting age is reached, immunisation effects take place. Put simply, this arises from the practice of going to the polling place and voting. The act of voting for a specific party, if repeated over and over can affirm the psychological identification that voters have with the party that they cast the ballot for. According to Butler and Stokes (1974), once a voter supports the same party three times, they are immunised against change. This effect is, arguably, even more pronounced in Australia, as compulsory voting ensures that most voters are 'immunised' at an early age. As a result of these processes, voters become partisan and identify with one party over another. This is referred to in the literature as party identification.

The concept of party identification has been revised since the early forays into political behaviour. First, as McAllister (2011, 35) notes, if the party a voter is aligned to introduces a policy particularly offensive to the voter they may vote for another party. However, party identification theory predicts the 'homing tendency' will eventually lead that voter back to the party they identify with. Second, it has become accepted that party identification is used as a short-cut for many voters. With an avalanche of information available to voters to digest when considering which party to vote for, identifying with one party over another simplifies the voter's decision. For Australia's major parties, these voting processes have ensured that the ALP and LPA have remained the dominant choices for Australian voters for decades. However, the strength of these ties is weakening.

Australia had long been seen as an outlier when it came to partisanship as the levels of identification with the major parties remained high, while elsewhere significant declines were evident (McAllister 2002, 387). In recent years, however, two important changes have occurred which means Australia is now less an outlier; partisanship is declining and the strength of the ties between the partisans and their party is weakening. The major parties are certainly still dominant, but this dominance is now under threat from forces that seem beyond their control. The global anti-establishment movement sweeping advanced democracies is showing signs of contagion here like it has in North America and Western Europe. Whether this is enough to shake the foundations of Australian parliamentary democracy like it has elsewhere is hard to say, but the effect is certainly evident. The capacity for parties to respond to the depth of the democratic crises sweeping the globe will be fundamental to their long-term success. Certainly, the evidence points in contradictory directions here; voters are unhappy with the establishment, but they also oppose what they perceive as instability, such as minority government.

THEORISING AUSTRALIA'S MAJOR PARTIES

Liberal democracy is often referred to as party-based democracy. Political parties play a critical role in aggregating and articulating the views of the electorate at large as well as acting as representatives of the people in the legislature, which is decided via the mechanism of the democratic election. The centrality of parties in the liberal democratic tradition has meant that they have received significant theoretical attention. This has not only been about the evolution in how political parties are organised and structured, but also focuses on the ways that they can affect one another as part of the **party system**. Yet for all the theorising about political parties, including that on Australia's major parties, it is important to remember that they are a relatively new phenomenon, as discussed earlier in this chapter. While results in Australian federal elections from 2010 onwards suggest that the stranglehold that the major parties had over Australian political life is, if not coming to an end, severely weakened, we know from the history of these parties and many other parties internationally that they will attempt to evolve as necessary to ensure their survival.

> **party system:** Relates to the interaction between political parties in a democratic system. Often discussions about party systems will include a discussion of the 'relevant' number of parties as well.

ELECTORAL SYSTEMS AND AUSTRALIA'S MAJOR PARTIES

It is also important to recognise that a strong relationship exists between the type of electoral system a jurisdiction uses and the type of party system and parties that are likely to emerge. This includes how dominant the major parties will often be in terms of their number of seats in the legislature. For example, consider the results in the 2015 UK General Election to that of the 2016 Australian federal election as shown in Table 8.1. While the UK utilises the Single Member Plurality electoral system, often referred to as first-past-the-post, Australia uses a mixed electoral system consisting of the Alternative Vote system in the House of Representatives and a form of proportional representation known as Single Transferrable Vote (PR-STV). While it is important to note that Senate elections in Australia occur at the state and territory level rather than the national level, one can still easily see how the use of different electoral systems has a significant effect on the votes to seats ratio for the major parties. It is particularly worth noting how proportional representation alters the dynamics within the legislature. While the use of PR-STV in the Senate is now widely seen as one of the checks and balances employed to prevent executive over-reach and ensure a wider range of views are present in this chamber, it also produces a result more consistent with the wishes of voters.

TABLE 8.1 MAJOR PARTIES AND ELECTORAL SYSTEMS COMPARED

COUNTRY AND ELECTION	NATIONAL VOTE FOR MAJOR PARTIES IN %	% OF SEATS WON
United Kingdom 2015 General Election	67.3% – 36.9% for the Conservative Party and 30.4% for the Labour Party	563/650 = 86.6% of the seats
Australia 2016 Federal Election House of Representatives	76.77% – 42.04% for the Liberal and National parties and 34.73% for the ALP	145/150 = 96.6% of the seats
Australia 2016 Federal Election Senate	64.72% – 34.93% for the Liberal and National Parties and 29.79% for the ALP	50/76 = 65.7% of the seats

Source: UK Political Info (2015) and AEC (2016)

While there are many who suggest proportional electoral systems should be introduced for all major elections to best capture the will of voters, the effect of these reforms on the functioning of the chamber is also important. Introducing PR for elections to the House of Representatives would almost certainly lead to minority government becoming a regular feature. Whether this would be the right approach considering the system already in place in the Senate is open to some debate. Nonetheless, we have seen quite recently in Australia with the Gillard-led minority government that minority governments can work and these type of administrations are not necessarily an impediment to the passage of legislation (Prosser and Denniss 2015). Indeed, the relationship between electoral systems and the representation of Australia's major parties goes to much larger questions about whether the dominant two-party model, which is a Westminster legacy, remains an appropriate model for governing the nation. A plausible argument can be made that if our politics is going to become less polarising and confrontational it needs to also be more **deliberative**. As it stands, with the current electoral system the major parties are not incentivised to engage with a diverse range of voices and views. Given the medium-term trend emerging, which is a shift away from the major parties in Australia, their hand may be forced, and electoral reform may be required.

What 'type' of party are Australia's major parties?

One of central theoretical debates about political parties is about how to classify them. This debate has many dimensions including: what characteristics can be used to distinguish one party from another; whether parties are generally evolving in a particular direction; and what constitutes a new type of party. While there have been some notable Australian contributions to this scholarship (for example, Jaensch and Mathieson (1998) have identified 13 different types of parties in Australian political history), much of this debate has occurred in the international scholarship, as summarised by Katz and Mair (1995) (also see Krouwel 2006).

When thinking about what type of parties Australia's major parties are, party scholars often compare them to some of the **ideal-types** proposed in the academic literature. The most common ideal-types used include the elite or cadre party, the mass party, the catch-all party and the cartel party. When compared, as is displayed in Table 8.2, these ideal-types are often used to show the evolution of political parties in modern democracies starting with the emergence of the elite or cadre parties in the 19th century all the way up to the present-day cartel parties. Debates about this story of the evolution of political parties are hotly contested and some party scholars contend that this narrative about party

deliberative: Processes which lead to anyone who is subject to the consequences of a decision to have a say over the decision are generally seen as deliberative, and deliberative democrats argue that their methods can improve collective decision-making in democracies.

ideal-types: In the political science literature, ideal-types are often used as a heuristic device which aims to explain how, for example, parties have changed over time. Ideal-types are not identifiable empirically as they are often based on evidence from hundreds of different cases.

TABLE 8.2 IDEAL PARTY TYPES IN THE COMPARATIVE POLITICS SCHOLARSHIP

CHARACTERISTICS	ELITE OR CADRE PARTY	MASS PARTY	CATCH-ALL PARTY	CARTEL PARTY
Time-period	19th century	1880–1960	1945-	1970-
Nature of party work and party campaigning	Irrelevant	Labour intensive	Both labour intensive and capital intensive	Capital intensive
Principal source of party's resources	Personal contacts	Members' fees and contributions	Contributions from a wide variety of sources	State funding for electoral participation and success
Relations between ordinary members and party elite	The elite are the 'ordinary' members	Bottom up; elite accountable to members	Top down; members are organised cheerleaders for elite	Mutual autonomy
Character of membership	Small and elitist	Large but not very diverse	Membership open to all	Small

Source: Adapted from Katz and Mair (1995, 18)

change being linear, oversimplifies significant complexity and diversity. Nonetheless, thinking about how contemporary parties in Australia have changed since Federation is a useful exercise to determine the ways that parties are able to adapt to changing economic and political conditions, and whether parties really are the drivers of social and political change or they are merely the effect.

Australia's major parties are relatively easy to classify when compared in such a way. The ALP, as discussed earlier in this chapter, came into being as a proto-typical mass party. Some scholars contend that the ALP then became a catch-all party as their policies became focused more on winning the middle-class suburban vote. Others, however, argue that the party reflects many of the characteristics of the cartel party (Jaensch 2006, 30). In contrast, the Liberal Party under the leadership of Robert Menzies was never truly a mass party in the same way that the ALP was. The Liberal Party was created as an anti-Labor Party to represent the interests of business and a 'forgotten' middleclass and to win elections. Hence, the Liberal Party is seen by many as a catch-all party. This is primarily because while there are strands of conservatism and liberalism within the Liberal Party, neither is entirely dominant. The same scholars who refer to the ALP as a cartel party, naturally make this claim about the Liberal Party as well and this debate is worth considering in more detail.

REFLECTION QUESTIONS

Are Australia's major parties a cartel?

The cartel party thesis is the single most important – and hotly debated – contribution to the study of political parties since the 1990s. Its creators, Richard Katz and Peter Mair, had spent years considering hundreds of individual cases of how political parties had changed, primarily in Western Europe, but also in North America. The argument they put forth suggested that two fundamental changes had occurred. One of these relates to the way political parties are organised and structured. The second, which is related to the first, is that party systems have also evolved due to the changes to parties. At its core, the cartel thesis is about the historical evolution of political parties, making it similar to earlier stories of parties changing from elite or cadre parties into mass parties and so on. But it is also about how parties cooperate and compete within democratic competitive party systems.

The cartel party, as a theoretical party type, has few party members. The way the party campaigns will be primarily capital intensive, which generally means spending money on expensive advertising. As the party has very few party members, it cannot rely on membership fees as mass parties did to fund their activities. Instead, cartel parties are heavily reliant on the state funding their participation in the electoral process. In most countries, this means that after elections, the relevant electoral authority – in Australia this is the Australian Electoral Commission – will provide funding to parties based on their share of votes. The second part of the thesis considers the cooperation and competition between the major parties. When we think about cartels in business, we generally think of a group made up of competitors who form to fix prices. This analogy is useful for considering this thesis for the major parties. Do the major parties act in unison to prevent competitors entering the market or taking market share? There is significant disagreement about this.

RESEARCH QUESTION

UNDERSTANDING AUSTRALIA'S PARTIES FROM A COMPARATIVE PERSPECTIVE

The ALP and the LPA share a pattern of family resemblances with political parties in other wealthy liberal democracies. An understanding of the similarities and differences with these parties helps to illuminate what is distinctive about our own major parties, and the historical and political contexts in which they have developed. The ALP, for example, is often compared with Labour parties in the English-speaking world, and with social democratic parties in Europe and Scandinavia. The similarities with the former are especially striking. Like their Australian counterpart, the British and New Zealand Labour parties grew out of the union movement, still have significant union involvement, and were and are subject to many of the same pressures as the ALP. All of these parties have been agents of progressive social change – universal public health systems, mass public housing projects, welfare safety nets and regulated labour markets – but they have also had the difficult task of reconciling the interests of their working-class constituents with the demands of the profit system. This has periodically led to splits in the Labour movement, and allegations that these parties betray the interests of those that they claim to represent.

This was especially the case in the Australian and New Zealand Labour parties in the 1980s and 1990s. Unlike in Britain where it was Margaret Thatcher's Conservative Party who spearheaded the neo-liberal restructuring of the economy and welfare state, it was Labour governments that initiated these policies in Australia and New Zealand. This demoralised many party members and put pressure on the link between the industrial and political wings of the labour movement, though without severing it. But the process in the two countries was not identical. Federalism and bicameralism in Australia, as opposed to the unitary and unicameral system of government in New Zealand, meant that ALP parliamentarians were more constrained than their New Zealand counterparts. The latter could launch a veritable blitzkrieg on the welfare state, whereas the ALP's project of restructuring was slower and more incremental, and undertaken with the support of the union leadership under the auspices of the Accords (Cox 2006). Today, the union movement retains more influence over the ALP than do unions over the New Zealand Labour Party. This speaks to the importance of institutions in shaping what parties can and cannot do.

The ALP is also often compared to the US Democratic Party. It is sometimes assumed that the Democratic Party is to the Republican Party what the ALP is to the Liberal Party. This is very misleading. Although it is true that many American unions support the Democratic Party, and that the latter has often advocated welfare measures and state involvement in the economy, the differences with the ALP are more important than any superficial similarities. Historically, the US Democratic Party was the party of white supremacy in the southern states of the US. It has never had the organic links with the union movement that is a core feature of the ALP. Unions are not an integral part of the Democratic Party's form or function, and nor do they exercise a strong influence over the Party's political platform. Membership is not dependent on joining one's relevant union, if available, as it still is with the ALP. Politically, the Democratic Party is probably closer to Australia's Liberal Party than to the ALP.

The LPA is also often compared with its non-Labour counterparts in other wealthy countries. As one of the two major parties, structurally the LPA does indeed perform a similar function to Britain's Conservative Party, New Zealand's National Party, and the US Republican Party. Even in multi-party European systems of government, one can note certain similarities between Christian Democratic parties (e.g. in Germany, Italy and Austria) and the LPA. Most obvious here is the explicitly pro-business, pro-free market bias that these parties exhibit, which places them on the centre-right of an ideological continuum. They are all, to varying degrees, committed to an anti-collectivist ideology that emphasises the virtues of small governments and individual responsibility. More fine-grained comparisons, however, reveal very significant differences that reflect divergences in the political cultures and institutional contexts in which they developed.

For example, while bearing certain similarities to the British conservatives, the LPA is very different. The British Conservative Party has its roots in British landed interests of the 18th and 19th centuries, and still strongly bears the imprint of its aristocratic, class heritage. While its detractors would say the same of the LPA, the latter has always been more of an urban-based, moderate party. Historically, although it has had its conservative moments as under Howard's leadership, the LPA has more typically sought to position itself as a liberal rather than conservative party, as we saw with Menzies' determination that the LPA should orient to the middle class and be 'a progressive party'. Here the LPA has been shaped by a broader political culture that values, at least rhetorically, egalitarianism. Although many would plausibly argue that the LPA's commitment to egalitarianism is only skin deep, the fact that it must pay lip service to this ethos constitutes a constraint that the British Conservative Party does not face.

If the LPA is different from the British Conservative Party, it is even more different from the modern US Republican Party. Although the US Republicans emerged in the mid-19th century as a progressive anti-slavery party, they would go on to become the party of Wall Street and big business, and by the early 1980s a party increasingly wedded to the ultra-conservative ideas of the Christian Right. By contrast, the LPA has always been, broadly speaking, a secular party, even if those holding religious views have sometimes exercised considerable influence within its ranks. Once again, this reflects a political culture in Australia that is relatively irreligious and intolerant of religious meddling in politics.

RESEARCH
QUESTION
REFLECTION
QUESTIONS

SUMMARY

Learning objective 1: Understand where Australia's major parties came from and why they emerged

In this chapter, the history and evolution of the major parties were discussed. What is evident from this is that the major parties each emerged in response to a distinct set of political and economic challenges. The ALP emerged because of the desire of working class trade unions to have the capacity to have a say, while the modern Liberal Party created by Robert Menzies responded to the crisis in conservative politics after the demise of the UAP in 1943 and as an avenue for non-Labor forces to promote their agenda.

Learning objective 2: Recognise some of the ways that the major parties have been theorised

Like major parties across advanced industrial democracies, scholars of political parties frequently try to theorise what type of parties Australia's major parties are. Australia's major parties have, at times, been referred to as mass parties, catch-all parties, electoral-professional parties as well as cartel parties. While debate about this will continue unabated, in thinking about how we understand and theorise Australia's major parties, two facets remain critical: how they are organised and their ideologies. Thinking about the combination of these two facets allows us to categorise Australia's major parties and compare them to international comparators.

Learning objective 3: Explain how the relationship between the major parties and voters has changed

The relationship between the major parties has significantly changed as a result of changing economic, cultural and social conditions in Australia. Most notably, the vote share that the major parties could previously rely on is under threat as increased support for a variety of other parties and candidates is apparent. The strength of the bonds between many Australian voters and the major parties has also weakened. This is not to say that these voters will not return to the major parties, they certainly could, and this phenomenon may be cyclical. However, there are certainly serious challenges for the major parties in maintaining their unparalleled dominance of Australian electoral politics.

Learning objective 4: Describe how Australia's major parties are different to major parties in other comparable advanced democracies

Australia's major parties may appear like those in the UK or the US, but there are clear differences. In each country, the parties are products of the environment they work in. Hence, institutional, social and cultural differences need to be accounted for in any discussion of how they are similar or different. For example, Australia's major parties are different for the simple reason that they work in a parliamentary system in a federation as opposed to presidential and federal in the case of the US and parliamentary and unitary in the case of the UK. This has a significant impact on the way these parties are organised.

DISCUSSION
QUESTIONS

DISCUSSION QUESTIONS

1.   What does the history of Australia's major parties tell you about the institutional structure of Australian federal politics?

2.   Is contemporary federal politics just a continuation of a battle between Labor and non-Labor forces like it was from 1910 onwards?

3.   How could Australia's major parties improve their standing in the eyes of most voters? Or is this impossible?

4.   What technological, cultural or economic forces are altering the relationship between the major parties and young voters?

5.   Are Australia's major parties effectively the same and has Australian federal politics become nothing more than a battle between competing brands?

FURTHER READING

Brett, J. (2003). *Australian Liberals and the Moral Middle Class: From Alfred Deakin to John Howard*, Melbourne: Cambridge University Press.

Brett, J. (2005). *Relaxed and Comfortable: The Liberal Party's Australia, Quarterly Essay number 19*, Melbourne: Black Inc.

Brett, J. (2007). *Robert Menzies' Forgotten People*, Carlton: Melbourne University Press.

Jaensch, D. (1989). *The Hawke-Keating Hijack: The ALP in Transition*, Sydney: Allen & Unwin.

Johnson, C. (1989). *The Labor Legacy: Curtin, Chifley, Whitlam, Hawke*, Sydney: Allen & Unwin.

Johnson, C. (2011). Gillard, Rudd and Labor tradition. *Australian Journal of Politics & History*, **57**(4), 562–79.

Kelly, P. (1983). *The Dismissal: Australia's Most Sensational Power Struggle – The Dramatic Fall of Gough Whitlam*, London; Sydney: Angus & Robertson.

Kelly, P. (1984). *The Hawke Ascendancy: A Definitive Account of Its Origins and Climax, 1975–1983*, London; Sydney: Angus & Robertson.

Kelly, P. (1993). *The End of Certainty: The Story of the 1980s*, St Leonards, NSW: Allen & Unwin.

Marsh, I. (2006). *Political Parties in Transition*, Sydney: Federation Press.

REFERENCES

Australian Electoral Commission. (2016). 2016 Federal Election. URL: http://vtr.aec.gov.au/senatedownloadsmenu-20499-csv.htm

Australian Labor Party. (2011). National Platform. URL: www.alp.org.au/austraian-labor/our-platform/

Bamford, J. (2004). *A Pretext for War: 9/11, Iraq, and the Abuse of America's Intelligence Agencies*, New York: Anchor Books.

Barns , G. (2003). *What's Wrong with the Liberal Party?* Melbourne: Cambridge University Press.

Beilharz, P. (1994). *Transforming Labor: Labour Tradition and the Labor Decade in Australia*, Cambridge: Cambridge University Press.

Bongiorno, F. (2001). The origins of caucus: 1856–1901. In S. Macintyre and J. Faulkner, eds. *True Believers: The Story of the Federal Parliamentary Labor Party*, Crows Nest, NSW: Allen & Unwin, pp. 3–17.

Bongiorno, F. and Dyrenfurth, N. (2011). *A Little History of the Australian Labor Party*, Sydney: UNSW Press.

Brett, J. (2003). *Australian Liberals and the Moral Middle Class: From Alfred Deakin to John Howard*, Melbourne: Cambridge University Press.

Brett, J. (2004). The new liberalism. In R. Manne, ed., *The Howard Years*, Melbourne: Black Inc, pp. 74–93.

Brett, J. (2007). *Robert Menzies' Forgotten People*, Melbourne: Melbourne University Press.

Butler, D. and Stokes, D. (1974). *Political Change in Britain: Basis of Electoral Choice*, Basingstoke: Palgrave Macmillan.

Castles, S. (1988). *Mistaken identity: Multiculturalism and the Demise of Nationalism in Australia*, UK: Pluto Press.

Cavalier, R.M. (2010). *Power Crisis: The Self-destruction of a State Labor Party*, Melbourne: Cambridge University Press.

Costar, B.J. and Strangio, P. (2005). *The Great Labor Schism: A Retrospective*, Melbourne: Scribe Publications.

Cox, L. (2006). The Antipodean social laboratory, labour and the transformation of the welfare state. *Journal of Sociology*, **42**(2), 107–24.

Disney, J. (2004). Social policy. In R. Manne, ed., *The Howard Years*, Melbourne: Black Inc, pp. 191–215.

Faulkner, J. (2001). Splits: Consequences and lessons. In J. Faulkner and S. Macintyre, eds, *True Believers: The Story of the Federal Parliamentary Labor Party*, Crows Nest: Allen & Unwin.

Goot, M. (2004). Convergence of the major parties and the emergence of minor parties: A response to Lavelle. *Australian Journal of Political Science*, **39**(3), 651–5.

Jaensch, D. (2006). Party structures and processes. In I. Marsh, ed., *Political Parties in Transition?* Sydney: Federation Press, pp. 24–46.

Jaensch, D. and Mathieson, D.S. (1998). *A Plague on Both Your Houses: Minor parties in Australia*, St Leonards: Allen & Unwin Academic.

Katz, R.S. and Mair, P. (1995). Changing models of party organization and party democracy the emergence of the cartel party. *Party Politics*, **1**(1), 5–28.

Kefford, G. (2015). *All Hail the Leaders: The Australian Labor Party and Political Leadership*, Melbourne: Australian Scholarly Publishing.

Kelton, M. (2008). *'More than an Ally'? Contemporary Australia–US Relations*, Aldershot: Ashgate.

Krouwel, A. (2006). Party models. In R. Katz and W. Crotty, eds, *Handbook of Party Politics*, Thousand Oaks: Sage Publications, pp. 249–69.

Langman, J. (1992). The Labor government in a de-regulatory era. In B. Galligan and G. Singleton, eds, *Business and Government Under Labor*, Melbourne: Longman Cheshire, pp. 75–90.

Lloyd, B. and Weller, P. (1975). *Caucus Minutes, 1901–1949: Minutes of the Meetings of the Federal Parliamentary Labor Party*, Carlton: Melbourne University Press.

Loveday, P. and Martin, A.W. (1977). *The Emergence of the Australian Party System*, Sydney: Hale & Iremonger.

Macintyre, S. (2001). The first caucus. In S. Macintyre and J. Faulkner, eds, *True Believers: The Story of the Federal Parliamentary Labor Party*, Sydney: Allen & Unwin, pp. 17–29.

Maddox, G. (1996). *Australian Democracy in Theory and Practice*, 3rd edn, Melbourne: Longman.

Manne, R. (2004). The Howard years: A political interpretation. In R. Manne, ed., *The Howard Years*, Melbourne: Black Inc, pp. 3–53.

McAllister, I. (2002). Political parties in Australia: Party stability in a utilitarian society. In P. Webb, D. Farrell and I. Holliday, eds, *Political Parties in Advanced Industrial Democracies*, Oxford: Oxford University Press, pp. 379–408.

McAllister, I. (2011). *The Australian Voter: Fifty Years of Change*, Sydney: UNSW Press.

Peetz, D. (2006). *Brave New Workplace: How Individual Contracts are Changing Our Jobs*, Sydney: Allen & Unwin.

Prosser, B. and Denniss, R. (2015). Minority government and marginal members: New issues for political and policy legitimacy in Australia. *Policy Studies*, **36**(4), 434–50.

Pusey, M. (1991). *Economic Rationalism in Canberra: A Nation-building State Changes Its Mind*, Melbourne: Cambridge University Press.

Sexton, M. (2005). *The Great Crash: The Short Life and Sudden Death of the Whitlam Government*, Melbourne: Scribe.

Simms, M. (1994). The end of pragmatism? The coalition parties in the early 1990s. *Australian Journal of Political Science*, **29**(1), 28–41.

Starr, G. (1980). *The Liberal Party of Australia: A Documentary History*, Richmond: Drummond/ Heinemann.

Stilwell, F.J. (1986). *The Accord . . . and Beyond: The Political Economy of the Labor Government*, Sydney: Pluto Press.

UK Political Info. (2015). 2015 General election results summary. URL: http://www.ukpolitical .info/2015.htm

Van der Eijk, C. and Franklin, M. (2009). *Elections and Voters*, Hampshire: Palgrave Macmillan.

Warhurst, J. (1996). Transitional Hero: Gough Whitlam and the Australian Labor Party. *Australian Journal of Political Science*, **31**(2), 243–52. doi:10.1080/10361149651210

Warhurst, J. and Parkin, A. (2000). *The Machine: Labor Confronts the Future*, St Leonards: Allen & Unwin.

Weller, P.M. (1989). *Malcolm Fraser PM: A Study in Prime Ministerial Power in Australia*, Sydney: Penguin Books.

Whitlam, G. (1979). *The Truth of the Matter*, Ringwood: Penguin Books.

CHAPTER 9

A GROWING INFLUENCE: MINOR PARTIES AND INDEPENDENTS

LEARNING OBJECTIVES

After reading this chapter, you should be able to:

1. Recognise the growing importance of minor parties and independents

2. Describe the key post-war non-major parties who have been in coalition with or in key veto positions with the major parties

3. Describe the recent insurgent minor parties who have been successful

4. Explain the differences between major and minor parties

5. Recognise the way that other institutional factors of electoral systems affect minor parties and independents in Australian politics

INTRODUCTION

It is often asserted that Australia has a two-party system. This not only is empirically incorrect, but it also demonstrates the worst aspects of what Henry Mayer (1980, 345) called the 'big party chauvinism'. The contemporary Australian party system is a rich and diverse subsystem. While it is true that the parties of government dominate the House of Representatives, Australia's use of a mixed electoral system at the federal level means that the situation in the Senate is vastly different with significant diversity often present. The fact that these other parties are not parties of government does not make them irrelevant or not part of the party system. In fact, as prime ministers and members of Cabinet would tell you, they have become so intertwined with political and policy outcomes that it is rare for legislation to be passed without some negotiation or compromise between the government and the crossbench. Considering how central these parties are to Australian federal politics, they need to be taken seriously, they need to be rigorously analysed and they need to be understood.

Independents have also had a significant impact on shaping political outcomes in Australia. Most notably this has come in times of minority government where they have had to negotiate with the major parties on political and policy outcomes. While less common at the federal level than the subnational level, we do not need to go too far into the past to see the last time that independents not only had a big say on policy outcomes but also on who governed. The Gillard-led minority government between 2010 and 2013 was one of the most successful in Australian federal history in terms of the number of pieces of legislation that were passed. This would not have been possible without the presence of three independents who supported the Gillard-led Australian Labor Party (ALP). Australia is one of only a handful of democracies around the world where independents not only exist but thrive in meaningful numbers. Considering the fragmentation of the Australian political landscape, it would not be a surprise if **minority government** became more common and the role of independents became more pronounced.

In the first section of this chapter, we will consider the increase in support for minor parties and independents in recent years. We will then describe and evaluate two different sets of minor parties. First, we deal with the minor parties who have played key roles as coalition partners or as veto players in Australian federal politics. Second, we examine some of the minor parties that have successfully achieved parliamentary representation, referred to as the 'insurgent' parties. Following this, we consider the role independents have played in Australian federal politics, and the advantages and disadvantages for minor parties and independents in the Australian system. The chapter concludes by outlining some of the core challenges that minor parties and independents face in the future. What this chapter shows is that within a system in which compulsory voting and the electoral system for the House of Representatives has been used since 1918, and the electoral system used in the Senate has been largely the same since 1948, the voting patterns and political behaviour of Australian voters has shifted dramatically. In turn, this has made elections more volatile and has also meant that governments frequently have to build a consensus with a range of new players to pass legislation.

minority government: This occurs when no party or parties in a formal coalition with one another have a clear majority on the floor of the House of Representatives, often also referred to as a 'hung parliament'.

AUTHOR PANEL

AUSTRALIA'S MINOR PARTIES AND INDEPENDENTS

In 2002, Ian McAllister wrote that, 'Placed in a comparative perspective, the hallmark of Australian politics is the dominance of party. The vast majority of voters identify with, and vote for, one of the major political parties: gaining election at the federal level is next to impossible without the benefit of one of the party labels – Liberal, National or Labor; and minor parties have played little role in shaping the development of the party system' (2002, 379). While identification with the major parties remains comparatively high (McAllister 2011), there is also evidence that the strength of these ties are weakening and that voters are more open to considering options beyond the major parties (McAllister 2011; Evans et al. 2016). Election results from 2007 onwards have highlighted this, as the number of voters supporting minor parties and independents has increased sharply, as illustrated in Figure 9.1. Whether this fragmentation is likely to continue or is cyclical and voters will return to the major parties is a source of much debate. But for now it appears that within the institutional structure of Australian federal politics, voting habits have changed.

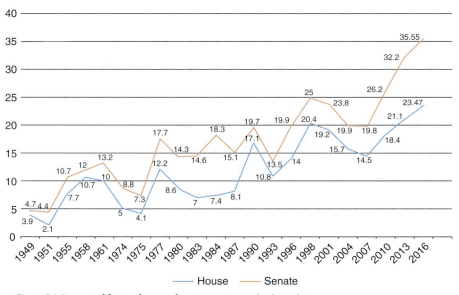

Figure 9.1 Per cent of first preferences for minor parties and independents
Source: Green (2015a, 400), AEC (2016) and Kefford (2017a)

It is also important to recognise that very few parties have been able to build a national profile to compete with the major parties. As will be shown in the discussion on the parties who have broken through, these parties have often been very well supported in one state, and in some other cases they have had some support elsewhere. The only serious exception to this in recent times has been the Australian Greens. They have grown to a position where they are competitive in Senate contests in every state in Australia. Yet even the Greens have found the challenge of winning House of Representatives seats exceedingly difficult, only managing it three times in federal elections (Adam Bandt won the seat of Melbourne in 2010 and retained it in 2013 and 2016). New parties, full of ambition and bravado, rise and fall each election cycle. This is now part of the rhythm of Australian federal politics. While most understand that the best opportunity to break through the major party dominance comes in the Senate, serious challenges remain in sustaining any sort of impact. What can be said for Australia's minor parties, then, is that the medium-term voting trend provides opportunities. However, significant challenges remain in translating this into effective and stable constituencies that first lead to election and second to entrenchment in the Australian party system.

The situation for independents is more complex. Without the advantages that party status brings (discussed in more detail later), independents face the major party machines alone. It makes the task of being elected to the Senate near impossible. It has been done, but it is very rare, with Nick Xenophon the last to do so in 2007. The fact he already brought name recognition with him when contesting the Senate tells us plenty about the challenges independents face. The success of independents in federal life is more associated with the House of Representatives. It is here that independents can make or break governments and where they have their best chance. At the 2016 election, two independents were re-elected, Andrew Wilkie in the seat of Denison in Tasmania and Cathy McGowan in the seat of Indi in Victoria. As has often been the case for other independents who have been successful, both Wilkie and McGowan have been able to entrench themselves and they will be very difficult to dislodge.

the political
establishment:
Generally seen as the
major parties, any
other established
parties as well as the
bureaucracy and elites
in the mainstream
media.

Australia's minor parties and independents, therefore, have never had a better opportunity to succeed. Australian voters are dissatisfied with the quality of Australian democracy, which is generally bad news for the major parties. They increasingly think politicians who are part of **the political establishment** are in it for themselves, they think inequality is rising and are increasingly pessimistic about their and their children's future prospects. These ingredients provide strong medium-term opportunities. Nonetheless, the major party machines should never be underestimated. They have financial, organisational, and institutional advantages that ensure they will remain pre-eminent for the foreseeable future.

REFLECTION
QUESTIONS

AUSTRALIA'S MINOR PARTIES

Given the level of de-alignment and the weakening of the ties between the major parties and voters we have seen in Australia, it is no surprise that there are a number of recent cases of minor party success. The 2013 and 2016 elections have seen the Palmer United Party (PUP) rise sharply and disintegrate just as quickly; Pauline Hanson's One Nation (PHON) re-emerge from total obscurity; and the Nick Xenophon Team (NXT) burst onto the Australian political scene. Each of these cases is important and tells us a great deal about the contemporary state of Australian federal politics. But there are a number of earlier cases that are worthy of examination in their own right and also in comparison to these new cases. The Democratic Labor Party (DLP), the Australian Democrats and the Australian Greens are three earlier cases of minor party success, with only the Greens surviving in any meaningful way to the current day. These are certainly not the only cases of minor party success, but each of these parties won multiple seats in at least one federal election. They are – or at least were – therefore serious players in the party subsystem. By analysing the organisational structures, ideology, success and failures of these minor parties, we can learn a great deal about the Australian party system, the incentives within it, as well as about the Australian voter. We also need to consider another minor party, the

Nationals, who have played a different role, that of coalition partner to the Liberal Party of Australia (LPA). This role presents a different set of opportunities and challenges than that faced by the other minor parties that have been successful at the federal level.

THE COALITION AND VETO PLAYERS IN THE POST-WAR PERIOD

While the origins and politics of the Nationals, the DLP, the Australian Democrats and the Greens are very different, these minor parties have all had a major impact on Australian politics. The Nationals, whose vote share has declined significantly, remain a key part of the party system due to their ongoing coalition with the LPA. This coalition has been a blessing and a curse for them. While giving them access to the government benches, there is a perception that they do not truly reflect the views of their base as they are drowned out by the LPA. The other three parties have shared a similar structural position within Australia's political landscape, while also grappling with many of the same issues. These have included how to remain politically relevant while maintaining a voice distinct from the big parties; how and for what ends to use their Senate representation, especially when holding the balance of power; and how, or indeed whether, they should seek to extend their influence beyond the confines of the Senate.

The Nationals

While sharing similarities with other minor parties, the National Party of Australia (NPA) is unique in two respects: first, it operates as part of a more or less permanent Coalition with the Liberal Party of Australia, which gives it power and influence beyond the relatively modest vote that it receives in elections; second, the NPA positions itself as the conservative political voice of rural and regional Australia, with support particularly concentrated in New South Wales and Queensland (in 2008, the Nationals and Liberals merged in Queensland). It is a self-consciously agrarian party, one of the oldest in the world (Davey 2010; Costar and Woodward 1985). Although it is the junior party in the Coalition, the NPA's history is longer, and arguably its roots in its favoured constituency are deeper, than those of the LPA. That history begins a century ago.

The Country Party, as the NPA was called up until 1975, officially formed in 1920. Representatives of state-based Farmers and Settlers' Associations that had coalesced in the previous decade constituted the new party (Graham 1966). These organisations viewed both the Liberal and Labor Parties, and the new Nationalist Party that formed after the split in Labor in 1916, as representing essentially urban-based interests, although the ALP was clearly regarded with greater hostility. The ideology of the new party was firmly rooted in agrarian myths of rugged individualism and personal responsibility, and thus imbibed a conservative moral ethos that has animated the party's policies throughout its history. Australia's prosperity was, the Country Party claimed, derived from the sheep's back and the soil that the farmers' labour tendered. These were the core constituents of the Country Party, although it tried to broaden its appeal in 1975 by changing its name to the National Country Party, and then dropping 'Country' altogether in 1982 and simply becoming the National Party.

From the outset, the new party campaigned within parliament for the interests of land-owning primary producers. As such, it rejected the commitment to high tariffs from both the main parties (a position that shifted considerably in the decades after the Second World War), rejected government price fixing, argued for reduced government spending and championed the rights of returned servicemen, many of whom had roots in rural and regional Australia. It won the balance of power in the 1922 election, and soon after would enter into a coalition with Stanley Bruce's nationalist government. The Coalition did not survive the loss of government in 1929, nor did it immediately reconvene when the United Australia Party won and kept government in its own right after 1931. It would not be until the formation of the modern LPA in 1944 that the Liberal–Country Coalition would take on its contemporary form.

At the founding of the new Liberal Party in 1944, its leader Robert Menzies was clear that a stable Coalition with the Country Party was essential to the fortunes of the non-Labor side of Australian politics (Costar 1994). The price that Menzies and subsequent Liberal leaders have been prepared to pay to preserve a stable Coalition Agreement has not been trivial. The Nationals' leader is always Deputy leader of the joint party caucus, which means they are Deputy Prime Minister when the Coalition is in Government (this tradition has been in place since 1968, when the position of Deputy Prime Minister was formally created). Moreover, some key ministerial portfolios in Cabinet are reserved for the Nationals – such as trade and agriculture – irrespective of the talents and experience of Liberal contenders for these coveted positions. The National Party has also had a strong track record of extracting concessions from its Coalition partner that the latter might not always be predisposed to giving, in the absence of having to preserve the Coalition. Thus the NPA has a strong track record of winning government subsidies and other handouts for farmers and miners, which more free-market oriented Liberals may not have given if they were governing alone (Maddox 1996, 327). A related issue has revolved around tariff protection. From the 1950s, under leader John 'Black Jack' McEwan whose name became synonymous with protectionism, the party moved to a position of supporting high tariffs (Davey 2010, 110–11). In an effort to broaden its appeal beyond rural sectional interests, it argued that city workers and their manufacturing employers provided the customers for rural goods, and therefore manufacturing should be protected from foreign competition. This position was eroded in the 1980s and 1990s, often under pressure from a Liberal Coalition partner enamoured with free trade and globalisation. This speaks to one of several challenges that the contemporary NPA faces.

If the NPA's relationship with the LPA has enabled it to win certain concessions for its rural and regional constituents, that same relationship has also led it to make compromises that have alienated some of those same supporters. The Coalition's general commitment to market-oriented solutions to economic and social problems has frequently had losers in rural and regional Australia. This has periodically led to charges that the National Party has sold its soul to the LPA, and in so doing betrayed the bush. The NPA is said to have subsumed itself to the interests of its Coalition partner, thereby diluting what is distinctive about its politics and making itself largely irrelevant. One consequence has been occasional bitter recriminations against the NPA's parliamentary leadership, and the splitting away of some high-profile figures who have run against the Nationals as independents or as representatives of new parties (e.g. Bob Katter). The Nationals have also had to contend with the political challenge posed by One Nation, in the late 1990s and more recently. This anti-immigration, populist party has appealed to some traditional NPA voters, which has meant that the National Party has had to position itself further to the right of the political spectrum than it otherwise would. Finally, a longer-term structural challenge to the NPA has been demographic change. There has been an ongoing decline in the population of rural and regional Australia relative to urban areas, which threatens to further dilute NPA representation in Australia's federal parliament in the future.

Despite these challenges, the NPA has exhibited a resilience that has proved its detractors and doomsayers wrong more than once. As long as they remain an integral part of the Coalition, they will remain an important force in Australian politics for the foreseeable future.

The Democratic Labor Party

The Democratic Labor Party formed in August 1957, out of the assembled fragments of state-based organisations that had crystallised in the wake of the ALP's 1955 split (Costar et al. 2005). It drew together those disaffected, socially conservative, and predominantly Catholic elements of Labor that had waged an internal campaign against alleged communist influence in the unions and the party (Fitzgerald 2003). It exercised a political influence disproportionate to its size and electoral support. The DLP helped to keep the ALP from winning federal government until 1972 and supported the Coalition from its position in the Senate. As such, it was a minor party with a major influence that anticipated future developments with the Australian Democrats and the Greens.

If the roots of the DLP were in the ALP's split, the roots of the split can be traced back to the 1930s. Catholics of Irish heritage constituted around 40 per cent of ALP membership and delegates to conferences, and a section of them were deeply troubled by the growing influence of the Communist Party of Australia (Love 2005, 3). This led to the publication of *Catholic Worker* from 1936, under the editorship of B.A. Santamaria. This crusader against both communism and free market capitalism would later form the Catholic Social Studies Movement, a secret society dedicated to fighting communism in the labour movement (Fitzgerald 2003). When the ALP set up Industrial Groups to support its own candidates running against communists in union elections, they were often infiltrated or taken over by fellow travellers of Santamaria. 'Groupers', as they were called, became a source of sharp division within the ALP membership and leadership in the early 1950s, years of heightened anti-communist hysteria. Internal relations turned poisonous after Labor's 1954 election defeat, with leader Doc Evatt accusing 'a small minority group of members, located particularly in the state of Victoria' of being 'increasingly disloyal to the Labor Movement and the Labor leadership … ' (cited in McMullin 1991, 275). Many of these members were expelled or left the party in early 1955 and formed anti-communist Labor parties in their respective states. These became the basis for the formation of the federal DLP in 1957.

The new party was labourist in its economic policy, but more conservative than the ALP on social issues, industrial relations and foreign affairs. Its staunchly anti-communist ideology made it a strong supporter of Australia's alliance with the United States, in contrast to the ambivalence often expressed by many on the left of the ALP. But more important than its ideology and policies was its hostility to the ALP. The DLP consistently directed its preferences to the Coalition in federal and state elections, on the basis that 'my enemy's enemy is my friend' (Reynolds 2005, 294). This helped keep Labor from office in Victoria and Queensland for 27 and 34 years, respectively, and helped deny federal Labor an election win until 1972.

From the outset, the DLP secured Senate representation for itself, which grew into holding the balance of power from 1964 to 1974. It developed an effective and consistent preference strategy that always placed the Coalition above the ALP, to the great electoral disadvantage of the latter. Despite its small size (around one tenth of Labor's membership) and comparatively low vote (usually in single digits), it was able to use its Senate position to generally support the Coalition, but also to sometimes wring concessions from it. The DLP effectively ended as a force in Australian politics in the double dissolution election of 1974, at which it lost all of its Senate representation (Reynolds 2005, 300). Its relentless dedication to destroying Labor, rather than developing a positive, distinctive voice that could attract new layers of supporters, contributed to its demise. This would serve as a warning to the other balance of power parties that emerged in the 1970s and 1980s, principally the Democrats and Greens. The DLP did re-emerge briefly following the 2010 federal election when John Madigan was elected as a Senator for Victoria for the party. However, before the 2016 federal election contest he split from the party and established a new party. Madigan was not re-elected in 2016.

SHORT-ANSWER
QUESTIONS

The Australian Democrats

Like the DLP before it, the Australian Democrats were a party formed of political fragments that split away from one of Australia's main parties, in this case the Liberal Party of Australia (LPA). Created in 1977, former Liberal Minister Don Chipp was the driving force behind the party's establishment and was also its first leader. His legacy was a party that would become the most successful third force in Australian politics until the mid-2000s, with the Democrats' promise to 'keep the bastards honest' resonating with many in the electorate demanding greater accountability from Labor and the Coalition (Warhurst 1997).

The origins of the Democrats can be located in the divisions within the Liberal Party between social liberals and social conservatives. More specifically, these differences had led to a split in the South Australian branch of the LPA, and the formation of the Liberal Movement and later the New Liberal Movement. Chipp entered into discussions with the latter when he resigned from the LPA in March 1977. His reasons for doing so are revealing:

> I wonder if the ordinary voter is not becoming sick and tired of the
> vested interests which unduly influence political parties and yearns for
> the emergence of a third political force, representing middle-of-the-road
> policies which would owe allegiance to no outside pressure group. Perhaps
> it may be the right time to test that proposition (Chipp and Larkin 1978,
> 179–80).

And test that proposition he did, with the newly formed Australian Democrats winning two Senate seats in the election of December 1977. From those small beginnings, the Democrats enlarged their influence and Senate representation to the extent that they held the balance of power for 16 consecutive years between 1980 and 1996. During that time the Democrats sought to position themselves as a centrist party between Labor and the Coalition, though their early support came more from former Liberal Party voters (Tilby Stock 1997). As both of the big parties shifted further to the right, however, the Democrats were increasingly perceived to be a left-of-centre party. This created frictions within the party and its leadership in the late 1990s and early 2000s, which often turned on the question of how and for what ends to use its Senate power.

As with the DLP before it, and the Greens after it, the Australian Democrats periodically found themselves in a position to have a disproportionate influence on Australian politics and government policy. At such times, particularly when the government of the day relies on the Senate votes of a minor party to pass legislation, these parties are confronted with the extent to which they are prepared to compromise principle in order to exercise power and influence. The argument is sometimes put that simply standing on principle and refusing to make pragmatic compromises with the government of the day makes minor parties irrelevant. Worse, it can also make them, critics would suggest, impediments to the realisation of the democratic will expressed in the fact of the government's majority in the House of Representatives.

It was considerations such as these that informed the then leader Meg Lees' decision to negotiate the passage of the Coalition's goods and services tax (GST) through the Senate in 2000. That decision placed the Democrats at the centre of events for a time, but with damaging longer-term consequences. Leadership instability ensued, Lees was replaced by the more left-wing Natasha Stott Despoja, the Democrat vote retreated and by 2007 had collapsed, to leave it without Senate representation. Without a parliamentary platform from which to promote the party and exercise influence, the Australian Democrats had effectively lost the mantle of the third force in Australian politics. Their demise was hastened by the growth of the Australian Greens, who face many of the same challenges as the Democrats.

SHORT-ANSWER
QUESTIONS

REFLECTION
QUESTIONS

The Greens

In mid-2017, the Greens were experiencing a period of political turbulence, mostly of their own making. After the 2016 election, the parliamentary leadership had been critical of the explicitly anti-capitalist position taken by some sections of its NSW division. Subsequently, NSW left-wing senator Lee Rhiannon was excluded from the Greens' party room, when she followed the lead of her NSW colleagues and supporters to actively campaign against the Gonski 2 education package, whose passage through the Senate was being negotiated by her parliamentary colleagues. The ensuing public spat damaged the Greens, and also revealed very different visions for the Greens' future. These divisions revolve around questions about the relative importance of parliamentary as opposed to activist politics, the degree of autonomy that state divisions should have, and how Greens' parliamentary representatives should use their Senate power. They are divisions that have been shaped by the Greens' evolution from being largely a single issue, extra-parliamentary social movement, to a multi-issue, national political party focused on using parliament to achieve political change (Jackson 2016; Miragliotta 2006).

The Greens can trace their political ancestry to social movements and political organisations that emerged in the 1970s and 1980s, for whom environmental and social justice issues were front and centre of progressive politics (Miragliotta 2006, 586–90). What was possibly the world's first green party – the United Tasmania Group (UTG) – had been established in Tasmania in 1972. While the UTG did not survive beyond the original campaign around which it fought (the inundation of Lake Pedder for hydro-electricity), one of its young activists and state election candidates would play a crucial role in environmental politics in the 1980s, and the formation of a national Greens Party in 1992.

The Director of the Tasmanian Wilderness Society, Bob Brown, won something of a national profile when he was arrested at the Franklin Dam blockade in 1983, and was later elected to the Tasmanian Legislative Assembly. Four other environmental activists would join him in the Tasmanian Parliament, where they began caucusing and eventually held the balance of power. This helped galvanise the green political organisations that had emerged in other eastern states. Meanwhile, in Western Australia the short-lived Nuclear Disarmament Party produced an activist – Jo Vallentine – who would in 1990 become Australia's first Green Senator. These various strands came together in 1992 to form a national Greens Party, the Australian Greens, with a loose, confederated structure that preserved the autonomy of the state-based parties (Miragliotta 2012, 102–4). By 2004 they had surpassed the Democrats as the third political force, with four federal Senators. Their fortunes improved further in subsequent election cycles, winning over 13 per cent of first preference votes at the 2010 election (the high watermark for Greens votes so far). Green support was even greater in inner urban areas, which was sufficient to win a House of Representatives seat in the electorate of Melbourne in 2010 (Adam Bandt retained the seat in the 2013 and 2016 elections). Clearly the Greens now have a core constituency of **cosmopolitan**, progressive voters, actuated by what is often described in the literature as 'post-materialist' values. But these undoubted successes harboured growing pains that go to the heart of the Greens' political identity.

Many commentators have observed that the Australian Greens, and Greens parties more generally, embody two, sometimes contradictory, political traditions (Jackson, 2016; Miragliotta 2006; Radcliffe 2002). On the one hand, these parties are motivated by a radical ethos that seeks to fundamentally transform economic and political structures that are viewed as the root causes of environmental destruction and social injustice. Capitalist economies and their preoccupation with endless growth, consumerism and materialism, are seen as fundamentally incompatible with an ecologically sustainable, just and equitable world order. On the other hand, a more pragmatic tradition has informed those Greens who are mindful of the realities of existing power structures. For them, compromising principles is sometimes necessary in order to win real improvements in the here and now, which would not be possible in the absence of compromise. The tensions between these traditions are also made manifest around organisational issues. Radicals regard grassroots activism and bottom-up, decentralised democratic processes as being the essential organisational supports for their radical, emancipatory ideals. Parliaments and mainstream electoral politics can be useful forums for pursuing these ideals, but they should not be fetishised. In contrast, pragmatists tend to emphasise the importance of strong, centralised leadership within political parties and the centrality of parliamentary representation for achieving real and meaningful change, even if this sometimes involves compromising one's principles.

The Australian Greens are a living embodiment of these tensions. Their charter reads like a radical manifesto for the abolition of existing conditions: 'We aim to transform the political, social and economic structures that disempower and oppress people and to develop a rich, participatory cultural life that enables the flourishing of new democratic movements for progressive change' (Australian Greens 2017). Contesting elections, and securing representation in parliaments, is seen as a necessary but not sufficient condition to this end. Instead, the emphasis is on participatory democracy and consensus forms of decision-making. Moreover, the Greens' Constitution explicitly licenses political decentralisation, stating that the constituent, state-based groups 'have the autonomy to make decisions relating to their own affairs according to their own state constitution', as long as such decisions conform to the charter and take into account national and state campaign priorities. The various state constitutions need only be 'compatible' with the

cosmopolitan:
Cosmopolitan values (often expressed as cosmopolitanism) are values which emphasise equality and the human experience beyond the nation-state.

national Constitution, not identical with it. These decentralising principles – shaped by both the federal nature of Australian politics and the separate state origins of the constituent Green groups (Miragliotta 2012, 98–100) – frequently clash with the pragmatic imperatives of the Greens' parliamentary leadership.

The unifying label 'Green', and the media visibility of the Greens' parliamentary leadership, can give a misleading impression of homogeneity to the Greens Party. In fact, it is perhaps more accurate to speak of eight state- and territory-based Greens parties – joined by a common charter – that have different origins and political practices. It is not an unreasonable generalisation to say that the Tasmanian and Queensland parties, with their roots firmly in anti-logging and environmental campaigns, and with their early formation dominated by charismatic individuals, have tended to be more centralist in their organisation than other states (Miragliotta 2012, 103–4). These other states have had more varied political progenitors that encompass broader leftist concerns, and they have placed greater emphasis on grassroots organising. This is particularly the case with the NSW branch, whose Constitution enshrines the democratic principle according to which elected representatives should be directed by the broader division on how to vote. This contradicts efforts by the parliamentary leadership – Richard di Natale today, but Christine Milne and Bob Brown before him – to act in a more disciplined, authoritative and centralised fashion. It was this contradiction that led to Lee Rhiannon's exclusion from the party room in mid-2017, when she chose to defy the national leadership and follow the directions of her state branch in denouncing so-called Gonski 2, whose passage through the Senate was being negotiated by Richard di Natale.

This was a perfect illustration of the sorts of challenges that the Greens faced, and are bound to face again in the future, as they grapple with how to reconcile their parliamentary power with their grassroots base.

SHORT-ANSWER
QUESTIONS
VIDEO

RECENT MINOR PARTY INSURGENCIES

While lacking the sustained success of the Nationals, DLP, Democrats and the Greens, a number of other important minor parties have achieved success in recent years. These parties, referred to here as the new minor party insurgents, have pursued very different policy agendas, but each has benefitted at least partially by the growing dissatisfaction with the major parties. These insurgents are a mixture of totally new players, one that rose quickly and has already disappeared and another which, long thought dead, re-emerged at the 2016 federal election. These parties, which will be discussed below, are the Palmer United Party (PUP), Pauline Hanson's One Nation (PHON) and the Nick Xenophon Team (NXT).

PUP

The Palmer United Party burst onto the Australian political scene in 2013 with one of the best debut election results for a totally new party in Australian federal political history. But less than three years later, the party was in tatters. PUP's rise and fall should be seen as a cautionary tale; a well-resourced party can make a deep impact on Australian federal politics, but managing the growing egos of those who have been elected, not to mention the broader party organisation, is a task beyond many. While most of the other successful minor party insurgencies have had a clear ideological profile, PUP was something altogether different. It was the classic catch-all party, which presented a series of crowd-pleasing policy proposals without much concern for coherence (Kefford & McDonnell 2016). The party was also unique in Australian federal history as it 'started big' contesting every electorate in the House of Representatives and every Senate contest in its first federal election. This was possible because the party's eponymous leader, Clive Palmer, bankrolled the party's campaign, splashing cash on advertising and supporting candidates on the ground with cash to manage their campaigns. Unsurprisingly, given most candidates and those in the party's head office – which was run out of one of Palmer's business interests – were political novices, it wasn't long before chaos and disorganisation reigned. This stretched the full gamut of orthodox party functions and responsibilities, including the selection and management of candidates, campaign coordination and the production of campaign material. The fact that the party would win the seat of Fairfax in the House of Representatives as well as Senate seats in Queensland, Tasmania and Western Australia was indicative of the rising levels of dissatisfaction in the electorate at this time (Kefford and McDonnell 2016).

As other parties who have broken through have found, winning seats, while incredibly difficult, is actually easier than **institutionalising** within the party system. PUP, for a short while, held the balance of power in the Senate and had a chance of cementing this with an agreement with Ricky Muir from the Australian Motoring Enthusiasts Party. But negotiations would break down and shortly afterwards the party's Tasmanian Senator, Jacqui Lambie, would leave the party to sit as an independent. The party's Queensland senator, Glenn Lazarus, followed her shortly afterwards. When Palmer unveiled the party, he said that his intention was to become the prime minister of Australia. The question left after the party's demise is whether his real intention was simply to remove policies that negatively affected his business interests. Most notable were the 'carbon tax' and the mining tax. While we may never know the answer to this question, it is clear from the PUP case that parties that are well resourced and which run on an anti-major party sentiment have a chance to be successful in contemporary Australian federal politics.

Pauline Hanson's One Nation

In the lead up to the 2016 federal election, it was widely believed that the reign of Pauline Hanson as the queen of the radical right in Australia was largely over. She was given an outside chance of election personally but no-one else in her party was given a realistic hope of election. However, the government's decision to go to a double dissolution election, which halved the threshold to win representation, changed the party's fortunes and allowed One Nation to regain a significant foothold in the Senate. The party would go on to win four Senate seats in total: two in Queensland, including one for the party's eponymous leader, one in New South Wales and one in Western Australia. But the story and impact of Pauline Hanson and One Nation runs much deeper and much further back than 2016.

Hanson was first elected to the federal parliament in the House of Representatives in 1996 in the seat of Oxley. She had been pre-selected by the Liberal Party, but during the campaign was disendorsed as a result of her inflammatory comments in a letter she wrote to the *Queensland Times* newspaper about Indigenous Australians. In 1997, with the help of co-founders David Oldfield and David Ettridge, Hanson formed PHON. Less than a year after its formation, the party did spectacularly well in the June 1998 Queensland state election, winning 22 per cent of first preferences and 11 seats in the unicameral legislature.

institutionalising:
The capacity of political parties to institutionalise in the party system; in other words, this means that parties can consolidate and remain as part of the institutional structure in the long-term. This is seen as contributing to political stability.

SHORT-ANSWER QUESTIONS

When the federal election was held in October later that year, however, Hanson failed in her bid for re-election after moving to the seat of Blair and the party only secured one Senate seat. Since that time, Hanson contested every federal election except 2010. However, this has not always been for One Nation. Hanson has also stood as a candidate in four state elections. This includes standing as an independent in the 2003 and 2011 NSW Legislative Council elections, and the 2009 and 2015 Queensland state elections.

Despite the party being named after Hanson (though this has changed multiple times), her relationship with others involved in the party has not always been easy. The fate of PHON as an electoral force has been largely wedded to that of Hanson, and in the nearly 20 years since its formation most of the significant results have been achieved when Hanson has been the leader of the party. In the period after the 2001 federal election, up until the 2013 federal election when Hanson was not involved with the party, the results were modest (Ghazarian 2015, 135–9). In this period, the party was dysfunctional; splinter groups broke away, some of the remaining parliamentarians left to become independents or joined other parties and the party was even deregistered by the Electoral Commission.

While the coverage of PHON is partially a product of the media's fascination with Hanson, it is also due to the policies PHON proposes. These policies are consistent with that of radical-right populists globally such as Marine Le Pen in France and Geert Wilders in the Netherlands. At present for PHON, this includes policies on immigration, refugees, Halal certification and Islam. In the party's first incarnation, the 'others' who were targeted were Asians and Indigenous peoples. These have been primarily replaced by Muslims. But political and economic elites remain the enemy as they have been seen as acting in their own self-interest. Climate change, acceptance of refugees and anything resembling cosmopolitanism is rejected outright.

The xenophobic nationalism of PHON is what separates it from all of Australia's other successful minor parties. This message is most successful in outer metropolitan and rural and regional areas. In the party's first period of success, their voters were predominately white, male, over the age of 50 and with modest education. While it is not entirely clear whether the demographics of the PHON voter remain the same, it can be said that the success of PHON is related specifically to the discourse and policies of the major parties. The more the major parties emphasise the inevitability of the market, global capitalism and the need for Australia to embrace immigration and refugees, the more traditional working-class voters are frustrated with a system they think is unwilling to consider their grievances. This is the niche that PHON works in and if they can maintain some level of organisational unity, there is a small but enduring market for their policies in contemporary Australian politics.

**RESEARCH
QUESTION**

The Nick Xenophon Team

At the 2016 election, the Nick Xenophon Team secured three Senate seats in South Australia and the seat of Mayo in the House of Representatives, also in South Australia. In doing so, NXT positioned itself as a force to be reckoned with and what's more, the party has a strong presence to entrench itself on the South Australian political scene for the foreseeable future. In some ways, NXT appears to resemble another minor party that was successful in South Australia – the Australian Democrats. Nick Xenophon, the party's eponymous leader, brought considerable name recognition to his party as a result of the decade he spent in the South Australian Legislative Council. According to Manning (2007), when Xenophon was elected to the Senate in 2007, he made 'history as the first

South Australian elected to the Senate. As Xenophon's six-year term in the Senate came to an end in 2013, he decided to form his own party. He argued: 'The current federal laws are stacked against independents running for the Senate, which is why there have only been a handful of independent senators in 112 years' (AAP 2013).

When he has been asked to describe the party in ideological terms, Xenophon says the party is in the 'political centre' (Grattan 2016). This positioning has also extended to the advertising the party has used, with one piece suggesting that the party wanted to 'break the duopoly' of the major parties. When the policies of NXT are analysed, what can be said is that they are largely protectionist in nature, with a heavy emphasis on Australian manufacturing and government intervention into markets. There is also a strong emphasis on infrastructure, improving education and health outcomes, and acting on predatory gambling and poker machines. On social issues the party is, for the most part, socially progressive. Support for same-sex marriage and constitutional recognition for Indigenous Australians are examples of this. The obvious historical comparison with NXT is the Democrats. Both parties have tried to position themselves as centrists, performed well in South Australia, and broad policy comparisons can be made with their socially liberal, economically protectionist and interventionist range of policy measures (Sugita 1997). The ideological profile of NXT is, therefore, certainly not as incoherent as that of PUP (Kefford and McDonnell 2016), but neither is it as clear-cut as the Greens or PHON.

The inevitable problem for NXT in both organisational and electoral terms is that the party is seen first and foremost as an advocate for the interests of South Australians. This view appears to have some basis when the party constitution is examined (NXT 2014). John Warhurst (2016) noted prior to the 2016 federal election that the Australian federal system has never really generated a successful state-based regional party compared to Canada as even those parties which have been strong in one state 'have also had wider national aspirations and representation right from the beginning'. NXT has the potential to break the mould in this respect but the challenges for the party are still significant, just as they are for any minor party.

RESEARCH QUESTION

AUSTRALIA'S 'INSURGENT' MINOR PARTIES

What should be evident from this discussion is that there is no one organisational structure, ideological mix, geographic region or strategy that guarantees the success of a minor party. Nonetheless, if there is one attribute they share, it is that each, in different ways, has tapped into grievances about either one or both of the major parties. Whether this grievance has been elite driven and led to a secessionist movement from one of the major parties, as occurred with the DLP and the Democrats, or whether this was more organic and grassroots, as is the case with the Greens, the major parties are the key. This is inevitable as while the conditions since 2007 have been ripe for minor party insurgencies, the major parties remained favoured by the electoral system and Australian political culture. What is also evident from these six cases is that despite the significant challenges for the minor parties, opportunities exist for parties who can position themselves against the major parties and can authentically engage with voters. It is no surprise that the Greens are the most successful of the insurgent parties as they have built slow and from their base. This approach should be instructive if other minor parties want to attain the level of success that the Greens have achieved across the country.

MINOR PARTIES AND THE PARTY SYSTEM

It is often assumed by supporters of parties that you refer to as a 'minor party' that you are declaring them irrelevant or that this is a pejorative label applied to a party that you disagree with. Nothing could be further from the truth. It is critical to understand that the classification of parties as 'major' and 'minor' is based on how we understand party systems to function. While in recent decades the focus of party-based research has been on how parties are organised and their ideologies, the study of party systems had previously been the dominant theme in the party literature (for example, see Blondel 1968; Duverger 1969). Discussions of party systems started by scholars counting the number of parties in the system, generally defined as those that won seats, and comparing systems that were similar to one another. Hence, discussions of a two-party system or multi-party system emerged from this starting point.

However, scholars soon realised that this approach was inadequate and did little to explain the ways that parties compete and cooperate with one another. While there have been a number theoretical innovations designed to improve the way party systems are analysed, the work of Sartori (2005) remains the most famous and widely used. In particular, it is the rules for relevance Sartori (2005, 108) devised that remains the dominant approach. Put simply, when considering how many parties in the party system are relevant, Sartori suggests we start by including those parties that have the potential to govern in their own right. You then add those parties that regularly form coalitions with these governing parties. In the Australian context, if we stopped here, we would be left with the ALP, the LPA and the Nationals. This partially explains why the Australian system is often referred to as a two or two and a half party system. But this view is dated.

According to Sartori, the next step is to consider which of the remaining parties can be considered relevant, no matter how small they are. They are relevant in the party system if they have either coalition potential or blackmail potential. This is where contemporary Australian politics is significantly different to earlier eras. While there may have been a few parties who might have met these criteria in the past, there are now far more parties who find themselves in potential blackmail positions.

In the Australian federal political landscape, the most common way that minor parties are going to find themselves in a blackmail position is through their presence in the Senate. Often, one or more minor parties can find themselves in a position in the Senate where they can extract concessions from the government of the day for supporting their legislation. The Greens, Democrats, PHON, NXT and PUP have all found themselves in these positions in recent times. Hence, if we use Sartori's framework for determining which parties are part of the party system, the Australian party system is anything but a two-party system. In fact, it is closer to a multi-party system more commonly associated with some Western European democracies. This is no surprise as many advanced industrial democracies are moving in a similar direction, especially if Sartori's model is used as a theoretical lens.

What of the other parties not included as part of the party system though? While Sartori had described these parties as irrelevant, more recent research suggests we need to think about how party systems operate. According to Kefford (2017b), 'Referring to these parties as "irrelevant" … limits our capacity to understand what is going on within the party system'. Hence, to more systematically classify parties in the party system, he has created a typology building on the pre-existing party system scholarship. Parties in the party system then can be classified as one of the following:

» Major parties are parties which regularly can be expected to form government in their own right or which can regularly be expected to become the biggest party out of government.

» Minor parties are parties which are not regularly expected to be able to form government on their own, or to be the biggest party out of government. They still, however, play an important role in the party system. They could hold balance of power or veto positions, have coalition potential or, dependent on the electoral system, could shape party competition.

» Peripheral parties are parties which have no effect on the party system. They may have parliamentary representation and/or play an important role in the polity. However, they will not have blackmail or coalition potential.

REFLECTION QUESTION

INDEPENDENTS IN THE AUSTRALIAN FEDERAL PARLIAMENT

What exactly is an independent? This seemingly straightforward question is difficult to answer. As Weeks (2017) has noted, for some, a key question as to the meaning of 'independent' is: 'independent' of what?'. For example, what makes Andrew Wilkie an independent but not Jacqui Lambie? Or why is Cathy McGowan an independent but Derryn Hinch is not? There is debate about this and many commentators and journalists make no distinction at all. This is problematic for a few reasons. First, true independents have challenges that candidates who run under a party label do not, these are important to acknowledge. Second, there is an important difference between candidates who are the only elected official of their party, such as Lambie and Hinch, and those who run under their own steam such as Wilkie and McGowan.

The independent needs to be given their proper historical context too. According to Weeks (2017, 5):

> Before the evolution of parties in Britain into their current form in the nineteenth century, independence originally meant independent of the monarch and of the great families, and later, in the eighteenth century, independent of the government. In that pre-nineteenth century era, independence therefore implied that a politician had a sufficient level of financial resources, which meant that he neither had to kowtow to the aristocracy or leave himself open to the corrupting influences of parliament.

The fact that independents not only exist, but flourish in Australia needs to be understood for how rare it is in comparative terms. There are three advanced democracies where independents exist in any significant numbers: Australia, Ireland and Japan. In the Australian context, independents have found most of their success in House of Representatives seats in regional and rural areas. The historical basis of this has been explained by Curtin (2004, 3), who contends that even in the early years of the Australian federated nation, 'many in rural and regional Australia also believed the party system would favour a particular set of interests: in their view, those of the city; and so without 'independent' representation, rural needs and values would be overlooked'. If the most common geographic area for the success of an independent is in the regional and rural areas of Australia, it should then be no surprise that this has the largest impact on previously safe Nationals and LPA seats. Independents, therefore, who have a large local profile – often this means being a former local government official and a mayor of the key town in the electorate is a good start – can be very competitive in these House of Representatives seats. This is only accentuated by the electoral system.

As mentioned in Chapter 7, in House of Representatives elections, the Alternative Vote (AV) system is used. Commonly referred to as preferential voting, this system requires voters to number the candidates in order of the candidate you like the most to the candidate you like the least. As Curtin (2004, 6) notes, 'ironically, although it was designed by and for major parties, Australia's electoral system of compulsory, preferential voting in single-member districts aids the cause of independents. Those voters disillusioned with their traditional party of choice are compelled to vote; Labor and the Coalition are more likely to direct preferences to independents than to each other; and, unlike some proportional systems, electorates are small enough to allow a candidate without the support of a party machine to assemble sufficient primary votes to win'. As votes are counted and preferences distributed until a candidate has a majority of votes in the electorate, which is effectively 50 per cent plus one vote, it means that independents only need to finish second in many districts to be successful. It is worth exploring an example of this to see how exactly this can work in the favour of independents.

The example of Andrew Wilkie in 2010 is telling here. On first preferences, Wilkie trailed both the candidates from the ALP and the Liberal Party. However, once all the preferences were distributed as was needed, Wilkie was able to win the election narrowly from the ALP candidate. The underlying message here is that if an independent candidate can win enough first preferences to be competitive with the major parties they have a chance of winning. In most instances, this will require them to finish at least second on first preferences, but it is still possible to win, albeit unlikely if they finish third, like the Wilkie example here demonstrates.

TABLE 9.1 ANDREW WILKIE ELECTION TO HOUSE OF REPRESENTATIVES IN 2010

CANDIDATE NAME	PARTY AFFILIATION	VOTES	PERCENTAGE
Andrew Wilkie	Independent	13 788	21.26%
Jonathan Jackson	Australian Labor Party	23 215	35.79%
Mel Barnes	Socialist Alliance	856	1.32%
Cameron John Simpkins	Liberal	14 688	22.65%
Geoffrey Alan Couser	Australian Greens	12 312	18.98%
Andrew Wilkie	Independent	33 217	51.21%
Jonathan Jackson	Australian Labor Party	31 642	48.79%

Source: AEC 2010. Copyright Commonwealth of Australia 2017

INDEPENDENTS AND MINORITY GOVERNMENT

Independents, of course, not only play a role in these local contests, they can on occasion be the king and queen makers of Australian federal politics. While far more common at the subnational level (see Moon 1995; Costar and Curtin 2004), there has been one notable case in recent times. The Gillard-led minority government between 2010 and 2013 is an interesting case study of the potential opportunities and pitfalls for independents taking part in minority governments. Gillard became prime minister after Kevin Rudd resigned from the position after realising he had little support to continue in the role. Early in their first term, the ALP looked in an invincible position to win re-election, but eventually limped into the 2010 poll. Alternatively, the Opposition Leader, Tony Abbott, had since taking over the role, improved the fortunes of the Coalition and they had displayed significant discipline in the lead-up to the poll. On election day, the result was a hung parliament with neither the ALP nor the Coalition able to govern in their own right by securing a majority on the floor of the house. This meant who would govern was dependent on who the six crossbench members would support.

One of these, from the WA Nationals, was always likely to side with the Coalition for the simple fact that while the WA branch was not officially affiliated with the broader Nationals organisation, they were at worst a cousin organisation. Another, Bob Katter, independent for the large Queensland seat of Kennedy, decided he would also support the Coalition. The Green, Adam Bandt, almost immediately threw his support behind the Gillard-led ALP. He was followed by Andrew Wilkie, the independent representing the Tasmanian electorate of Denison. Who would form government was left in the hands of two rural independents, Rob Oakeshott and Tony Windsor. While both represented electorates who leaned towards the conservatives, both would commit their support to the Gillard-led ALP (Costar 2012). The strength of the position that independents find themselves in when circumstances like this present themselves is hard to fathom. One example from the 2010 case is instructive. So desperate was the Abbott-led Coalition to form government, they offered Andrew Wilkie $1 billion to rebuild a hospital in Tasmania. Katter, who eventually sided with the Coalition, gave both sides a 20-point list of demands and said he would support whoever agreed to implement the most of these (Costar 2012).

Windsor and Oakeshott said that driving their decision was policy, as well as the politics. They cited, in particular, regional education, the National Broadband Network and climate change as key policies which they thought the Gillard-led ALP were best positioned to deal with. But they also noted the makeup of the Senate and believed that stability would be best served with the ALP in power as the ALP and Greens were in control of the Senate, so the Coalition would struggle to govern effectively in any case. They both did, however, extract a number of concessions from the Gillard ALP. As Costar (2012, 364) detailed, they both signed formal agreements which comprised four parts:

> a covering letter detailing proposed initiatives in each one's electorate; the 'agreement' proper, which related to supply and confidence and access of the Independents to the Prime Minister and other ministers; Annex A, which contained detail of proposed reforms to parliamentary and governmental procedures; and Annex B, which committed the government to a broad range of regional policy initiatives. The covering letters contained some

remarkably local and specific commitments; Oakeshott, for example, was promised the upgrade of the Bucketts Way at Krambach—the main regional road between Gloucester and Taree.

As Costar and Curtin (2004, 28–30) have detailed, there is now a long history of independents and the major parties coming together under a 'charter of good governance'. These various charters have, over the years, committed governments to a range of measures including parliamentary reform, increased expenditure on service delivery and greater focus to specific policy areas such as the environment. The 2010 minority government at the federal level can be seen as a continuation of these trends and demonstrates that when placed in a king or queen maker position that independents can be measured, shrewd and extracting. They also have a tendency to focus on process and attempt to improve the quality of the democratic institutions which make up Australian politics.

VIDEO

WHAT DETERMINES THE SUCCESS AND FAILURE OF MINOR PARTIES AND INDEPENDENTS?

Quite evidently from our discussion so far, minor parties and independents have to overcome significant challenges to be elected to either the House of Representatives or the Senate. The electoral system is the most obvious of these but is by no means the only challenge. These include organisational challenges, which as evidenced in the discussion of those parties who have broken through, has rarely been managed successfully. Resources are another key challenge and unless a candidate or party has the resources that PUP had at their disposal due to the personal and business wealth of their eponymous leader, Clive Palmer, this will remain a key challenge. Finally, the problem of institutionalising and entrenching oneself into the fabric of the country's political culture is a challenge, especially for minor parties. Each of these challenges will be discussed below.

In the House, minor parties and independents find themselves in a very similar position. They have to run against the machines of the major parties, which is exceedingly difficult even in a time when dissatisfaction with the political establishment is high. As demonstrated in the discussion of the election of Andrew Wilkie in 2010 in the seat of Denison, minor parties and independents have to put themselves in a position to generally have the second highest number of first preferences and, then, depending on preference flows, might be able to get over the 50 per cent + 1 vote threshold. Without name recognition this is almost impossible. Candidates from minor parties and independents who generally do well in the House usually come from one of two groups: they were local mayors or other elected officials, or they have a large profile as a result of sporting, military or cultural achievements.

The Senate is more complex. The changes to the electoral system introduced before the 2016 federal election have closed a loophole that minor parties had available to them. Before this change, parties who were registered with the Australian Electoral Commission (AEC) would immediately be placed above the line on the Senate ballot paper. As the overwhelming majority of voters – in excess of 90 per cent in most states – would only vote '1' above the line, rather than number every candidate below the line, minor parties could prearrange an exchange of preferences with other like-minded parties by utilising what was known as their 'Group Voting Tickets' (GVTs). The use of the GVTs led to a number of unusual outcomes. The most well-known of these was the election of Ricky Muir from the Australian Motoring Enthusiasts Party to a Victorian Senate spot in 2013. Muir, who only won 0.51 per cent of first preferences, was subsequently elected after he met the 14.29 per cent quota for election at a normal half-Senate election. Through prearranged deals with many other smaller political parties, each party agreed to preference the established major parties last and to send their preferences to one another (Green 2014, 2015b). The success of these tactics, which had initially been trialled at the state level in New South Wales, led to a huge number of new parties registering with the AEC and flooding the ballot. In 2013, for example, the New South Wales Senate ballot paper was estimated to be almost two metres long. The electoral reforms of 2016 for the Senate ballot paper have all but closed these loopholes as they mean that voters no longer have to either simply vote '1' above the line or number all the numbers below the line. Voters now need to number at least six boxes above the line or at least 12 boxes below the line. So, while voters now have more flexibility in determining how their preferences are distributed, this has increased the challenge for minor parties.

Quite evidently, from the earlier discussion on the minor parties who have been successful, party organisation and the resources the party has at its disposal are also important. But these are not panacea to all a party's problems. As was evident in the case of PUP, having near unlimited financial resources does not make up for party dysfunction and disorganisation. While difficult, parties and independents that can work out ways to manage the various challenges they face are going to perform the best. These challenges include, for example, how to manage the exploding egos of elected officials, the relationship between party elites and the grassroots, how to make policy, how to determine when and when not to deal with the government and the opposition, and who to hire as staff in the offices of elected officials. If minor parties and independents can successfully manage these challenges, there are opportunities for them in the Australian federal system in the contemporary climate and, thus, challenges for the major parties in needing to negotiate and work with them.

What is the process for political parties registering to contest an Australian federal election?

SPOTLIGHT

If an individual or group of individuals want to start their own party and stand as a candidate or group of candidates for election to the Commonwealth parliament, they have to follow a registration process administered by the AEC. As part of this process, a party constitution needs to be created which sets out at least some of the aims of the party, who the registered officers of the party will be and what the party will be known as.

Before this occurs, however, the new party needs to meet the conditions for registration. Either the party needs to have over 500 members who are on the electoral roll, or a new party can be registered by any current member of parliament. This is the way that a number of relatively new minor parties have been created. For example, the Jacqui Lambie Network and the Nick Xenophon Team. The party then needs to complete an application for party registration form, attach all documents plus a $500 application fee.

If the AEC accepts that these documents are in order, they will advertise that an application for new party registration has occurred on their website as well as in major newspapers. During this period, objections can be lodged with the AEC about the new party registration. Objections generally relate to whether the name of the party is too similar to other parties or if there is a challenge to whether the party has met the requirements for registration. If the party successfully passes this stage, they can be officially registered as a party that can contest Australian federal elections.

QUESTION

Do you think parliamentarians who have defected from other parties, like Jacqui Lambie and Corey Bernardi did, should be allowed to start their own parties?

pre-poll: The period in the lead up to the day that an election is held where voters can cast their ballots early at specific polling places.

The organisational challenges for both minor parties and independents are vast. For example, who do they ask to campaign on their behalf? Considering the major parties often struggle to have members and supporters present at each booth or **pre-poll** venue, how are minor parties and independents meant to meet this challenge? Nick Xenophon once said that he and NXT were not working on a 'shoestring budget but a dental floss budget'. This anecdote, while amusing, contains a kernel of truth for all minor parties and independents. They are under-resourced and out-gunned when they come up against the major party machines. To overcome this, candidates will often invest their own money in their campaigns. On one level, this is admirable and demonstrates that democratic politics below the major parties is filled with people who want to participate in the political process. But it also reveals a fundamental truth about Australian federal politics. The major parties, with their history, hundreds of elected officials in each state and territory at local, state and federal levels, can and do use the resources and prestige that each layer of government provides them to ensure their colleagues in other layers of government are also elected. Minor parties and independents, with the exception of the Greens, have nothing close to this.

Even those parties who do manage to break through the cartel face serious organisational and resource challenges if they want to last longer than one term. The case of PUP is instructive here. The party had enormous financial resources but were unable to manage the pressures of public office and the inevitable ballooning egos of their elected representatives. Panebianco (1988, 18–19) articulated the challenge that new parties face when they move from a phase 'in which organizational identity is manifest (the objectives being explicit and coherent), to a phase in which the organisational ideology is latent (the objectives being vague, implicit, and contradictory)'. For parties such as NXT and PHON, their goals were to turn Xenophon and Hanson's personal popularity and name recognition into something larger than themselves. What are the objectives once they have achieved this aim? Successfully managing this transition will require party elites to clarify what the objectives of the party are, and to think about ways to include candidates, members and supporters in party decision-making. If this cannot be achieved, these parties may replicate the fate of PUP who faded as quickly as they rose due to internal party chaos.

SUMMARY

Learning objective 1: Recognise the growing importance of minor parties and independents

Minor parties and independents are playing an increasingly important role in Australian federal politics. Since 2007, there has been a steady increase in the vote share for minor parties and independents. This has led to a record number of crossbenchers being elected following the 2016 federal election.

Learning objective 2: Describe the key post-war non-major parties who have been in coalition with or in key veto positions with the major parties

This is not to suggest that Australia does not have a long history with minor parties. In the post-war period, Australia has had a number of key minor parties. One particular set of these minor parties, who have been described here as the 'veto players', have been able to, as a result of their balance of power position in the Australian Senate, play a disproportionately large role on political and policy outcomes. Three key examples of this are the DLP, the Australian Democrats and the Australian Greens.

Learning objective 3: Describe the recent insurgent minor parties who have been successful

Beyond these three 'veto players' a number of insurgent minor parties have emerged. These parties are organisationally and ideologically varied. Some appear to have followed in the footsteps of now defunct veto players, like NXT has for the Democrats, others rose suddenly and disappeared even quicker, while others have reappeared from obscurity. This suggests that there is fertile ground for minor parties in Australian federal politics.

Learning objective 4: Explain the differences between major and minor parties

In considering the role that minor parties play and how they have influenced Australian federal politics, they need to be distinguished from Australia's major parties. This can be done by thinking about the role they play in the Australian party system. Major parties are parties of government; minor parties are parties that still play an influential role and are 'relevant' but are unable to form government in their own right.

Learning objective 5: Recognise the way that other institutional factors of electoral systems affect minor parties and independents in Australian politics

Clearly, minor parties and independents are affected by the institutional structure of the political system they work in. This is most pronounced in terms of the electoral system. In elections where majoritarian electoral systems are used, like that in the House of Representatives, minor parties can often struggle as they are outmatched by the major party machines. They have far greater opportunities in the Senate as a result of the proportional system that is employed. Independents, in contrast, are in almost the exact opposite situation. While independents have found success in the House, they are rarely elected to the Senate, as they are lost on the ballot paper, being below the line.

DISCUSSION QUESTIONS

1. What do the varied types of minor parties that have been successful tell you about Australian federal politics?

DISCUSSION
QUESTIONS

2. Is Australia becoming a multi-party system like there are in some Western European democracies?
3. What challenges beyond the electoral system do Australia's minor parties and independents face in being elected to the Commonwealth parliament?
4. What role beyond holding the major parties to account do minor parties and independents play in Australian federal politics?
5. Why have independents been successful in Australian federal politics?

FURTHER READING

Bartlett, A. (2009). The Australian Democrats. *Australian Cultural History*, **27**(2), 187–93.

Blondel, J. (1990). *Comparative Government: An Introduction*, New York and London: Philip Allan.

Bolleyer, N. (2012). New party organization in Western Europe: Of party hierarchies, stratarchies and federations. *Party Politics*, **18**(3), 315–36.

Bolleyer, N. (2013). *New Parties in Old Party Systems: Persistence and Decline in Seventeen Democracies*, Oxford: Oxford University Press.

Crabb, A. (2015). Protest parties have all the answers until reality bites, *The Sydney Morning Herald*, 14 March. Retrieved from: http://www.smh.com.au/comment/annabel-crabb-protest-parties-have-all-the-answers-until-reality-bites-20150313-1435t9.html#ixzz3uwhxgmok

Ghazarian, Z. (2015). Organisational approaches of the right-of-centre minor parties. In N. Miragliotta, A. Gauja and R. Smith, eds, *Contemporary Australian Political Party Organisations*, Melbourne: Monash University Publishing, pp. 50–61.

Jaensch, D. and Mathieson, D.S. (1998). *A Plague on Both Your Houses: Minor Parties in Australia*, St Leonards, NSW: Allen & Unwin Academic.

King, T. (2015). The advent of two new micro parties: The Palmer United Party and Katter's Australia Party. In C. Johnson, J. Wanna and H.A. Lee, eds, *Abbott's Gambit: The 2013 Australian Federal Election*, Canberra: ANU E-Press, pp. 293–310.

Mair, P. (1991). The electoral universe of small parties in postwar Western Europe. In F. Müller-Rommel and G. Pridham, eds, *Small Parties in Western Europe: Comparative and National Perspectives*, London: Sage, pp. 41–70.

Novák, M. and Cassling, R. (2000). The relevance of small parties: From a general framework to the Czech 'Opposition Agreement'. *Czech Sociological Review*, 27–47.

Richmond, K. (1978). Minor parties in Australia. In G. Starr, K. Richmond and G. Maddox, eds, *Political Parties in Australia*, Melbourne: Heinemann Educational Australia, pp. 317–85.

Smith, G. (1991). In search of small parties: Problems of definition, classification and significance. In F. Müller-Rommel and G. Pridham, eds, *Small Parties in Western Europe: Comparative and National Perspectives*, London: Sage, pp. 23–40.

REFERENCES

AAP. (2013). Independent senator Nick Xenophon to form his own political party, 22 May. URL: http://www.theaustralian.com.au/national-affairs/politics-news/independent-senator-nick-xenophon-to-form-his-own-political-party/story-fn59nqld-1226648186859

Australian Electoral Commission. (2016). 2016 Federal Election. URL: http://vtr.aec.gov.au/senatedownloadsmenu-20499-csv.htm

Australian Electoral Commission (2010). TAS Division – Denison. URL: http://results.aec.gov
.au/15508/website/housedivisionfirstprefs-15508–194.htm

Australian Greens. (2017). *The Australian Greens Charter and Constitution*. URL: https://greens
.org.au/sites/greens.org.au/files/AG_Constitution_amended May_2017.pdf

Blondel, J. (1968). Party systems and patterns of government in Western democracies. *Canadian
Journal of Political Science*, **1**(2), 180–203.

Chipp, D. and Larkin, J. (1978). *Don Chipp: The Third Man*, Adelaide: Rigby in association with
Beckett Green.

Costar, B. (ed.). (1994). *For Better or for Worse: The Federal Coalition*, Carlton: Melbourne University
Press.

Costar, B. (2012). Seventeen days to power: Making a minority government. In M. Simms and J.
Wanna, eds, *Julia 2010: The Caretaker Election*, Canberra: ANU Press, pp. 357–70.

Costar, B.J. and Curtin, J. (2004). *Rebels With a Cause: Independents in Australian Politics*, Sydney:
UNSW Press.

Costar, B. and Woodward, D. (eds). (1985). *Country to National: Australian Rural Politics and
Beyond*, Sydney: Allen & Unwin.

Costar, B., Love, P. and Strangio, P. (eds). (2005). *The Great Schism: A Retrospective*, Carlton North:
Scribe Publications.

Curtin, J. (2004). Independents in Federal Parliament: A new challenge or a passing phase? *Politics
Program, School of Political and Social Inquiry*, Melbourne: Monash University.

Davey, P. (2010). *Ninety Not Out: The Nationals 1920–2010*, Sydney: UNSW Press.

Duverger, M. (1969). *Political Parties: Their Organization and Activity in the Modern State*, London:
Methuen.

Evans, M., Stoker, G. and Halupka, M. (2016). Now for the big question: who do you trust to
run the country? *The Conversation*, 3 May. Retrieved from https://theconversation.com/
now-for-the-big-question-who-do-you-trust-to-run-the-country-58723

Fitzgerald, R. (2003). *The Pope's Battalions: Santamaria, Catholicism and the Labor Split*, Brisbane:
University of Queenland Press.

Ghazarian, Z. (2015). *The Making of a Party System: Minor Parties in the Australian Senate*,
Melbourne: Monash University Publishing.

Graham, B.D. (1966). *The Formation of the Australian Country Parties*, Canberra: ANU Press.

Grattan, M. (2016). Grattan on Friday: In conversation with Nick Xenophon, *The Conversation*, 9
June. Retrived from https://theconversation.com/grattan-on-friday-in-conversation-with-nick-
xenophon-60798

Green, A. (2014). Ricky Muir's strange path to the Senate, 7 August. Retrieved from http://blogs.abc
.net.au/antonygreen/2014/08/ricky-muirs-strange-path-to-the-senate.html

Green, A. (2015a). Explaining the results. In C. Johnson, J. Wanna and H.A. Lee, eds, *Abbott's
Gambit*, Canberra: ANU Press, pp. 393–410.

Green, A. (2015b). The origin of senate group ticket voting, and it didn't come from the major parties,
23 September. Retrieved from http://blogs.abc.net.au/antonygreen/2015/09/the-orogins-of-
senate-group-ticket-voting-and-it-wasnt-the-major-parties.html

Jackson, S. (2016). *The Australian Greens: From Activism to Australia's Third Party*, Melbourne:
Melbourne University Press.

Kefford, G. (2017a). Minor parties. In A. Gauja, P. Chen, J. Pietsch and J. Curtin, eds, *Double
Dissolution: The 2016 Australian Federal Election*, Canberra: ANU Press.

Kefford, G. (2017b). Rethinking small political parties: From micro to peripheral. *Australian Journal
of Political Science*, **52**(1), 95–109.

Kefford, G. and McDonnell, D. (2016). Ballots and billions: Clive Palmer's personal party. *Australian Journal of Political Science*, **51**(2), 183–97.

Love, P. (2005). The Great Labor Split of 1955: An overview. In B. Costar, P. Love and P. Strangio, eds, *The Great Schism: A Retrospective*, Carlton North: Scribe Publications, pp. 1–20.

Maddox, G. (1996). *Australian Democracy in Theory and Practice*, 3rd edn, South Melbourne: Longman.

Manning, H. (2007). *South Australians at the Polls – The 2007 National Election*, School of Political and International Studies, Flinders University.

Mayer, H. (1980). Big party chauvinism and minor party romanticism. In H. Mayer and H. Nelson, eds, *Australian Politics: A Fifth Reader*, Melbourne: Longman Cheshire, pp. 345–60.

McAllister, I. (2002). Political parties in Australia: Party stability in a utilitarian society. In P. Webb, D. Farrell and I. Holliday, eds, *Political Parties in Advanced Industrial Democracies*, Oxford: Oxford University Press, pp. 379–408.

McAllister, I. (2011). *The Australian Voter: Fifty Years of Change*, Sydney: UNSW Press.

McMullin, R. (1991). *The Light on the Hill: The Australian Labor Party, 1891–1991*, Melbourne: Oxford University Press.

Miragliotta, N. (2006). One party, two traditions: Radicalism and pragmatism in the Australian Greens. *Australian Journal of Political Science*, **41**(4), 585–96.

Miragliotta, N. (2012). Federalism, party organization and the Australian Greens. *Australian Journal of Politics & History*, **58**(1), 97–111.

Moon, J. (1995). Minority government in the Australian states: From Ersatz majoritarianism to minoritarianism. *Australian Journal of Political Science*, **30**, 142–63.

Nick Xenophon Team. (2014). Constitution. URL: https://nxt.org.au/assets/uploads/6-constitution-19.12.14-final.pdf

Panebianco, A. (1988). *Political Parties: Organization and Power*, Cambridge and New York: Cambridge University Press.

Radcliffe, J. (2002). *Green Politics: Dictatorship or Democracy?* London: Palgrave.

Reynolds, P. (2005). The Democratic Labor Party: A retrospective. In B. Costar, P. Love and P. Strangio, eds, *The Great Labor Schism: A Retrospective*, Carlton North: Scribe Publications, pp. 291–300.

Sartori, G. (2005). *Parties and Party Systems: A Framework for Analysis*, Colchester: ECPR Press.

Sugita, H. (1997). Ideology, internal politics and policy formulation. In J. Warhurst, ed., *Keeping the Bastards Honest: The Australian Democrats' First Twenty Years*, Sydney: Allen & Unwin, pp. 155–76.

Tilby Stock, J. (1997). The Australian Democrats and minor parties. In D. Woodward, A. Parkin and J. Summers, eds, *Government, Politics, Power and Policy*, South Melbourne: Addison-Wesley Longman, pp. 168–83.

Warhurst, J. (ed.). (1997). *Keeping the Bastards Honest: The Australian Democrats' First Twenty Years*, Sydney: Allen & Unwin.

Warhurst, J. (2016). Federal election 2016: All aboard the NXT express with Nick Xenophon, 22 June. Retrieved from http://www.smh.com.au/comment/the-nxt-express-20160621-gpo5fo.html

Weeks, L. (2017). *Independents in Irish Party Government*, Manchester: Manchester University Press.

CHAPTER 10

FOLLOW THE LEADER: POLITICAL LEADERSHIP IN AUSTRALIA

LEARNING OBJECTIVES

After reading this chapter, you should be able to:

1. Understand the tension between leadership and liberal democracy

2. Recall some of the theoretical debates about the importance of leaders

3. Explain the different arenas leaders work in and the different skills they require

4. Summarise the debate about Australia's 'leadership problem'

5. Describe the leadership gender gap and some of the methods employed to remedy this

INTRODUCTION

Political gridlock, policy failures, tight election contests. No matter the circumstances, one thing is certain: **political leadership** will be cited as both the cause and the solution. But is leadership really as important as it is made out to be or, alternatively, are the institutional and structural contexts in which leaders work the key determinant of success and failure? This question has long been debated in political science and scholars have sought to understand the relationship between actors and the agency they possess and how structures shape, mould and bend to the will of actors. Debates about leadership churn are especially relevant in Australia given the number of political leaders that were replaced in the decade following the 2007 federal election.

While questions about leadership can appear abstract at first, understanding the friction between leadership and liberal democracy provides scholars and students with a deeper grasp of our institutional setup. Hence, questions about whether it really matters who are the leaders of the major parties, or even the prime minister, are not merely theoretical or philosophical pursuits. In considering political leadership in Australia, this chapter begins by considering the tension that exists between leaders in liberal democracies and the democratic institutions they work within. It then outlines some of the theories about leaders and leadership. It goes on to investigate and discuss Australian political leadership by considering the different types of political leadership in Australia. This extends beyond the parties and includes the bureaucracy, interest groups and NGOs. Following this, debates about recent leadership failure and supposed 'poor leaders' in Australia will take place. This chapter also deals with questions related to structure and **agency** as well as the political leadership gender gap in Australia.

political leadership: Leadership involves more than occupying a leadership position; it is the capacity to take and build support for difficult policy decisions by motivating followers.

agency: The ability of social actors to act freely and independently. Social scientists debate the extent to which agency is restricted by context and structure – by the institutions and processes which define social roles.

AUTHOR
PANEL

LEADERSHIP AND DEMOCRACY

Is it possible to both lead and be a representative of the people? This seemingly simple question goes to the central conundrum for political leaders in liberal democracies. They are meant to represent electorates, parties and nations, acting as the delegate for these different groups with disparate interests, but they are also required to demonstrate their initiative and capacity to drive political and policy progress. While not impossible, the tension between the need to represent and to lead are often incompatible. This explains many of the problems that leaders in liberal democracies face. Indeed, when we think about what democracy means, this problem is further illustrated. Democracy literally means rule by the people and 'Democracy is about an autonomous **demos** governing itself as a collective, which entails that rulers who control the coercive power of the state need to be constrained' (Hendriks and Karsten 2014, 41).

demos: Effectively refers to the population of a democratic state and was used to refer to the citizens of the Ancient Greek states.

While there are alternatives, such as rule by an elite few (aristocracy) or the rule by an individual with absolute power (autocracy), it has long been accepted that democracy is the best of the options available. Combining popular rule with organisational structures to maintain the social and political order that allows nations to try to resolve complex problems is extremely challenging. Democratic leadership is therefore inherently problematic, as how can societies be simultaneously governed by the people and by their leaders? Indeed, this reveals the difference between modern representative or liberal democracy and earlier types of democracy. In its original Athenian form, democracy involved the direct participation of a small number (500) of male citizens in their government. However, today's democracy is more often understood as rule by the people's representatives and is marked by popular elections, political parties and parliamentary representation. Like elsewhere, these are the institutions and processes that characterise the Australian political system.

According to Kane and Patapan (2012, 14), leadership has often been overlooked by scholars and students of democracy; and 'inherent in this neglect is the suspicion that leadership, if inevitable, is inevitably "elitist"'. This is particularly prescient for a number of reasons. First, considering the focus on freedom or liberty in liberal democracies this suspicion is, in part, understandable. Liberal democracies like to compare themselves to authoritarian regimes to highlight how good their citizens have it. Second, the rise of various populist parties and movements around the globe have shown that this suspicion is felt strongly by many voters who espouse democratic but illiberal values. This means that these voters may support democracy but they seek greater direct influence over decisions by the 'people', who they perceive to have been shut out of the decision-making (Mudde and Kaltwasser 2014, 385).

The tension between leadership and democracy and how this tension should be resolved has been an endless source of debate by political scientists and philosophers. Kane and Patapan (2012, 15) suggest that 'democratic theory since 1915 can be interpreted as a variety of attempts to affirm, modify, or transcend what Robert Michels then described as the iron law of oligarchy'. Michel's (1962) thesis is that all organisations, including those with democratic ideals, will inevitably become dominated by a few elites. Other theorists have sought to redefine liberal democracy as not rule by the people but elite rule with public approval (Schumpeter 1961, 246). But this particular view inverts the logic of representative democracy. It rejects the suggestion that voters choose a parliament which, in turn, chooses and holds leaders accountable. Instead leaders are thought to manufacture public opinion and shape the electoral choices voters will make.

While these approaches show that there are a variety of theories about how leadership and democracy shape one another, they generally consign voters to the passive role of bystanders. This is a step too far for those who emphasise the importance of the participation of citizens in their government in so far as this is possible in a complex, diverse society such as Australia's. In a representative democracy, voters must be able to determine who governs, both by electing representatives to parliament to form and then hold governments accountable and – in between elections – by actively participating via grassroots activism in various units of civil society, through expressing their views in opinion polls, surveys, petitions or via social media. Leadership is absolutely necessary in all of these processes and forums as will be discussed in the rest of the chapter. However, the tension between these leaders and those who are led are as acutely felt in these organisations as they are in society as a whole.

SHORT-ANSWER
QUESTIONS

THEORISING POLITICAL LEADERSHIP

The theoretical literature on political leadership is incredibly diverse. It traverses a variety of areas in political science with little consensus on why and how leaders are important. Nonetheless, there are a number of theories which are helpful in unpacking the opaque nature of leadership in liberal democracies. One such theory comes from Heywood (2013, 301–3), who suggests leadership can be understood in four ways: as a natural gift, as a sociological phenomenon, an organisational necessity and as a political skill. The idea that leadership is a natural gift is an ancient premise that men, as they all were at this time, were born with some special attributes that allowed them to change the course of history. Very few, if any, social scientists would still subscribe to such a view, which would be seen as simplistic as it underestimates the institutions, history and social forces that shape political contexts. As Heywood notes (2013, 302), from this perspective leaders 'do not so much impose their will on the world as act as a vehicle through which historical forces are exerted'. Hence, the personalities of individuals are not as important as the conditions these leaders find themselves working in. A more instrumental view of leadership is to view it simply as a necessity that needs to be met. In this view, leadership is therefore a part of bureaucratic politics and the more complex and bureaucratic that politics becomes, the more that leaders and leadership will be required. The final theory of leadership, that it is a political skill, suggests that leadership is something that can be learned, whereby leaders can try to use their personality as well as the resources available to them to convince others of their position and to drive political and policy outcomes. Whichever we think best describes leadership, it is evident that attempts to create theoretical models are likely to be contested.

PRIME MINISTERS AND POWER

Prime ministers, as the most well-known face of political leadership in Australia, have received significant academic scrutiny. While this literature has a number of dimensions, one important theoretical and empirical debate is about whether the capacity of political leaders to 'get their way' and to lead with little interference from colleagues and institutions has increased. While there has been much written in recent decades about how and why leaders may have more power or authority than they once had, Bennister (2008, 336–7) argues that:

> In contrast to the burgeoning study of leadership in other disciplines, political science has been slow to make systemic analyses of political leadership. The keenness of scholars to concentrate on institutions and structures has led to a downplaying of the role of leadership. Prime Ministers, in particular, are viewed as constrained actors, dependent and contingent.

This has certainly been true of how leaders, but specifically prime ministers, have been viewed in Australia. But these debates are not new. In fact, they have a long and storied history. Within Westminster parliamentary democracies, this can be traced back to debates in the UK that considered whether cabinet government remained an accurate description of how the executive functioned. Critics contended that, in fact, a better description was prime ministerial government (Bennister 2008, 337; 2012; Honeyman 2007, 4; Crossman 1963). These debates continued for decades in Westminster settings, but two important theoretical contributions have emerged since. The first of these is known as **personalisation**, while the second is referred to as **presidentialisation**.

While these will be discussed in more detail in the section that follows, it is worth considering the language we use to describe governments. It has now become commonplace that when we talk about Australian federal governments, that we refer to them as the 'Rudd Government', the 'Abbott Government' or the 'Turnbull Government'. By doing this, we are assigning the success and failure of these governments to the prime minister and the leader of one of the major parties. In one way, this makes sense as the responsibility stops at the top, or at least it should. However, it also simplifies the complexity of the system, the way parties and parliament work. Depending on who you ask, this may or may not matter, but it is a simplification of some of the features of the personalisation debate, which is where we will now turn.

A PERSONALISED OR PRESIDENTIAL POLITICS?

Explanations vary widely for the causes of personalisation. However, the media is generally seen as central. According to McAllister (2007): 'The electronic media have been seen as crucial in shaping the way that governments communicate with voters and seek to convert them; at the same time, party leaders have exploited their exposure in the electronic media in order to attract votes'. While there is considerable debate about it (Karvonen 2010), a weakening of the major parties is often seen as contributing to personalisation. The effect of which is generally said to be that potential leaders will attempt to build a support base outside the party as well as within it. Most important in this regard was the evolution of the media landscape and this starts with the rise of television. From the 1960s onward television gave a new prominence – and new political opportunities – to leaders. But the media is no magic bullet and broader changes to democratic politics and our societies also need to be considered. Indeed, in the view of McAllister 'Whatever the importance of the media in this process, no single explanation accounts for the increasing personalisation of politics in democratic societies' (McAllister 2007, 573).

While related to the idea of personalisation, presidentialisation goes much further (Kefford 2013; Dowding 2013a; Dowding 2013b). According to Poguntke and Webb (2005,1), 'presidentialisation denotes a process by which regimes are becoming more presidential in their actual practice without, in most cases, changing their regime type'. In other words, presidentialisation describes circumstances in which leaders acquire more resources and autonomy within the institutional parameters of their regime. Poguntke and Webb (2005, 7) perceived that this process has three distinct faces: the executive face, the party face and the electoral face. In their view, each 'revolves around the tension between political parties and individual leaders'. The crux of the claim is that prime ministers have accumulated presidential-like powers in that they can govern over or around their Cabinet and party. Thus, the executive face of presidentialisation is supposedly apparent in the expansion of the Department of Prime Minister and Cabinet as well as an array of advisers working in close contact with the prime minister. The party face of presidentialisation involves a shifting balance of power within parties to the advantage of leaders and can be seen in the political leverage prime ministers today have because they carry extra responsibility to sell their party to voters. The electoral face of presidentialisation is evident in the pivotal role

personalisation: A theory that suggests that individual political actors have become more prominent at the expense of political parties and other collective actors.

REFLECTION
QUESTIONS

presidentialisation: A theory that suggests that the expanding powers of the office, the media attention they command, and their pivotal place in election campaigns has seen prime ministers accrue a now considerable authority and autonomy.

that party leaders have in modern-day election campaigns; in the ready-made opportunity they have to speak directly to voters, which flows from the focus that news media give to leaders; and the increasing tendency for voters to rely upon their perceptions of leaders in choosing which party to support at the ballot box.

Not all political scientists agree that parliamentary politics has become presidentialised. There are after all fundamental structural differences between presidential and parliamentary systems. Tiffen (2017, 155) points out that in Australia: 'Party leadership is, first of all and inescapably, leadership of the party room, of a relatively small group of MPs'. Relations in the closed party room are 'crucial to the leader's survival'. The circumstances of presidents are very different. They are directly elected by voters, which can be advantageous but have the problem of dealing with a legislature that they often have little control over. Compare this to a prime minister in Australia, who will already have control of the House of Representatives, and this is why many scholars argue that prime ministers are more powerful than presidents already, so describing the phenomenon as presidentialisation is misleading (Dowding 2013). There are many dimensions to this debate, and they are hotly contested. Their importance is that they allow us to think about the ways that political actors respond to incentives in the Australian political system, and the ways that norms develop and are abandoned.

SHORT-ANSWER
QUESTIONS

NO, PRIME MINISTER

In considering the ways that political leaders exercise power, James Walter and Paul Strangio (2007) investigated five Australian prime ministers seeking to explain the growing importance of the office. Their study examined the (different) leadership styles of Whitlam, Fraser, Hawke, Keating and Howard and sheds light on what distinguishes leadership from holding office. Their analysis also draws attention to long-term structural factors that explain the growing importance of prime ministers – factors such as the growing web of ministerial advisers, the expanding influence of the Commonwealth vis-á-vis the states, the politicisation of the public service and the changing nature of parties. They consider that democracies require both leaders who are able to provide the political community with direction, and the support of robust institutions, including advisers and an independent public service able to say 'no, prime minister' along with an effective opposition able to provide alternative policy advice.

One maxim often repeated in the large literature on leadership is that 'the most effective leaders surround themselves with the right people' (Rath and Conchie 2008, 2). Walter and Strangio (2007) also make this point. While the capacity of prime ministers to lead is shaped by institutional context and by their personality, style and skill, governing inescapably entails working with a wide range of other players. Prime ministers do not govern alone, and prime-ministerial leadership is always co-dependent on colleagues and followers. Their relationship with their party is a 'critical source of leadership empowerment and constraint' (Strangio, 't Hart and Walter 2013, 2–3). Put another way, the capacity of prime ministers to exercise the authority their office brings – their *agency* – is both enhanced and contained by *structure* – by their dependence on public servants, advisers, ministers and their party. This may seem contradictory; however, this is part of the chimerical nature of leadership and why successful leaders accrue and exercise power in different ways (Heifetz 2010, 16).

Ultimately, there are no recipes for success for Australian prime ministers. While there are some templates that are often cited, such as the way that John Howard or Bob Hawke managed their Cabinets, what works for one leader may not necessarily work for another. Prime ministers are dependent on their colleagues, the public service and those within their party. As leaders, prime ministers will not always have a determining influence on issues (Strangio, 't Hart and Walter 2013, 11). To further complicate matters, prime ministerial leadership is also conditional on the 'historical moment', on the political climate and current institutional conditions. For all their informal authority, style and skill, prime ministers may find themselves unable to exercise the leadership they would like (Strangio, 't Hart and Walter 2013, 9).

REFLECTION
QUESTIONS

Leadership theorists: Max Weber and James McGregor Burns

SPOTLIGHT

Here, leadership theory from Max Weber and James McGregor Burns is discussed to demonstrate the way we can analyse leadership in Australian federal politics.

Nineteenth and early 20th century German sociologist and philosopher, Max Weber, asked in what circumstances followers accept the authority of leaders. He concluded that authority takes three pure forms. Traditional authority derives from tradition and custom and is on show where monarchs rule. Rational-legal authority attaches to office: it is apparent where the holder of an office is able to issue authoritative rulings and is typical of modern governments. Charismatic authority attaches to an individual who, through sheer force of personality, commands the loyalty and trust of others. People follow charismatic leaders not because of custom or tradition or because rules require it, but because they believe in them (Weber 1978, 226–245).

Weber understood that, in practice, leaders possess overlapping kinds of authority. A prime minister will have a formal-legal authority – say the right to convene Cabinet meetings, appoint ministers, call elections, and so on. But their authority and the loyalty they command may also derive from their personal charm and have a charismatic component. Moreover, one form of authority might morph into another. Leaders who initially win power by exercising a charismatic authority over their followers may then construct rules and procedures that will confer a rational-legal authority should their charismatic appeal wane.

American historian and political scientist, James MacGregor Burns, also made a significant contribution to leadership theory by distinguishing transactional from transformational leadership (1978). The first is a managerial style of leadership devoted to securing and retaining power. Followers are offered tangible rewards for their support and loyalty. Transactional leaders motivate followers by appealing to their self-interest – compliance is achieved through a mix of reward and punishment. Prime ministers who offer voters tangible benefits such as tax cuts or subsidies for their support, or who reward their party room supporters with ministerial positions are exercising transactional political leadership.

In contrast, transformational leaders do not seek power for its own sake. They appeal to their followers' higher ideals and values and encourage their followers to put shared interests ahead of their own. Burns (1978, 4) considered that transformational leadership involves a process (rather than a series of discrete transactions) in which people engage with others 'in such a way that leaders and followers raise one another to higher levels of motivation and morality'. Transformational leadership is characteristic of periods of challenge and reform where the opportunity exists for a leader's intellectual, moral, heroic capacities to impact the solution of larger societal problem.

QUESTION

Which contemporary or recent leaders have shown transformational or transactional leadership? Think about the types of leaders mentioned earlier from outside parliament, including Indigenous leaders, leaders of business, movements, interest groups and so on.

POLITICAL LEADERSHIP IN AUSTRALIA

While parliamentary leaders, and especially prime ministers, are important and deserve significant attention, political leadership in Australia should never be seen simply as the purview of parliamentarians. Political leadership crosses cultural, social and economic lines and should not be seen as simply a top-down, hierarchical phenomena. Political leadership is evident in everyday grassroots politics within social movements, NGOs, interest groups and any number of other disparate units of civil society. Leadership is therefore not just about managing the people or institutions of the state.

Equally important to understand is that political leadership is not just about administration and decision-making by political elites behind closed doors. There is quite evidently a rhetorical aspect to political leadership. Structures and the institutional context are no doubt important but so is the capacity to use language to persuade, cajole and negotiate colleagues, political opponents as well as the citizenry. Again, this does not always need to be the grand sweeping oratory of an election victory or defeat or other significant occasion, it can also be at the grassroots, at the micro-level of democracy. Political leadership in Australia needs to be understood then as part of the everyday rhythm of politics.

It would be expected then that this broader view of what constitutes political leadership in Australia should be evident in any of the recent lists of Australia's greatest political leaders. However, disappointingly, in many of these, leadership is viewed through a very narrow prism. For example, one such list was devised by John Adams, former political adviser, and public servant. In designing his list, Adams said he hoped to kick-start public debate about the nature of genuine leadership. Australia's 'current political class', he worried, were 'obsessed with obtaining and maintaining power', unprepared 'to lead and take significant political and personal risks', attached to 'deeply ideological agendas' which do not align with 'the pressing public policy concerns of the Australian people', and are addicted to 'hyper-partisan divide and conquer tactics'. In his view, great political figures show the qualities of personal courage, willingness to act in the public and national interest, leadership, foresight, and their tenure is marked by consistency and impact (Adams in Hildebrand 2017).

Adams' complaint about the dearth of leadership within Australia's political class will resonate with many. There is a deep disappointment with the current crop of political leaders, which is evident in the growing support for anti-establishment, outsider and protest parties. But his top 10 list of leaders should raise eyebrows. To begin with, all those listed are white males. Predictably it contains figures such as wartime prime minister John Curtin, and Paul Keating who, as treasurer and prime minister, reshaped his party and Australia's economy. However, it omits Australia's longest-serving prime minister and Liberal Party founder R.G. Menzies; it has former prime minister Joseph Lyons sitting atop the list; and, perhaps even more surprising, Julian Assange, founder of Wikileaks, ranks second. While the presence of someone from outside the parliamentary ranks is laudable, the lack of diversity within this and many lists like it suggest embedded cultural expectations remain around an overtly masculine and aggressive style of leadership in Australia (Davis Musgrove and Smart 2011).

The reality is that political leadership is on display every day in public service departments and agencies, in non-government organisations and social movements, in Indigenous communities, within industry sectors, in trade unions, in think tanks, and in bodies such as the Reserve Bank of Australia (which sets monetary policy at arm's length from the government of the day). It also cannot be forgotten that those who are not normally classified as working in politics can also show political leadership. Business leaders, for example, often seek to exercise leadership in policy areas that do not directly mirror their business interests. One prominent example of this was Qantas CEO Alan Joyce being a prominent advocate of marriage equality and financially backing the Yes campaign in 2017. Another example is mining magnate Andrew Forrest who is well known for his campaigns to end slavery and to encourage fellow employers to employ Indigenous Australians. There are many more examples. Governments have even recruited business leaders to provide policy leadership. Thus, David Gonski was asked in 2010 to lead efforts to find a better model for school funding.

Of course, there are also more concerted attempts by individual leaders and groups of leaders to influence politics via the interest groups they are a part of as well. The Business Council of Australia, comprising the CEOs of some 100 of Australia's largest companies, sets out to steer policy debate – to exercise leadership – across issues ranging from tax reform to remaking Australia's Federation. The Australian Council of Trade Unions, similarly try to influence debate around industrial relations. Nonetheless, in asking what are the qualities that an effective political leader displays, it is important to consider the attributes of different types of leaders. This is important as while there is invariably significant focus on the prime minister, the unique set of institutions that they work in are atypical. Take, for example, the Aboriginal activist, leader and founder of the Cape York Institute for Policy and Leadership, Noel Pearson. Some of the methods that prime ministers or opposition leaders use, Pearson also uses, but he is free of the millstone of party and parliamentary representation. This provides Pearson with the capacity to utilise other sets of skills and to engage with a wider set of stakeholders. Parliament therefore may be the institution from which our most visible political leaders emerge, but there are many who do not hold public office, with vision and influence, who are shaping and moulding Australia's future.

REFLECTION
QUESTIONS

CHALLENGES FOR POLITICAL LEADERS

If we accept that political leaders are an inevitable feature of representative democracy, the question then is what types of demands are placed on them. This is not just a theoretical or abstract pursuit. 'Political leaders in democracies face a multitude of demands, which are hard to reconcile' (Hendriks and Karsten 2014, 42). Prime ministers require the support of political parties to win regular elections and to secure the support of parliament for their legislative program. To retain this support, they may need to make decisions that reward their party supporters and that will not be seen as being in the wider public interest. For example, when Malcolm Turnbull replaced Tony Abbott as prime minister in 2015, it was widely anticipated that he would pursue some of the 'small l' liberal policies with which he had previously advocated (such as introducing same-sex marriage and support for an emissions trading scheme to deal with climate change). But he was hamstrung by the need to placate a conservative bloc within the Liberal party room. Inevitably this weakened Turnbull's authority as prime minister and added to a growing public disillusionment with his leadership and also his government.

Another challenge for those leaders who work in the daily cut and thrust of Australian federal politics has been the ever-growing number of new players that have appeared in parliament. All recent prime ministers have had to deal with a Senate in which a historically large number of minor party and independent senators have been able to block legislation when they work together. Prime ministers have either been unable to legislate policies they had promised to introduce or been forced to engage in 'horse trading' to pass modified versions of laws they had initially proposed. In the view of many critics, this shows why the institutional structure of Australian politics no longer works the way it should, as Senators, some elected on tiny numbers of votes, should not dictate policy to the major parties who have received millions of votes. Leaving this to one side, the point is that political leadership, especially at times when there is a fragmentation in the political landscape, is hard. It requires expert negotiation skills and interpersonal skills. Moreover, the Westminster-inspired majoritarian politics, which has been dominant in Australia for decades, is largely incompatible with the new realities that leaders face.

Claims that political leaders are beholden to opinion polls has been presented as another challenge. Hugh White (2010), for one, declares that it is 'weak politicians [who] allow their policies to be dictated by public opinion. Political leadership changes public opinion to support good policy.' But this is to simplify the constraints that democracy imposes on political leaders. In 2007 Kevin Rudd declared climate change 'the greatest, moral, economic and environmental challenge of our generation' (Van Onselen 2010). This was an appeal to Australians to put higher ideals and values ahead of narrow self-interest that James MacGregor Burns (1978) might recognise as an attempt at transformational leadership. And indeed as prime minister, Rudd was able to convert lofty ideals into meaningful policy that would deal with climate change.

Had Rudd been able to secure a Senate majority, worked harder to get a deal done with the Greens or even gone to a double dissolution election on the issue, events may have followed a different course. Instead he was forced into a policy retreat, which proved especially damaging because of expectations raised by his earlier efforts at transformational leadership. Indeed, the harm to Rudd's public standing was such that his party colleagues would conclude that the ALP's best chance of retaining power lay in replacing him as party leader and prime minister. Changing public opinion to support good policy is therefore not so easily done. Leaders will not always be able to bring their party or the electorate with them. They may not always be fairly or accurately reported in the media. When public opinion is polarised, they will inevitably face a trenchant opposition able to freely voice its concerns online and in the news media. Democracy itself can therefore create circumstances that prevent transformational leadership.

SHORT-ANSWER QUESTIONS

DOES AUSTRALIA HAVE A LEADERSHIP PROBLEM?

An election defeat in 2007 ended John Howard's (11 years, 267 days) tenure as prime minister. In the decade that followed, the prime ministership changed hands five times. Rudd, Gillard, Rudd again, Abbott and then Turnbull all held the office. Three of these – Rudd, Gillard and Abbott – were overthrown by their own party. In the entire previous century, this had occurred on just three occasions. More noteworthy still, in the politically turbulent decade following Howard's defeat, each major party removed an election-winning prime minister before they had completed a full term. Labor replaced Rudd in 2010 after two years and 76 days, and the LPA replaced Abbott one year and 327 days into his first term. It appears that prime ministers today are indeed 'more vulnerable to being displaced by their own side' (Tiffen 2017, 2). If we look at the evidence in the state and Commonwealth parliaments between 1970 and 2016, the evidence suggests that leaders are viewed as dispensable. Rather than being rejected by voters or allowed to retire, 68 of the 138 leaders who have headed major parties were overthrown by their colleagues (Tiffen 2017, 2).

R.G. Menzies' 16-year tenure as prime minister is unlikely to be matched. It is equally unlikely that we will ever again see a state premier stay in office as long as Tom Playford did in South Australia (from 1938 to 1965). Internal wars over the leadership of political parties and the prime ministership are not new. Similar battles were fought in the 1980s and 1990s on both sides of politics. In the ALP, Hawke and Keating fought for the leadership and the keys to the Lodge; while in the Liberal Party, Howard and Peacock were the central protagonists in the battle for the leadership. Today party leaders are more closely scrutinised by the news media and on social media, and their performance is routinely measured by opinion polling and low favourability ratings, encouraging both voters and their party room colleagues to question their leadership.

When a leadership challenge occurs, it has also become common for the media to report voters saying that they voted for the leader and their colleagues should not be able to replace them. Leaders will often invoke this direct relationship they share with voters too. For example, when Abbott was replaced by Turnbull he said, 'It's the people that hire, and frankly it's the people that should fire' (Bourke 2015). However, there are a few problems with this analysis. To begin with, this is not how liberal democracy works in a parliamentary system. But more than this, while voters might say this is their view at the time, longitudinal survey data tells us that when voters express why they voted the way they did, individual leaders usually fall well behind a long list of policy preferences. Hence, while we need to recognise that some voters do feel that they develop a bond with various leaders, it is equally important to recognise that the evidence suggests that whether voters like or are comfortable with a particular leader's style, does not determine the way they vote. Nonetheless, cutting down leaders, especially when it is seen as unnecessary, is unlikely to be rewarded by Australian voters.

RESEARCH QUESTION

Is the recent leadership churn unusual?

Australia has been described as the 'coup capital of the democratic world' for the manner and the frequency that political leaders are replaced (Bryant 2015). But is this just hyperbole? Is the recent period all that different to earlier periods of Australian politics?

TABLE 10.1 'LEADERSHIP CHURN' IN CONTEMPORARY AUSTRALIAN POLITICS

DATE	ALP	LIBERAL PARTY
29 Nov 2007		Brendan Nelson becomes leader of the Liberal Party and Opposition Leader following the 2007 election loss
3 Dec 2007	Kevin Rudd sworn in as PM after leading ALP to 2007 election victory	
15 September 2008		Malcolm Turnbull replaces Brendan Nelson as Opposition Leader
1 December 2009		Tony Abbott replaces Malcolm Turnbull as Opposition Leader
24 June 2010	Julia Gillard replaces Kevin Rudd as PM	
26 June 2013	Kevin Rudd replaces Julia Gillard as PM	
18 September 2013		Tony Abbott sworn in as PM after leading the Coalition to the 2013 election victory
10–13 October 2013	Bill Shorten becomes leader of the ALP and Opposition Leader after 2013 election loss	
14 September 2015		Malcolm Turnbull replaces Tony Abbott as PM

While it is hard to dispute that there have been a significant number of leadership changes, whether this period is unique is worth considering. One example in modern times has been the Liberal Party during the period that the Hawke and Keating governments were in power. After the Hawke-led ALP defeated the Fraser Government at the 1983 federal election, Andrew Peacock was elected as leader of the Liberal Party. He would subsequently be replaced by John Howard in 1985, who would then be replaced again by Andrew Peacock in 1989. In 1990 it was John Hewson's turn. By 1994, Alexander Downer was the leader. And then in 1995, Howard returned to lead the Liberal Party again. He would remain as leader till the defeat of his government at the 2007 federal election, where he also lost his own seat of Bennelong. Nonetheless, while in opposition, the party changed leaders six times across the space of 12 years. While the ALP was in government, there was also significant ongoing friction about leadership although the leadership of the party and the government only changed hands once in 1991. When the most recent period is compared to this earlier period, you could argue there is a slight increase in leadership turnover but to call it unique in Australian politics is an exaggeration. The important questions are whether the turnover of leaders is healthy for Australian politics and what is driving such turnover?

QUESTION

What are the different types of justification given for leadership changes in Australia and which of these are the most defensible? For example, personality, electoral success or failure, ideology.

WHY HAS THERE BEEN A 'REVOLVING DOOR' OF LEADERS?

The larger question scholars and commentators of Australian democracy need to ask is whether the problem is not the actors, but the incentives in the system itself. In other words, does the institutional structure and political culture incentivise the 'coup culture' that has dominated Australian federal politics from 2007 onwards. While there is much discussion about politicians being in it for themselves, feathering their own nests and just waiting for their supposedly exorbitant pensions, the reality is that the pressure and sacrifices to serve as an elected official in the federal parliament are enormous and should not be underestimated. For one, even backbenchers work very long hours and have to be away from home for large parts of the year. The higher up the ranks one goes, the greater the demands. Relationships with family and friends weaken or cease to exist as the Canberra 'bubble' becomes the lives of those who walk the corridors of power. Who would want to be away from friends and family for over half the year and who would want to be working seven days a week and, in many cases, 16–18 hours per day?

The answer to this question is that only a very small minority of the Australian population would want to live this life and make these sacrifices. Within this group there will be those who are willing to make these sacrifices for the betterment of Australia, but there will also be others for whom this sacrifice is a means to an end. Their goal will be to climb the ladder of Australian democracy and one day, ideally, their achievements will finally match their ambitions. That this latter group exists is not necessarily a bad thing, but the intense scrutiny and personal sacrifices that need to be made to serve in Canberra are not to be underestimated. Clearly this has some effect on not only who is elected to parliament, but also the types of personalities that are incentivised in the Australian political system.

While in the Spotlight box above, we suggested that the major parties changing their leader frequently is not unique, we do need to recognise that leaders are remaining in their positions for shorter periods than previously. According to Gauja (2015), this is partially attributable to domestic factors but we also need to recognise that the nature of party politics is changing: 'Citizens are less engaged with formal political institutions; are more likely to use social media and act as citizen reporters and run their own issue campaigns; are more educated and likely to be more critical of, and less loyal to, parties'. But there is another factor that has also been overlooked so far. This is how Australia's political parties select their leaders. Increasingly, who votes for the party leader has changed in other parliamentary democracies. An interesting counterpoint here is the way the UK parties select their party leaders. In the case of the UK's three biggest parties, the Conservatives, the Labour Party and the Liberal Democrats, leaders are selected by a broader range of people than simply the political representatives in parliament. While it differs in each case, party members, supporters and affiliated groups have a say over who will be the parliamentary leader. Broadening the number of people who are involved in making leadership decisions does a few things. First, the process takes more time, so this slows down any 'night of the long knives', as has been common in Australia. Second, it changes the relationship between potential leaders and the grassroots of the party, as being a 'factional powerbroker' in and to itself is no longer enough. Third, it allows those beyond the elected officials to prevent what they see as overreach and the removal of a leader that the base support. For example, this may have saved Kevin Rudd in 2010 and Julia Gillard in 2013.

Only the ALP has moved to such a model in Australia. Following the 2013 election defeat, this process was used for the first time. The model implemented had the following rules. First, that the votes of the parliamentary representatives would be worth 50 per cent. The other 50 per cent would be made up of the rank and file grassroots party members. The other critical change the ALP implemented was that if a parliamentary leader wins an election, they remain leader for the duration of the term. The exception to this is if the leader resigns, requests a leadership election, or if 75 per cent of caucus members sign a petition calling for a leadership ballot on the grounds that the current leader has brought the party into disrepute. Candidates for the leadership must be nominated by 20 per cent of caucus, and ballots to decide the leader will occur automatically following an election loss. When utilised for the first time, the result was a win for Bill Shorten (52.02 per cent compared to Anthony Albanese's 48.98 per cent). While Shorten received 63.95 per cent of the votes of his parliamentary colleagues, he only received 40.08 per cent of those of the broader membership (Griffiths 2013). It was estimated that 30 000 ALP members voted in the 2013 leadership ballot.

VIDEOS
SHORT-ANSWER
QUESTIONS

GENDER AND LEADERSHIP

While the question, 'Does Australia have a leadership problem?' has been answered so far in terms of the institutional environment and processes used to select leaders, there is another way to answer this question. Australia has a leadership problem for the simple fact that in well over a century Australia has had: one female prime minister; 11 female state premiers or territory chief ministers; one female High Court chief justice; and one female Governor-General. Neither the ALP nor LPA have ever chosen a woman as federal opposition leader. Just three of the 30 Speakers of the House of Representatives, and just one of the 36 Attorneys-General of the Commonwealth parliament have been women. Women remain under-represented in the senior ranks of the Commonwealth public service. One State – South Australia – has never had a female premier. The federal Liberal Party has never had a female leader. This list could go on and on.

Similar observations might be made about the dearth of Indigenous Australians in Australian parliaments: only 38 have ever sat in a national, state or territory legislature and only two in the House of Representatives. So too with ethnic minorities, for example, it took until 2010 before a Muslim was elected to the Commonwealth parliament. But it is the failure to recruit women into leadership roles in Australian politics which is especially striking, since, at its birth, Australia was a pioneer in progressing the enfranchisement of women. The fact that women are notably absent from Australia's political leadership ranks points to gender bias and to a particularly insidious leadership problem.

The experiences of Julia Gillard as Australia's sole female prime minister are worthy of further analysis. While Gillard endured significant attacks from within parliament, as Summers (2012) has shown with great detail, the attacks from parts of the community were disturbing. This included violent and sexually explicit images of the prime minister that were distributed widely. In reflecting on her time in office, Gillard (2014, 106–7) said:

> As early as 1975, in her book *Damned Whores and God's Police*, feminist and author Anne Summers explained that during our nation's history,

women were always categorised in one of these two roles. It felt to me as prime minister that the binary stereotypes were still there, that the only two choices available were good woman or bad woman. As a woman wielding power, with all the complexities of modern politics, I was never going to be portrayed as a good woman. So I must be the bad woman, a scheming shrew, a heartless harridan or a lying bitch.

While some will attest that the attacks on Gillard were no more or less than any other prime minister has endured, this overlooks the gendered nature of much of the material disseminated about Gillard. Ultimately, the way that the Gillard's prime ministership is defined, and what it says about Australian democracy, is in the eye of the beholder: some view it as the end of a bad era of ALP government; others view the personal and misogynistic attacks on Gillard as key to understanding the period; and there are many views between and beyond this. No matter the view, there can be little doubt that there are likely to be significant challenges for Australia's next female prime minister.

REFLECTION
QUESTIONS

AFFIRMATIVE ACTION AND THE KEYS TO THE LODGE

Between them the two major parties have controlled the keys to the Lodge since the Country Party provided a stop-gap prime minister in the summer of 1967–68. Each has taken a different approach to encouraging women to enter the national parliament, which is the first hurdle that every future leader must leap. In 1994, the ALP adopted a quota and set itself the challenge of endorsing women in at least 35 per cent of winnable seats by 2002. This has since been refined. Labor's constitution presently provides for 'comprehensive affirmative action' and requires that men and women each fill a minimum of 40 per cent of seats in parliament, with candidates of either sex able to occupy the remaining 20 per cent. Legislated or voluntary quota systems (such as Labor's 40:20:40 scheme) operate in a

TABLE 10.2 COMMONWEALTH PARLIAMENT GENDER DIVERSITY AS OF JULY 2016

Party	M	F	%F
ALP	52	43	45.3
LP	65	18	21.7
NATS	18	3	14.3
CLP	1		0
GRN	5	5	50
AC	1		0
DHJP	1		0
JLN		1	100
KAP	1		0
LDP	1		0
NXT	2	2	50
PHON	3	1	25
IND	1	2	66.7
Total	151	75	33.2

Source: APH (2017)

number of countries (McCann 2013). But such schemes have their critics. For critics, fixed quotas for women are seen as incompatible with merit. This is the view that has prevailed within the Liberal Party.

Sussan Ley, for example, has said she wants to be seen 'to be here for my ability, for my merits' (Mills 2014). Instead of introducing quotas, the Liberal Party has sought to provide networked support and encourage women to stand for preselection to enable them to crash through the '**glass ceiling**'. However, the evidence suggests that quotas have been the only effective mechanism that has improved female representation. One Australian study, which analysed female representation in 250 parliaments in 190 countries, found that when the three common strategies employed to deal with representation gaps were analysed – namely, no targets, targets, or quotas – that the only strategy that led to increased female representation were quotas. Moreover, targets had the same effect as having no target at all (Sojo et al. 2016). Increasing female representation will not by itself solve the issue of a lack of female leaders. Clearly, there are deeper cultural and social issues at play. Nonetheless, by increasing the number of female elected officials it raises the prospect for these women, who otherwise may not have had the opportunity to make their case for the leadership of their respective parties.

glass ceiling: An invisible but very real pattern of discrimination that prevents women rising to the top of hierarchical organisations such as corporations, government agencies and political parties.

CASE STUDY

Julia Gillard speaks in London in memory of Jo Cox MP, 11 October 2016

Let me share with you what that gender discrimination can look and feel like. As Prime Minister, day after day, time after time, I would find myself in a room, often a business boardroom, where I was the only woman, apart perhaps from a woman serving coffee or food.

Because politics at senior levels … has been almost always the pursuit of men, the assumptions of politics have been defined around men's lives – not women's lives. It is assumed a man with children brings to politics the perspective of a family man, but it is never suggested that he should be disqualified from the rigours of a political life because he has caring responsibilities. This definitely does not work the same way for women.

Even before becoming prime minister, I had observed that if you are a woman politician, it is impossible to win on the question of family. If you do not have children, then you are characterised as out of touch with 'mainstream lives'. If you do have children then, heavens, who is looking after them? I had already been chided by a senior conservative Senator for being 'deliberately barren' …

Before becoming prime minister, I had also worked out that what you are wearing will draw disproportionate attention. … Undoubtedly a male leader who does not meet a certain standard will be marked down. But that standard is such an obvious one: … a well-tailored suit, neat hair, television-friendly glasses. … Being the first female prime minister, I had to navigate what that standard was for a woman.

It is galling to me that when I first met NATO's leader, predominantly to discuss our strategy for the war in Afghanistan, where our troops were fighting and dying, it was reported in the following terms: 'The Prime Minister, Julia Gillard, has made her first appearance on the international stage, meeting the head of NATO, Anders Rasmussen, in Brussels. Dressed in a white, short jacket and dark trousers she arrived … and was ushered in by Mr Rasmussen …' This article was written by a female journalist. It apparently went without saying that Mr Rasmussen was wearing a suit …

This gender stereotyping was at the very benign end compared to much of what I faced: 'Ditch the witch' on placards at rallies. The ugly ravings about how 'women are destroying the joint' from a conservative and cantankerous radio shock jock. The pornographic cartoons circulated by an eccentric bankrupt. The vile words on social media.

It may be easy and comforting for you to conclude that all this is something about the treatment of women in Australia. I regret doing this but I have to disabuse you of that notion. Indeed, some of the sexist insults thrown at me were not original. Rather they had originally been hurled at Hillary Clinton … in 2008.

Source: Gillard (2016)

QUESTION

In this extract from a speech she made in 2016 in tribute to the slain British MP Jo Cox, Julia Gillard reflects on some of the challenges she faced as Prime Minister. Are gender stereotypes still embedded in our understanding of political leadership?

VIDEO
RESEARCH
QUESTION

SUMMARY

Learning objective 1: Understand the tension between leadership and liberal democracy

Ultimately their party colleagues will regard prime ministers as successful if they are winning elections or they retain the confidence and majority support of the voting public. Democracy and the need for popularity poses leaders with a particular dilemma. Leaders who follow public opinion are seen as 'weak'. Leaders who steer their own policy course and seek to bring the public along with them risk being seen as autocratic and 'out of touch'. Political theorists have long reminded us that while leadership is vital, it always sits uncomfortably with the democratic principle of popular sovereignty.

Learning objective 2: Recall some of the theoretical debates about the importance of leaders

What makes a good leader is much debated. Prime ministers need a variety of strengths, skills and talents to manage the Cabinet; to rally supporters in Question Time; to understand and explain complicated legislation; to negotiate with powerful vested interests; to out manoeuvre opponents; and to identify and win support for public policy solutions to the problems Australia faces. Unsurprisingly, there is little agreement about the particular attributes successful leaders require. But there have been some theoretical approaches that have dominated. The 'great man' tradition imagined that, when needed, leaders would emerge to change the course of history. Political psychologists search for the personality and other traits that mark individuals out as charismatic leaders. Political scientists are more prone to ask about the relations of leaders with Cabinet and party colleagues, advisers, public servants and others on whom they depend – to emphasise that the structures of executive government restrict the agency of leaders. While Burns (1978) distinguished between transactional leaders who cultivate supporters by appealing to their self-interest and by offering rewards and threatening punishment, and transformational leaders able to articulate and build support for their vision of a better society.

Learning objective 3: Explain the different arenas leaders work in and the different skills they require

Leadership is not easily defined, but we intuitively recognise that it is central to politics and government – and often complain that the current crop of leaders fail the test of making and explaining difficult but necessary decisions. While it is party leaders and prime ministers who first spring to mind, leadership is displayed in the public service, in industry, in communities and displayed by NGOs and interest groups.

Learning objective 4: Summarise the debate about Australia's 'leadership problem'

The perceived problem that Australia has with leadership relates to both the number of leadership changes and the process that leads to these changes. In the period 2007–14, there were a large number of changes in the leaders of the major political parties. Australia, until recently stood largely alone in the way that leadership changes occurred. Most other comparable parliamentary systems have changed the process whereby leaders can change in the middle of a term. The changes the ALP introduced in 2013 are similar to changes in other countries like the UK and Canada.

Learning objective 5: Describe the leadership gender gap and some of the methods employed to remedy this

Just one woman – Julia Gillard – has served as Australian prime minister. Her party turned to her – as in the case of several of the women who became state premiers – at a time of flagging political fortunes and then later turned on her when her own political fortunes appeared to be falling. In the two major parties, women are under-represented – even in the ALP which employs a quota system to boost the numbers of women in caucus. This under-representation reduces the likelihood that female political leaders will soon be commonplace. The evidence suggests that targets that are often advocated for in the Liberal Party, have no effect on increasing the representation of women and will, therefore, have no effect on the number of women in leadership positions either.

DISCUSSION QUESTIONS

DISCUSSION
QUESTIONS

1. What makes an effective leader?
2. Who are some of Australia's most important political leaders outside of parliament?
3. What agency do prime ministers have?
4. Have prime ministers become more presidential-like figures?
5. Why have there been very few female prime ministers and state premiers?

FURTHER READING

Daly, F. (1977). *From Curtin to Kerr*, South Melbourne, Victoria: Sun Books.

Foley, M. (2000). *The British Presidency*, Manchester: Manchester University Press

Grattan, M. (ed.). (2003). *Australian Prime Ministers*, Sydney: New Holland Publishers.

Helms, L. (ed.). (2012). *Comparative Political Leadership*, Basingstoke: Palgrave Macmillan.

Kane, J., Patapan, H. and 't Hart, P. (2009). Dispersed democratic leadership revisited. In J. Kane, H. Patapan and P. 't Hart, eds, *Dispersed Democratic Leadership: Origins, Dynamics, & Implications*, Oxford: Oxford University Press, pp. 299–321.

Kane, J., Patapan, H. and 't Hart, P. (eds). (2009). *Dispersed Democratic Leadership: Origins, Dynamics, & Implications*, Oxford: Oxford University Press.

Walter, J. (2008). Can Kevin Kick the Command Culture? Paper presented to APSA 2008, URL: http://www.polsis.uq.edu.au/APSA-2008

REFERENCES

Australian Parliament House. (2017). Composition of Australian parliaments by party and gender: a quick guide. URL: http://www.aph.gov.au/About_Parliament/Parliamentary_Departments/Parliamentary_Library/pubs/rp/rp1617/Quick_Guides/PartyGender.

Bennister, M. (2008). Blair and Howard: Predominant prime ministers compared. *Parliamentary Affairs*, **61**(2), 334–55.

Bennister, M. (2012). *Prime Ministers in Power*, London: Palgrave Macmillan.

Bourke, L. (2015). Only voters have the right to 'hire and fire' their leaders, says embattled Tony Abbott, *The Sydney Morning Herald*, 2 February. Retrieved from http://www.smh.com.au/federal-politics/political-news/only-voters-have-the-right-to-hire-and-fire-their-leaders-says-embattled-tony-abbott-20150202-133xno.html

Bryant, N. (2015). Australia: Coup capital of the democratic world, *BBC*. Retrieved from http://www.bbc.com/news/world-australia-34249214

Burns, J.M. (1978). *Leadership*, New York: Harper & Row.

Crossman, R. (1963). Introduction. In *The English Constitution*, London: Fontana, pp. 1–57.

Davis, F., Musgrove, N. and Smart, J. (2011). Introduction. In F. Davis, N. Musgrove and J. Smart, eds., *Founders, Firsts and Feminists: Women Leaders in Twentieth-century Australia*. eScholarship Research Centre, University of Melbourne.

Dowding, K. (2013a). The prime ministerialisation of the British Prime Minister. *Parliamentary Affairs*, **66**(3), 617–35.

Dowding, K. (2013b). Presidentialisation again: A comment on Kefford. *Australian Journal of Political Science*, **48**(2), 147–9.

Gauja, A. (2015). This is why Australia churns through leaders so quickly, Monkey Cage Blog, 18 September. Retrieved from http://www.washingtonpost.com/news/monkey-cage/wp/2015/09/18/this-is-why-australia-churns-through-leaders-so-quickly/?utm_term=.6953a5f1096b

Gillard, J. (2012). Transcript of Speech, *The Sydney Morning Herald*, 12 October. Retrieved from http://www.smh.com.au/federal-politics/political-news/transcript-of-julia-gillards-speech-20121009-27c36.html

Gillard, J. (2014). *My Story*, Melbourne: Random House.

Gillard, J. (2016). Julia Gillard speaks in London in memory of Jo Cox MP. Retrieved from http://juliagillard.com.au/articles/julia-gillard-speaks-in-memory-of-jo-cox-mp/

Griffiths, E. (2013). Bill Shorten elected Labor leader over Anthony Albanese after month-long campaign, 13 October. URL: http://www.abc.net.au/news/2013-10-13/bill-shorten-elected-labor-leader/5019116

Heifetz, R. (2010) Leadership. In R.A. Couto, ed., *Political and Civic Leadership: A Reference Handbook*, Thousand Oakes: Sage.

Hendriks, F. and Karsten, N. (2014). Theory of democratic leadership. In R.A.W. Rhodes, and P 't Hart, eds, *The Oxford Handbook of Political Leadership*, Oxford: Oxford University Press, pp. 41–56.

Heywood, A. (2013). *Politics*, 4th edn, Basingstoke: Palgrave.

Hildebrand, J. (2017). Assange, Keating named among Australia's top 10 figures of all time, 3 June. Retrieved from http://www.news.com.au/finance/work/leaders/assange-keating-named-among-australias-top-10-figures-of-all-time/news-story/5152c5c6dc20c0382d5246b97514cb17

Honeyman, V. (2007). Harold Wilson as Measured Using the Greenstein Criteria. Paper presented to PSA Conference, University of Bath, 11–13th April 2007. Retrieved from http://www.psa.ac.uk/2007/pps/Honeyman.pdf

Kane, J. and Patapan, H. (2012). *The Democratic Leader: How Democracy Defines, Empowers and Limits its Leaders*, Oxford: Oxford University Press.

Karvonen, L. (2010). *The Personalisation of Politics: A Study of Parliamentary Democracies*, Colchester: ECPR Press.

Kefford, G. (2013). The presidentialisation of Australian politics? Kevin Rudd's leadership of the Australian Labor Party. *Australian Journal of Political Science*, **48**(2), 135–46.

McAllister, I. (2007) The personalisation of politics. In R.J. Dalton and H. Klingemann, eds, *The Oxford Handbook of Political Behavior*, Oxford: Oxford University Press.

McCann, J. (2013). Electoral quotas for women: an international overview, 14 November. Parliamentary Library. Retrieved from http://www.aph.gov.au/About_Parliament/Parlia mentary_Departments/Parliamentary_Library/pubs/rp/rp1314/ElectoralQuotas#_ftnref47

Michels, R. (1962). *Political Parties: A Sociological Study of the Organizational Tendencies in Modern Democracies*, New York: Free Press.

Mills, T. (2014). Sussan Ley rejects gender quota call. *Border Mail*. 10 March.

Mudde, C. and Kaltwasser, R. (2014). Populism and political leadership. In R.A.W. Rhodes and P. 't Hart, eds, *The Oxford Handbook of Political Leadership*, Oxford: Oxford University Press, pp. 376–88.

Poguntke, T. and Webb, P. (2005). *The Presidentialisation of Politics in Democratic Societies: A Framework for Analysis*, Oxford: Oxford University Press.

Rath, T. and Conchie, B. (2008). *Strengths Based Leadership*, Omaha: Gallup Press.

Schumpeter, J. (1961). *Capitalism, Socialism and Democracy*, London: Allen & Unwin.

Sojo, V.E., Wood, R.E., Wood, S.A. and Wheeler, M.A. (2016). Reporting requirements, targets, and quotas for women in leadership. *The Leadership Quarterly*, **27**(3), 519–36.

Strangio, P., 't Hart, P. and Walter, J. (eds.) (2013). *Understanding prime-ministerial performance: Comparative perspectives*, Oxford: Oxford University Press.

Summers, A. (2012). Her Rights at Work (R-rated version). Retrieved from http://www.annesummers .com.au/speeches/her-rights-at-work-r-rated-version/

Tiffen, R. (2017). *Disposable Leaders*, Sydney: UNSW Press.

Van Onselen, P. (2010). Politics trumps a moral challenge, *The Australian*, 29 April.

Walter, J. and Strangio, P. (2007). *No, Prime Minister*, Sydney: UNSW Press.

Weber, M. (1978). *Economy and Society*. Edited by G. Roth and C. Wittich. Berkley: University of California Press.

White, H. (2010). It's about leadership, not awareness, *The Interpreter*, 22 March. Retrieved from https://www.lowyinstitute.org/the-interpreter/its-about-leadership-not-awareness

CHAPTER 11

THE FOURTH ESTATE: NEWS MEDIA IN THE DIGITAL AGE

LEARNING OBJECTIVES

After reading this chapter, you should be able to:

1. Understand what the public sphere is, how the news media is said to contribute to it, and its connection to political discourse

2. Differentiate between liberal democratic (chaos) and political economy (control) theories of the media

3. Explain key changes to the Australian media landscape from the 20th to the 21st century

4. Describe the opportunities and challenges that digital technologies present to media organisations and their journalism

INTRODUCTION

According to liberal democratic theory, a free press is necessary for a well-functioning democracy. In its 'ideal' form, the news media play an essential role in informing the **public sphere** by mediating the exchange of ideas, providing diverse political communications.

However, examples such as the 2011 revelations in England of phone hacking of celebrities and citizens, like murdered schoolgirl Milly Dowler, by tabloid journalists at the now defunct *News of the World* reveal how this ideal notion of the media can fall short (Davies 2014). Consider also other factors that might hinder the media's performance beyond the practice of reporting, such as how media institutions are structured in society. For example, the Australian news media has one of the most concentrated press ownership structures of any liberal democracy (Finkelstein and Ricketson 2012, 60). This raises questions about the number and diversity of voices, and the operation of media power in this public space designated for critical debate.

This chapter aims to provide a better understanding of the Australian media's contribution to the public sphere and its role to critically inform Australians about politics and policy. We do this by discussing two largely contrasting theories about how the media functions in society: the chaos (pluralist) and control (propaganda) paradigms. We consider questions such as whether having fewer media proprietors affects what stories journalists pursue, or what their editors consider fit to print. How much does the news we read, watch and listen to, affect how we, as individuals, think about everyday issues? Are certain stories missing or some issues or groups in society under-represented? Does Australia's concentrated media ownership matter in the 21st century when online news is instantly available to us from all corners of the world?

We also explore key 21st century challenges to media institutions by mapping the rise of the digital public sphere. The emergence of social media and other online communications has both positive and negative consequences for newsrooms. The negative includes the viral spread of **fake news** that leaves people unsure of what is true, and what is not, and can damage public trust in news. We consider the implications of the migration of advertising to online competitors such as Google and Facebook, which has interrupted media's century-old business model and led to journalism job losses and outlet closures.

On the positive side, the digital era enables journalists to reach new audiences beyond traditional geographical boundaries. Journalists can source information and reach audiences more cheaply and quickly than before. Online communication technologies serve politicians, political parties and interest groups too. They are harnessing digital tools to communicate directly with citizens and – importantly for their organisational survival – to recruit volunteers and to fundraise.

In plotting these dynamic shifts in the Australian media landscape, this chapter provides an overview of the challenges and opportunities for media institutions and political journalism in the digital age. We begin by examining some theories that are useful to help us understand the news media's role in democratic society.

public sphere: A communicative space where public opinion about politics and policy are formed. Freely expressed and diverse voices are regarded as a precondition for a healthy democracy.

fake news: There is little agreement on what constitutes fake news. The Collins English Dictionary made it the 2017 word of the year, defining it as 'false, often sensational, information disseminated under the guise of news reporting'. Some, such as Harvard's First Draft at Harvard's Shorenstein Centre, argue it is about more than news and encompasses the whole information ecosystem. This includes different types of misleading content (misinformation, disinformation and mal-information). These different categories speak to the motives for producing fake news, and the form it takes whether it be a hoax or a badly reported story.

THE PUBLIC SPHERE

German sociologist Jürgen Habermas outlined a concept of the public sphere in his 1962 book, *The Structural Transformation of the Public Sphere*. It contributes to democratic theory by critically examining the role of mass media in political debates, public opinion formation, and legitimacy of state power in the 17th through to the 20th centuries. Habermas's thesis focused on the role of private persons coming together in rational-critical debate about public issues (Calhoun 1992, 1). This contest of ideas by private people in a public space, in the words of Habermas, was important because it compelled 'public authority to legitimate itself before public opinion' (1989, 25–6). In other words, it allowed the governed to have opinions of their rulers and their laws, and publicly airing these views was one way to hold authority to account. Until this time, 'public opinion' was not a well-known phrase, and arose at about the same time as the emergence of the public sphere (Habermas 1989, 26).

In Europe, the public sphere's 'preeminent institution' for exchanging ideas was the press (Habermas 1989, 181). But it was also made possible by political conversations in British coffee houses, French tea salons, scholarly German journals and academic societies. In the United States, the public sphere emerged in the political and professional pamphlets like Thomas Paine's *Common Sense* in 1776 (Schudson 2011, 66). The production of newspapers and related publications was made possible by Johannes Gutenberg's much earlier invention of the printing press, in 1440.

Central to this chapter, the press provided a means for freely sharing diverse viewpoints. Habermas (1989, 171) chronologically plots the rise and fall of the public sphere, finally characterising it in the 20th century as little more than an illusion, corrupted by the commercialisation of the mass media. His later writings revise this very pessimistic conclusion, finding that the media in the digital age could still serve as the backbone of the public sphere but with significant qualifications including that, for democracy's sake, the state must undertake to 'protect the public good of the quality press' (Habermas 2010, 136).

REFLECTION QUESTION

CRITIQUING THE HABERMASIAN PUBLIC SPHERE

normative: The expression of value judgements or prescriptions. In relation to the media, it refers to the expression of its 'ideal' role as opposed to how the media actually performs.

There has been much thoughtful scholarly criticism of both the historical and **normative** aspects of Habermas's conception of the public sphere (see Calhoun 1992 for details). While there is not the space here to elaborate on these critiques, they collectively tackle underlying assumptions of, or lack of attention to, class, gender, religion, culture and ethnicity (Calhoun 1992, 466). Historians and political scientists also question the neglect of the role of social movements and the overestimation of the degeneration of the public sphere, especially the uniform negativity applied to the modern media (Calhoun 1992, 33 & 37).

Another criticism is that the public sphere is conceived as being singular, whereas critics argue for the notion of multiple public spheres, which co-exist and may overlap or compete. Also criticised is Habermas's distinction of the public from the private. These two concerns are particularly useful when we consider the rise of the digital public sphere and blurring of public and private communications in online environments, such as Facebook, where users post both personal and public information, often without clearly distinguishing one from the other. To understand the idea of plural public spheres, Twitter might be considered as a separate public sphere, for the exchange of ideas, from Facebook.

The existence of multiple public spheres could also be construed from how the Canberra press gallery reported former prime minister Julia Gillard's' 'misogyny speech' compared to reactions of international and social media. In the very different responses to Gillard's speech in 2012 we see different public spheres in action. In her speech, which you can hear in the VitalSource Video link, Gillard, under heavy opposition fire for appointing the controversial Liberal-turned-independent Peter Slipper as the Speaker of the House, accused Opposition Leader Tony Abbott of being a hypocrite and mysogynist. While mainstream journalists mainly focused on the immediate political context of the speech, the public and overseas media saw it from a broader perspective, labelling it as a watershed moment in public life against sexism.

VIDEOS
REFLECTION
QUESTIONS

While it is contested that the public sphere should be conceived as a singular or plural space, the overall concept is useful here for considering the ideal role of the media in a democracy. It offers us a framework and starting point for thinking about how the Australian media should ideally inform our democracy in the digital age. It does this by providing us with the concept of a shared communicative space (or spaces) for Australians to engage in public debates and weigh up policy issues that may, in turn, inform who we vote for. It is also important for informing us as to whether our political parties and leaders are using their power appropriately.

RESEARCH
QUESTIONS

THE DIGITAL GLOBAL PUBLIC SPHERE

Since the commercialisation of the internet in the mid-1990s, and the development of digital technologies, the opportunities for connecting the peoples of the world have never been greater. The emergence of Facebook in 2004, YouTube in 2005 and Twitter in 2006, among other forms of social media, has further enabled citizens to participate, comment and engage with political ideas in various ways whether in comment sections of online newspapers, online forums or Tweets and status updates. These interactions occur beyond the press and physical coffee houses and tea salons of Habermas's first conception of the public sphere. Indeed, the capacity of this digitised network information space is not just considered a digital public sphere but a globalised public sphere by some scholars (see McNair et al. 2016, ix; Volkmer 2014).

For Manuel Castells (2008, 89), 'the contemporary global public sphere is largely dependent on the global/local communication media system'. This media system includes both the traditional media of television, radio and the press, as well as digital communications, including what Castells labels 'mass self-communication'. This is using communication networks for the many-to-many transmission and reception of messages in ways capable of bypassing mainstream media and often government controls (2008, 90).

If, as Castells argues, the public sphere is where citizens come together to express their autonomous views to influence the political institutions of society, then civil society is the 'organised expression of these views' (2008, 78). In a democracy, the relationship between the state and civil society is key as 'without an effective civil society capable of structuring and channelling citizen debates over diverse ideas and conflicting interests, the state drifts away from its subjects' (Castells 2008, 78). Put another way, democratic representation is called into question. Castells (2008) argues that the digital communication tools and networks available to us in the 21st century pave the way for the formation of global civil society enabling 'ad hoc forms of global governance' to address problems that transcend the nation-state. There are many reasons why nation-states might not cooperate in this possibility of global governance, but it is not for want of global communication networks.

information and communication technologies (ICT): A broad term that refers to technologies that provide access to information through communication technologies that include the internet, wireless networks, mobile phones and other communication forms to give society new communication capabilities.

The development of **information and communication technologies** (ICTs) has for some time lifted hopes of a more inclusive public sphere that will allow greater democratic engagement between political parties, candidates, other political actors, and voters. Kellner (1999, 101) predicted that political actors excluded by traditional media would use technology to advance their interests and have their views heard more broadly.

However, other scholars have highlighted how social media is failing to live up to this democratic promise of greater inclusion and deliberation. Cass Sunstein (2007, 1) identifies a narcissistic trend, colloquially named the 'DailyMe', whereby online users engage with a self-selected narrow range of interests to focus on themselves. This is commonly called the 'echo-chamber effect'.

SPOTLIGHT

What are 'echo chambers' and 'filter bubbles'?

An echo chamber is where like-minded participants group together to share similar viewpoints and are cordoned off from alternative views or information. The concern is that these groups can tend towards polarisation and hyper political partisanship that, in turn, can foster division and intolerance towards others (Curran, Fenton and Friedman 2012, 10).

Studies suggest that this type of polarising online behaviour presents a challenge to mainstream politicians in at least two ways. First, because they seek to engage broadly without alienating any voters, politicians may be 'risk averse' in their online communications and tend toward broadcasting messages as they would with analogue media rather than engaging in dialogue with social media users. This involves *talking* rather than *listening* and does not fully utilise social media's capabilities to engage in conversations with voters (Macnamara and Kenning 2014; Lukamto and Carson 2016).

Second, an individual's filter settings on websites, along with digital platforms' algorithms, may result in a 'filter bubble'. This results in intellectual isolation. It is caused by algorithms personalising online content to filter information based on the user's past online behaviours (Pariser 2011). It can result in us missing out on information and debates contrary to our pre-existing views, which may reinforce our preconceptions and biases (Sunstein 2007, 116).

More recent studies suggest fears of the echo chamber effect are exaggerated. In 2016, a national survey by the US Pew Research Center during the US Presidential election campaign found that most users of Facebook and Twitter had a mix of people, with a variety of political beliefs, in their networks (Duggan and Smith 2016). Moreover, a fifth of those surveyed reported changing their minds about a political or social issue because of their engagement with social media (Duggan and Smith 2016, 18). This finding questions the echo chamber theory. In a multi-nation study, the Reuters Institute at the University of Oxford found social media users, and users of search engines, engage with more online news brands than non-users. This suggests that social media use might actually increase an individual's exposure to diverse news, rather than limit it (Newman et al. 2017, 43). In some Australian Twitter studies, the echo chamber effect has also been discounted, except for a minority of 'hardcore partisan online communities' (Bruns 2017).

QUESTION

Think about the way you use social media: do you engage with a wide range of political viewpoints online, or is the information you receive mainly about things you already agree with?

THEORIES OF THE MEDIA IN A DEMOCRACY

For the purposes of this chapter, when discussing the media and its role in sharing ideas and engaging in political discourse, we are largely reflecting on the news media. This includes newspapers, television and radio news programs and online content, whether it be on Facebook, Twitter or Reddit, that is about the news of the day and current affairs and events. Other forms of media such as film, literature, art and written music, also form part of the media environment that surrounds us every day (Croteau and Hoynes 2014, 2). These types of media, while important, are outside the scope of what we consider here as news media. News, as the name suggests, is describing happenings, phenomenon or events that are new. It is difficult to define exactly as it can be described in terms of its production processes, its content, or its function in society. Here are some examples of different approaches.

What is news?

SPOTLIGHT

Media scholar Michael Schudson argues that news is the product of journalistic activity (2011, 5). This might have been true in the past, but we should consider if this will be so in the future. For example, technology companies such as Google are partnering with media outlets in Europe to fund artificial intelligence news machines to produce news stories (Williams 2017). Is this to be considered journalistic activity if it is automated by robots? Some describe news as providing a shared experience of the world. In this case, news is 'new information about a subject of some public interest that is shared with some portion of the public … News is, in effect, what is on a society's mind' (Stephens 1988, 9). Another way to think about news is as a 'manufactured good' like other consumable goods in society. Schudson (2011, 6) sees this good as 'the product of a set of social, economic, and political institutions and practices'. If news can be fashioned like a product, who or what determines what is news? Why are some stories considered news and others not? This way of thinking about news is helpful because it introduces the notion that news makers have power in society: to emphasise some issues over others. Again, this idea relates to groups and voices in society that are under-represented in news coverage because newsrooms often consist of similar types of people who think about news in similar ways. Studies of the types of journalists and values that dominate newsrooms in Britain and the United States show that white middle- to upper-class men dominate the people behind the news (Conboy 2013, 46). This also underscores that news is produced, as opposed to the news being a 'mirror of reality'. From this perspective, news is seen as a construction 'dependent on professional routines and also on broader forces such as ideological powers exercised by elites within society (Wall 2005). Following this logic, news reproduces society's dominant paradigms and power structures (Hall et al. 1978). As we shall see in the next section, some scholars view news media as having normative functions in society. Geoffrey Craig, for example, reminds us that the news media is not just any old business but has the important role of informing the public sphere: 'The media are businesses and yet they are ascribed a special function in the democratic health of a society' (2004, 3). Schudson warns us to be wary of smuggling 'democracy' into the description of journalism, but does define it as 'information and commentary on contemporary affairs taken to be publicly important' (2011, 7).

QUESTION

What are the different ways that researchers have thought about how to define news? What do these different ways of thinking tell us about the idea that news can be 'objective'?

LIBERAL DEMOCRATIC THEORY ('CHAOS' PARADIGM)

As discussed in Chapter 8, the liberal tradition emphasises the virtues of freedom and liberty. A democracy, briefly, is a political system that involves citizens in governing their own affairs. It is predicated on a commitment to the rule of law in which political leaders are elected in free and fair elections, which are contestable, and allows for the greatest possible adult public participation in the election process (suffrage), guaranteed by various civil and political rights.

Important elements of liberal democratic society include: 'elections, competitive political parties, free mass media, and representative assemblies' (Almond et al. 2010, 23). It is the virtue of a 'free mass media' to inform public opinion in a democracy that is the foundation of liberal democratic theory of the media. Why is this considered so important? Italian political philosopher Norberto Bobbio argued that liberal democracy presumes that not only do citizens have the right to choose who governs them, but that they must be well informed to 'vote for the wisest, the most honest, the most enlightened of their fellow citizens' (1987, 19). Speaking broadly, the media is one means by which the public can be informed about rival political candidates' values, beliefs and the issues for which they stand.

A second role of the media is what is often called the 'fourth estate' role. Openness, transparency and accountability of the elected representatives to the people have been considered central tenets of a well-functioning democracy for the past 200 years in the West. The media have been formally recognised for this role – for example, in the First Amendment to the US Constitution.[1] In Australia, the role is not codified in its Constitution, but has been, at various times, recognised in High Court interpretations of it. The 'fourth estate' role of the media was acknowledged in successive inquiries into the print and news media.[2]

Further, in recognition of the media's role to provide diversity of voices, Australia and some European democracies, including the United Kingdom, Norway, Finland and Sweden subsidise or fund sections of the media. In Australia, this involves taxpayer funding of the Australian Broadcasting Corporation (ABC) and partial funding of the Special Broadcasting Service (SBS). Government funded, or subsidised, media is considered by one school of thought necessary for a commercially sensitive industry where popular and sensational news can be 'interesting to the public', but not necessarily 'in the public interest'. From this perspective, public broadcasting is regarded as important to a free public life (see Garnham 1990, 104–14). The former Editor of Britain's *Guardian* newspaper provides an example of this distinction of 'public interest' from what is 'interesting':

---

[1]   The First Amendment to the US Constitution: 'Congress shall make no law respecting an establishment of religion, or prohibiting the free exercise thereof; or abridging the freedom of speech, or of the press; or the right of the people peaceably to assemble, and to petition the Government for a redress of grievances.'

[2]   This includes the 'Norris Inquiry' by Sir John Norris on behalf of the Victorian Government in 1981; the report of the House of Representatives Select Committee on the Print Media, News & Fair Facts: The Australian Print Media Industry, Canberra: Australian Government Publishing Service, March 1992; and the 2012 'Report of the independent inquiry into the media and media regulation' by Ron Finkelstein QC with Professor Matthew Ricketson.

> What's the public interest in a cricketer having a love romp in a hotel room …
> But if elected representatives are arguing a case in Parliament but not revealing
> that they are being paid to do so, then that strikes at the heart of democracy.
> That's public interest; this is an easy distinction (de Burgh 2000, 15).

Democracy depends on the state accepting criticism of its power. Through the liberal democratic lens of the media, citizens should encounter diverse and multiple viewpoints, including those of dissenting and critical voices of the state, in the public sphere. In Britain, the media's reputation as providing this monitorial role of state power was coined the fourth estate, reportedly when Thomas Carlyle used the word in reference to House of Commons politician Edmund Burke: 'Burke said there were Three Estates in Parliament; but, in the Reporters' Gallery yonder, there sat a *Fourth Estate* more important far than they all' (1840, 392).

Media scholar Brian McNair (1999, 17) draws on the defining characteristics of the liberal tradition broadly conceived as 'constitutionality, participation and rational choice'. Constitutionality refers to the rule of law and ensuring that the processes of democracy such as elections are lawful. Participation includes those of legal age able to vote, which should be as universal as possible. Rational choice is the notion that voters have enough information to choose what Bobbio calls the 'wisest' candidate. This implies also that voters have a sufficient choice of candidates. Bringing these three elements together in the context of the public sphere, McNair highlights the key normative roles of the news media in the public sphere of a democracy.

THE 'IDEAL' ROLE OF MEDIA

The news media is ascribed several specific functions in a democracy. Brian McNair (1999, 21–2) identifies five:

» To <u>inform</u> citizens

 This is the monitoring function of the media.

» To <u>educate citizens</u> as to the meaning and significance of the 'facts'

 This role is often linked to the need for 'objectivity' or 'professional distance' in reporting rather than opinion or emotive reporting.

» To provide a <u>platform</u> for public political discourse

 This is to enable public opinions to be formed by facilitating public conversations.

» To give <u>publicity</u> to governmental and political institutions

 This puts the media spotlight on those with power and includes the accountability or watchdog role of the media.

» To serve as a channel for the <u>advocacy</u> of political viewpoints

 This includes allowing parties and other political actors to say what they stand for. It also can include the media taking a stand on issues, sometimes called 'campaigning journalism'. These stories are usually labelled as having a particular editorial stance.

Investigative journalism

Of the above functions, a much-celebrated role of the media is its accountability role. This was made famous by the Watergate scandal, unearthed by *Washington Post* reporters Carl Bernstein and Bob Woodward in the early 1970s, leading Richard Nixon to resign the presidency. Also known as watchdog reporting, investigative journalism can provide a check on the excesses of government and on powerful private interests. Among others, de Burgh (2000), Ettema and Glasser (1998), and Schudson (2008) find the investigative journalist's role is to expose wrongdoing in the public interest. This may include: exposing injury and injustice; revealing information that would otherwise remain hidden; or promoting legal, policy or regulatory reforms to correct a wrong or close a loophole. Investigative journalism is not the only means of exposing transgressions – parliamentary hearings, police and whistleblowers do this too – but it is a powerful one. For example, Schudson (2008) argues the mere existence of investigative journalism in democracies serves as a deterrent to politicians and others against engaging in wrongdoing.

Twenty-first century examples of watchdog reporting in Australia, such as the 2017 exposure of the mistreatment of youths at the Don Dale Youth Detention Centre in the Northern Territory, highlight the investigative journalist's role to expose hidden information in the name of the public interest. Caro Meldrum-Hanna, an investigative reporter with the ABC's TV program *Four Corners*, unearthed videos showing several boys being maltreated by the centre's staff. The footage included a 13-year-old being stripped naked, and a 17-year-old boy strapped to a chair with a hood over his head. After screening of the program on 25 July 2016, a public outcry led the Prime Minister Malcolm Turnbull to announce a Royal Commission into the abuse of youths in the Northern Territory corrections system.

VIDEO

CASE STUDY

'The journalist's perspective of the media's role in democratic society' – Nicole Chvastek, ABC Radio presenter and former TV reporter, Channel 7 and ABC

When I think of journalism and its role in a democracy I think of game changing exposes like *Four Corners* Moonlight State, a story that shone a disinfecting sunlight on the corruption poisoning aspects of the Queensland government in the 1980s. I think of the Panama and Paradise Papers leak of millions of documents that shed light on how the rich and powerful set up systems to redirect their profits into tax havens to avoid paying the full tax rate.

It is the work of journalists who dig for information and report in hostile environments which have brought these stories to the surface, triggering debate and often action.

You will rarely be welcomed by the powerful when you work as a journalist. Nor should you be. Your role is to ask difficult questions, to scrutinize and to hold to account fearlessly, impartially and accurately.

If the story has revealed illegality or abuse, expect the backlash. It may be from lawyers. It may be from an angry spin doctor. It may be from an angry crook.

My advice: Fact check, get it right and report. And if you report in places where the rule of law doesn't hold as it does in Australia, and even here where it does, expect to be threatened. It won't happen for every story you write, but it's coming.

It is interesting to reflect on the roles of modern Australia's journalism greats. Chris Masters. Laurie Oakes. Kerry O'Brien. There's the TV, radio and newspaper investigative teams who put their own safety to one side to secure justice for total strangers. Witnesses to truth who hunt down and meticulously research strands of information from dark places. Reporters who sift the legitimate from the fraudulent and through publication bring that information into the light in order for you and I to truly understand the system we live under and the forces that construct and manipulate it or honour it. Only when we are informed can we make informed choices.

When I first started reporting I remember naively asking the manager of a building site for permission to film. He politely asked everybody including my TV crew to leave the room and then rushed at me, standing over me, his face contorted in menace, a hot breath near mine, roaring physical threats at me with wild eyes. I remember a union official doing much the same thing as I tried to report from a picket line. I remember a Bikie with a gun who answered the door when I knocked and a drug addict with nothing to lose wielding a needle my way as I reported on a stabbing at an inner-city housing estate.

A media adviser recently barked a series of ultimatums and insults at my new and impressionable junior producer because the minister he was advising was getting interview questions (asked by me) that the staffer didn't like. The politician tried to walk out of the interview. He lodged a complaint with my organization. He banned my program and favoured others. Not everyone operates like this, but you'll encounter the ones that do.

If you are operating within the law, fairly, accurately and in the public interest these tactics should be expected. Accept criticism with grace but understand the environment in which you operate. Be safe and always wary when you are reporting on the road. Understand that no-one has an obligation to speak to you, but you have a duty to shine that light.

And remember, journalism is not all *Moonlight State*. Recently Rose, a pensioner from Creswick rang into my radio show and explained with gentle fury how Centrelink had robo-called her demanding she repay $60,000 in welfare payments they alleged had been overpaid to her. Rose had never had $60,000 in her life and was never likely to. With gentle fury, she spoke about the trauma this had triggered in her as she fought for a year to prove she, in fact, owed them nothing. She detailed the months of tracking down documents and records from years ago while the powerful bureaucracy insisted she come up with the money.

As it happened, she didn't owe the money. But no one can return the peace of mind and the year she lost fighting them. Journalism gives people who do not have a giant bureaucracy at their disposal a voice and a chance to be heard. Not by a recorded robot message but by hundreds of thousands of other people who think and who act, and who respond.

We are fortunate in Australia that we rarely face threats to our lives when we take on the powerful. This is not Russia. It is not Syria. But here, in wealthy democratic Australia, lives can also be lost and diminished when people feel they are invisible and despair sets in.

So, when Rose goes on air she'll never have a million-dollar Public Relations machine behind her that studies focus groups for months before she speaks, and workshops a list of slogans for her to recite. Her voice is where the real people speak from. There's something about the polite but determined quiver in her delivery that tells you she's your neighbor, or your grandma.

And in that moment, like a thousand other moments when you work as a journalist, people hear Rose's story and respond, and the power imbalance is righted, just a little bit. And a 70-year-old pensioner knows her complaint is valid and her voice has been heard.

QUESTION

Where does this example situate the journalist in terms of the elite in society and the average citizen? Using McNair's list of five 'ideal' functions of the media in democratic society, which functions are identified by the journalist here as central to how she sees the reporter's role?

THE 'CHAOS' PARADIGM

Investigative reporting in the example of the exposé of the mistreatment of youths at Don Dale Youth Detention Centre could be considered an example of the liberal democratic role of the media. The way the journalist used the medium of television to inform the public sphere (audience) about the abuse of institutional power, in this case the prison wardens employed by the state, fits within this pluralist (or chaos model) of the media in society.

The chaos model is a pluralist theory for understanding the democratic function of the news media. Coined by McNair, the term is often contrasted with control theories of media (see below), which have a top-down approach to the flow of power in society. The chaos approach rejects the idea that power only flows in one, and the same, direction all the time. Chaos theory's emphasis is on mechanisms of the media for 'dissent, openness and diversity rather than closure, exclusivity and ideological homogeneity' (McNair 2006, vii).

Media scholars referencing this stream generally view media technologies as liberating, providing citizens with greater opportunities for participation, engagement and political accountability. Political scientist John Keane argued that the digital age is a time of 'communicative abundance' and provides exciting new opportunities for observing and reporting abuses of power in society. He argues that in the digital age, 'power-monitoring and power-controlling devices have begun to extend sideways and downward through the whole political order' (Keane 2010, xxvii).

The International Consortium of Investigative Journalists' (ICIJ) reporting of global tax evasion in the 'Panama Papers' in 2016, and the 'Paradise Papers' in 2017, are examples of 'new mechanisms for observing and reporting abuses of power' in the global public sphere.

Reporting of the Panama Papers is the largest example to date of many journalists from different countries collaborating and using mass data leaks to convey a story of international importance. It tells the global story about how the world's rich and famous use offshore tax havens to cut their tax bills. Other mass data dumps to reporters have included Edward Snowden's National Security Agency (NSA) file leaks about how governments spy on their citizens, and WikiLeaks' Iraq war files that showed how the US covered up the killings of innocents in the crossfire of war.

This type of collaborative reporting is in line with what Castells identified as the 'global/local communication media system'. In the case of the Panama Papers, 400 journalists from different nations, including Australia, worked together using digital tools to expose global tax evasion and corruption. By exposing wrongdoing, this new global collaborative journalism can strengthen democratic accountability and tell a local story about an individual or company's tax avoidance. At the same time the reports tell a broader story of how the rich and powerful across the globe use these purpose-built offshore schemes to maintain their wealth and privilege. Exemplifying the chaos paradigm, collaborative investigative reporting challenges the top-down power of elites in the international political order. In other words, power and flow of information is multi-directional and, in this way, McNair uses 'chaos' as a positive term to speak of structure rather than as signifying something that is negative.

The Panama Papers had many real-life impacts such as costing Icelandic Prime Minister Sigmundur Davíð Gunnlaugsson his job. It also highlighted the power of 'big data' leaks in the digital age. A year later, in 2017, the ICIJ again formed a collaboration of almost 100 media outlets including Australia's online *Guardian* newspaper and ABC TV's *Four Corners* program to reveal the leaked Paradise Papers. This leak of 13.4 million documents, mostly from Bermuda, revealed how companies and individuals – including royalty, politicians, rock stars and sporting heroes – use offshore entities to avoid paying their share of national taxes.

However, it is important to note that a challenge in the 'communicative abundance' era is that communications are not evenly distributed across the globe, and there exists a power gap between the information-poor and the information-rich. Keane has argued that the information-poor may suffer because they are deemed to be 'almost unneeded as communicators, or as consumers of media products' (2010, xxvii).

Another contemporary challenge in the communicative abundance era is the rise of fake news. In the second decade of this century, the technological advances that have engendered the global public sphere also allow for the 'weaponisation' of information. As used by politicians, non-mainstream media, hoaxers, and other political actors, fake news undermines the public's confidence in mainstream news (McNair 2018, 91).

In contrast to the chaos model, which views media reporting as diverse and as a public good, the control paradigm conceives of news media as shaped by 'a number of influences, [which] all work in the same conservative direction' to reinforce the existing power structures in society (Miliband 1973, 203). It conceives the mass media as largely reflecting the 'corporate good' rather than the 'public good' by upholding the interests of elites and capital (see Herman and Chomsky 2002).

VIDEO

POLITICAL ECONOMY THEORY (CONTROL PARADIGM)

Walter Lippmann wrote in his 1922 book *Public Opinion* that the mass media were altering the nature of public political discourse. He argued that 'a revolution is taking place, infinitely more significant than any shifting of economic power … [through] the manufacture of consent' (Lippmann 1922 [1997], 158). Lippmann, a political columnist and a leader of the 'interpretative style' of journalism – where journalists saw their role as not just reporting, but also explaining events – was not of the view that news was a mirror of reality. Rather, he was among the first to describe the transformative role of the media and its power to create or recreate the way we see the world, and thus mediate reality. Having seen the effects of war propaganda in the First World War, Lippmann was cautious of the misuse of media power for political purposes. He warned 'the creation of consent is not a new art', nor was it a 'daring prophecy to say that the knowledge of how to create consent will alter every political calculation and modify every political premise' (Lippmann 1922 [1997], 158).

In a similar vein, and influenced by the context of the Cold War, Edward Herman and Noam Chomsky (2002) address the economic and political power of the mass media to act as **gatekeepers** of information. They seized on Lippmann's famous phrase 'manufacturing consent' to write a significant account of how the media reinforce the economic, social and political agendas of the powerful in society through their construction of what is news. *Manufactured consent: The political economy of the mass media* applies a propaganda model, through the lens of political economy, to understand the behaviour of the mainstream media in the 20th century.

Herman and Chomsky argued that Western media subliminally activate news filters to pander to powerful commercial and political interests when deciding what has news

gatekeeper: Someone who decides if access will be granted. In terms of the media, 'gatekeeping' refers to access to information. It occurs at many stages of the news gathering process including what sources a reporter decides to consult, who is quoted, how the sub-editors and editors arrange the story, and the prominence that it is given on the webpage or in the newspaper or television bulletin. Politicians' press secretaries also play a gatekeeping role by determining what information goes to which media outlet and how much information is released. Gatekeeping theory was conceptualised by social psychologist Kurt Lewin in 1943.

value. The essential elements informing their propaganda model were: (1) the size of the media outlet, its ownership structures and wealth; (2) the influence of advertising as the primary media income source for the mass media; (3) reliance on information provided by government and business 'experts' who reinforce the dominant paradigms; (4) reliance on information provided by perceived purveyors of propaganda, such as public relations specialists and government lobbyists; and finally, (5) what they termed anti-communism – the negative reaction to any news that seemed to support communist ideology (Herman and Chomsky 2002, 2). In the 21st century, anti-communist rhetoric is less prevalent, and this last point could be reasonably perceived as another 'other' that challenges western ideology: Islamism, for example.

Herman and Chomsky's work remains salient in the 21st century because, notwithstanding new media digital entrants, the owners of existing large media companies have continued to consolidate. In the 19th century, the press was likely to be family-owned enterprises. Then, as these businesses were acquired, society witnessed the rise of the media baron. In turn, in the 20th century, large numbers of these businesses were sold to corporate conglomerates. By the 21st century, media businesses had acquired further holdings to become global media empires such as the announcement of the US$52.4 billion merger of Disney Corporation and Rupert Murdoch's 21st Century Fox in late 2017.

Scholars such as Ben Bagdikian, Robert McChesney, Thomas McPhail and Eli Noam among others, have critiqued global media ownership structures, raising concerns about their increasing concentration and the associated cultural imperialism that may follow. For example, Bagdikian (2004, 3) before his death found that from 1983 to 2004, due to media acquisitions and mergers, corporate media ownership in the United States had consolidated from 50 major media enterprises to just five, including Time Warner, The Walt Disney company and Rupert Murdoch's News Corporation. All had commercial interests across different aspects of the supply chain (called 'vertical integration') and disseminated their media products across multiple media platforms and markets. Bagdikian's conclusions were stark:

> They are American and foreign entrepreneurs whose corporate empires control every means by which the population learns of its society. And like any close-knit hierarchy, they find ways to cooperate so that all five can work together to expand their power, a power that has become a major force in shaping contemporary American life.

More than a decade later, the media corporations have been joined by social media giants in shaping contemporary society. In November 2017, the United States Senate committee hearings in Washington into the 2016 US Presidential election heard how before and after the election of Donald Trump, 146 million Facebook users may have seen Russian disinformation about the election. Similarly, Google's YouTube bosses conceded that the platform had housed 1108 Russian-linked propaganda videos. Twitter also revealed it had been home to more than 36 000 Russian-linked accounts that generated 1.4 million election related tweets (*The Economist* 2017). While it is not easy to measure the impact this mischievous content had on how Americans voted in November 2016, the cultural power of these digital monoliths to spread all types of information is unprecedented. This global cultural power provides a new basis for taking note of Lippmann's warning about 'manufactured consent', and for revisiting Herman and Chomsky's structural analysis of media power.

VIDEO
SHORT-ANSWER
QUESTIONS

THE CHANGING AUSTRALIAN MEDIA LANDSCAPE

As in other developed economies, Australia's traditional media outlets of newspapers, radio and television are in a state of flux in the digital age. On one hand, media technologies and the internet have made it faster, cheaper and easier to access, share and produce news stories across the globe. But, as discussed earlier in this chapter, the speed, volume and spread of news come with costs.

The rise in digital technologies has contributed to falls in Australia's traditional media outlets' revenues, as audiences and advertising have migrated online. Advertising revenue was the major income source for commercial news last century. That tight bond between the business of selling advertising and providing news has broken. Journalism was the lure to attract what Australian advertisers call 'eyeballs', or consumers, to its news pages. Today, non-media companies beyond Australia's borders attract advertisers, offering cheaper rates and data analytics for the sophisticated targeting of ads to consumers.

Australian newspapers that relied heavily on classified advertising revenues have been hardest hit with job losses, market write-downs and asset sales. Marshall McLuhan (1964, 207) predicted in his book *Understanding Media: The Extensions of Man*: 'The classified ads (and stock market quotations) are the bedrock of the press. Should an alternative source of easy access to such diverse daily information be found, the press will fold.' American media academic Clay Shirky (2014) describes the revenue downgrades of old media companies as the 'slow divorce between advertising and editorial'.

However, it is important to note that as much as the internet and global companies such as Google and Facebook take the lion's share of the online advertising market, the reasons for the decline in the established media are multifaceted. Australian daily newspapers' hard-copy circulation declines began *before* the internet took hold, in the early 1990s (Simons 2007, 29). This suggests that other factors contributed to the falls in newspaper profitability, such as changes to Australian ownership laws, political imperatives leading to those law changes, and cultural factors such as busy lifestyles leaving little time to buy and read a printed newspaper, or to watch a television news broadcast at a set time.

Also noteworthy is that the OECD (Wunsch-Vincent et al. 2010) found that the decline of newspapers is not a worldwide trend. Less economically developed nations such as India have experienced growth in their newspaper markets, and the number of titles worldwide increased in the first decade of this century.

The changes to the media market and arrival of social media have important implications for the reporting of politics in Australia and elsewhere. Compared to last century, the news cycle is faster, continuous and ravenous for content. In the words of former British prime minister Tony Blair (2007, 477):

> Make a mistake and you quickly transfer from drama into crisis … A vast aspect of our jobs today – outside of the really major decisions, as big as anything else – is coping with the media, its sheer scale, weight and constant hyperactivity. At points, it literally overwhelms.

Blair made this point in 2007. Ten years later, the information available to us through social media, online sites and established media has increased. This highly competitive environment has made it more difficult for politicians to get a sustained message heard without the distraction of new stories competing for the audience's attention. The consequence of this, said Blair, is a more toxic relationship between politicians and the media that results in increased public cynicism of both. He argues that new forms of media have further blurred the line between fact and opinion:

> The new forms can be even more pernicious, less balanced, more intent on the last conspiracy theory multiplied by five … we are all being dragged down by the way media and public life interact. Trust in journalists is not much above that in politicians (Blair 2007, 479).

REFLECTION
QUESTIONS

AUSTRALIAN MEDIA OWNERSHIP

Concurrent with technological and cultural change, Australian newspaper ownership structures altered in the later part of the last century, resulting in fewer overall owners and a greater concentration of ownership.

Australian media takeovers, due to cross-media ownership law changes in the late 1980s, significantly contributed to Australia losing *all* its daily evening newspapers. This caused irreversible falls in newspaper penetration by 50 per cent (Tiffen and Gittins 2009, 181). Whether it was the lack of newspaper choice, or the loss of a favourite masthead, many readers abandoned the newspaper-buying habit altogether during this time.

Concentration of media ownership is of interest to us because it can narrow editorial choices for readers. For example, watchdog reporting is generally more expensive and time consuming to produce than everyday news stories. Under a corporate structure, newspaper publishers must consider diverse internal interests, some of which are competing. These interests can include shareholder, advertiser and reader considerations, which need to be balanced alongside responsible economic management. Consequently, concerns about journalism standards such as a potential lack of plurality of opinion and diversity of stories can arise in cities with concentrated media ownership (House of Representatives Select Committee report 1992, xxi).

Among liberal democracies, Australia has the most concentrated press ownership structure. It has two major metropolitan print media owners and a third smaller proprietor. Measured by circulation, the third is Seven West Media controlled by businessman Kerry Stokes. Among Seven West's diverse media businesses (television, magazines, radio, online and regional newspapers) it owns the daily tabloid, *The West Australian*, which has the largest circulation in that state. The second largest print proprietor is Fairfax Media, which is owned by investors and individual shareholders and has media interests in magazines, radio, online and metropolitan and regional newspapers. Fairfax Media owns the daily national financial masthead the *Australian Financial Review* and three capital city daily mastheads, *The Age, The Sydney Morning Herald* and *The Canberra Times*.

The largest of Australia's print proprietors is News Corp. Like Fairfax, it is a multiplatform media company but with more interests in pay television, magazines, online and newspapers. It owns about 200 national, metropolitan, suburban, regional and Sunday print titles, including daily metropolitans sold in every state and territory except in Western Australia (Battersby 2017). News Corp owns Australia's only general news national daily broadsheet, *The Australian*.

One hundred years ago, Australia's print newspapers were flourishing. By 1848, there were 11 daily Australian newspapers (Mayer 1964, 10). By 1886 there were 48 daily papers, including regionals. In the 20th century, by 1958, the total number of dailies had grown to 55. This peaked at 56 in 1984 – when profits were high, and advertising revenues were considered 'liquid gold'. It was not to last, as Figure 11.1 shows.

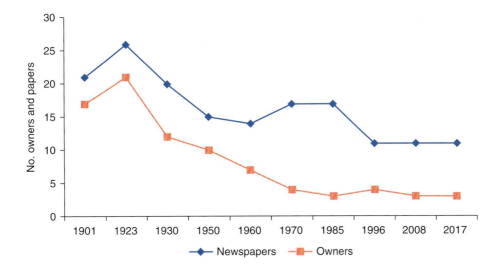

Figure 11.1 The number of Australian mastheads and newspaper owners over time

During the print media company acquisitions and mergers of the late 1980s, 12 of Australia's 19 metropolitan daily newspapers changed hands; two of them changed ownership twice, *The Canberra Times* and *The West Australian* (Tiffen 2015, 67). By 2008, the overall number of Australian daily papers – including regionals – slipped back to its late 19th century figure of 49. Twelve were daily capital city papers, half the number produced at the turn of the 20th century. By 2015, this number appears to have stabilised and Australia has around 46 daily papers, regional and metropolitan (Tiffen 2015, 70) and 12 daily metropolitan papers. There are three proprietors of these 12 mastheads and two of them, News Corp and Fairfax Media, own 11 between them. This gives these owners a daily newspaper circulation share of about 85 per cent. This is the highest of any developed democracy (Tiffen 2015, 65).

RESEARCH
QUESTION

Media freedom and Australian democracy

Australia's concentrated media ownership has implications for how the nation is evaluated in terms of its media freedoms. Two international watchdogs on media freedom, Reporters Without Borders and Freedom House, assess freedom of the media in nation-states as one measure of a nation's democratic legitimacy. Both ranked Australia below other democracies in 2017 at 19th and 22nd, respectively. Freedom House has measured media freedom since 1979 and Australia has had a noticeable drop in its ranking. It has shifted from 8th place in 2002 to 22nd in 2017.

Australia's media are considered free, but Australia's ranking suffers because of its concentrated media ownership, combined with political and legal environments that restrict reporting in various ways. In the watchdogs' recent annual reports, they identified, as violations of press freedom, new laws related to national security. The Australian Parliament passed a 2014 law that introduces jail terms for journalists who disclose 'special' intelligence operations. The watchdogs also identified a 2015 law to compel internet and mobile phone providers to store user metadata for two years, which could threaten the ability of journalists to freely interact with sources (Freedom House 2016). Both organisations cite restricted media access into immigration detention centres, onshore and offshore at Nauru and Papua New Guinea, as harmful to Australia's media freedom. Further, Australia's legal environment does not allow for constitutionally guaranteed press freedom at the federal level (Freedom House 2016).[3]

Reporters Without Borders considers Australia's public broadcaster as a positive for media freedom, but criticises Australia's heavily concentrated press ownership. It also identified the raiding of Labor Party offices in federal police raids during the 2016 federal election campaign – initiated to determine the source of a leaked story about the National Broadband Network that embarrassed the Commonwealth Government – as a violation of confidentiality of sources. The organisation stated that it 'showed that the authorities were more concerned about silencing the "messengers" than addressing the issues of concern to the public that had been raised by their revelations' (Reporters Without Borders 2017).

The watchdogs' 2017 reports found that all countries had media restrictions that had worsened this century, with only 13 per cent of the world's population living with a free press. In a worrying trend, Freedom House found that democratic leaders were attempting to shape news coverage by delegitimising the mainstream media through labels such as 'fake news', exerting political influence over public broadcasters, and playing favourites with 'friendly private outlets' (Freedom House 2017).

Freedom House ranked Australia's internet freedom slightly more open than the established media, with a score of 21. However, since these measurements began, Australia's net freedom score has deteriorated from 17 in 2011 to 21 in 2017. This is due to legislative changes allowing greater government surveillance in the name of national security. On the positive side, Australia's internet penetration is relatively high (92 per cent) and internet access continues to improve in rural and regional areas (Newman et al. 2017, 115).

REFLECTION
QUESTION

IMPACTS OF MEDIA ECONOMICS

The political economy of media contributes to concentrated media ownership in Australia through company mergers and acquisitions in response to changes to the economic and political landscape in which they operate. This has led to fewer professional journalists working in the major news outlets in Australia (MEAA 2017, 6). Newspaper companies, free-to-air (FTA) television and the national broadcaster, the ABC, have seen their newsrooms shrink in recent years due to cost cutting. After several rounds of editorial job cuts during the Global Financial Crisis, the largest single cuts were in 2012 when Fairfax Media, Channel 10 and News Corp combined cut almost 3000 staff (Carson 2013). In 2014, federal government budget cuts to the ABC caused it to shed 10 per cent of its workforce including journalists (Carson 2014). Again, in March 2017, Fairfax's daily metropolitan mastheads *The Age* and *The Sydney Morning Herald*, shed a quarter of its remaining editorial staff: 125 full time jobs (Ward 2017).

Regional towns and rural Australia are particularly vulnerable to cuts to local media services as large companies such as Fairfax find ways to cut costs to their holdings outside the capital cities. Fairfax-owned regional newspapers like the *Cooma-Monaro Express* with a 130-year old history of delivering news to locals stopped printing its paper in 2016. Fairfax also closed the *Summit Sun* in Jindabyne. Regional television and radio news have also been affected with the ABC shutting five regional radio posts in 2014, and ending the

---

3   It is explicitly protected in Victoria through the Charter of Human Rights and Responsibilities.

popular national rural program, 'The Bush Telegraph'. At the same time, the ABC closed Adelaide's television studio and wound back television production in smaller states.

Of the commercial television networks, Channel Ten has been hardest hit by media market changes. It was put into voluntary administration in mid-2017. The network had a last-minute reprieve when US TV, network giant CBS made a winning bid to take over the company. Channels Nine and Seven have also reported massive losses with advertising revenue falls in recent years. Pay TV, streaming video on demand with services like Stan and Netflix, Apple TV and YouTube, also impact FTA TV's advertising revenues. Top rating shows that would attract significant advertising dollars like *Stranger Things, Game of Thrones* and *Breaking Bad* are not available on free TV in Australia.

New digital entrants

There have been many new digital media entrants to the Australian media market, including international companies since the major newsroom job losses in 2012. These include *The Guardian, Daily Mail, Huffington Post, New York Times, Buzzfeed* and the academic digest, *The Conversation*. These newsrooms are generally smaller than the newsrooms of the past. Thus, they do not attempt to cover everything, but rather focus on more niche aspects of news. Generally, Australian politics is part of the reporting mix of these new entrants, although the tone of reporting tends to be more conversational and engaging than traditional outlets (Carson and Muller 2017).

The 2016 Australian federal election coverage highlighted how both new and established media were using digital technologies to report politics in ways not previously possible. Political journalists updated audiences constantly with campaign news using social media including Twitter, Snapchat, Facebook and Instagram. *The Guardian*'s Katharine Murphy through her 'Australia politics live' blog was one of several examples that threaded breaking political news and pictures with social media posts and memes. Online political site *Crikey* tracked election promises and calculated how much parties were allocating to spend on them. Veterans of the press gallery teamed up to produce regular podcasts with their extended analysis of the campaign. Among them were 'Two Grumpy Hacks – an Australian election podcast' with national political editor of *news.com.au* Malcolm Farr and *Courier-Mail* stablemate Dennis Atkins. The ABC's *7.30* host Leigh Sales teamed up with ABC TV host of *Kitchen Cabinet* Annabel Crabb in their 'Chat 10 Looks 3' series. Likewise, *Guardian* editor Lenore Taylor partnered with colleague Katherine Murphy to podcast 'Australian Politics Weekly'. These examples show the hybridity of established media figures using new media methods to report Australian politics.

AUTHOR
PANEL

OPPORTUNITIES AND CHALLENGES OF DIGITAL MEDIA TECHNOLOGIES

As we have discussed in this chapter, the development of digital technologies raises formidable challenges for newsrooms and the public sphere in the form of lost revenues, downsizing of newsrooms and fake news, yet the digital media environment also heralds unprecedented opportunities for journalists and political reporting. Three areas of opportunity arising from digital technologies that we will elaborate on here are media collaborations, the use of data reporting, and greater audience participation in public discourse.

OPPORTUNITIES FOR JOURNALISM

Collaboration

The same conditions that allow for the viral spread of fake news – internet connectivity, and many-to-many digital networks – have also enabled a new collaborative model of multiple newsrooms (and countries) sharing information to expose wrongdoing. We saw this with the example of the ICIJ and the worldwide collaborative reporting efforts that produced the Panama and Paradise papers. Another example is the not-for-profit US online newsroom *ProPublica*. Their newsroom of 50 journalists work with established media outlets in Europe and America to produce investigative journalism. *ProPublica* has partnered with more than 150 media outlets since its beginnings in 2008 and has won numerous Pulitzer Prizes. Its first Pulitzer was for working with the *New York Times Magazine* in 2010 to trace the devastating consequences of local hospital workers' decisions when cut off by Hurricane Katrina's flood waters (Fink 2009). Through media collaborations, *ProPublica* reduces costs by pooling resources and using different media platforms to reach bigger audiences for stories of public interest (Carson and Farhall 2017). In this way, it has highlighted how we can tell stories in different ways depending on the platform, and that some stories are more suited to one platform over the other. Some stories can be told in multiple ways: podcast, online print, infographics and so forth.

On a smaller scale, Australian media outlets are also starting to collaborate with each other, and with non-media outlets such as academia, and winning Walkley Awards for their efforts. These collaborations have been mainly between Fairfax Media and ABC journalists on investigative stories. They include, among others, exposing the Commonwealth Bank's unscrupulous tactics in providing life insurance to customers but avoiding insurance pay-outs. *The Guardian* Australia has partnered with the ABC and US whistleblower Edward Snowden to show how Australian spy agencies attempted to monitor the telecommunications of the Indonesian President Susilo Bambang Yudhoyono and his wife. While University of Technology Sydney journalism students collaborated with experienced *Sydney Morning Herald* reporters to reveal the free trips and gifts that Australian politicians receive. This won the 2012 Walkley Award for Best Digital Journalism.

This is just a sample of some of the Australian collaborations that have formed. It reveals an innovative adaptation by media outlets in times of cost-cutting to newsrooms. This trend is a major shift away from the 20th century model of reporting where single newsrooms competed against one another for 'scoops'. This century, journalists are seeing the value in collaborations to share resources, reach a bigger audience and to tell public interest stories across different platforms. These stories, as the awards recognise, can lead to important public outcomes such as policy and law reforms, criminal charges, public sackings and Royal Commissions (Carson and Farhall 2017).

Data journalism

The digital era also offers reporters new ways to use numbers to tell stories. In a data-rich age, it is possible for journalists to show their evidence behind a story to increase public trust in the veracity of a report. This might involve displaying original documents online, embedding data in news reports, or using data to produce infographics to tell the news in interesting and interactive ways. News stories about the 2016 Australian census findings and annual federal budgets are excellent examples of this type of interactive story-telling using numbers. Journalists are also using big data leaks to crowdsource stories by asking their audiences to help. An early example was Britain's *Guardian* newspaper inviting its readers to scrutinise politicians' expenses after the paper uploaded half a million leaked documents relating to the claimed expenses of members of parliament in 2009. In Australia, former *Sydney Morning Herald* journalist, Linton Besser, was awarded the 2010 investigative journalism Walkley Award for exposing the Department of Defence's spending of millions of dollars on luxury items that were unrelated to its role. The newspaper built a database to enable the public to trawl through 70 000 defence contracts and to report back any unusual findings.

Pulitzer Prize-winning investigative journalist David Barstow (Interview with author, 5 May 2016) of the *New York Times* argues that investigative reporting is of a higher quality than ever before due to new tools and use of data:

> The very best investigative reporting is a cut above what used to be the best. The highest levels are in part because we have a whole bunch of new tools, our ability to interrogate data, our ability to display original documents, to embed original documents online, digital presentations, our growing sophistication with graphics, growing sophistication with how to integrate all of the different forms of storytelling.

New audiences and participation

Modern newsrooms use data analytics to track audience receptiveness to stories. Academic research with Facebook in 2017 found that understanding the audience through analytics is central to the news process. In-depth case studies with seven Australian digital-only media outlets showed that data analytics allowed for a better knowledge of their audiences. When a story is uploaded, many newsrooms will have the live analytics on a big screen to see what the immediate interest is in the story. Outlets also track their individual page impressions each month to see if readers and viewers are growing (Carson and Muller 2017, 12). Outlets use social media to distribute stories to grow audience and to track what stories social media users engage with.

Social media enables two-way conversations. Through social media, audience interaction is an opportunity to source story ideas and for reporters to get more information and story tip-offs. The research found that social media played a vital role in decisions about how to shape and present the news. Shareability is a key criterion in news judgements, and for this reason video had become an increasingly popular means of presenting a story. The study found contemporary reporters need to consider the audience in every step of the news process: gathering information, posting the story and responding to comments (Carson and Muller 2017, 7).

Finally, scholars such as Wright (2012) and Wojcieszak and Mutz (2009) have revisited the concept of the public sphere in the digital age in their examination of how internet users' 'everyday talk' online can become political. They argue that these online spaces, which are varied, and include comment sections of newspapers, online community forums for shared interests, or advice forums on topics such as parenting, can become a space for political participation and deliberation that was not available last century.

CHALLENGES FOR JOURNALISM

It is important to acknowledge the challenges for journalism when considering news media in the digital age. Unsurprisingly, this section expands on funding journalism and examines ways that companies are addressing revenue shortfalls. Another challenging issue for media outlets is public trust, which has been falling in democracies. Among other factors, we consider how this might be linked to the rise in fake news.

Funding journalism

Newspapers do attract new audiences by posting their stories online. In Australia their readership has never been larger; however, the problem is not size. Studies show that most people do not pay for online news; for example, Deloitte's Sixth Annual Media Review (2017) found 90 per cent of people surveyed did not pay for online news. Of those who did, they paid mainly for specialist news, in-depth reporting and trusted brands. Here is a conundrum. Liberal democratic media theorists would argue that newsroom cost-cutting that leads to the shedding of journalists who report on those who wield power – politicians, councils, corporates, statutory authorities and so forth – limits media's watchdog role and this has serious implications for the health of a democracy. The 2012 Finkelstein media inquiry stated that job cuts at Australian newspapers could affect democratic accountability:

> With the growing influence of the internet as an advertising medium and the consequential reduced capacity of newspapers to use advertising revenue to support news production efforts, there is a fear that the civic watchdog, or Fourth Estate, function of news organisations will be permanently weakened with consequential damage to democracy and society's wellbeing (Finkelstein and Ricketson 2012, 305).

The question, then, is who is going to pay for professional journalists to maintain the fourth estate function while there is an expectation that online news is free? What are the 21st century media business models for survival?

Twenty-first century business models

While there is, as yet, no single silver bullet funding model for journalism, there are some options, and what works best depends on the type of media outlet it is. For some, the economic answer has been found in wealthy benefactors (think of Jeff Bezos, the owner of Amazon who bought the ailing *Washington Post,* or Russian businessman Alexander Lebedev who took ownership of Britain's *The Independent*, or billionaire hedge-fund owner John Henry and *The Boston Globe*). But, a rich proprietor might invite new problems for media outlets, such as conflicts of interest. Others, like *ProPublica* and *The Texas Tribune,* rely on philanthropy and seek public donations, using a non-profit model. *The Guardian* in Australia is pursuing this model too. Other media outlets are finding new revenues by diversifying their business interests. For example, Bloomberg has a professional services business that provides market data. *The Economist* has a proprietary research arm and an events business to supplement its journalism.

Analysis of new business models for newspapers by the Pew Research Center (Rosenstiel et al. 2012) found that 44 per cent of papers are looking at some form of non-traditional revenue. These included holding events, consulting, and selling new business products. Yet, the news industry has not moved very far in finding a model that would replace the once thriving print advertising model of last century. This is a great challenge ahead for traditional news media organisations. Academic research with Facebook found that Australian digital newsrooms are using a hybrid business model to pay their journalists. This model combines several revenue-raising methods. The combination varies depending on the target audience. The most common methods were: advertising, **native advertising**, building databases and selling access to them; hosting events related to the media content; using market research to develop and offer new media products; crowdsourcing funds and philanthropy; and the least popular model for digital newsrooms was the electronic **paywall** (Carson and Muller 2017, 35). The study showed that this hybrid funding model was working for many online-only Australia news outlets and that consequently most had increased staff numbers in the past five years (Carson and Muller 2017, 48).

Fake news and public trust

Public confidence in the veracity of public information is being challenged by fake news. The internet and computer algorithms make it easier for false information to spread, whether deliberately (fake news) or not (sloppy reporting). A century ago the 'yellow press', so named because of the yellow pages of the newspapers, fostered scuttlebutt and sensationalism. What is different in the 21st century is that fake news stories, through digital technologies, spread further and faster than before. Since US President Donald Trump's election, public apprehension has intensified about Trump's 'alternative facts', his 'war' on journalists, and fake news. A recent US Pew Research study found 88 per cent of Americans believe fake news confuses the public about basic facts (Barthel et al. 2016). The Oxford English Dictionary declared fake news its 'word of the year' for 2016, and in 2017 the Collins Dictionary followed suit. Collins defined it as 'false, often sensational, information disseminated under the guise of news reporting'.

However, scholars and commentators are not in agreement about how to define fake news. Some, such as Harvard University's First Draft, look at the motives for, and types of, misleading information under the broad banner of fake news. US President Donald Trump uses the term to describe parts of the mainstream media with which he disagrees. Brian McNair (2018, x) argues that it is a cultural phenomenon that 'is one expression of a wider crisis of trust in elites, including political and mainstream media elites'. McNair also makes the point that the term is deployed by a subsection of the elites, often on the fringe of mainstream politics, as an ideological weapon across the political spectrum.

Wrong information, whether deliberate (disinformation), malicious (mal-information) or incorrect (misinformation) in the public sphere matters because news needs to be accurate to inform the public and for the public to have confidence in the information they receive (Wardle and Derakhshan 2017). This is part of the normative functions that liberal democratic theorists ascribe to news media in democracies. Inaccurate reporting has consequences for media's role to provide for a well-informed citizenry, particularly during election campaigns when voters decide who to elect.

There were many examples of fake news during the 2017 Brexit campaign in the United Kingdom. One instance was the use of billboards on buses by the Leave campaign claiming that Britain's exit from the EU would free up £350 million per week for allocation to their National Health Service. Official figures clearly showed this claim to be untrue. In fact, the accurate figure was £250 million per week and even then, much of this funding returned to the country under various schemes. Once caught out in the lie, Leave campaigners denied that they had meant the £350 million figure to be taken literally (McNair 2018, 28). This

native advertising: Where advertising has the same presentation style as news stories so that consumers feel like the ad belongs with the content. It can be hard to tell apart from news because it looks so similar.

paywall: An electronic 'fence' used to charge for online content. A hard paywall requires readers to pay before they can access any story online. Soft paywalls allow some free access.

is what McNair calls the 'weaponisation' of information for political gain. Consider what misinformation does for public trust in the media.

We know that public trust in the media is declining in Australia, as it is in other democracies. The Edelman Trust Barometer, which researches public trust in the media across 28 countries, found Australians trust in the media had fallen to 32 per cent in 2017. This was a drop of 10 points from 2016 (Edelman 2017, 75). Australian research also finds trust in the Australian media across different outlets is falling, but confidence in some organisations is higher than others. For example, Essential Research (2017) polling found 63 per cent of surveyed Australians said they had 'a lot' or 'some' trust in the Australian Broadcasting Corporation compared to only 20 per cent having the same level of trust in blogs. Trust in local newspapers was marginally higher (44 per cent) than for daily metropolitan papers (42 per cent), news and opinion websites had similar levels of public trust at 40 per cent. How these trust levels relate to fake news is a developing area of study.

RESEARCH
QUESTIONS
SHORT-ANSWER
QUESTIONS

SUMMARY

Learning objective 1: Understand what the public sphere is, how the news media is said to contribute to it, and its connection to political discourse

The public sphere is a normative concept regarding the role of the news media in providing the public with information so that they can ultimately make rational choices about who to elect to best represent them. It is a physical and figurative space for people to come together, engage in political discourse and form their opinions. In the 21st century, the public sphere extends to the online environment and, through social media and other digital networks, has the capacity to be global. Many scholars think of the public sphere as being plural rather than a singular space for discussing political issues and ideas.

Learning objective 2: Differentiate between liberal democratic (chaos) and political economy (control) theories of the media

Media theorists have different views on the news media's role in a democracy. Liberal democratic theorists tend to view it as serving the public sphere in a positive way. Theorists such as McNair, Schudson, Kellner and Keane generally view the media as supporting the wellbeing of democracy through several functions including acting as a check on the (mis) use of power. They understand the media to be diverse and open with the power to disrupt the established social order. Control theorists such as Herman and Chomsky do not share this view. Rather, they see the media as activating filters that serve to reinforce the interests of the wealthy and powerful.

Learning objective 3: Explain key changes to the Australian media landscape from the 20th to the 21st century

Australian media are in a state of flux. On one hand, the business model that linked advertising to journalism has broken, and the established media has suffered from cost cutting and professional journalism job losses. On the other hand, the digital age has lowered the barriers to entry to make it easier and cheaper for anyone to purport to be a journalist and to act as a check on power. This century has also seen many international media brands enter the domestic market giving Australians more media options, but these newsrooms tend to be smaller and do not attempt to cover every story as was the endeavour of 20th century newspapers.

Learning objective 4: Describe the opportunities and challenges that digital technologies present to media organisations and their journalism

As with other sectors, the development of digital technologies has affected media organisations. They provide both opportunities and challenges to journalism and the reporting of politics. On the positive side, digital technologies provide the communication and data sharing means for greater collaboration between journalists and newsrooms, domestically and abroad. Collaborations offer journalists greater resources, audiences and safeguards against persecution than going it alone. Software developments to parse large amounts of data have enabled data journalism to thrive. Journalists can tell stories using numbers in new and engaging ways. The use of data analytics means that the audience is central to every decision including: what story to pursue, how to tell it and on which platform. Likewise, people have more options for engaging with stories, reacting to them, and for telling their own.

But media organisations also face challenges. Among the most pressing is finding a sustainable funding model to employ professional journalists. Every indication so far is that this is likely to be a hybrid model whereby media outlets rely on more than one revenue stream to finance their journalism. Another great challenge is how to address the proliferation of fake news and falling levels of trust in the media. Public confidence in journalism is declining in democracies and Australia is no exception. What this means for future Australian political reporting is less clear. What is clear is that fake news and falling levels of public trust in the media should concern us. Former US President Barack Obama (2016) stated: 'If we are not serious about facts, what's true, and what's not, if we can't discriminate between serious arguments and propaganda, then we have problems'.

DISCUSSION
QUESTIONS

DISCUSSION QUESTIONS

1. In what century was the Habermasian public sphere thought to have emerged, and how did it exist? In Habermas's view, what triggered its demise?

2. How might the idea of the public sphere be relevant today in the digital age of global communications?

3. Can you think of examples of how the media in the 21st century plays a role informing the global public sphere about matters in the public interest?

4. Where do Australian audiences get their news from in the 21st century? What concerns exist about contemporary sources of news?

5. What does it mean when voters are increasingly relying on social media to get news? What is the democratic 'promise' of 'new media'? Does the existence of alternative views mean they are *equally* influential? Can new media forms such as blogs and Twitter have significant influence compared to mainstream commercial media?

FURTHER READING

Blair, T. (2007). Tony Blair's 'media' speech: The Prime Minister's Reuters speech on public life. *The Political Quarterly*, **78**(4), October–December, 476–87.

Carson, A. and McNair, B. (2016). Still the main source: The established media. In A. Gauja, P. Chen, J. Curtin and J. Pietsch, eds, *Double Dissolution: The 2016 Election Book*, Canberra: ANU Press.

Carson, A. and Muller, D. (2017). *The Future Newsroom*, Sydney: Facebook. Retrieved from http://arts .unimelb.edu.au/__data/assets/pdf_file/0003/2517726/20913_fnreport_sept2017_web-final.pdf

Errington, W. and Miragliotta, N. (2011). The liberal democratic tradition and the media. *Media and Politics: An Introduction*, Melbourne: Oxford University Press, pp. 1–19.

Este, J. (2012). *Kicking at the Cornerstone of Democracy: The State of Press Freedom in Australia*, Sydney: MEAA.

Herman, E.S. (2000). The propaganda model: A retrospective, *Journalism Studies*, **1**(1), 101–12.

Kang, C. (2016). Fake news onslaught targets pizzeria as nest of child trafficking, *The New York Times*, 21 November. Retrieved from http://www.nytimes.com/2016/11/21/technology/fact-check-this-pizzeria-is-not-a-child-trafficking-site.html

Macnamara, J. and Kenning, G. (2014). E-electioneering 2007–13: Trends in online political campaigns over three elections. *Media International Australia*, 152, 57–74. doi:10.1177/13298 78X1415200107

McNair, B. (2018). *Fake News: Falsehood, Fabrication and Fantasy in Journalism*, London: Routledge.

The Economist, (2017). Do social media threaten democracy? *The Economist*, 4 November. URL: https://www.economist.com/news/leaders/21730871-facebook-google-and-twitter-were-supposed-save-politics-good-information-drove-out

Young, S. (2011). Creating election news: Journalists. In S. Young, *How Australia Decides: Election Reporting and the Media*, Melbourne: Cambridge University Press, pp. 107–25.

REFERENCES

Almond, G.A., Powell, G.B., Dalton, R.J. and Strom. K. (2010). *Comparative Politics Today: A World View*, 9th edn, Longman: New York.

Bagdikian, B.H. (2004). *The New Media Monopoly*, Boston: Beacon Press.

Barthel, M., Mitchell, A. and Holcomb, J. (2016). Many Americans believe fake news is sowing confusion, Pew Research Centre, 15 December. Retrieved from http://www.journalism.org/2016/12/15/many-americans-believe-fake-news-is-sowing-confusion/

Battersby, L. (2017). News Corp and the Murdochs starting 2017 with more news and influence than before, *The Sydney Morning Herald*, 14 January. Retrieved from http://www.smh.com.au/business/media-and-marketing/news-corp-and-the-murdochs-starting-2017-with-more-news-and-influence-than-before-20170110-gtoo2a.html

Blair, T. (2007). Tony Blair's 'media' speech: The Prime Minister's Reuters speech on public life. *The Political Quarterly*, **78**(4), October–December, 476–87.

Bobbio, N. (1987). *The Future of Democracy*, Cambridge: Polity Press.

Bruns, A. (2017). *Echo Chamber? What Echo Chamber? Reviewing the Evidence*. St Lucia: University of Queensland. Retrieved from http://snurb.info/files/2017/Echo%20Chamber.pdf

Calhoun, C. (1992). *Habermas and the Public Sphere*, Baskerville: MIT Press.

Carlyle, T. (1908) [1840]. Lecture V: The hero as man of letters: Johnson, Rousseau, Burns. *On Heroes, Hero-Worship, & the Heroic in History. Six Lectures*, London: Dent.

Carson, A. (2013). *Investigative journalism, the public sphere and democracy: The watchdog role of Australian broadsheets in the digital age*. Unpublished doctoral thesis, University of Melbourne.

Carson, A. (2014). ABC cuts a tale of two Australias: Sydney-Melbourne and also-rans, *The Conversation*, 24 November. Retrieved from theconversation.com/abc-cuts-a-tale-of-two-australias-sydney-melbourne-and-also-rans–34424

Carson, A. and Farhall, K. (2017). The rise of global collaborative journalism in the 'post-truth' age. Presented at *Future of Journalism 2017* conference Cardiff School of Journalism, Media and Cultural Studies.

Carson, A. and D. Muller. (2017). *The Future Newsroom*, Sydney: Facebook. Retrieved from http://arts.unimelb.edu.au/__data/assets/pdf_file/0003/2517726/20913_fnreport_sept2017_web-final.pdf

Castells, M. (2008). The new public sphere: Global civil society, communication networks, and global governance. *Annals of the American Academy of Political and Social Science*, **616**(1), 78–93.

Collins English Dictionary. (2018). *fake news*. Available at: https://www.collinsdictionary.com/dictionary/english/fake-news

Conboy, M. (2013). *Journalism Studies: The Basics*, Abingdon: Routledge.

Craig, G. (2004). *The Media, Politics and Public Life*, Sydney: Allen & Unwin.

Croteau, D. and Hoynes. W, (2014). *Media/Society: Industries, Images, and Audiences*, 5th edn, Thousand Oaks: Sage.

Curran, J., Fenton, N. and Friedman, D. (2012). *Misunderstanding the Internet*, Abingdon: Routledge.

Davies, N. (2014). *Hack Attack: The Inside Story of How the Truth Caught Up with Rupert Murdoch*, New York: Faber.

De Burgh, H. (2000). *Investigative Journalism*, London: Routledge.

Deloitte. (2017). *Media Consumer Survey 2017: Australian media and digital preferences* – 6th edition. URL: http://landing.deloitte.com.au/tmt-media-consumer-survey-2017-inb-lp-ty.html

Duggan, M. and Smith, A. (2016). *The Political Environment on Social Media*, Washington, DC: Pew Research Center. Retrieved from http://assets.pewresearch.org/wp-content/uploads/sites/14/2016/10/24160747/PI_2016.10.25_Politics-and-Social-Media_FINAL.pdf

Edelman Trust Barometer. (2017). Asia Pacific, Middle East and Africa, *Edelman Trust Barometer: Annual Global Study*. URL: http://www.edelman.com/trust2017/trust-asia-pacific-middle-east-africa

Essential Research. (2017). Trust in Media, *Essential Report*, 4 October. URL: https://www.essentialvision.com.au/?s=media&searchbutton=Search

Ettema, J. and Glasser, T. (1998). *Custodians of Conscience: Investigative Journalism and Public Virtue*, New York: Columbia University Press.

Fink, S. (2009). Deadly choices at memorial, *ProPublica*, 27 August. Retrieved from https://www.propublica.org/article/the-deadly-choices-at-memorial-826

Finkelstein, R. and Ricketson, M. (2012). Report of the Independent Inquiry into the Media and Media Regulation, Australian Government: DBCDE, 2 March. Retrieved from https://www.dbcde.gov.au/digital_economy/independent_media_inquiry

Freedom House. (2016). *Freedom of the Press 2016*. URL: https://freedomhouse.org/report/freedom-press/freedom-press–2016

Freedom House. (2017). *Freedom of the Press 2017*. URL: https://freedomhouse.org/report/freedom-press/freedom-press–2017

Garnham, N. (1990). *Capitalism and Communication*, Sage: London.

Habermas, J. (1989). *The Structural Transformation of the Public Sphere*, trans. T. Burger, Cambridge: MIT Press.

Habermas, J. (2010). *Europe: The Faltering Project*, trans. C. Cronin, Cambridge: Polity Press.

Hall, S., Critcher, C., Jefferson, T., Clark, J. and Roberts, B. (1978). *Policing the Crisis: Muggings, the State, Law and Order*, Basingstoke: Macmillan Education.

Herman, E.S. and Chomsky, N. (2002). *Manufacturing Consent: The Political Economy of the Mass Media*, New York: Pantheon.

House of Representatives Select Committee on the Print Media. (1992). *News & Fair Facts: The Australian Print Media Industry*, Canberra: Australian Government Publishing.

Keane, J. (2010). *The Life and Death of Democracy*, London: Pocket Books.

Kellner, D. (1999). Globalisation from below? Toward a radical democratic technopolitics. *Angelaki: Journal of the Theoretical Humanities*, **4**(2), 101–13. doi:10.1080/09697259908572039

Lippmann, W. (1922) [1997]. *Public Opinion*, New York: Harcourt Brace.

Lukamto, W. and Carson, A. (2016). POLITWEETS: Social media as a platform for political engagement between Victorian politicians and citizens. *Communication Research and Practice*, **2**(2), 191–212.

Macnamara, J. and Kenning, G. (2014). E-electioneering 2007–13: Trends in online political campaigns over three elections. *Media International Australia Incorporating Culture and Policy*, **152**, 57–74. doi:10.1177/1329878X1415200107

Mayer, H. (1964). *The Press in Australia*, Melbourne: Lansdowne Press.

McLuhan, M. (1964). *Understanding Media: The Extensions of Man*, New York: McGraw-Hill

McNair, B. (1999). *An Introduction to Political Communication*, 2nd edn, London: Routledge.

McNair, B. (2006). *Cultural Chaos: Journalism, News and Power in a Globalised World*, London: Routledge.

McNair, B. (2018). *Fake News: Falsehood, Fabrication and Fantasy in Journalism*, London: Routledge.

McNair, B., Flew, T., Harrington S. and Swift. A. (2016). *Politics, Media and Democracy in Australia*, London: Routledge.

Media, Entertainment and Arts Alliance (MEAA). (2017). Submission to the Senate Select Committee Inquiry into Public Interest journalism, 14 July. Parliament of Australia. URL: https://www.aph.gov.au/Parliamentary_Business/Committees/Senate/Future_of_Public_Interest_Journalism/PublicInterestJournalism/Submissions

Miliband, R. (1973). *Parliamentary Socialism*, London: Merlin.

Newman, N., Fletcher, R., Kalogeropoulos, A., Levy, D.A.L. and Nielsen, R.K. (2017). *Reuters Institute Digital News Report 2017*, Oxford: Reuters Institute for the Study of Journalism. Retrieved from https://www.digitalnewsreport.org/

Obama, B. (2016). Remarks by President Obama and Chancellor Merkel of Germany in a Joint Press Conference. The White House Office of the Press Secretary, 17 November. Retrieved from obamawhitehouse.archives.gov/the-press-office/2016/11/17/remarks-president-obama-and-chancellor-merkel-germany-joint-press

Pariser, E. (2011). *The Filter Bubble: What the Internet is Hiding From You*, London: Penguin.

Reporters Without Borders. (2017). *2017 World Press Freedom Index*. URL: https://rsf.org/en/ranking_table

Rosenstiel, T., Jurkowitz, M. and Hong, J. (2012). *The search for a new business model*, Pew Research Centre, 5 March. Retrieved from https://www.journalism.org/2012/03/05/search-new-business-model

Schudson, M. (2008). *Why Democracies Need an Unlovable Press*, Cambridge: Polity Press.

Schudson, M. (2011). *The Sociology of News*, 2nd edn, San Diego: Norton.

Shirky, C. (2014). Last Call: The end of the printed newspaper, *Medium*, 19 August. Retrieved from https://medium.com/@cshirky/last-call-c682f6471c70

Simons, M. (2007). *The Content Makers: Understanding the Media in Australia*, Melbourne: Penguin.

Stephens, M. (1988). *A History of News*, New York: Viking Press.

Sunstein, C. (2007). *Republic.com 2.0*, Princeton: Princeton University Press.

The Economist. (2017). Do social media threaten democracy? *The Economist*, 4 November, 19–22.

Tiffen, R. (2015). From punctuated equilibrium to threatened species: The evolution of Australian newspaper circulation and ownership. *Australian Journalism Review*, **37**(1), 63–80.

Tiffen, R. and Gittins, R. (2009). *How Australia Compares*, 2nd edn, Melbourne: Cambridge University Press.

Volkmer, I. (2014). *The Global Public Sphere: Public Communication in the Age of Reflective Interdependence*, Cambridge: Polity Press.

Wall, M. (2005). Blogs of war: Weblogs as news. *Journalism*, **6**(2), 153–72.

Ward, M. (2017). Fairfax Media to axe 125 editorial jobs as part of $30 m restructure, *Mumbrella*, 3 May. Retrieved from https://mumbrella.com.au/fairfax-media-axe-125-editorial-jobs-part-30 m-restructure–442106

Wardle, C. and Derakhshan, H. (2017). Information disorder: Toward an interdisciplinary framework for research and policymaking, *The Council of Europe*. Retrieved from https://shorensteincenter.org/wp-content/uploads/2017/10/PREMS-162317-GBR-2018-Report-de%CC%81sinformation.pdf?x78124

Williams, B. (2017). Journalists, look out: Google is funding the rise of the AI news machine in Europe, *Mashable*. Retrieved from https://mashable.com/2017/07/07/google-ai-journalism-funding-europe/#cgw1ydf63sq8

Wojcieszak, M. and Mutz, D. (2009). Online groups and political discourse: Do online discussion spaces facilitate exposure to political disagreement? *Journal of Communication*, **59**(1), 40–56.

Wright, S. (2012). From 'third place' to 'third space': Everyday political talk in non-political online spaces. *Javnost – The Public*, **19**(3), 5–20.

Wunsch-Vincent, S., Vickery, G., Serra Vallejo, C. and Youn Oh, S. (2010). Evolution of news and the internet. *OECD Working Party on the Information Economy*, Paris: Organisation for Economic Co-operation and Development.

CHAPTER 12

HAVING A VOICE: CITIZEN PARTICIPATION AND ENGAGEMENT

LEARNING OBJECTIVES

After reading this chapter, you should be able to:

1. Describe the organisational landscape of political participation in Australia and the variety of tactics employed by citizens' groups

2. Outline and evaluate the ways in which Australian governments engage with citizens' groups

3. Discuss the challenges arising from the growing demand for political participation and engagement in the 21st century

INTRODUCTION

In the 21st century, political participation by a diverse range of citizens' groups in Australia is expanding. While conventional accounts of the political landscape highlight Australia's well-established formal institutions such as the electoral system, parliament, federalism, the public service and judiciary, a holistic approach to the study of Australian politics must also include the political contributions of a wider range of citizens and the various ways in which governments attempt to structure their input.

The chapter begins with a description of the organisational landscape of citizens' groups in Australian politics and an overview of the various terms used to describe them, including **interest groups**, pressure groups, non-governmental organisations (NGOs) and the non-profit sector. It surveys the most common political strategies employed by groups seeking to influence political debate. These comprise the organisation of public protests and demonstrations, the dissemination of campaign material through various media, consumer activism, and engaging with formal institutional politics. The chapter summarises the main advantages and drawbacks for the political system arising from the active participation and engagement of citizens' groups.

Australian governments provide a range of opportunities for citizens to contribute to political debate and public policy. Key examples include invitations to submit written and/or oral statements; hosting public forums and conventions such as 'community cabinets'; forming issue-specific stakeholder groups; administering surveys and national votes; and establishing more formal **collaborative governance** arrangements, particularly for managing natural resources. The relative merits and drawbacks of these government-initiated arrangements are discussed with reference to theoretical modelling of community engagement.

The final section of the chapter examines the new challenges arising from the growing citizen participation and demand for community engagement in Australian politics. These comprise debates over the extent of representativeness and transparency of citizens' groups and their resulting legitimacy, the appropriate level of public funding for citizens' groups, state governments' legislative attempts to curtail public demonstrations, and the phenomenon of '**slacktivism**'. The discussion of these issues demonstrates how the participation and engagement of citizens' groups is evolving in 21st century Australia.

interest groups: Associations of individual people or organisations with shared objectives, which aim to influence the political process.

collaborative governance: Governments delegating some degree of decision-making power to citizens' groups and/or other stakeholders, such as business actors and other levels of government.

slacktivism: A pejorative term for activism conducted via online media.

AUTHOR PANEL

THE ORGANISATIONAL LANDSCAPE OF CITIZEN PARTICIPATION

In Australia, a nation with relatively few restraints on political freedom, a vast array of citizens' groups is actively engaged in politics and public policy, both within formal processes as well as external to governments. Australian citizens' groups are extremely diverse, hailing from all facets of organised Australian social life – many also have global linkages – and include, for example:

» Australian Red Cross
» Australian Christian Lobby

» Business Council of Australia

» Oxfam Australia

» Australian Council of Social Service

» National Rifle Association of Australia

» Catholic Church

» Sea Shepherd

» Australian Council of Trade Unions

» Australian Government Primary Principals Association

» Australian Medical Association

» United Patriots Front

» Birdlife Australia

» Smith Family

» GetUp!

» Australian Childcare Alliance

» Australians for Constitutional Monarchy

» Minerals Council of Australia

» Media, Entertainment and Arts Alliance

» Australian Conservation Foundation

» Beyond Blue

» National Union of Students.

In political science, and more generally, a variety of terms are used to describe such groups. Among these are interest groups, NGOs, **civil society** groups, community organisations, pressure groups, associations, social enterprises, lobby groups, non-profit organisations, social movements, charities, activist groups and cooperatives. While this seemingly crowded field indicates complexity in the realm of citizens' political participation, four common elements may be identified. First, citizens' groups attempt to exert influence from outside parliament and do not typically seek to become formal representatives. Second, they represent a relatively narrow set of citizens and/or limited issue-based concerns in contrast to major political parties, which tend to develop comprehensive sets of policies across most issue-areas. Third, participation in citizens' groups is voluntary. And fourth, the primary motivation for such groups is not usually to generate a financial profit. Citizens' groups are thus conceptually located above the level of the family but separate from government and the market.

civil society: The sphere of society that is distinct from governments and business and above the level of the family.

The organising principle for citizens' groups is affiliation, or a sense of affiliation, that individuals may have with a broader set of citizens. Citizens' groups are organised at all levels of politics at the grassroots, municipal, regional, state/territory, national and global levels. They include groups such as local community clubs and churches to environmental NGOs, trade unions, professional bodies and business associations. It is important to note that business entities are increasingly engaged in public advocacy on a range of issues alongside regular citizens' groups, and in this sense, they may reasonably be included in such discussions. A prominent example is the more than 1300 businesses operating in Australia that have pledged their support for marriage equality. Indeed, Qantas, Airbnb, Fairfax Media and Foxtel even produced and distributed marriage equality 'acceptance rings' to support the cause (Urban 2017).

CATEGORISING CITIZENS' GROUPS

In attempting to discern the field of citizens' groups, several different classification systems are on offer. Among the most common is the notion of 'insider' versus 'outsider' groups (Grant 1978). Outsiders are said to have little access to governments, few economic resources, and mainly focus on public channels to air their grievances and elicit support. Examples include animal liberation groups, anti-vaccination organisations or the Occupy Wall Street protesters. Outsider groups employ various tactics of persuasion, but they often rely on evocative language, images and public protest to generate support.

In contrast, insider groups enjoy relative ease of access to elected representatives and bureaucrats, considerable economic resources, and consequently employ less visible political strategies. Examples of Australian insider groups include the Australian Council of Trade Unions (ACTU), National Farmers' Federation, Australian Chamber of Commerce and Industry, and Returned Servicemen's League. Because members typically pay fees, insider groups often have a professional staff, management structure, annual budget and the capacity to undertake research to inform their policy positions.

While the insider/outsider typology provides insights into citizens' groups relative access to governments and economic resources, in practice, many groups straddle both camps according to the preferences of the government of the day. On occasions, the insider status of some groups fails to result in the desired level of influence, prompting instead media campaigns that seek to rally citizens to their cause and thereby pressure governments from the outside. In 2010, the use of a $22 million national advertising campaign by the Minerals Council of Australia to argue against the Rudd Government's proposed 'super-profits' mining tax is one such example (Davis 2011).

A second method for categorising citizens' groups is on the basis of their primary function. Distinguishing groups according to whether they serve a promotional (public interest) or sectional (private interest) role (Warhurst 2009, 329) highlights the political motivations of various groups and the range of citizens they aim to represent. For example, **promotional groups** often publicise underreported dimensions of issues that they believe are neglected by the media and policy-makers. Dr Philip Nitschke's group Exit International, which advocates the legalisation of euthanasia, is one such organisation. Promotional groups often seek to make claims about the moral, rights-based or ethical dimensions of an issue and group membership is rarely restrictive. In fact, the primary aim of some promotional groups is not to represent a broader set of citizens but publicise the philosophical merits of a principle or idea, regardless of the number of supporters. In contrast, **sectional groups** are said to primarily exist to serve the interests of members and membership is often restricted by occupation, business type or industry sector. Examples include the Housing Industry Association, Pharmacy Guild of Australia or Transport Workers Union. Sectional groups are likely to be relatively well-funded due to the financial contributions of members.

The promotional versus sectional typology is closely linked to the public/private dichotomy, which similarly distinguishes business associations, occupational lobby groups and trade unions from groups seen as representing the broader public interest. In other words, private interest groups are viewed as largely self-interested and instrumental organisations while public interest groups are seen as selflessly working toward the betterment of society. In reality, however, the distinction between promotional (or public interest) and sectional (private interest) groups is murky. At face value, trade unions, for

promotional groups: Citizens' organisations working toward public interest rather than private, instrumental objectives.

sectional groups: Organisations that seek to represent the interests of a particular sector or cohort of society, often a particular profession or industry.

instance, are primarily sectional groups seeking to advance the rights of members, but they also play promotional roles that may serve the broader public interest. Groups such as the ACTU and the Australian Medical Association concurrently represent members while campaigning to promote social justice more broadly through their support for campaigns against domestic violence and gender discrimination. Meanwhile, business associations such as the Clean Energy Council, which officially represents the Australian renewable energy industry, may be understood as serving a simultaneous public interest function by promoting low emissions energy alternatives to fossil fuels. Further, business associations often engage in philanthropic causes not directly related to advancing their private interests. The Small Business Association of Australia, for instance, supports the Act for Kids support service, which aims to treat and prevent child abuse and neglect.

Classifying citizens' groups according to their orientation towards existing policy settings is yet another system for distinguishing between groups. Such a scheme might divide groups into the categories of 'conformer', 'reformer' or 'radical' (Scholte, O'Brien and Williams 1999, 112). Conformer groups seek to maintain the policy status quo and typical examples include business groups, such as the Australian Hotels Association seeking to preserve existing policy approaches to poker machines, or religious groups striving to uphold the traditional conception of marriage. Alternatively, radical groups may wish to overhaul existing policies in their entirety and replace them with fundamentally different approaches to organising public life. Examples might include far-right nationalist groups such as United Patriots Front, 'deep green' environmental groups such as Earth First! Australia or the Socialist Alliance. Meanwhile, situated between conformers and radicals, reformer groups work within existing political frameworks to adapt policies according to their particular issues and priorities. Notable Australian examples include the Australian Conservation Foundation, Australian Council of Social Service and the ACTU. A strength of this classification method is that it avoids distinguishing between the moral and instrumental goals of citizens' groups, instead highlighting their degree of support for the status quo. However, the boundary between proposing reform and advocating radical change is open to interpretation. Some might view the harm minimisation objectives of the Australia Drug Law Reform Foundation as radical, while others perceive it as advocating sensible policy change.

In short, while there is no one recognised way to classify citizens' groups, the various typologies outlined above encourage consideration of citizens' groups' proximity to elected representatives, the main functions they undertake, and their general policy orientations. Together, these are important factors in understanding the varied roles and significance of citizens' groups in Australia and elsewhere.

POLITICAL STRATEGIES FOR PUBLICISING CITIZENS' CONCERNS

Citizens' groups employ an extensive repertoire of tactics in an effort to influence politics and public policy. These may be divided into four key strategies, often employed simultaneously: conducting public activities and performances, developing and disseminating documentation via a range of media, consumer activism, and engaging with formal political structures. While these generic political strategies are also used by elected representatives and governments to influence public life, they are cornerstones of citizens' groups' *modus operandi* given that they typically lack formal authority through which to realise their goals. In particular, the use of new media and consumer activism by citizens' groups has proliferated in the 21st century, which has proved challenging for governments and especially business actors targeted by such activities.

Conducting public activities and performances

Citizens groups regularly engage in public activities or performances designed to attract media coverage. These activities include organising and participating in public demonstrations and protests; acts of civil disobedience; media appearances, such as interviews on news and current affairs programs; and staging press conferences.

Public demonstrations are a staple of Australian public life. They involve people marching in the streets or assembling at specific venues such as parliaments, armed with signs and slogans summarising their cause and a range of speakers rallying the crowd. In a globally coordinated event in November 2015, for instance, thousands of citizens participated in a Peoples' Climate Rally, comprising a march through city streets in Sydney, Canberra, Perth and Hobart, plus a number of regional Australian towns, to call for stronger measures to address global warming in the lead up to the Paris UN climate conference. In August 2017, citizens from trade union, youth, conservative Christian, and LGBTIQ groups clashed in Canberra's Civic Square advocating their opposing views about the Safe Schools program initiated by the Victorian Government, which promotes the inclusivity of same-sex attracted, intersex and gender diverse students. Similarly, Reclaim Australia supporters have repeatedly conflicted with anti-racism groups such as No Room for Racism at rallies around Australia in recent years. In short, public demonstrations attract media attention to an issue, demonstrate the strength and depth of concern among citizens, attract supporters and detractors, and may ultimately result in a governmental response in the form of policy change.

Acts of civil disobedience are another avenue for citizens' groups – and individuals – aiming to attract public attention in order to influence the political process. These may comprise 'sit-ins' or the chaining of individuals to buildings or equipment requiring a police presence and forcible removal. In essence, civil disobedience is a principled refusal to adhere to a particular law for moral or ethical reasons. Indeed, in 2016, the secretary of the ACTU, Sally McManus, contentiously stated that the right of citizens to defy 'bad laws' is an essential aspect of democratic participation (ABC News 2017). In the early 1980s, civil disobedience was prominently employed by environmental activists opposed to hydroelectric dams in Tasmania. It resulted in 1500 citizens arrested and a further 500 detained in prison for purposefully breaking a state law making 'lurking, loitering or secreting' in the Franklin river forests area illegal (Tierney 2003). More recently, in regard to health policy and illicit drug use, terminally ill people and those with chronic pain are challenging laws that criminalise the use of cannabis for medicinal purposes by continuing to source and administer cannabis for pain relief. Civil disobedience has also been employed by journalists refusing to reveal sources of information, gay law reform activists, and illegal workers' actions, such as strikes.

Representatives of citizens' groups contribute frequent media appearances and even conduct their own press conferences and media forums to publicise their causes. Indeed, the vast majority of news reports include input not only from government and opposition party spokespeople but community and stakeholder representatives from industry, trade unions and an array of other citizens' groups. In 2016, the proposed restrictions on lever-action shotguns, an issue that pitted civil libertarians and conservatives against gun control and greens groups, resulted in numerous media appearances by citizens' groups including Gun Control Australia, Alannah and Madeline Foundation, Australian Medical Association, Sporting Shooters Association of Australia, Firearm Owners United, National Farmers' Federation, and National Rifle Association. In regard to hosting forums, ACOSS's (Australian Council of Social Service) regular NGO Media Forums bring together journalists, professional experts, and researchers to discuss the community services sector. And in 2012, Greenpeace and the Sydney Aquarium held a joint press conference to highlight the vulnerability of the Great Barrier Reef to coal mining in Australia (Greenpeace International 2012). Regardless of the particular format employed, media engagement is a crucial method for citizens' groups to publicise their concerns to governments and the wider electorate.

Producing and disseminating documentary material

Citizens' groups produce documentary material in many different forms in their effort to influence public debate. These include press releases, public statements, position papers, reports, newsletters, open letters, petitions, posters, pamphlets, advertisements, opinion pieces, letters to the editor, films, books and public announcements. Such materials are disseminated via newspapers, television, radio, citizens' groups' websites, social media, billboards, car bumpers and the postal service. Examples of these contributions are endless, but a number of recent noteworthy instances include:

» Lock the Gate's films about the social and environmental impact of coal mining and gas extraction, *Fractured country: an unconventional invasion* and *undermining Australia: coal vs communities*

» *Ban the super-trawler* car stickers and associated campaign material targeting factory fishing vessels in Australian waters involving Greenpeace, Stop the Trawler Alliance and recreational fishers' groups, among others

» Australia Defence Association's letter to the *Australian Financial Review* in November 2015 advocating that Defence Housing Australia remain in public hands

» United Voice's report, *Who pays for our common wealth: tax practices of the ASC 200*, and associated video advertisements about corporate tax avoidance and wealth inequality in Australia

» People with Disability Australia's Twitter, YouTube, Pinterest and Facebook pages advocating funding for the National Disability Insurance Scheme

» Australians Together's four-episode DVD *Sharing our story* about Australian history and the current generation of Indigenous people

» Sustainable Population Australia's media releases, submissions, brochures, books, and articles available on their website.

Consumer activism

In the 21st century, consumer activism has emerged as a significant and increasingly common strategy for citizens' groups in promoting their causes. It involves groups promoting the purchase of ethically and/or sustainably produced goods that reflect a political belief or set of beliefs; or it may involve calls to boycott particular products or corporations on the basis of perceived deficiencies in their production processes. The rise of ethical investment, organically certified goods, free range meats and eggs, fair trade coffee and a host of global groups that set voluntary standards such as Fairtrade International, Forest Stewardship Council and Marine Stewardship Council are indicative of the recent surge in consumer activism. The market mechanism of consumption offers a potentially significant source of leverage because accusations made by citizens' groups about unethical and unsustainable production practices may affect corporate reputations and ultimately profitability. The eventual goal of consumer activism is to persuade governments to enhance their regulation of industrial activity to reflect contemporary community values about corporate production processes.

In regard to ethical and sustainable consumption, there are numerous certification schemes administered by a range of groups. In addition to those mentioned above, notable examples include Rainforest Alliance certification, Aquaculture Stewardship Council certification, Fair Tax Mark, the UTZ Certified program, Ethical Clothing Australia certification and Responsible Investment Australia Association certification. These schemes typically involve the setting of standards and development of product labels by citizens' groups, applications by producers to be certified as compliant with a scheme's standards and use of the scheme's label on product packaging and in advertising material. Such labels are signposts to consumers seeking to align their political beliefs with their consumption choices, subject to their ability to pay premium prices. A recent example of a corporate boycott in Australia is the 'NoHarveyNo' campaign orchestrated by GetUp! and Markets for Change (GetUp! 2017). The groups demanded that retailer Harvey Norman cease selling furniture produced from native forest timber. In general, consumer activism strategies aim to pressure businesses to adhere to higher social and/or environmental production practices without necessarily resorting to the coercive power of the state.

Engaging with formal politics

Alongside the evolving strategies outlined above, many citizens' groups continue to employ more traditional advocacy methods. In broad terms, traditional advocacy may be understood as engaging with formal political structures – the agents and institutions of the state. This may take a number of forms. First, citizens' groups may use the legal system to test existing or proposed government policies and corporate activities. This is often referred to as 'lawfare'. In 2016, for example, the Australian Conservation Foundation sought to challenge Adani's Carmichael coal mine in Queensland's Galilee Basin in the Federal Court. Similarly, in 2017, Environmental Justice Australia initiated Federal Court proceedings against the Commonwealth Bank for not disclosing sufficiently the risk that climate change poses to its business and the resulting impacts on shareholders.

The contribution of financial donations to political parties and individuals running for office by citizens' groups is another aspect of citizen participation in formal politics. The National Shop, Distributive and Allied Employees' Association, for instance, donated $657 395 to the Australian Labor Party (ALP) in the 2015–16 financial year while the Alliance of Australian Retailers donated $90 000 to the Liberal Democratic Party; the Australian Hotels Association SA branch donated $80 000 to the Liberal Party in South Australia; and the Sporting Shooters Association of Australia (Queensland) donated $75 000 to Katter's Australia Party (Elvery 2017).

Further, citizens' groups engage in behind-the-scenes lobbying and cultivate personal relationships with members of parliament (MPs), ministers and bureaucrats. As Jacobs (2014) explains, parliamentarians see 'a steady stream of lobbyists through the door' making such relationships a routine aspect of day-to-day formal political life. The Australian Council for International Development, for example, has a long history of regular meetings with public servants, ministers and politicians to discuss foreign aid policy (Kilby 2015), while the Australian Women Against Violence Alliance lobbies parliamentarians at the state and federal levels in its efforts to positively influence gender equality. Other groups have firm preferences for relationships with particular parties. While trade unions and groups espousing progressive values have well-publicised relationships with the ALP, business, libertarian and conservative groups have traditionally been associated with the Liberal Party and the Nationals. The Institute of Public Affairs, for instance, has long standing informal links to the Liberal Party and several shared personnel (Kelly 2016).

Third, more visibly, citizen's groups schedule their campaigns to coincide with the electoral cycle to influence citizen's voting decisions. For the 2016 federal election, the group GetUp! targeted the seats of conservative Liberal MPs. In Tasmania, GetUp! spent close to $300 000 on campaign advertising alone to unseat Andrew Nikolic MP (Morton 2016). For the 2013 federal election, the Australian Chamber of Commerce and Industry launched their campaign to promote the goals of small business, emphasise the need to reduce 'red tape', simplify the tax system, improve infrastructure and promote flexibility in employment. Similarly, Australian trade unions mobilised against the Howard Government at the 2007 federal election with the 'Your Rights at Work' campaign targeting the government's liberal approach to workplace flexibility. According to Reece (2013), in the context of elections, 'advocacy groups are using all the campaign tools and techniques that were once the sole preserve of the political parties'.

THE BENEFITS AND DRAWBACKS OF CITIZENS' GROUPS

Citizens' groups perform a range of roles and activities in Australian politics including agenda-setting, public education and service delivery, and therefore confer a variety of benefits on the political system at large. Indeed, democratic theorists praise open citizen participation, not just at election time, because citizens' groups are viewed as important intermediaries between communities and government (Dryzek 2000). They provide a channel for consultation about, and access to, the views of disadvantaged or marginalised groups, which may lead to the formulation of more effective policies (Maddison and Denniss 2013). Additionally, citizens' groups provide public commentary, feedback and evaluation of existing public programs as well as deliver government and privately funded programs in their own right. In doing so, they promote public debate and facilitate wider community understanding of, and input into, public policy (Yeatman 1998). Citizens' groups therefore serve an important accountability and policy effectiveness function in liberal democracies. Significantly, their participation may boost the legitimacy of government decisions by creating at least the veneer of democratic participation, representativeness and transparency.

In contrast, there are a number of concerns about the roles and impact of citizens' groups in the political process. It has been argued that citizens' groups often seek to advance their own private interests, which they disguise as being in the public interest (see Hamilton and Maddison 2007). Citizens' groups may not be representative, and the internal structures of groups may not be transparent or democratic. The idea that some groups will have a disproportionate influence is a chief concern of public choice theorists who emphasise the self-serving, utility maximising behaviour of citizens' groups (Johns 2000). Critics are particularly wary of public funding for citizens' groups, which is seen to distort citizens' views, elevating some over others (Kelly 2014). Another issue is that citizens' groups are typically focused on one particular issue area, or group of issues, and

VIDEO
SHORT-ANSWER
QUESTIONS
REFLECTION
QUESTIONS

therefore have the luxury of making niche demands that do not have to be weighed against competing priorities or whole-of-government objectives. A final criticism is that citizens' groups tend to consist of citizens who are willing and regular participants in the political process (Alver 2016). Often dubbed the 'usual suspects', these citizens, rather than being representative, are unique simply because they are willing and able to devote their time and resources to getting involved in public debate, while the vast majority of citizens are busy with their day-to-day lives.

SPOTLIGHT

Citizen group in profile: Australian Hotels Association

The Australian Hotels Association (AHA) is a membership-based industry association established in 1839. It currently represents over 5000 industry employers around Australia via a networked organisation of branches in each state and territory and a Canberra-based National Office. The aim of the AHA is to represent the interests of the hotel and hospitality industry on a range of state and federal policy issues including gambling and alcohol regulation, trade practices matters, taxation, workplace relations, tourism, music licensing and business regulation. It is governed by a National Board staffed by delegates from each of its state/territory branches. The number of delegates from each state/territory is based on the number of members located in each region.

The AHA works with other industry bodies whose interests coincide with the hotels and hospitality industry including the Australasian Gaming Council, Clubs Australia, and the Australian Chamber of Commerce and Industry. In recent years, the AHA has been active in public debates about several contentious policy issues. The AHA has advocated a reduction in the 'backpacker tax', supported the reduction of workers' penalty rates for weekend and public holiday work, opposed 'lockout laws' in Australian cities to target late night alcohol-related violence, opposed poker machine reform, opposed the 'plain packaging' tobacco laws and supported greater regulation of holiday accommodation via the sharing economy (e.g. Airbnb). The AHA's political strategies include employing lobbyists, maintaining a national office in Canberra, producing written submissions for governmental consultation processes, and financial donations to the major political parties. Indeed, various branches of the AHA are some of the largest donors among gaming and hospitality industry groups. In total, for 2015–16, the AHA donated close to $800000 to the Coalition parties while the ALP received over $500000 (Livingstone and Johnson 2017).

QUESTION

Discuss the influence of the AHA in Australian politics. How should this group be classified and what roles does it play in policy debates?

Citizen group in profile: GetUp!

Paul Oosting, National Director, Getup!

GetUp! is a national-level campaigning group that brings together its one million members with experts, strategists and movement partners to promote progressive change in Australia. The organisation is independent and driven by values, rather than party politics. GetUp! aims to achieve its vision of a fair, flourishing and socially just Australia by campaigning on human rights, environmental justice, economic fairness and democracy.

One of the most notable successes of GetUp! was its influential 2016 federal election campaign, which saw conservative MPs lose their place in parliament, and several MPs were left clinging to once safe seats. GetUp! sought to be nimble with its campaign tactics, pivoting to focus on the issues most important to its members. It aimed to make the economic fight of the election about protecting Australia's 'world class' public health and education systems, the iconic Great Barrier Reef, and the future of the clean energy industry. GetUp! aimed to shift votes away from MPs who failed to support action on these issues. It achieved:

- an average swing of 4.9 per cent against conservative MPs in its target seats
- eight conservative MPs or those considered to be opposing progress on GetUp!'s issues lost their place in parliament and swings were recorded against other notable conservative MPs George Christensen and Peter Dutton
- Australia-wide conversations from all sides of politics about investing in hospitals and renewable energy and addressing corporate tax avoidance.

Prior to the election, GetUp!'s nationwide phone banks saw 3736 volunteers donate 17 471 hours to have 40 218 conversations with swinging voters. These conversations were paired with the use of targeted social media, especially Facebook, which reached 6.2 million users over the course of the campaign. On election day, 3031 GetUp! members reached 1.1 million voters with 'how to vote' cards across 500 polling booths in marginal seats. The 'all-angle' combination of campaign tactics and the rapid mobilisation of members aims to keep GetUp! at the forefront of Australian political change.

QUESTION

What key factors explain the rise in prominence of GetUp! in recent years?

BEYOND THE ELECTORAL CYCLE: GOVERNMENT MECHANISMS FOR ENGAGING CITIZENS

Aware of the potential benefits of, and increasing demands for, citizen participation in the political process in the 21st century, governments employ a range of techniques and measures to elicit community input into policy-making. These include inviting written and oral submissions, hosting public forums, establishing stakeholder groups, conducting surveys and polls on particular issues, and initiating formal collaborative governance arrangements that delegate decision-making authority to groups of citizens. These arrangements, which allow citizens to participate in various ways and to differing degrees, are discussed in more detail below.

WRITTEN AND ORAL SUBMISSIONS

Governments frequently employ the engagement strategy of inviting written and oral submissions from citizens' groups and individuals on a particular policy matter under consideration, often in response to a government produced 'issues paper'. For example, the Department of Foreign Affairs and Trade invited written submissions, ranging from short emails to entire analytical papers, from citizens' organisations and individuals on the potential impacts and opportunities of an Australian free trade agreement with Hong Kong. The Department provided possible key topics that it saw as significant in the proposed agreement and subsequently received submissions from the Australia China Business Council, Australian Fair Trade and Investment Network, Australian Forest Products Association, Australian Red Meat Industry and Certified Practising Accountants Australia, among others (Department of Foreign Affairs and Trade 2017). In the interests of transparency, it is common practice for governments to publish all submissions unedited on their websites.

PUBLIC FORUMS

Public forums or 'town hall' meetings are typically hosted by governments to provide information to communities from a particular geographical area or policy sector. Such meetings allow large groups of citizens to come together to ask questions of elected representatives, senior public servants and/or consultants, and permit governments to gauge a community's reception to particular policies or programs. In reviewing its Disability Employment Framework, for example, the Department of Social Services hosted 38 public forums across 11 Australian cities with a total of 740 participants comprising people with disability and their families, carers, service providers, employers and industry associations (Department of Social Services 2015). From 2008, the Rudd Government conducted federal level 'community cabinets' in locations around Australia (a mechanism initiated in Queensland in the 1990s) as a method for bringing the workings of government closer to regular citizens (McCann 2012). Community cabinets typically include an hour-long public forum featuring the prime minister or state premier/territory chief minister plus several cabinet ministers with opportunities for one-on-one meetings between citizens and ministers.

STAKEHOLDER GROUPS

Governments frequently construct policy stakeholder groups, small representative groups of citizens, that meet once or periodically over several months or even years as a method to elicit citizen feedback on programs and policies. In late 2016, for instance, the Turnbull Government announced a Forum on Western Sydney Airport, a project with vast economic benefits for the region, and called for community, stakeholder and local government nominations. Subsequently, in March 2017, it named a 22-member panel comprising representatives from the local community, relevant stakeholder groups and those nominated by the affected local governments (Department of Infrastructure and Regional Development 2016). According to the Department of Infrastructure and Regional Development (2016), the group 'will provide a communication channel for the community's engagement in the development of the airport and ensure community's views are taken into account […][and] will play an important role in the airspace and flight path design process'. Not all attempts to form stakeholder groups, however, follow an effortless path. In 2010, Prime Minister Gillard's idea for a citizens' assembly on climate change consisting of up to 200 people to elicit community views on a carbon price was criticised as a 'community gobfest' and a stalling mechanism by groups wanting rapid and decisive governmental action to address climate change (Rodgers 2010).

SURVEYS AND POLLS

In Australia, plebiscites and referenda refer to one-off polls on issues of national significance. A referendum is a national yes/no vote on altering the Australian Constitution, while a plebiscite or advisory referendum is used to determine voters' will on a non-constitutional issue with verdicts not binding on governments. Plebiscites and referenda are the broadest possible citizen participation mechanism employed by governments because they give (indeed compel given Australia's compulsory system of voting) all citizens to cast a ballot. Elected representatives, citizens' groups and individual citizens are often collectively involved in leading arguments for and against a proposed change.

Since Federation, Australian citizens have approved just eight of 44 proposed constitutional changes via 19 referenda (Parliamentary Education Office 2017). The most recent, the referendum on an Australian republic in 1999, was unsuccessful. The generally low rate of success is at least partly due to Australia's referenda rules, which require a double majority in order to be approved: this comprises a majority of voters across Australia *and* a majority of voters in a majority of states. Most recently, a possible referendum on recognising Indigenous people in the preamble of the Australian Constitution that received bipartisan parliamentary support was debated by Aboriginal and Torres Strait Islander representatives at a constitutional convention at Uluru in May 2017 (Zillman 2017). However, participants ultimately expressed a preference for representation measures beyond symbolic constitutional recognition. In regard to plebiscites, only two have been held, in 1916 and 1917 on military conscription, which were both defeated. The 2017 national postal vote on same-sex marriage is another such national vote, albeit non-compulsory and non-binding on parliament. Despite its informal status, the majority of Australian citizens participating in the postal vote supported the change and before the close of 2017, the Turnbull Government had overseen parliament's endorsement of same-sex marriage. While national polls on specific issues bypass the problems of representative democracy by giving every citizen a voice, the minimum level of citizen participation required is simply a registering of support for, or against, change.

At the state and territory as well as local levels, governments regularly deploy voluntary surveys of relevant groups of citizens on particular issues that affect them. In Queensland, for example, the Queensland Government Statistician's Office conducts official surveys involving individual citizens, their households, businesses and other citizens' groups. The data generated by such surveys aim to reflect a representative cross-section of the community and, to the extent that surveys require greater than yes/no input, they may provide policy-makers with more in-depth, nuanced understandings of citizens' views.

COLLABORATIVE GOVERNANCE

In the 21st century, governments are increasingly turning to 'collaborative governance' arrangements to enlist the active contribution of citizens in the political process. Such arrangements are similar in intent to the establishment of stakeholder groups, but the degree of decision-making authority conferred to citizens in collaborative governance is intended to be substantive, rather than simply advisory. Alternative descriptions of such arrangements include devolved or decentred governance, polycentric governance and participatory democracy (Gunningham 2009). For example, in the early 2000s, in regard to the governance of the Murray–Darling Basin, the New South Wales Government established local committees to develop recommendations for allocating water rights across competing industry sectors and the environment. Each of the 36 committees contained between 12 and 20 members with representatives of environmental groups, Indigenous people, elected representatives and local and state government public servants (Bell and Park 2006). In the area of social services, in 2010 the Rudd Government established a National Compact: a policy framework document setting out a new era of relations between government and the non-profit service and advocacy sector (Butcher 2010). And in regard to the Tasmanian forest industry, business, union and environmental group representatives were involved in a collaborative 'forest peace process' arrangement for three years from 2010 to negotiate the future of the controversial sector (Schirmer, Dare and Ercan 2016). While collaborative governance processes in their various forms offer selected citizens a substantial degree of input, in practice, due to the degree of deliberation required, they are often difficult to administer due to value conflicts, accusations of non-representativeness and/or stalemate in negotiations. Consequently, it may be incumbent on governments to appropriately design and administer such arrangements from the outset in order to promote their effectiveness (Bell and Hindmoor 2009).

SPOTLIGHT

Collaborative governance: the case of the Tasmanian forest peace process

From 2010 to 2012, after decades of conflict over Tasmania's forest sector, representatives of the forestry industry, trade unions and environmental groups participated in a collaborative governance process to help bring an end to one of the nation's most entrenched environmental debates. With support from the Tasmanian and Commonwealth governments, the so called 'peace process' was initiated by the group Our Common Ground to develop a plan for the future of the Tasmanian forest industry.

It involved several meetings over three years between a range of citizens' groups including the Australian Conservation Foundation, Australian Forest Contractors Association; Australian Forest Products Association; Construction, Forestry, Mining and Energy Union; Environment Tasmania; Forest Industries Association of Tasmania; Tasmanian Forest Contractors Association; Timber Communities Australia; Tasmanian Sawmillers Association; and The Wilderness Society. In late 2010, the Gillard Government appointed former ACTU Secretary Bill Kelty to serve as an independent facilitator.

Over a tense period of negotiations that verged on collapse on multiple occasions, the negotiation process culminated in the 2012 Tasmanian Forest Agreement, which provided for new areas of forest conservation, reduced timber harvesting, and was supported by a $276 million Commonwealth industry restructuring package. To become law, however, the Agreement had to pass both houses of the Tasmanian Parliament. In April 2013, the Upper House made significant amendments but leading environmental groups including The Wilderness Society continued to support the Agreement on the basis that it remained 'the best we've ever had'.

Despite this, when the Liberal Government was elected in 2014, it repealed the Agreement on the basis of it costing forestry jobs, but with a six-year moratorium on the harvesting of the 400 000 hectares of native forests set aside in the Agreement. In 2017, the government attempted to bring forward the end of the moratorium by two years, but environmentalists joined forces with the Forest Industries Association to oppose the move, which in turn convinced Tasmania's Upper House members to defeat the Bill. Consequently, the hard fought 'peace' brokered by this collaborative governance process is currently in a state of temporary limbo, slated to be reassessed in 2020 at the expiry of the moratorium.

QUESTION

What does the Tasmanian forest peace process reveal about the factors influencing the fate of collaborative governance initiatives?

EVALUATING CITIZEN ENGAGEMENT MECHANISMS

While community engagement is said to involve 'working collaboratively with and through groups of people affiliated by geographical proximity, special interest, or similar situations to address issues that affect them' (Lowe and Hill 2005, 170), not all engagement mechanisms are aptly described as collaborative. In order to assess the degree of citizen involvement in policy-making, Sherry Arnstein's 'ladder of citizen participation' model (1969) is one potential evaluative framework. It describes eight rungs or levels for evaluating the degree of engagement between governments and citizens comprising, from the bottom, manipulation, therapy, informing, consultation, placation, partnership, delegated power and, at the highest level, citizen control (Arnstein 1969). However, this model, as the pejorative terms of 'manipulation', 'therapy' and 'placation' for lower levels of citizen input attest, is geared towards dissecting *and* promoting citizen participation.

Another influential and more recently developed method for assessing citizen participation is the International Association for Public Participation's 'public participation spectrum' (2014) comprising a five-point continuum. The five nodes on the continuum range (from the lowest level of citizen participation to the highest) are informing, consulting, involving, collaborating and empowering (International Association for Public Participation 2014). *Informing* involves governments sharing information with citizens. Contemporary examples may include regular newsletters from local governments to citizens, fact sheets published on departmental websites, government advertisements on TV or social media. *Consulting*, the second node on the continuum, additionally involves a process of feedback from citizens to governments, but only with the obligation by government to acknowledge rather than act upon citizen responses. Examples include surveys, calls for submissions and other public comment arrangements. Further along the continuum, the node of *involving* involves some level of government action in response to citizen participation, even if this is marginal. Similar types of engagement could be involved as for the consulting stage, but with a greater level of government feedback. *Collaborating* is the fourth node and represents processes that join citizens with decision-makers whereby citizen input will be reflected in the final decisions made. The final, and highest node on the continuum, is *empowering*, whereby citizens are responsible for decision-making and governments will act upon citizen decisions. Empowering is said to guarantee that decision-making is delegated to citizens or citizens' groups. However, as the real-world arrangements outlined above demonstrate, the delegation of decision-making authority in Australia is rare and when it does occur, difficult to administer and far from conflict-free. Indeed, most citizen engagement by governments in Australia is best described as informing, consulting and involving on the International Association for Public Participation's spectrum.

VIDEO
REFLECTION
QUESTIONS
SHORT-ANSWER
QUESTIONS

KEY CHALLENGES FOR CITIZEN PARTICIPATION AND ENGAGEMENT

The contemporary field of citizen participation and engagement has given rise to a new set of issues and challenges for the Australian political system. These comprise debates over the extent of representativeness and transparency of various citizens' groups, the appropriateness of public funding for citizens' groups, recent governments' legislative attempts to minimise citizen protest at sites deemed workplaces, and the phenomenon of 'slacktivism'.

REPRESENTATIVENESS AND TRANSPARENCY

Among the key attributes of citizens' groups is that they offer marginalised people opportunities for political participation and publicise neglected issues and problems that might otherwise remain peripheral. However, the degree to which 'noisy' citizens' groups may dominate or distort debates about public issues is a concern for those who prioritise representativeness as a key value underpinning the participation of citizens' groups. Without a valid claim of representation, such groups, and their contributions to public debate, may be said to lack legitimacy. Compounding this issue is that citizens' groups are often accused of being staffed by elites and/or professional activists with few links to regular citizens (Johns 2000). Indeed, 'community representatives' are often atypical precisely because, unlike most people, they are willing to become involved. However, this affliction may also be true of elected representatives and party officials.

Further compromising the legitimacy of citizens' groups, at least in the eyes of critics, is the source of their funding. The Sunrise Project, for example, a group campaigning against

Australian coal mining, is funded by a US-based organisation, the Sandler Foundation (Kelly and Shanahan 2016; Shanahan 2016). Such arrangements raise questions about the accountability of citizens' groups and the interests they serve, particularly where funding emanates from international sources. In contrast, other groups may have limited access to external funding and may suffer resource constraints that severely hamper their operations. State and Commonwealth governments seek to address such unevenness across the sector of citizens' groups by providing a variety of funding opportunities.

Another difficulty in the practice of citizen engagement is NIMBYism or 'not in my backyard' syndrome, which is a particular issue for governments in decisions about the siting of new commercial developments or industries, whereby citizens residing in close proximity to proposed developments protest most loudly. When such groups gain traction, governments may be motivated to put the public good on hold for a minority of citizens disproportionately affected by government projects or commercial activities. In Melbourne, the controversial Skyrail public transport project to replace congested level crossings, for instance, prompted a local protest group, Lower Our Tracks, to challenge the project in the Victorian Supreme Court (Willingham 2016).

For governments, a key challenge in mediating the input of citizens' groups is that they 'rarely speak with one voice' and, in fact, communities may be deeply fragmented (Foley and Martin 2000, 486). In regard to efforts to curb spending on gambling, drugs and alcohol by those receiving welfare payments, government attempts to introduce a welfare card have been simultaneously met with praise and opposition. At its worst, such fragmentation may result in endless consultation, delayed decision-making or governments watering down their policy positions in an effort to placate dissenting groups at the expense of robust public policy.

PUBLIC FUNDING FOR CITIZENS' GROUPS

While citizens' groups are considered separate to governments, the reality is that many, at least partially, rely on some degree of public funding. This may take the form of government contracts to deliver services, grants and/or the receipt by various groups of tax deductible gift recipient (DGR) status, which incentivises citizens to contribute financial donations. Tax deductible donations alone are said to cost the government up to $1.3 billion per year (Martin 2017). The rationale for public funding is that it supports a pluralistic society in which a diverse range of voices and issues may be heard. In recent years, however, this status, particularly for environmental groups, has been subject to scrutiny by Coalition governments and conservative think tanks such as the Institute for Public Affairs (Kelly and Shanahan 2016). Scepticism about public funding for citizens' groups rose to prominence during the Howard Government, which initiated a process of defunding various citizens' groups, particularly those engaged in political advocacy over service delivery (Hamilton and Maddison 2007). More recently, a Parliamentary Inquiry into the Register of Environmental Organisations initiated in 2015 brought attention to environmental groups' DGR status and, currently, many environmental groups face the possibility of having their status revoked for engaging in political advocacy. However, a 2010 High Court decision on *Aid/Watch Incorporated v Commissioner of Taxation* upheld the notion that advocacy, lobbying and similar activities do in fact constitute charitable activity.

SPOTLIGHT

Public funding for citizens' groups? The Parliamentary Inquiry into the Register of Environmental Organisations

The Register of Environmental Organisations, established in 1992, is a Commonwealth tax deductibility scheme allowing eligible environmental groups to receive deductible gift recipient (DGR) status by the Australian Taxation Office. Donations made to organisations listed on the Register are tax deductible for the donors. There are currently more than 600 groups listed on the Register of Environmental Organisations.

The purpose of the Register is to increase the fundraising capacity of conservation groups by incentivising citizens and corporations to donate. As Friends of the Earth's Cam Walker contends 'like every environmental organisation across the country that employs staff, tax deductibility is the lifeblood of our organisation' (Duffy 2015).

In order to be eligible for DGR status, organisations must have a principal purpose of: 'the protection and enhancement of the natural environment or of a significant aspect of the natural environment; or, the provision of information or education, or the carrying on of research, about the natural environment or a significant aspect of the natural environment' (Department of the Environment and Energy 2017).

However, in recent years, environmental organisations have been accused of misusing their DGR status. Former MP Andrew Nikolic stated that '[t]here are some of those groups that unfortunately abuse that privilege, they engage in untruthful, destructive attacks on legitimate business and undertake political activism, which shouldn't attract those very generous concessions from the taxpayer' (ABC News 2014).

On the back of such criticisms, a 2016 Parliamentary Inquiry examined the Register in the context of how it supports citizens to preserve the environment. The Committee received more than 700 submissions, thousands of letters and other correspondence, met with representatives, held public hearings and conducted discussions (Standing Committee on the Environment 2016, 2–3).

The Inquiry report concluded that the Register should only approve DGR status for environmental non-government organisations involved with 'practical' conservation work. However, the federal government is yet to formally respond to the report beyond releasing a discussion paper on potential reforms.

QUESTION

What are the key arguments for and against government funding for citizens' groups engaged in political advocacy?

ANTI-PROTEST LAWS

The rights of peaceful assembly and freedom of expression are seen as core values within Australia and other liberal democracies and are included in the International Covenant on Civil and Political Rights (1966). However, a number of Australian states have recently developed anti-protest legislation to limit the locations at which activists can conduct political demonstrations. For example, in Tasmania in 2014, the Liberal Government introduced the *Workplaces (Protection from Protesters) Act* as a way to curb protest activity in forestry areas while the New South Wales Liberal Government recently granted police the power to stop, search and detain protesters, and shut down protests that disrupt traffic. Further, the New South Wales Government expanded the offence of 'interfering' with mining sites, including coal seam gas exploration and extraction (de Kretser 2016). Such legislation is criticised as curtailing a vital aspect of Australian democracy and prioritising business interests ahead of citizens' concerns relating to environmental conservation and social justice. In highlighting the trend to stifle citizen advocacy, in early 2016, a coalition of Australian citizens' groups collectively launched a report *Safeguarding Democracy* (Human Rights Law Centre 2016). According to the Human Rights Law Centre, the key architect of the report, since 2001, 'the Australian Parliament has passed over 200 new laws that infringe many of our basic fundamental freedoms. As a result, more and more government decisions are now made about peoples' lives by bureaucrats or Ministers behind closed doors' (Howie 2016).

SLACKTIVISM OR THE NEW CITIZEN ADVOCACY?

Also known as 'armchair activism', 'keyboard activism' or 'hashtag activism', slacktivism refers to political advocacy performed online, especially via social media. The most commonly used online platforms for such advocacy in Australia include Change.org Australia, GetUp! and Dosomething.org. Critics argue that unlike traditional forms of protest such as street demonstrations, strikes or hard-copy petitions, slacktivism does not require the same degree of effort and dedication on the part of citizens. Indeed, it is often derided because it requires minimal input, often just a 'click and share' on social media, which results in little real-world impact other than a 'feel good' effect for the contributor. In other words, people who support various causes in this way are criticised as not being truly engaged or sufficiently committed to social change. This has led critics to argue that internet campaigns or social media campaigns should not be treated with the same seriousness as campaigns conducted in real time involving face-to-face communication (Robertson 2014).

In support of internet advocacy, the Director of Change.org Australia, Karen Skinner, cites the increased number of citizens engaged in political advocacy that may previously have been politically inactive: '[p]eople talk about slacktivism and clicktivism or whatever term you want to use, but it's not the case. We're seeing 3.7 million Australians starting online petitions. It shows Australians have issues that they care about, and they want to see things change. We're also seeing a petition win every 24 hours. Change is being enacted. Slacktivism is just a dismissive term, it's not the reality' (Gillespie 2016). In this regard, the online public sphere may in fact facilitate an active citizenry by mobilising supporters to a cause and disseminating campaign material far more rapidly than traditional methods. For example, in 2016 an online petition succeeded in bringing about the cancellation of Australian meetings of the men's rights activist group Return of Kings, the capping of credit card surcharges by federal Treasurer Scott Morrison, specialised training for emergency department staff in Queensland on responding to suicidal patients, and a pay rise for the Australian Defence Force among many more instances.

RESEARCH
QUESTION

SUMMARY

Learning objective 1: Describe the organisational landscape of political participation in Australia and the variety of tactics employed by citizens' groups

In the 21st century, the scale, scope and complexity of citizens' demands for political input in Australia has increased. A broad range of local, regional and national citizens' groups – many with membership of international groups – actively strive for political influence utilising an array of traditional and newly evolved strategies. Citizens' groups are thus becoming an increasingly ubiquitous force in Australian political life.

Citizens' groups employ four key strategies, often concurrently. These comprise public performances and activities, developing and disseminating documentation via a range of media including new media, consumer activism, and engaging with formal political structures. In doing so, citizens' groups confer a range of benefits on the political system at large. They may serve a public education function, broaden citizen participation and highlight neglected issues. Alternatively, critics often contend that they distort public debate, are self-serving, and do not represent regular citizens' concerns.

Learning objective 2: Outline and evaluate the ways in which Australian governments engage with citizens' groups

From the perspective of governments, citizens' groups may serve a functional role in providing local knowledge, expertise and feedback that may improve the quality of public policy. Governments therefore facilitate the involvement of citizens' groups in the political process in a number of ways. These include through advertising for written and oral submissions; arranging public forums, meetings and briefings; forming stakeholder advisory groups; administering surveys and votes on specific issues; and establishing formal collaborative governance processes with some degree of decision-making authority. Each consultation mechanism involves a different degree and style of citizen input, which can be assessed by various participation models such as the International Association for Public Participation's model.

Learning objective 3: Discuss the challenges arising from the growing demand for political participation and engagement in the 21st century

With the increase in demand for citizen participation in the 21st century, a number of new issues and challenges have arisen. First, the degree to which citizens' groups are representative of a broader set of citizens is an ongoing debate that goes to claims about their degree of legitimacy. This entails debates over funding sources, staffing, NIMBYism and fragmentation. Second, contention over public funding for citizens' groups has re-emerged with a Parliamentary Inquiry focused on environmental groups in particular. Third, governments have recently sought to place limits on the locations where public protest is permitted. Finally, the merits of 'slacktivism' or online activism is variously derided as an inferior form of advocacy or hailed as the new face of citizen activism.

DISCUSSION QUESTIONS

DISCUSSION QUESTIONS

1. What factors facilitate the active presence of citizens' groups in Australian politics?
2. Why is it difficult to classify citizens' groups?

3. What is the significance of the outsider/insider typology of citizens' groups?
4. Why do governments choose to engage with citizens between elections?
5. What is the biggest challenge for citizen engagement in 21st century Australia?

FURTHER READING

Alver, J. (2016). What makes participatory processes democratic? From external to internal inclusion, *The Policy Space*, 20 September. Retrieved from http://www.thepolicyspace.com.au/2016/20/144-what-makes-participatory-processes-democratic-from-external-to-internal-inclusion

Australian Charities and Not-for-profits Commission. (2017). *Background to the not-for-profit sector*. Retrieved from https://www.acnc.gov.au/ACNC/About_ACNC/Research/Background_NFP/ACNC/Edu/NFP_background.aspx

Bell, S. and Hindmoor, A. (2009). Governance through community engagement. In *Rethinking Governance: The Centrality of the State in Modern Society*, Melbourne: Cambridge University Press, pp. 137–61.

Bell, S. and Hindmoor, A. (2009). Governance through associations. In *Rethinking Governance: The Centrality of the State in Modern Society*, Melbourne: Cambridge University Press, pp. 162–85.

Casic, M. (2016). Offshore detention and the new face of civil disobedience, *The Drum*, 8 February, ABC News. Retrieved from http://www.abc.net.au/news/2016–02-05/cosic-civil-disobedience-in-australia/7142316?pfmredir=sm

Hamilton, C. and Maddison, S. (2007). *Silencing Dissent: How the Australian Government is Controlling Public Opinion and Stifling Debate*, Crows Nest, NSW: Allen & Unwin.

Human Rights Law Centre. (2016). *Safeguarding democracy*, Human Rights Law Centre. URL: http://static1.squarespace.com/static/580025f66b8f5b2dabbe4291/5812996f1dd4540186f54894/581299ee1dd4540186f55760/1477614062728/HRLC_Report_SafeguardingDemocracy_online.pdf?format=original

Jacobs, C. (2014). The secret life of lobbyists, *Crikey*, 16 July. Retrieved from https://www.crikey.com.au/2014/07/16/the-secret-life-of-lobbyists/

Johns, G. (2000). NGO way to go: Political accountability of non-government organizations in democratic society. *IPA Backgrounder*, **12**(3), 1–16.

REFERENCES

ABC News. (2014). Liberal MP moves to strip charity status from some environmental groups, *ABC News*. URL: http://www.abc.net.au/news/2014–06-29/andrew-nickolic-moves-to-strip-charity-status-from-some-environ/5557936

ABC News. (2017). ACTU boss Sally McManus has no problem with workers breaking 'unjust laws', *ABC News*. URL: http://www.abc.net.au/news/2017–03-15/actu-boss-happy-for-workers-to-break-unjust-laws/8357698

Alver, J. (2016). What makes participatory processes democratic? From external to internal inclusion, *The Policy Space*. Retrieved from http://www.thepolicyspace.com.au/2016/20/144-what-makes-participatory-processes-democratic-from-external-to-internal-inclusion

Arnstein, S.R. (1969), A ladder of citizen participation, *Journal of the American Institute of Planners*, **35**(4), 216–24.

Bell, S. and Hindmoor, A. (2009). *Rethinking Governance: The Centrality of the State in Modern Society*, Melbourne: Cambridge University Press.

Bell, S. and Park, A. (2006). The problematic metagovernance of networks: Water reform in NSW. *Journal of Public Policy*, **26**(1), 63–83.

Butcher, J. (2010). An Australian compact with the third sector: Challenges and prospects. *Third Sector Review*, **17**(1), 35–58.

Davis, M. (2011). A snip at $22 m to get rid of PM, *The Sydney Morning Herald*. Retrieved from http://www.smh.com.au/business/a-snip-at-22 m-to-get-rid-of-pm-20110201-1acgj.html

de Kretser, H. (2016). NSW anti-protest laws are part of a corrosive national trend, *The Sydney Morning Herald*. Retrieved from http://www.smh.com.au/comment/nsw-antiprotest-laws-are-part-of-a-corrosive-national-trend-20160321-gno10h.html

Department of Foreign Affairs and Trade. (2017). *Australia-Hong Kong Free Trade Agreement: submissions and public consultations*. URL: http://dfat.gov.au/trade/agreements/a-hkfta/pages/submissions.aspx

Department of Infrastructure and Regional Development. (2016). *Factsheet: Forum on Western Sydney Airport*, Department of Infrastructure and Regional Development. URL: http://westernsydneyairport.gov.au/files/factsheet_fowsa.pdf

Department of Social Services. (2015). *Disability Employment Framework – Round One – Consultation report*. URL: https://engage.dss.gov.au/disability-employment-framework/consultation-report/

Department of the Environment and Energy. (2017). *Register of Environmental Organisations*, Department of the Environment and Energy. URL: http://www.environment.gov.au/about-us/business/tax/register-environmental-organisations

Dryzek, J.S. (2000). *Deliberative Democracy and Beyond: Liberals, Critics, Contestations*, Oxford: Oxford University Press.

Duffy, C. (2015). Environmental groups face tax deductibility loss in Government push, *ABC 7.30*. Retrieved from http://www.abc.net.au/7.30/content/2015/s4214478.htm

Elvery, S. (2017). Who did the political parties receive donations from? Search the full dataset, *ABC News*. Retrieved from http://www.abc.net.au/news/2017–02-01/australian-political-donations-searchable-database-2015–2016/8208090

Foley, P. and Martin, S. (2000). A new deal for the community? Public participation in regeneration and local service delivery. *Policy and Politics*, **28**(4), 479–91.

GetUp! (2017). The ad they don't want us to see, viewed. URL: https://www.getup.org.au/campaigns/save-our-forests/no-harvey-no/the-ad-they-dont-want-us-to-see

Gillespie, K. (2016). The Director of Change.org Australia Explains How Slacktivism Is a Myth, *VICE*. Retrieved from https://www.vice.com/en_au/article/bnkdad/the-director-of-changeorg-australia-about-medicinal-cannabis-gay-panic-and-the-myth-of-slacktivism

Grant, W. (1978). *Insider Groups, Outsider Groups and Interest Group Strategies in Britain*, Department of Politics, University of Warwick.

Greenpeace International. (2012). *Press conference at the Sydney Aquarium*, Greenpeace International. Retrieved from http://www.greenpeace.org/international/en/multimedia/photos/press-conference-at-the-sydney-aquarium/

Gunningham, N. (2009). The new collaborative environmental governance: The localization of regulation. *Journal of Law and Society*, **36**(1), 145–66.

Hamilton, C. and Maddison, S. (2007). *Silencing Dissent: How the Australian Government is Controlling Public Opinion and Stifling Debate*, Crows Nest, NSW: Allen & Unwin.

Howie, E. (2016). *It's time to safeguard our democracy*, Human Rights Law Centre. Retrieved from https://www.hrlc.org.au/news/its-time-to-safeguard-our-democracy

Human Rights Law Centre. (2016). *Safeguarding democracy,* Human Rights Law Centre. URL: http://static1.squarespace.com/static/580025f66b8f5b2dabbe4291/5812996f1dd4540186f548 94/581299ee1dd4540186f55760/1477614062728/hrlc_report_safeguardingdemocracy_online .pdf?format=original

International Association for Public Participation. (2014). *IAP2's public participation spectrum*, IAP2 International Federation. URL: https://www.iap2.org.au/tenant/c0000004/00000001/ files/iap2_public_participation_spectrum.pdf

Jacobs, C. (2014). The secret life of lobbyists, *Crikey.* Retrieved from https://www.crikey.com .au/2014/07/16/the-secret-life-of-lobbyists/

Johns, G. (2000). NGO way to go: Political accountability of non-government organizations in democratic society. *IPA Backgrounder,* **12**(3), 1–16.

Kelly, D. (2016). With friends like these: just how close are the Liberal Party and IPA? *The Conversation.* Retrieved from https://theconversation.com/with-friends-like-these-just-how-close-are-the-liberal-party-and-ipa-60442

Kelly, J. and Shanahan, D. (2016). Eight biggest green groups net $685 m windfall over decade, *The Australian.* Retrieved from http://www.theaustralian.com.au/national-affairs/climate/eight-biggest-green-groups-net-685 m-windfall-over-decade/news-story/2c5c2a5b7e2f553fc6c25139 4458cc09

Kelly, P. (2014). New climate change battlefront pits Abbott against the anti-coal brigade, *The Australian.* Retrieved from http://www.theaustralian.com.au/opinion/columnists/paul-kelly/ new-climate-change-battlefront-pits-abbott-against-the-anticoal-brigade/news-story/0d6e84a d0ae845a2f5f4d045a01e9808

Kilby, P. (2015). *NGOs and Political Change: A History of the Australian Council for International Development*, Canberra: ANU Press.

Livingstone, C. and Johnson, M. (2017). Gambling lobby gives big to political parties, and names names, *The Conversation.* Retrieved from https://theconversation.com/gambling-lobby-gives-big-to-political-parties-and-names-names-73131

Lowe, J. and Hill, E. (2005). Closing the gap between government and community. In A. Rainnie and M. Grobbelaar, eds, *New Regionalism in Australia*, Aldershot: Ashgate, pp. 165–80.

Maddison, S. and Denniss, R. (2013) *An Introduction to Australian Public Policy: Theory and Practice*, 2nd edn, Melbourne: Cambridge University Press.

Martin, F.A. (2017). Explainer: why are some donations to charities tax deductible? *The Conversation.* Retrieved from https://theconversation.com/explainer-why-are-donations-to-some-charities-tax-deductible-72968

McCann, J. (2012), Community cabinets in Australia, Parliament of Australia. Retrieved from http://www.aph.gov.au/about_parliament/parliamentary_departments/parliamentary_library/ pubs/bn/2012–2013/communitycabinets

Morton, A. (2016). Election results: Abbott-backer Andrew Nikolic blames GetUp! for swing that cost him seat of Bass, *The Sydney Morning Herald.* Retrieved from http://www.smh.com.au/ federal-politics/political-news/election-results-abbottbacker-andrew-nikolic-blames-getup-for-swing-that-cost-him-seat-of-bass-20160704-gpy38y.html

Parliamentary Education Office. (2017). Referenda and plebiscites, Parliamentary Education Office. URL: https://www.peo.gov.au/learning/fact-sheets/referendums-and-plebiscites.html

Reece, N. (2013). *The rise and rise of issues campaigners*, Election Watch Australia; The University of Melbourne. Retrieved from http://past.electionwatch.edu.au/australia-2013/campaign-ads/ rise-and-rise-issues-campaigners

Robertson, C. (2014). Slacktivism: the downfall of millennials, *HuffPost* (US edition). Retrieved from https://www.huffingtonpost.com/charlotte-robertson/slacktivism-the-downfall-_b_5984336.html

Rodgers, E. (2010). Gillard defends climate change 'gobfest', *ABC News*. Retrieved from http://www.abc.net.au/news/2010–07-23/gillard-defends-climate-change-gobfest/917416

Schirmer, J., Dare, M. and Ercan, S.A. (2016). Deliberative democracy and the Tasmanian forest peace process. *Australian Journal of Political Science*, **51**(2), 288–307.

Scholte, J.A., O'Brien, R. and Williams, M. (1999) The WTO and civil society. *Journal of World Trade*, **33**(1), 107–23.

Shanahan, D. (2016). Green campaign against Australian coal: trail leads to John Podesta, *The Australian*. Retrieved from http://www.theaustralian.com.au/opinion/columnists/dennis-shanahan/green-campaign-against-australian-coal-trail-leads-to-john-podesta/news-story/42784b8b30e0ab18d7386054189a0933

Standing Committee on the Environment. (2016). *Inquiry into the Register of Environmental Organisations*, Canberra: House of Representatives.

Tierney, J. (2003). Tassie's Franklin River – 20 years on, *ABC News*. Retrieved from http://www.abc.net.au/7.30/content/2003/s892579.htm

Urban, R. (2017). Firms ring in campaign for marriage equality, *The Australian*. Retrieved from http://www.theaustralian.com.au/national-affairs/firms-ring-in-campaign-for-marriage-equality/news-story/0539ca1821754e570cd16a08dc7b6586

Warhurst, J. (2009). Interest groups and political lobbying. In D. Woodward, A. Parkin and J. Summers, eds, *Government, Politics, Power and Policy in Australia*, 9th edn, Frenchs Forest, NSW: Pearson Education Australia.

Willingham, R. (2016). Sky rail: Supreme Court dismisses residents' bid to derail project, *The Age*. Retrieved from http://www.theage.com.au/victoria/sky-rail-supreme-court-dismisses-residents-bid-to-derail-project-20161220-gtepu5.html

Yeatman, A. (1998). *Activism and the Policy Process*, St Leonards, NSW: Allen & Unwin.

Zillman, S. (2017). Symbolic constitutional recognition off the table after Uluru talks, Indigenous leaders say, *ABC News*. Retrieved from http://www.abc.net.au/news/2017–05-27/uluru-calls-for-treaty-puts-constitutional-recognition-off-table/8565114

CHAPTER 13

CONCLUSION

LEARNING OBJECTIVES

After reading this chapter, you should be able to:

1. Outline some of the overarching challenges for Australian democracy

2. Consider whether domestic politics still matters or whether international politics is the key

INTRODUCTION

Contemporary Australia is buffeted by forces which it has little control over. Its climate is growing harsher as a by-product of climate change. The global refugee crisis ensures the number of refugees seeking safe-haven from conflicts elsewhere is ever increasing. The economy, now interconnected with other nation-states via a system of bilateral and multilateral trade agreements and the free flow of capital, is affected by economic developments elsewhere. Changing modes of political communication driven by socio-political and technological changes have upended liberal democracy. While a wealthy advanced industrial economy, Australia has little capacity to act as a global change agent. Hence, it attempts to engage with the international community and for good reason too. Abrogating our responsibilities to the international community would indicate that the closed-minded, colonial thinking that Australia had seemingly unshackled itself from still lingers in the national psyche.

The scale of these international challenges is matched by a domestic set of economic, political and social problems which, at times, appear intractable. Economic inequality is on the rise. Corporate profits are enormous, yet wage growth is stagnant. Meaningful engagement with Australia's first peoples is routinely sacrificed at the altar of political expediency. The 'Australian dream' of home ownership seems further away than ever for many. The difficult-to-amend Constitution needs modernisation. Witness the significant numbers of federal politicians whom the High Court found during 2017 to be dual citizens, in breach of an arcane section of the Constitution, and therefore ineligible to sit in the parliament.

By highlighting *some* of the problems Australia faces, our goal is not to suggest that Australian democracy is broken beyond repair. Indeed, there is much to be optimistic about. But it is only by analysing the challenges we as a nation face, that students of Australian politics can truly evaluate the future of Australian democracy. This chapter provides an opportunity to engage in analysis of contemporary Australian politics and question some of the challenges chosen for further discussion in this chapter. It also aims to bring together much of the discussion through the previous 12 chapters.

SIX KEY CHALLENGES FOR AUSTRALIAN DEMOCRACY IN THE 21ST CENTURY

Some of the overarching problems that Australian democracy faces today are enduring challenges also faced by other liberal democracies. Working out how to, for example, best manage the institutions of the state or developing strategies to engage with and empower interest groups and NGOs are problems that democracies across the globe are confronted with. Equally, how well nation-states manage social and political inclusion and equality can define how successful and representative liberal democracies are. However, the importance of the domestic context should not be underestimated. Australia's unique mix of institutions, its history and culture ensure that the problems it faces and the challenges to its democracy are never quite the same as in other comparable countries like New Zealand, the United Kingdom or Canada.

In what follows, six key challenges for Australian democracy in the 21st century are outlined. Undoubtedly, there are a number of others that could have also received attention. The environment is one that immediately springs to mind. The effect of climate change is not just on the immediate livelihoods of humans through global warming. The long-term effects of changes to farming and food production impact the Australian economy, as much as they do our capacity to feed ourselves. There is the problem of a loss of faith in democracy itself, which is revealed by opinion polls showing that half of Australians now attach no particular importance to it (see Lowy Institute 2017). The increase in nationalism and the threat of isolationist foreign policy from the US is another challenge. Australia's relationships with regional and global partners has been prefaced on the notion that the US will remain actively engaged in our region and in global affairs. If this changes, Australia faces a set of new challenges.

The key political challenges we have chosen to be discussed here are governance and the role of the state; the Australian Federation; globalisation and economic inequality; Australia's ongoing fiscal dilemmas; representation and participation; and the changing communications landscape.

GOVERNANCE AND THE ROLE OF THE STATE

As was discussed in Chapter 6, there has been a discernible shift from government to governance in recent decades. Changes to the Australian public sector and the ways that the government has delivered services since the 1980s, has undoubtedly changed Australian society. But have these changes produced more problems than they were designed to solve? Market-based approaches have become the favoured instruments of both major parties despite widespread opposition to their use in service delivery. The privatisation of government assets has also been a sore spot for many voters, who not only overwhelmingly oppose sales of government assets, but generally favour increased expenditure on services over tax cuts (Woods and Lewis 2015; Phillips 2016). Even the staunchly pro-market Australian Competition and Consumer Commission (ACCC) has bluntly refuted the benefits of these approaches, with ACCC chairman, Rod Sims, arguing in 2016 that asset sales had damaged the Australian economy (Hatch 2016).

Clearly, discussions about the use of market-based mechanisms cannot be separated from discussions of ideology and also how prevalent evidence-based policy *actually* is; however, these debates are also about what role the state is to play. For most of the final two decades of the 20th century, and the first two of the 21st century, voters were presented with a set of free-market policies that, for the most part, had bipartisan support from the major parties in Australia, the UK, the US and elsewhere. But can the major parties, which are by their very nature, vote-seeking, continue to advocate a set of policies which polling shows the majority of voters oppose? An interesting case study has been the Jeremy Corbyn-led Labour Party in the 2017 UK general election. The policies the party took to the election were some of the most radical in the Anglo-American democracies of the last 30 years. This included renationalising a variety of areas of the economy. While there are clearly a number of factors which contributed to the huge swing to the Labour Party, the potential for other parties in other jurisdictions to propose policies that contradict the bipartisan neo-liberal consensus appears possible.

SHORT-ANSWER
QUESTIONS

Breaking free of the ideological straightjackets the major parties in many countries are in is important for another reason too. Many of the radical-right populist political parties who pose a threat to liberal democracy are able to fill a niche in party systems by presenting themselves as not only the saviours of 'the people' from unaccountable political elites, but as the only parties who will smash the free-market consensus and deliver power back to the people. Few would dispute that free markets *can* work, but the challenge for Australia's political class is using market-based instruments when they are appropriate and not as panacea to *all* of our public policy problems.

THE AUSTRALIAN FEDERATION

Another challenge for Australian democracy in the 21st century is the state of the Australian Federation. As discussed in Chapter 2, Australia, as a federation, needs to resolve issues such as the distribution of the goods and services tax to and between states. However, the increasing centralisation of financial power at the Commonwealth level contrasts with the ongoing role that the states play in the heavy lifting service-delivery areas of policing, transport, health and education. Scholars have noted that, around the globe, national governments – even unitary governments – are devolving policy responsibilities to subnational levels of government. This trend points to the impossibility of governing complex societies from national capitals. But it does not also mean that national-level governments wield less influence. In Australia's case, the Commonwealth has been content to see the states run transport systems, schools and hospitals, but to use its own financial supremacy and authority to conditionally fund the states in order to direct transport, education and health policy. The ongoing challenge is to strike a balance between achieving national policy priorities while still allowing policy to be shaped to fit particular regional or local needs and circumstances.

Whether Australia has the right mix of national and regional-level political institutions is another matter. There is a widespread sense that Australia's particular federal structures need adjustment, if not wholesale reform. Some proposals for 'big picture' change extend to creating new states, formalising the role of the Council of Australian Governments and local government, and refashioning taxation responsibilities to end the financial dependence of states upon the Commonwealth. There are those who would enlarge the scope and authority of the states – and those who would replace them with more numerous, smaller-scale regional governments. But tempering the enthusiasm of all those who would reform Australia's federation is a harsh political fact: the Constitution is not easily changed. In recent decades, governments have shied away from seeking to amend the Constitution, fearing defeat and loss of face.

Section 128 was put in place to ensure that the more populous states of New South Wales and Victoria could not override smaller the states and reshape Australia's federal system to their advantage. It has effectively prevented constitutional amendment in circumstances where the major parties are not fully agreed on the merits of reform. Australia's federation is unlikely to be altered unless ways can be found to overcome short-term vested interests and party rivalries. Beramendi (2009, 764) observes that 'federalism sets the stage for central and subnational governments to behave non-cooperatively'. Invariably different political parties hold government in the various states and territories, and at Commonwealth-level. Inevitably the search for partisan advantage is ever-present in their dealings. It leaves reforming Australia's federation an intractable problem.

National security and the rhetoric of securitisation

Central to many debates in political science is the ongoing role of government (or the state) in our lives. This is also true of the challenges Australia faces in the 21st century. We live in an era of **securitisation**. Not only is national security high on the agenda for governments but decision-making in this and many other areas, such as how we deal with asylum seekers, are securitised. As discussed in Chapter 4, this is the process whereby particular issues are constructed as central to state security, and thus become the subject of extraordinary government measures that dilute civil liberties and judicial protections (Buzan et al. 1998, 25). Following the terrorist attacks on the US in 2001 and then the Bali bombing the following year, the belief that Islamic terrorism posed a real threat to Australia became widespread. As other governments did, Australia moved to introduce stricter anti-terrorism laws – beginning with legislation pushed through the parliament in 2001, followed by numerous other pieces of legislation including the 2005 Anti-Terrorism Acts (Gelber 2017).

Subsequent rounds of anti-terrorist measures (notably the 2014 *National Security Legislation Amendment Act*) have extended the powers of security agencies to covertly detain Australians not suspected of any crime; introduced a new broad offence of advocating terrorism; amended penalties for journalists and whistleblowers who might disclose information about special intelligence operations; and expanded the surveillance powers available to the Australian Security Intelligence Organisation. The volume and scope of legislation enacted has been extraordinary. New data retention laws, which came into effect in late 2015, now also require Australian internet service providers and telecommunications companies to store details of all internet access, emails, telephone calls and text messages for a two-year period, and to make this metadata available to security and law enforcement agencies. The question is whether the removal of rights and freedoms found in this rushed legislation is a necessary and proportionate way of defending Australian democracy. Some critics believe not and point to the hasty and excessive restrictions upon individual liberty and free speech.

Between 2003 and 2012 a total of 417 Australians died by falling out of bed. This is more than double the 113 who died as a result of terrorism in the period 1978 to 2014. Far more Australians are at risk from domestic violence, which claimed some 850 lives between 2003 and 2012, not to mention road accidents in which 8525 died in this same period (Keane 2014). This is not to deny that there is a real threat. At the end of 2017, the government reported that a total of 14 terrorist attacks had been thwarted in the previous three years (since the threat of attack had been upgraded to 'probable') (AAP 2017). But by any dispassionate assessment of the risks involved, Australia's response to terrorism appears disproportionate to the actual threat it poses. In 2017 the Commonwealth established a new Department of Home Affairs, bringing together responsibility for federal law enforcement, national security, criminal justice, emergency management, multicultural affairs, immigration, customs and border protection agencies in a single 'superministry'. Far fewer resources have been injected into road safety and mitigating the scourge of domestic violence, which cost far more Australian lives each year.

Free speech and free and open political communication are not simply abstract ideals which distinguish liberal democracies. They are in a real sense functional tools, which permit representative democracy to function. Free speech has a vital role in democratic deliberation and legitimation. If citizens are to willingly abide by laws that governments

securitisation: The process of constructing particular issues as central to state security, which then become the subject of extraordinary government measures that often erode civil liberties.

make, then they must have an investment in their making that comes with the capacity to freely discuss and openly debate issues of concern. That is, 'effective democracy is dependent on citizens' ability to criticise the government and to participate actively in deliberation over issues affecting them' (Gelber 2017, 205). The ongoing securitisation of a raft of policy areas is problematic for Australian democracy and as Pearson (2014) puts it, '[i]n a democracy, that means striking a reasonable balance between preserving the integrity of intelligence and police operations and allowing enough information flow to permit scrutiny and informed public debate'. Managing these, often contradictory, pressures remains a significant challenge in an era when there is declining trust in political institutions.

**VIDEO
RESEARCH
QUESTION**

GLOBALISATION AND ECONOMIC INEQUALITY

globalisation: A process of growing inter-connectedness across the globe; in particular, the ease of movement of people, ideas and capital are cited as examples.

In 2016, 37.7 million people travelled to and from Australia, up from 21.7 million in 2006. An estimated one million Australians now live and work abroad. One in four Australians is overseas born. These are measures of **globalisation** – of the trend toward an increasing, complex interdependency between Australia and other countries, which is both caused by, and found in, population movements, global trade patterns, financial flows, and communication technologies that transcend national boundaries. In the past half century, globalisation has transformed Australian society and, with it, changed the nature of its politics. It is widely championed – but also resented. A Lowy Institute opinion poll conducted in 2017 found that 78 per cent of Australians believe that globalisation is mostly good for Australia – up from 64 per cent in 2006 (Lowy Institute 2017). But beneath such evidence of its broad acceptance, there is a residual resentment. The emergence of One Nation is often seen as an early indication of an exasperation with globalisation and the winners and losers that it produces (Bean 2000; Goot and Watson 2001). A similar exasperation may explain why minor parties attracted a record 34 per cent of the Senate vote in 2016. While there is significant debate in the scholarly literature about the role of economics and culture in contributing to changing voting behaviour (Inglehart and Norris 2016), it is clear that economic inequality plays some role and that it has progressively increased. This is a serious challenge for Australian democracy.

Globalisation has led to the removal of trade barriers and a global shift in which manufacturing industries shifted from high-wage areas to cheaper wage areas of East Asia (see Knox, Agnew and McCarthy 2014). In Australia, 'traditional industries such as car making shut down and manufacturing moved offshore' (Marks 2017). During the past several decades, the nature of the labour market fundamentally shifted (ABS 2012). New employment opportunities emerged in the service and mining sectors. But as in North America and Western Europe, these were often in metropolitan areas leaving those living in regional and rural areas behind. Consumers benefitted enormously from cheaper imported goods. The salaries of CEOs sky-rocketed. Australia's economy entered a sustained period of growth. But Australia's manufacturing industry was hard hit and the labour market transformed. Unions count among the losers, undercut by the declining share of jobs held by blue-collar and factory workers and by a surge in self-employment, contract and casual work in areas (such as retail), which are difficult to organise (Burgman 2016, 54).

It also is clear that economic divisions within Australian society have deepened since the 1980s. There is now an emerging view that inequality has reached unacceptable levels matching those last seen in the 1940s. For example, in 2017 the newly elected

ACTU secretary blamed neo-liberalism for having made 'working people and ordinary Australians' its victims and caused inequality in Australia to reach a 70-year high (Karp 2017). A recent ACOSS (2015, 8) study found that Australians in the top quintile (20%) of income earners now earn around five times as much as Australians in the bottom quintile. Today the wealthiest quintile of Australians has a 'staggering 70 times as much wealth as a person in the bottom 20%'. In the first decade of this century, executive salaries increased some 70 per cent faster than average wages growth. These figures underscore the significant structural changes in Australia that have occurred during the past 30 years.

A deepening economic inequality (which is visible in the high cost of housing and in static or falling wage levels) presents a significant challenge to Australian democracy in the 21st century. There is now a substantial body of social research showing 'that inequality correlates negatively with [self-reported] happiness in Western societies'. This is something ameliorated only by 'trust in the institutions' which plays an important part in the relationship between income and wellbeing (Ferrer-i-Carbonell and Ramos 2014, 1016). For the moment, trust in government institutions is in short supply and the inability or unwillingness of political actors to reduce economic inequality is posited as one central cause of its decline.

SHORT-ANSWER QUESTIONS

AUSTRALIA'S ONGOING FISCAL DILEMMAS

In the wake of the 2007–08 Global Financial Crisis, and with the end of the mining boom, the ALP and Coalition governments alike have faced difficulties in balancing receipts and expenditure, bringing down **budget deficits** while promising 'to balance the Budget over time by keeping expenditure under control' (Treasury 2016). Inevitably, as Australia's population grows, governments must raise and spend more. Moreover, technological and other developments now require governments to deal with a wider array of different policy problems – something which explains why taxing and government spending counts for over a quarter of Australia's GDP, up from less than a fifth in the early 1970s.

The Commonwealth government's chief revenue streams derive from company and income taxation. This poses a particular set of political challenges. Reducing expenditure is difficult enough. Cuts to education, health or other programs will be vigorously resisted by interest groups affected. Asking employees to pay more personal income tax is also politically fraught. Other OECD countries may impose higher levels of income tax; but Australian taxpayers are now being asked to carry an increasing tax burden. In the 1950s, income tax accounted for 40 per cent of Commonwealth tax revenue. By the century's end (in 2000–01) it supplied 47 per cent of the taxes collected by the Commonwealth. By 2013–14 it accounted for half. In 2024–25 it is projected to account for 56 per cent (Treasury 2017). The nub of the political problem that governments face is that Australians who pay income tax are also voters.

In the 35 years following 1985, Commonwealth governments introduced budget deficits on 21 occasions (Tsiaplias 2016). Governments, the CEO of the Business Council of Australia says, have been too willing to 'accept deficits as normal' and to kick the can down the road. Burgeoning government debt arguably reduces the scope of governments to respond to economic downturns and to underwrite new infrastructure. It may have an even more 'devastating' consequence, shifting 'the burden onto future generations' and lumbering 'the students, apprentices and young workers of today' with 'crippling levels of tax to subsidise the self-serving generations who came before them' (Westacott 2017).

budget deficit: 'It is never the case that the government spends exactly what it raises in taxes, so in any given year there is either a budget surplus (tax revenues are more than spending), or a budget deficit (tax revenues less than government spending)' (Crosby 2015).

A way out of this dilemma would be to grow the number of taxpayers by stepping up immigration (Coombes and Dollery 2002, 8). But there are sizeable political obstacles to expanding the already high immigration intake given present levels of complaint that 'Australia's "breakneck" population growth is [already] flooding major cities' and threatening 'irreversible' environmental degradation (Carr 2016).

Globalisation has posed several challenges to the collection of company or corporate taxation. Multinational corporations such as Apple and Facebook now play a greater part in Australia's economy, yet they are well-placed to minimise the taxes they pay, as indeed are many other companies who operate across national borders and in a range of jurisdictions. In the 2013–14 tax year, 579 companies with an annual income exceeding $100 million did not pay tax (ABC 2015). Similarly, in the 2015–16 tax year, 732 of the 2043 largest companies operating in Australia paid no tax at all (Hutchens 2017). Of further concern, globalisation also means that individual national governments are engaged in a competition to lower the rates of company tax in order to retain or attract companies to their jurisdiction. Australia has not been immune to this pressure. Business groups have been enthusiastic, but voters less so, fearing that reducing the share of taxes paid by companies must require either cutbacks in government services or the shifting of the tax burden elsewhere.

Further complicating matters are a number of economic trends that restrict the capacity of government to raise revenue. These include a growing 'gig economy', the casualisation of the workforce, automation, a prolonged period of low wage growth, a shrinking manufacturing sector and a shift in terms of trade associated with contracting commodities markets. Beneath such economic changes lie long-term demographic shifts also having a direct impact on the budget. The number of Australians aged over 65 years has grown at more than twice the rate of the rest of the population, from some 11 per cent in the early 1990s to more than 15 per cent today (Tsiaplias 2016). This ageing of the population has placed greater demands on and explains the growth in government health and social spending. Moreover, it is set to constrain the government's capacity to raise income tax by diminishing the size of the working (or tax paying) population. The rate at which the Australian population is ageing is such that by 2040 one in every five people will likely be aged 65 or more years. However one looks at it, Australia faces serious and long-term fiscal problems.

VIDEO
SHORT-ANSWER
QUESTIONS

REPRESENTATION AND PARTICIPATION

The suggestion that Australian politics is unrepresentative, that Australians are disengaged, and few are participating in the democratic process beyond casting their ballots at elections is a well-worn critique. The leadership churn following John Howard's 2007 election defeat and the eruption of internal divisions within the major parties is often posited as both cause and effect of this new era of politics. Other pundits see deeper problems. In diagnosing 'our broken political system', Gordon (2016) ventures that the problem is not just that all the measures of the health of Australia's national politics are 'at or near, record lows', but that the underlying trend 'towards an alienated, angry, distrustful, unattached and disengaged electorate is accelerating at such a pace that it will prove very hard to arrest, let alone reverse'. The noted political commentator Paul Kelly (2014) largely agrees with Gordon, describing Australia's political system as malfunctioning. It is, he argues, incapable of producing the public policies needed to prevent Australia's long-term economic decline. Kelly described an alarming erosion of Australia's political culture 'tied to wider social and media trends' and leaving its political system unable to respond to Australia's needs. But do these diagnoses of a 'broken' politics overlook some fundamental problems?

Australia's electoral system remains first and foremost one which enhances the prospects of the major parties in lower house elections. While it may have produced legislative majorities broadly in line with public sentiment for much of the last century, as was noted in Chapters 7–9, this is no longer the case. Australian voting behaviour is increasingly trending towards its international comparators with de-alignment from the major parties and a significant increase in support for minor parties. Hence, instead of viewing voters as disengaged, angry, alienated and distrustful, perhaps the real problem is that the electoral system needs to be reformed to ensure election outcomes are representative of the will of voters.

Another concern is the continued lack of diversity in Australian political ranks. The failure to improve the representation of women in parliaments, especially on the conservative side of politics, suggests a serious flaw in Australian democracy. A properly functioning representative democracy ought to produce a political class that closely resembles the society from which it is drawn. That Australia does not has likely had political consequences. For example, it is probable that, given that one in four Australian women have suffered violence at the hands of their partner (ANROWS 2017), a better representation of women in the parliament might have seen a much greater priority given to combatting domestic violence. It is also likely that there would be a much greater focus on addressing the gender pay gap, which has remained almost unchanged for 20 years. The reality is that women still, on average, earn far less than men, are more often in part-time employment and are under-represented in the senior levels of the public service, on corporate boards and in the media. Any society that fails to adequately use the skills of half (or more) of the population will be underachieving. Equally, any political system which fails to fully represent women is similarly failing.

Figure 13.1 Australia Day protests

Of course, the challenge is not just to remedy the unequal representation of men and women. It is also about social inclusion, engagement and participation of first nations peoples, the LGBTIQ community as well as migrants. There are successes of course. The same-sex marriage postal survey result in 2017 was a significant moment for equality in Australia. The apology to the Stolen Generations by the Rudd ALP Government in 2008 was an equally powerful moment for the nation. But encouraging engagement and participation in the political process requires more than this. As has been evident in the decision of the federal government to reject the 2017 'Uluru Statement' which called for the establishment of a 'first nations voice' in the Constitution (McKay 2017), political expediency and an inevitable opposition to anything resembling significant change to Australia's institutions ensures progress is slow and hard-fought. As discussed in Chapter 12, participation and engagement has to be meaningful and it has to occur beyond election campaigns. The challenge at the grassroots of Australian democracy is to maintain an active and engaged civil society. Without this, Australian democracy will become a stale contest between vested interests.

REFLECTION
QUESTIONS
VIDEO

THE CHANGING COMMUNICATIONS LANDSCAPE

The changing communications landscape has not simply changed the way that citizens receive political news, it has altered the nature of the media and politics. These changes are significant, and their impact deeply felt. When television emerged as the dominant medium for political communication in the 1960s it offered political actors access to a large, mass audience. With the more recent rise of digital media, including social media platforms, how citizens engaged with politics changed. In 2017, seven in every ten Australians had a Facebook page. One in two used Facebook on a daily basis. For many, Facebook has become a source of news, not only about the activities of friends, but about political and economic issues generally. In 2015 Reuters emphasised that their annual survey of digital media use had revealed 'the rising importance of Facebook in the distribution of digital news' across numbers of countries. In Australia some four in every ten interviewed now say they use it as a news source (Liddy 2015; Reuters 2017). The algorithms which drive Facebook are designed to link individual users to content (including news and ads) which the data it holds about them suggests will be of interest. This points to the shifting nature of news itself.

The companies operating social media such as Facebook and Twitter are news distributors, not news generators. The lesson of the 2016 US presidential election is that social media can be exploited to rapidly and widely distribute 'fake news' stories having no factual basis (Allcott and Gentzkow 2017; Persily 2017). That social media is programmed to distribute content catering to individuals' known preferences and interests, compounds this. Users of social media are inadvertently subject to selective exposure that ensures that they receive information that matches their pre-existing political beliefs and isolates them from contrary news content and commentary that might challenge those beliefs. This isn't to say social media is an inherently negative influence. As was outlined in Chapter 11, this form of communication provides a participatory, collaborative tool, connecting users and building online communities. Social media also removes many of the barriers which political groups once faced in organising protest rallies or signature drives and collecting funds. They have allowed new, spatially diffuse forms of activism (such as the Occupy Wall Street movement in 2011) which at one and the same time bridge local-level and global politics.

Ideas quickly spill via social media and email across national borders and between activist groups. The internet and social media has 'supercharged' transnational activism. Of course, transnational campaigns are not new. Witness the proliferation of global organisations such as Greenpeace and Amnesty last century, or global struggles such as the international campaign of union bans, boycotts and demonstrations to end apartheid in South Africa. The sheer number of transnational NGOs which emerged in the last half of last century has been seen as 'a new force in international politics', which has transformed 'global norms and practices' (Khagram, Riker and Sikkink 2002, 4). And now new communications technologies have enhanced the spread and density of these activist networks. Australians can just as easily contribute to global campaigns that target international institutions, foreign governments and transnational corporations as in campaigns protesting the decisions of Australian state and national governments.

While new modes of communication provide significant opportunities for enhancing Australian democracy, they also pose significant challenges. Ensuring that government is still held to account via an effective fourth estate is one of these. Safeguarding the integrity of election campaigns is another. Limiting the effect of 'fake news' is a third. A fourth is the challenge of ensuring that Australian media sustain a genuinely national, public discussion of policy alternatives in an era when social media are designed to feed us with political news reinforcing our own views – and in which the digital environment extends an anonymity that encourages 'trolling' and incivility toward those with different political views.

REFLECTION QUESTIONS
RESEARCH QUESTION

DOES DOMESTIC POLITICS MATTER? HAS GLOBALISATION CONSTRAINED GOVERNMENTS?

While the challenges discussed thus far have primarily been about the domestic political environment, a question worth considering is whether domestic politics still matters? In other words, have international economic and political forces become so fundamental to our everyday lives that domestic politics has become nothing more than a reaction to the international context? In the wake of the 9/11 attacks on the US, the UN Security Council passed *Resolution 1373* requiring UN member countries including Australia to amend their domestic laws to ensure that acts of terrorism were treated as serious criminal offences, punishable in ways which underscore their seriousness. Australia willingly complied. The dramatic global news media coverage of the Al-Qaeda attack on New York's twin towers had done much to alert Australians of the potential threat that terrorism posed. When the Howard Government passed the *Security Legislation Amendment (Terrorism) Act* in 2002, it did so with bipartisan support and in response to shifting public opinion. But it was also responding to external pressures and not simply, nor only, to the wishes of voters who had elected it.

We may think of Australia as a democracy in which voters elect governments to implement policies they wish to see enacted. But the reality is that globalisation has inexorably produced an interconnected and interdependent world, and that the Australian government is obliged to comply with a raft of trade, defence, human rights, conservation and other international agreements that it has entered into over the past half century or more. One direct expression of globalisation is that Australia is, as other countries are, evermore engaged in negotiating and implementing both bilateral and multilateral agreements with other countries that allow them to jointly or collectively address the many economic, environmental, social and political problems requiring an integrated policy response. In some contexts, international agreements can directly shape the actions of national governments. The conventions and treaties that Australia has signed may influence the way it behaves, both domestically and internationally. But the ratification of an international agreement does not mean handing over **sovereignty** to an international agency.

sovereignty:
Governments are said to be sovereign when they exercise an authority over their people and territory which is not constrained by external influences.

Governments are said to be sovereign when they exercise an untrammelled authority over their people and territory. In recent decades the arrival of asylum seekers by boat has placed border protection and Australia's sovereignty at the very centre of political debate. Under the terms of the UN *Refugee Convention* to which it is a signatory, Australia agreed to provide asylum to refugees fleeing political persecution. Yet successive governments, including those formed by both the ALP and the Coalition parties, have been determined to withhold the right to remain in Australia from persons using the services of people smugglers to reach Australia, even if they are genuine refugees. Governments have insisted, and Australian courts have agreed, that as a sovereign country Australia has every right to control immigration, protect the integrity of its borders, and determine who may enter and reside within its territory.

Australia's detention of asylum seekers arriving by boat in offshore centres (in Nauru and on Manus Island in PNG) and its refusal to accept those classified as refugees by the United Nations High Commissioner for Refugees (UNHCR) has drawn extensive criticism. This includes criticism from the UNHCR which has questioned whether Australia has a policy regime that does afford the protection to persons fleeing persecution that Australia committed to providing when it signed on to the 1951 *Refugee Convention*. Australian governments may have challenged the validity of UNHCR criticism and re-asserted Australia's sovereign right to secure its borders. But ultimately it is in Australia's interests to protect its standing in the community of nations along with its investment in international cooperation by honouring its obligations under the various international agreements into which it has entered. Whether it is the case of asylum seekers, trade agreements or climate change accords, international and domestic politics are increasingly interconnected. The difficult challenge that governments now face in a world shaped by globalisation is to manage the tensions, where they arise, between the demands voters may make upon them and their obligations under the international agreements that Australia has entered into.

Ultimately, the domestic and international political environments are intertwined. While one may drive decisions in one policy area, the opposite may be true in another. The simple reality is also that the international community is still made up of nation-states all attempting to pursue their own agendas. The liberal democracies that are part of this community are ultimately accountable to their people via elections. The domestic politics of liberal democracies is never, therefore, solely driven by international politics. Put simply domestic politics still matters in this era of extended globalisation.

REFLECTION
QUESTIONS
VIDEO

SUMMARY

Learning objective 1: Outline some of the overarching challenges for Australian democracy

Australian democracy faces numerous challenges in the 21st century. While there are too many to list, six examples were provided in this chapter that have underpinned much of the previous discussion throughout this text. These include governance and the role of the state, the Australian Federation, economic inequality, Australia's ongoing fiscal dilemmas, representation and participation, and the changing communications landscape. There is, unsurprisingly, a degree of overlap between these challenges. Economic, cultural and historical forces all shape political outcomes. Likewise, the institutional architecture is likely to have an influence on political outcomes long after the reality of politics on the ground has changed from when those institutions were established. Indeed, this is one of the central challenges that Australian democracy faces: managing significant challenges at a time when its institutional structure is largely the same as it was over a century ago.

Learning objective 2: Consider whether domestic politics still matters or whether international politics is the key

In a globalised world, international politics may dominate the headlines, and it is clearly important, but the importance of domestic politics should never be underestimated. Beyond the corridors of power, at the grassroots of Australian democracy, at the meetings of NGOs, interest groups and fledgling political parties, Australian democracy in action can be witnessed. While this may not be what we think about when we consider Australia's sovereignty or the domestic political environment, it is only through an active civil society that Australian democracy flourishes at all. The reality is also that while Australia may be a signatory to a range of international agreements, enforcing these agreements is extremely difficult. The international community is nothing but a collection of nation-states. Hence, while international politics and events in the US, Europe and Asia have a meaningful impact on Australian democracy, the domestic political context remains central to political and policy outcomes for Australian citizens.

REFERENCES

AAP. (2017). Aust entering 'peak terrorism' period, *Shepparton News*, 11 December.

ABC News. (2015). Zero tax: Data reveals how much tax major Australian corporations pay, December 12. URL: http://www.abc.net.au/news/2015–12-17/tax-transparency-report/7036708

Allcott, H. and Gentzkow, M. (2017). Social media and fake news in the 2016 election. *Journal of Economic Perspectives*, **31**(2), 211–36.

Australian Bureau of Statistics. (2012). Fifty years of Labour force: now and then. 1301.0 *Year Book Australia, 2012*. URL: http://www.abs.gov.au/ausstats/abs@.nsf/Lookup/1301.0Main+Features 452012

Australian Council of Social Service. (2015). Inequality in Australia. A nation divided. *ACOSS*. URL: http://www.acoss.org.au/wp-content/uploads/2015/06/Inequality_in_Australia_FINAL .pdf

Australia's National Research Organisation for Women's Safety. (2017). Personal Safety Survey update 2017. URL: https://anrows.org.au

Bean, C. (2000). Nationwide electoral support for One Nation in the 1998 federal election. In M. Leach, G. Stokes and I. Ward, eds, *The Rise and Fall of One Nation*, Brisbane: University of Queensland Press, pp. 136–52.

Beramendi, P. (2009). Federalism. In C. Boix and S.C. Stokes, eds, *The Oxford Handbook of Comparative Politics*. URL: www.oxfordhandbooks.com.ezproxy.library.uq.edu.au/view/10.1093/oxfordhb/9780199566020.001.0001/oxfordhb-9780199566020-e-31?rskey=erp9kU&result=2

Burgman, V. (2016). *Globalization and Labour in the Twenty-First Century*, Abingdon: Routledge.

Buzan, B., Waever, O. and de Wilde, J. (1998). *Security: A New Framework for Analysis*, Boulder, Colo: Lynne Rienner.

Carr, B. (2016). Migration pushing Australia to 'third-world style population growth rate', *The Guardian*, 16 February. URL: https://www.theguardian.com/australia-news/2016/feb/16/migration-pushing-australia-to-third-world-style-population-growth-rate

Coombes, G. and Dollery, B. (2002). An analysis of the debate on intergenerational equity and fiscal sustainability in Australia, *Working Paper Series in Economics* No. 2002–5. University of New England School of Economics. URL: http://www.une.edu.au/febl/EconStud/wps.htm

Crosby, M. (2014). Budget explainer: Debts and deficits, is Australia really the worst? *The Conversation*, 11 May. Retrieved from https://theconversation.com/budget-explainer-debts-and-deficits-is-australia-really-the-worst-40086

Ferrer-i-Carbonell, A. and Ramos, X. (2014). Inequality and happiness. *Journal of Economic Surveys*, **28**, 1016–27.

Gelber, K. (2017). Freedom of political speech, hate speech and the argument from democracy: The transformative contribution of capabilities theory. *Contemporary Political Theory*, **9**(3), 304–24.

Goot, M. and Watson, I. (2001). One Nation's electoral support: Where does it come from, what makes it different and how does it fit? *Australian Journal of Politics & History*, **47**(2), 159–91, doi.org/10.1111/1467–8497.00226

Gordon, M. (2016). How to fix our broken political system, *The Sydney Morning Herald*, 23 December. Retrieved from http://www.smh.com.au/comment/how-to-fix-our-broken-political-system-20161223-gth6e7.html

Hatch, P. (2016). Privatisation has damaged the economy, says ACCC chief, *The Sydney Morning Herald*, 27 July. Retrieved from http://www.smh.com.au/business/privatisation-has-damaged-the-economy-says-accc-chief-20160726-gqe2c2.html

Hutchens, G. (2017). Australian tax office says 36% of big firms and multinationals paid no tax, *The Guardian*, 7 December. Retrieved from https://www.theguardian.com/australia-news/2017/dec/07/australian-tax-office-says-36-of-big-firms-and-multinationals-paid-no-tax

Inglehart, R. and Norris, P. (2016). Trump, Brexit, and the rise of populism: Economic have-nots and cultural backlash, *Working paper*, August 2016. Retrieved from https://research.hks.harvard.edu/publications/getFile.aspx?Id=1401

Karp, P. (2017). Neoliberalism 'has run its course', says ACTU boss Sally McManus, *The Guardian*, 29 March. Retrieved from https://www.theguardian.com/australia-news/2017/mar/29/neoliberalism-has-run-its-course-says-actu-boss-sally-mcmanus

Keane, B. (2014). The real threat of terrorism to Australians, by numbers, *Echo Net Daily*, 5 September. Retrieved from https://www.echo.net.au/2014/09/real-threat-terrorism-australians-numbers/

Kelly, P. (2014). Politics in crisis and a nation in denial, *The Australian*, 2 July. Retrieved from http://www.theaustralian.com.au/opinion/columnists/paul-kelly/politics-in-crisis-and-a-nation-in-denial/news-story/15dbcd6166cfc6a55fd7559109751c14

Khagram, S., Riker, J.V. and Sikkink, K. (2002). From Seattle to Santiago: Transnational advocacy groups restructuring world politics. In S. Khagram, J.V. Riker and K. Sikkink, eds, *Restructuring World Politics*, Minneapolis: University of Minnesota Press.

Knox, P., Agnew, J. and McCarthy, L. (2014). *The Geography of the World Economy*, 6th edn, Abingdon: Routledge.

Liddy, M. (2015). Australians don't trust the news – except when it comes from their favourite sources, *abc.news.com*, 16 June. Retrieved from http://www.abc.net.au/news/2015–06-16/australians-digital-news-trust/6548232

Lowy Institute. (2017). *2017 Lowy Institute Poll*. URL: https://www.lowyinstitute.org/publications/2017-lowy-institute-poll

Marks, K. (2017). The rise of populist politics in Australia, *BBC,* 1 March. Retrieved from http://www.bbc.com/news/world-australia-39111317

McKay, D. (2017). Uluru Statement: A Quick Guide. Parliament of Australia. Retrieved from https://www.aph.gov.au/About_Parliament/Parliamentary_Departments/Parliamentary_Library/pubs/rp/rp1617/Quick_Guides/UluruStatement

Pearson, M. (2014). Five reasons terror laws wreck media freedom and democracy, *The Conversation*, 13 October. Retrieved from https://theconversation.com/five-reasons-terror-laws-wreck-media-freedom-and-democracy–32791

Persily, N. (2017). The 2016 U.S. election: Can democracy survive the internet? *Journal of Democracy*, **28**(2), 63–76.

Phillips, B. (2016). The tax myths that cloud our judgement, *ABC*, 26 April. Retrieved from http://www.abc.net.au/news/2016–04-26/phillips-the-tax-myths-that-cloud-our-judgement/7357358

Reuters. (2017). *Digital News Report*. URL: http://www.digitalnewsreport.org

Treasury. (2016). Balancing the budget. URL: http://budget.gov.au/2016–17/content/glossies/budget_repair/html

Tsiaplias, S. (2016). Budget explainer: the structural deficit and what it means, *The Conversation*, 22 April. Retrieved from https://theconversation.com/budget-explainer-the-structural-deficit-and-what-it-means–57437

Westacott, J. (2017). Act now on budget deficit or our kids will bear the burden, *The Australian*, 25 March. Retrieved from https://www.theaustralian.com.au/news/inquirer/act-now-on-budget-deficit-or-our-kids-will-bear-the-burden/news-story/1c5bd424cfaf775ac2b141688a29a0ef

Wilkins, G. (2013). CEOs take home 70 times average salary, *The Sydney Morning Herald*, 20 September. Retrieved from http://www.smh.com.au/business/ceos-take-home-70-times-average-salary-20130919-2u2kl.html

Williams, G. (2011). The laws that erode who we are, *The Sydney Morning Herald*, 10 September. Retrieved from http://www.smh.com.au/federal-politics/political-opinion/the-laws-that-erode-who-we-are-20110909-1k1kl.html?deviceType=text

Woods, J. and Lewis, P. (2015). Hate privatisation? There's nothing new about that, *ABC*, 11 February. Retrieved from http://www.abc.net.au/news/2015–02-11/lewis-and-woods-voters-still-sceptical-of-privatisation/6083982

INDEX